DESK BOOK
FOR SETTING UP
A CLOSELY-HELD
CORPORATION

Robert P. Hess

INSTITUTE for BUSINESS PLANNING, Inc.
IBP Plaza • Englewood Cliffs, N.J. 07632

Third Printing.....September, 1980

Library of Congress Cataloging in Publication Data

Hess, Robert P
  Desk book for setting up a closely-held corporation.

  Includes index.
    1. Close corporations—United States.   2. Close
corporations—Taxation—United States.   I. Title.
KF1466.H45   346'.73'0668   79–19309
ISBN 0-87624-113-5

Printed in the United States of America

Dedicated to Kathy, Bobby and Scotty

ABOUT THE AUTHOR

Robert P. Hess is an attorney at law and a member of the California State and Los Angeles County Bar Associations. Mr. Hess is a partner in the Los Angeles, California law firm of Hill, Farrer and Burrill. He was educated at Lehigh University (B.A. in Economics, 1964), then Stanford Law School (J.D., 1967), and was certified by the State Bar of California as a Specialist in Taxation Law. He is a member of the American Bar Association Section of Taxation, a member of Committees on Employee Benefits and Standards of Tax Practice, and a panelist for California Continuing Education of the Bar.

His previous publications include: "Tax Factors in Organizing a Corporation," Prentice-Hall, Tax Ideas; "Planning a Lifetime Gift Program," *Taxation for Lawyers;* and "Restricted Stock Options," Title Insurance and Trust Company 21st Annual Tax and Probate Forum, 1969.

What This Desk Book Will Do for You

This book will save you time, and it will lead you to additional fees. It is easy to understand and enables you to have answers to tricky questions right at your fingertips. Corporate and tax questions that seemed complicated before are answered in easy to understand language.

This book will assist lawyers and accountants in advising clients who are considering the possibility of incorporating a business with a small number of owners. It discusses how to determine when incorporation may be desirable for purposes of income tax planning. It helps you assess ways of limiting the client's potential liability for damages that may result from the operation of his business. The book spells out the income tax consequences that result from operating a business in the corporate form. It also describes the specific steps to follow in setting up a corporation and the tax consequences to be considered at the time of incorporation. Numerous potential problems arise in connection with the establishment of a closely-held corporation, such as unintentional recognition of ordinary income or capital gain, locking assets in the corporation unnecessarily or improper timing of the incorporation process. This book covers the gamut of such problems and shows how they can be avoided.

In addition to the income tax savings and the limitation of potential liability which may be achieved by incorporating a small business, incorporation also provides flexibility for the owner's estate planning or other disposition of his business interests. This book explains the numerous opportunities for planning that are available to shareholders of a corporation but are unavailable to owners of an unincorporated business.

This book provides a crystal clear explanation of business planning techniques that most practitioners need to provide their clients with valuable advice, even if their specialty is some other area of law or accounting.

Quite often a professional who is not familiar with a particular area of the law may tend to avoid that area. This book provides its readers with a practical knowledge of the problems and benefits relating to a closely-held corporation and enables them to feel comfortable when advising their clients to take a course of action in that area.

In addition to the discussion of when to incorporate and how to incorporate, this book provides valuable checklists and forms such as sample employment contracts, stock buy-sell agreements, pension and profit sharing plans and other documents useful to maximize the benefits available to the owners of a closely-held corporation.

The sample documents in the final section provide you with a solid foundation for advising your client what to do and how to do it in connection with the incorporation of a closely-held corporation. By using the forms in this book, you will be able to give your clients the benefit of years of experience. You can spot potential problems and provide quick and accurate answers to questions involving tax considerations and other legal matters.

A Word from the Author

The chapters in this book are grouped into five parts. One of the most important areas in successful planning for closely-held corporations is the preparation of proper documentation to support various corporate programs. □ *Part Five* contains step-by-step procedures for preparing such documentation and has completely filled-in forms which have been used in actual practice. However, before you get to the point of utilizing these forms to establish and maintain a corporation, you must understand the essential requirements which have to be met to form a valid corporation.

□ *Part One* will help you to decide if incorporation is advisable. □ *Part Two* analyzes the tax aspects of operating a business in the form of a closely-held corporation. □ *Part Three* shows you how to determine the proper capital structure for the corporation. □ *Part Four* provides you with a discussion of the advantages of the various employee benefit plans.

Setting up a closely-held corporation is by no means a cut and dried procedure. There are numerous potential problems commonly encountered when forming a closely-held corporation. The advisable solutions to these problems are analyzed throughout this desk book.

At the outset, you should take a careful stock of what you expect to accomplish by setting up a closely-held corporation. Taking stock means asking fundamental questions about procedures and tax consequences. Highlighted below are some of the key questions to ask—and answer—before you begin:

□ The appropriate name of the corporation—if the first choice is unavailable, what are alternative choices?

- ☐ Who is to be responsible for forming the corporation, and how long will it take?
- ☐ What kind of capital structure is to be used?
- ☐ How many directors are to be elected?
- ☐ Who will the officers be?
- ☐ What type of agreements are contemplated among the stockholders to cover such things as transfers of stock either voluntarily or upon death or disability?

In addition to procedural questions, you must give consideration to the tax and other substantive consequences that are associated with establishing a corporation. Highlighted below are some of the key points to be evaluated:

- ☐ Is the business one that lends itself to the division of its activities into two or more separate entities? Sometimes such a division may produce tax savings.
- ☐ Do you want the formation of the corporation to be tax-free? Property can be transferred to a newly-formed corporation on a tax-free basis if the transferor or transferors end up owning at least 80% of the combined voting power of all classes of stock and at least 80% of all the nonvoting shares. This may be desirable if the property being transferred has increased in value since the time it was acquired by a transferor.
- ☐ Should property that is subject to encumbrances be transferred to the corporation?

  Advantage: If the corporation assumes the transferor's debt, it may be paid off with corporate earnings.

  Disadvantage: If the corporation assumes liabilities or takes property subject to encumbrances, the excess of the total assumed debt over the tax basis of the transferred property will result in taxable gain to the transferor.

- ☐ Should assets be leased to the corporation? Frequently a lease arrangement, rather than an outright transfer of property, can produce more favorable tax results to a corporation and its organizers.

Advantages: The lessor may use depreciation to offset income from the property. The corporation may also benefit if the deduction for rent paid exceeds the depreciation deduction the corporation could have taken.

☐ What type of capital structure will be most beneficial? The basic inquiry is how much equity capital (stock) and how much debt should be used. The considerations involved in making the decision are:

1. Interest paid is deductible by the corporation, but dividends are not.

2. Debt reduces the possibility of tax on improper accumulation of earnings.

3. Retirement of debt obligations does not create tax liability while stock redemption may.

4. Debt imposes fixed obligations for the payment of principal and interest. If the corporation defaults, control could be lost.

☐ Is there sufficient capital? If the original capital of a corporation includes both equity and debt, an undesirable tax effect can occur if the debt element is unrealistically high. If there is too much debt, the IRS may take the position that purported interest payments are really dividends. The IRS may also argue that repayment of the principal is a disguised stock redemption.

☐ Do you want to create a preference in earnings or equity by issuing preferred stock? If so, the preferred stock should be issued at the time of incorporation. If preferred stock is issued after incorporation, such stock runs the risk of being considered "Section 306 stock." This result will cause any gain on the sale of the stock to be treated as ordinary income to the extent of the corporation's earnings. If preferred stock is issued at the time of incorporation, it cannot be Section 306 stock.

☐ Have you overlooked the Section 1244 deduction? Normally, you should qualify the stock under Section 1244 of the IRS so that any loss on the investment will be deductible against the ordinary income to the extent of

$50,000.00 a year on an individual return or $100,000.00 on a joint return.

☐ The owners of a closely-held corporation should enter into an agreement to protect their ownership and control by placing restrictions on the sale or other disposition of stock to outsiders. For example, if a corporation makes a Subchapter S election, the benefits of the election could be lost if stock is transferred to an ineligible stockholder. In this connection, it is desirable to have the owners adopt a "buy-and-sell" agreement.

☐ You should be aware of the "collapsible corporation" rule if the corporation is being formed for a specific short-term purpose. If a corporation liquidates and more than 70% of the gain is attributable to appreciated corporate property which has been held for less than three years, then the capital gain may be converted to ordinary income.

☐ Organization expenditures may be treated as "deferred expenses" and may be written off as tax deductions over a period that is not less than 60 months beginning with the month in which the corporation commences business. In order to deduct such expenses, an election must be made not later than the time prescribed by law for filing the corporation's income tax return.

ACKNOWLEDGMENTS

I would like to express my sincere appreciation for the assistance of all my partners and associates, particularly Carl S. Stutsman, Jr., Leon S. Angvire, and John C. Westwater.

Contents

xvii

PART TWO: TAX CONSIDERATIONS

PART THREE: FIXING THE CAPITAL STRUCTURE

PART ONE

HOW TO DECIDE
IF INCORPORATION IS
ADVISABLE

1

Essential Considerations and the Steps to Be Taken Before Deciding to Incorporate

Before you can decide if it is advantageous for a client to incorporate, you must gather all pertinent facts relating to the client's business and personal needs and desires. After analyzing these facts, a decision can be made as to whether incorporation of the business will be both economically and practically beneficial.

What are the advantages of doing business in the corporate form?

- *Limited Liability*—personal assets of the business owner may be protected from business debts and other liabilities.
- *Tax Benefits*—a corporation provides flexibility for income tax planning and also permits the owner to take advantage of tax-favored fringe benefits that are not available to the owner of an unincorporated business.
- *Perpetual Life*--a corporation continues to be in existence regardless of changes in ownership resulting from transfers or death. Other forms of business entities may terminate upon the occurrence of such events.

- *Continuity of Management*—a corporation may easily acquire new owners by issuing shares of stock.
- *Easy Transfer of Ownership*—an entire business may be transferred to a new owner by simply transferring the ownership of the stock.
- *Estate Planning*—the corporate form of doing business provides flexibility in deciding how to transfer the business in the event the business owner dies.

[¶100] CHECKLIST FOR GATHERING THE DATA FOR INCORPORATING

☐ *What Is the Annual Net Income of the Business: First You Must Determine How Much Income the Business Is Creating.*

1. How to Determine Gross Business Income:

   The owner of a small business often keeps inadequate records. Many personal expenses are paid from business income. You must examine the income statement of the business to see whether personal expenses have been paid out of the business. If they have been, the apparent income from the business will have been understated.

   (*Note:* Some small business owners find it very tempting not to reflect all the cash in the business records. An advisor has an obligation to make sure that the owner is not avoiding taxes by concealing income. This book will show you how to help your clients minimize their taxes in a *legitimate* manner.)

2. How to Determine Annual Net Business Income:

   Once the gross income has been determined, figure out the net income. From a tax planning standpoint, it is the net income that is important—not the gross income. In reducing gross income to net income, *deduct* all business related expenses such as: Cost of Goods Sold; Rent; Accounting Fees; Legal Fees; Business Entertainment; Automobile Expenses; Advertising;

Business Taxes and Fees. The Internal Revenue Service does not consider personal expenses in net income in an incorporated business. Therefore, *add back* any personal expenses that the business has paid, such as: House Payments; Personal Entertainment; Personal Automobiles; Insurance Premiums; Medical and Dental Expenses; Daily Living Expenses.

By following this approach, you will be able to tell how much income the business is really making. If the net income of the business exceeds the living expenses of the owner and his family, incorporation may provide significant benefits. In order to take advantage of many tax-saving programs, it is necessary to have money to fund the programs.

□ How Is the Ownership Divided Up?

Is the business owned by one person or by several people? It is important to remember that what may be advisable for one person may not be advisable for someone else. Be sure to find out who controls the business. The success or failure of the business may be dependent on who has the controlling interest.

Are the owners strangers, or are they related? The relationship between the owners can have important tax consequences. Certain related persons, such as parents and children, are sometimes deemed to own each other's stock and this can cause problems. If a corporation redeems all of a person's stock in the corporation, this situation will be treated as if the stockholder sold the stock. However, if all of the stock owned by the person is not redeemed, the payment by the corporation may be treated as a dividend. Dividends may be taxed less favorably than payments received on the sale of stock. For example, if a father owned 50% of the stock of a corporation and his son owned the other 50%, a redemption of the father's 50% would not be considered to be a complete redemption.

Why?

Because the father would be deemed to own the son's stock for purposes of determining whether there was a complete termination of the father's interest in the corporation.

☐ *Does the Owner Have Income from Outside the Business?*

If the business owner or owners have income from sources outside the business, greater flexibility may be available for tax planning. If the owners do not have to use all the business income to live on, business income will be available to fund certain tax-favored programs. Also, it may be desirable to accumulate income in the corporation if the corporation is in a lower income tax bracket than the owners. Examples of outside income are: Interest; Dividends; Rent; Royalties; Gains on Sales of Property; Gifts or Inheritances.

☐ *What Are the Personal Financial Needs of the Owner?*

How much income does the business owner need to meet his personal financial obligations? Personal expenses include such things as: Rent or House Payments; Food; Car Payments; Clothing; Entertainment; Medical Expenses; Dental Expenses; Insurance Premiums; Travel; Education for Children.

If the personal expenses of the owner use up all of the business income, incorporation may not be advisable from an income tax point of view. Many tax-related benefit programs which are available to incorporated business require cash to fund them. For instance, a corporate profit-sharing plan would not be feasible if a corporation had no profits.

> *Suggestion:* Personal expenses such as medical and dental bills could be paid by a corporation on a tax-preferred basis as an employee benefit. This would provide more available cash.

> *Example:* Mr. Smith has an adjusted gross income of $40,000 and has incurred $1,000 worth of medical expenses.

> *Result:* Without incorporation, these expenses are not deductible because they do not exceed 3% of his adjusted gross income.

Comment: In analyzing Mr. Smith's financial needs, you should take this into account. If Mr. Smith incorporates, the medical expenses can be paid by the corporation and they will be tax deductible by the corporation.

☐ Does the Business Generate Surplus Funds?

After the net income of the business is determined and the other personal needs of the owner are analyzed, unallocated funds may remain. This is of critical importance if the owner intends to establish tax-favored fringe benefits for himself. For instance, the tremendous advantages which can result from establishing a corporate profit-sharing plan would not be available if the business did not have the income to fund such a plan.

☐ What Type of Business Is Involved?

One of the advantages of incorporation is that it can limit the owner's personal liability for corporate debts. If the business is risky (such as manufacture of explosives, making parts for airplanes, heavy construction, machine shop operation or manufacture of drugs), incorporation may be advisable to protect the owner from potential personal responsibility for a defective product or an accident. If the business is relatively safe (such as selling office supplies or other non-dangerous products or service business), the limited liability aspect of incorporation may be relatively insignificant. You should ask your client what his experience has been with respect to lawsuits being filed against him or other related businesses.

☐ How Are Corporate Profits Estimated?

A business should not be analyzed solely on the basis of facts as they exist at a particular time. Our economy is subject to severe fluctuations and a business that is successful today might be a failure tomorrow. Before you can adequately assess the financial condition of a business, you need to obtain information for several preceding years. Ask your client for his income tax returns for those years. This information will enable you to assess whether the business is expanding, contracting or merely maintaining a level income. The following worksheet could be used to assist in making projections:

FINANCIAL RECORD FOR XYZ BUSINESS

	19X4	19X5	19X6	19X7	19X8	19X9
Gross Sales						
Cost of Sales						
Gross Profit						
Net Worth						

In addition to looking at the records of the business involved, it is important to analyze present *industry conditions*. If the business is successful, is it something that looks like it will continue indefinitely, or is it just a fad? Trade journals can be reviewed to obtain information on an entire industry. Also, you might want to review the financial statements of publicly traded corporations in the same industry.

Before incorporating and establishing the fringe benefit programs, it is important to make projections as to the trend of the business. Unless the projections indicate continued financial success, incorporation could prove to be a disservice for your clients. In making projections, careful consideration should be given to assessing:

(a) Industry trends.

(b) Maturity and stability of the particular business being considered. For instance, how long has your client been in business? How long has the industry been in existence? Does the income of the business tend to fluctuate or remain constant?

(c) Dependability of client's profit.

(d) Necessity of new capital or retention of earnings to finance expansion.

(e) Possible changes in your client's personal financial needs, such as college educational expenses for children.

[¶101] PRELIMINARY PRE-INCORPORATION QUESTIONNAIRE

The following questionnaire will assist you in obtaining the information that is required to decide whether incorporation is advisable.

INFORMATION WORKSHEET—CORPORATION

1. Name of Client:

2. Income and Expense Information:
   - A. Business
     1) Get copies of income tax returns for the past several years.
     2) Ask client to project continuing income.
   - B. Personal
     1) Get copies of personal income tax returns for past several years.
     2) See if client anticipates any significant changes such as:
        a) Inheritances or gifts.
        b) Major expenses—e.g., college for children.
     3) List of assets and debts.

3. Who owns the business?

   - A. Just the client?
   - B. Several people?
     1) Who owns what percent?

   _____

   _____

   _____

     2) Who makes the decisions?
     3) Are the owners related?

Name	Relationship
_____	_____
_____	_____
_____	_____

     4) What would happen to business if one or more owners died?

4. Type of Business—for Risk Analysis
  A. What does the client, or his employees, do?
    1) Risk to outsiders?
      a) Truck driver
      b) Construction
    2) Risk to employees?
      a) Machine operator
      b) Window washer
  B. Type of product
    1) Dangerous, such as explosives?
    2) Product that could cause extensive damage if defective, such as airplane parts?
  C. Past Experience
    1) Any lawsuits against client?
    2) If so, what result?
    3) Any threatened lawsuits?

[¶102] EXAMPLES OF THE ECONOMIC BENEFITS OF INCORPORATION

After you have gathered the facts, you should be able to determine the economic benefits that are available to the business owner. You must analyze the financial situation of the owner *and* of the business.

Example 1: Suppose that ABC Corporation generates a profit of $20,000 before tax. The owner, Mr. Smith, decides he needs a bonus of $20,000 to meet his personal financial needs or needs to spend money on new equipment for the business. ABC Corporation may not be able to take advantage of certain fringe benefits, such as a profit-sharing plan.

Reason: There would be no funds to contribute to the plan.

Comment: Be sure to determine whether a business will generate sufficient cash surplus to be able to take advantage of corporate fringe benefits.

Example 2: Incorporation may be advisable even if a business has a modest income if the owner has substantial income from sources outside the business—say $20,000 from rent. The outside income may cover his personal financial needs, and he might very well want to incorporate to be able to take advantage of corporate employee fringe benefits.

Comment: Remember that it is the available cash in the business that determines whether many fringe benefit programs may be funded.

[¶103] SPECIFIC TAX-RELATED BENEFITS OF INCORPORATION

If it appears that the business will be able to generate a significant profit over a long period of time, then incorporation could bring numerous financial benefits to the owner. A significant profit generally means that a fair amount of money—say $25,000—is left over after paying business expenses and paying the owner enough to meet his personal financial obligations. The benefits available to the owner of such an incorporated business are:

- Personal *medical* and *dental* expenses may be paid by the corporation with tax-deductible dollars;
- Group-term *life insurance* premiums may be paid by the corporation with tax-deductible dollars;
- *Pension* and *profit-sharing* plans may be established; and
- *Disability insurance* coverage may be provided with tax-deductible premiums.

The specifics of these programs will be covered in detail in Chapter 8.

[¶104] HOW LIMITED LIABILITY WORKS TO THE OWNER'S ADVANTAGE

A corporation is a separate legal entity from its shareholders. The corporation, not the owner, is solely responsible for corporate debts and other corporate liabilities such as damage claims. If corporate liabilities exceed assets, the shareholders normally cannot be held personally responsible for such excess liabilities. If creditors can show that the corporation was set up as a sham to defraud creditors, the individuals may have personal liability.

Example: X Corporation manufactures a product that explodes and injures Mr. Jones. Jones sues X Corporation and gets a judgment of $100,000. X Corporation has a net worth of only $25,000.

Result: Jones can get the $25,000 from X Corporation, but he can't go after the owners for the other $75,000.

Comment: If the business were not incorporated, the owners would be personally responsible for the $75,000. Jones could take personal assets of the owners to satisfy the business liability.

Although the benefit of limited liability arises primarily in cases of involuntary product failure, be alert for other situations such as:

- Employee negligence;
- Trade creditors' claims in excess of corporate assets;
- Injuries to employees or others because of unsafe conditions on the business premises;
- In the case of professional corporations, malpractice by persons other than the shareholder himself.

Example: Dr. Smith and Dr. Jones form a corporation to practice medicine. Dr. Smith performs an operation on Mrs. Feeble and the operation causes permanent damage due to the negligence of Dr. Smith. She successfully sues Dr. Smith and the corporation for $100,000.

Result: Dr. Smith is personally liable because he was negligent. However, Dr. Jones is not personally responsible to pay anything to Mrs. Feeble.

Comment: If Smith and Jones were operating as a

partnership, Jones would also be responsible to see that Mrs. Feeble was paid.

[¶105] HOW LIMITED LIABILITY WORKS TO THE CORPORATION'S ADVANTAGE

The limited liability aspect of the corporation form of business operates in two ways:

1. The personal assets of the shareholders are protected from corporate liabilities; and
2. If your client engages in more than one business activity, the assets of one may be protected from the *liabilities of the other*. In order to provide this type of isolation from liability, it is necessary to set up a separate corporation to conduct each business activity of your client.

Example: Mr. Smith has one business that manufactures aircraft parts and another business that sells office supplies. Suppose the aircraft business makes a defective part that causes a plane crash. The victims of the crash (or their families) could wipe out the assests of both business.

Result: If neither business is incorporated, the assets of each business could be attached to satisfy the debts of the other.

If both businesses were conducted as separate corporations, the assets of the office supplies business would be protected.

[¶106] LIMITED LIABILITY WORKS TO THE BENEFIT OF SHAREHOLDERS

Shareholders are not responsible for corporate debts in their capacity as shareholders any more than they are personally responsible for other corporate liabilities. However, banks or other lenders normally will not loan money to a newly organized corporation without securing a personal guarantee of the loan by the shareholders. In such a situation, the individual shareholders would be responsible for the repayment of the loan because of their personal guarantees.

> *Example:* Mr. Smith forms a corporation, Smith, Inc., to conduct his business of manufacturing widgets. He transfers equipment worth $10,000 to the corporation and contributes $2,000 in cash. If Smith, Inc. went to a bank to borrow $20,000 for working capital, the bank probably would not loan the money without having Mr. Smith personally guarantee that the loan will be repaid.

> *Reason:* If Smith, Inc. did not repay the loan, and if there were no guarantee by Mr. Smith, the bank would only be able to recover the corporation's equipment and whatever other corporate assets were left.

> *Comment:* Until a corporation has significant assets of its own, the owner should be prepared to sign a personal guarantee and to supply the proposed lender with a financial statement before he can expect the corporation to obtain a loan.

[¶107] HOW TO LINE UP FINANCING

Borrowing by a corporation is similar to borrowing by an individual. The business owner should know how much credit his position justifies. He should not approach the situation as if he is asking the bank for a favor; he should realize that he is a potential customer of the bank and that the bank should want his banking business. He should have all the necessary financial facts and figures about his own business. The bank will be interested in determining whether the owner has the ability to evaluate the conditions of his business and the problems it faces and whether he has business ability.

A banker also will want to know how the borrowed funds will be used. Thus, the owner should be in a position to show that the purpose of the loan is reasonable and that the expenditure of the funds will still leave an adequate margin of safety for repayment of the loan. He should try to arrange a repayment schedule that he can reasonably meet. Along these lines, the owner should be prepared to make cash projections.

It is a good idea to have both personal and financial statements of assets and liabilities in addition to the financial statements relating to the projected business income.

What Bankers Want to Know About the Prospective Buyer. The banker is going to need additional information which he will get partially from discussion with the prospective borrower, partially from checking his credit files, and partially from checking with other creditors. The customer's or prospect's credit file and the accumulated information about a particular business and its owner are of tremendous importance in every loan decision. It is a marked trail which leads the experienced lending officer back through the history of the organization and its officers and enables him to uncover and evaluate information that might not otherwise be made available to him.

The banker will want to know these things about the prospective borrower:

(1) *Character, Ability, and Capacity:* Is the principal reliable? Does he made good on his commitments? Does he have the ability and the energy to carry out his plans? Does he have proven management ability? Does the organization have depth of management?

(2) *Capital Resources:* Is the equity in the business enough to carry the job? Are his own assets fully committed to the enterprise? Does the borrower have ability to supply further funds? Could he raise equity money outside? Is there a proper relationship between the capital commitments of the business and the amount of the loan requested, together with other debt which the business may be carrying?

(3) *Soundness of Company and Its Operations:* How good are its executives? Do they know where they're going? What has been the sales trend? Does it indicate acceptability of products? How competitive is the business? Is there product diversification? Is too much money going into new products? What is its reputation in the trade? How effective is its sales organization?

Are its plant and equipment old and uncompetitive? Are its financial records and controls adequate? Has the profit trend been healthy? Are its margins good enough to support the present level of overhead? Are disbursements for dividends, salaries and bonuses in balance with sales, profits, net worth and working capital?

(4) *Soundness of the Loan:* Is it for a proper purpose? Does the cash flow projection show that it can be repaid on the due date? Is working capital after scaling down past-due receivables and stale inventory sufficient to cover a reasonable loss and still provide reasonable protection for the loan and other creditors? Does the applicant have enough of his capital in the business as evidenced by net worth in relation to advances from trade creditors, other creditors and the new bank loan? Are any of the following conditions present to an extent which would throw doubt on the financial soundness of the business:

    (a) Heavy inventories in relation to sales?

    (b) Excessive dividends and salary withdrawals?

    (c) Heavy loans to officers of subsidiary organizations?

    (d) Large past-due receivables?

    (e) Top-heavy debt?

    (f) Too much investment in fixed assets?

    (g) An overextended position, indicated by excessive inventory receivables and debt and scrambling to apply income and funds to pay the most insistent creditors?

    (h) A revenue structure which indicates that any sharp drop in sales would throw the business into serious financial trouble?

Financial Ratios Lenders Check Into: Financial ratios are useful tools for evaluating a company's operations. There are many more, but it's likely that any lender will at least look at these:

(1) *The Current Ratio:* Current assets divided by current liabilities. This is a measure of the borrower's ability to meet current debt and his margin of working capital.

(2) *Net-Worth-to-Debt Ratio:* Tangible net worth divided by total debt; shows the relationship of the owner's investments to funds contributed by his trade creditors and others. It also shows the owner's equity and indicates his ability to stand up under pressure from his debtors.

(3) *Sales-to-Receivables Ratio:* Net annual sales divided by outstanding trade receivables; shows the relationship of sales volume to uncollected receivables. This indicates the liquidity of the receivables reflected on the balance sheet.

(4) *Cost-of-Sales-to-Inventories Ratio:* Cost of goods sold divided by inventory shows how many times the company turns over its inventory. This indicates the profitability of the business when weighed with the profit margin. It also shows whether inventories are fresh and salable and helps evaluate the inventory item in the balance sheet. It indicates the liquidation value of the inventory.

(5) *Net-Profit-to-Sale Ratio:* The annual net profit divided by annual net sales. This shows the relationship of net profits to the year's sales and the profitability and efficiency of the business.

(6) *Operating Ratio:* Relationship between net income and total net sales.

(7) *Earnings Ratio:* Gross earnings divided by total sales.

(8) *Capital-Employed Ratio:* Net profits divided by total capital employed.

(9) *Fixed-Property Ratio:* Total net sales divided by tangible fixed assets.

How Turnover Rates Figure as Financial Yardsticks: Monthly turnover rates also are important as a financial yardstick to bankers and credit men in evaluating the financial efficiency of various businesses. These financial tools, like ratios, show relationships between two elements of the business. Here are some of the most common types used:

(1) *Inventory Turnover:* The number of times that stocks

are sold out and replenished during a given period, such as a month, quarter, or year.

(2) *Accounts Receivable Turnover:* This indicates the number of times merchandise stocks are turned into sales during a specific period of time. It is the net sales divided by accounts receivable.

(3) *Turnover of Net Fixed Assets:* The amount of the net fixed assets required for each dollar of sales (total net sales divided by net fixed assets).

(4) *Turnover of Business Capital Employed:* Total net sales divided by total assets.

Other Yardsticks Bankers Use in Evaluating a Loan: Other things a banker will consider are whether the assets on the balance sheet should be marked down or up in value. He will look at the withdrawals which have been made from the business. The reconcilement of net worth will show the extent to which net worth has been increased by net profit for the accounting period, write-up of inventory valuations, profit on the sale of investments or real estate, profit on the purchase of the company's securities below book value, recoveries of items previously charged off or new cash investments. It will also show the extent to which net worth has been reduced by losses for the period, readjustment of plant or inventory values, and charge-offs of other fixed assets, and withdrawals and dividends.

[¶108] NON-FINANCIAL BENEFITS OF INCORPORATION

A corporation provides centralized management for the conduct of a business operation. It also provides a continuous life for the business. The corporation continues in existence even if its shareholders die.

Centralized Management and How It Works

The shareholders of a corporation are the ones who decide what the corporation does. However, since many corporations have too many shareholders to have them vote on matters of day-to-day business, a procedure is set up to delegate their authority.

The shareholders elect a Board of Directors who are responsible for managing the corporation's affairs. Since it is often necessary to make daily decisions without having time to consult all of the Directors, a procedure has also been set up to delegate authority to individuals who conduct daily operations. The Board of Directors elects the corporate officers (President, Secretary, etc.) for this purpose.

> *Comment:* In closely-held corporations, the shareholders, Directors and officers are frequently the same people. However, it is important to note that the President normally is the person with primary authority to make daily corporate decisions. For this reason, be sure that the personalities of the parties involved are conducive to centralized management.

> *Example:* Suppose Smith and Jones form a corporation in which they each own 50% of the stock. Smith is elected President and Jones is elected Vice-President. Both men have equal voice in the management of corporate activities, but Smith might appear to be the top man to outsiders. Be sure that in such a situation Mr. Jones is not a person who would resent being placed in a position of apparent inferiority.

> *CAVEAT:* If business owners are married, it is critical to determine how the spouses will react to centralized management. In many instances, the owners themselves will not be disturbed by having one person have more apparent authority than another, but their spouses might object.

A Corporation Has Continuous Life—What Happens if an Owner Dies or Becomes Disabled?

If the owner of stock in a corporation dies, the corporation remains in existence. The ownership of the shares merely changes hands. A corporation does not cease to exist unless the stockholders affirmatively take action to have it liquidated.

You should decide what role, if any, the family members should play in the management of the corporation at the following points in time:

- Currently,
- When an owner becomes disabled, or
- When an owner dies.

Normally, business owners have a compatible relationship among themselves. However, they may not want to have family members of their associates involved in the business. Therefore, it is important to outline who will be responsible for corporate management in the event of the occurrence of the contingencies mentioned above.

The death or disability of a corporate shareholder does not affect the operation of a corporation from a legal point of view. The corporation continues in existence, and it operates through its appropriate officers. If one of the officers dies, he is replaced by the Board of Directors. However, if the family of a deceased shareholder does not get along with the surviving shareholder, problems can arise.

> *Example:* Mr. Smith and Mr. Jones each own 50% of the stock of X Corp. Smith is an engineer and has been responsible for inventing the product that X Corp. sells. Jones, on the other hand, is a great salesman and has been responsible for promoting sales for X Corp. Smith and Jones are compatible and they each realize that the other is contributing valuable services to the corporation. However, the wives don't like each other.

> *Result:* If Smith or Jones becomes incapacitated, difficulties may occur. The wife of the shareholder who is unable to participate in corporate decisions will often interfere with the operation of a successful business venture.

> *Suggestion:* Consider all potential problems at the outset. It may be advisable to provide for the buy-out of

a deceased or incapacitated shareholder, as a means of avoiding problems.

[¶109] USING THE CORPORATE STRUCTURE IN ESTATE PLANNING

In many instances it is easier to transfer ownership of a corporation to heirs than it is to transfer ownership of a partnership interest. Specific ways in which corporate stock can be used to facilitate estate planning will be discussed in detail in Chapter 7.

[¶110] REVIEW PRE-EXISTING BUSINESS AGREEMENTS

If you are dealing with an unincorporated business that has more than one owner, it is quite likely that the owners may have entered into various agreements. A checklist of agreements might be:

- Buy–Sell agreement relating to the ownership of the business;
- Leases;
- Bank Accounts;
- Loans; and
- Other contracts.

All such agreements should be reviewed carefully to determine whether incorporation would cause any problems. Some questions to be answered are:

- Is it necessary for some third party to consent to the substitution of a corporation in place of the individual owners of a lease or a loan?
- Do existing contracts prohibit assignment to a new business entity?

The best plan for incorporation can be completely undermined if actions are called for which violate the terms of existing agreements.

> *Example:* Suppose ABC Partnership has leased a building which houses its manufacturing operations. The partnership incorporates and assigns all existing contracts and leases to the corporation. Unfortunately, the lease provided that it could not be assigned without the consent of the landlord.

> *Result:* ABC Partnership breached its lease.

> *Comment:* Lack of inspection of prior agreements may inadvertently cause your clients to incur penalties or damages for breach of a contract.

[¶111] HOW TO EXPLAIN THE COSTS INVOLVED IN INCORPORATION

Typical initial costs and expenses include:

• Filing fees with Secretary of State;

• Fee to obtain a permit to issue stock; and

• Costs of Minute Book and Stock Certificate Book.

It is prudent to advise your client of the total estimated expenses to get his corporation to the point where it will begin to provide benefits.

> *Example:* If limited liability is the motivating factor for incorporation, estimate only those legal fees involved in forming the corporation and transferring of assets. These fees would be for preparing the Articles of Incorporation, By-laws and Minutes of Organizational Meeting, and for preparing documents to actually transfer assets to the corporation.
>
> If establishing corporate fringe benefits is the primary reason, estimate the costs for setting up the fringe benefit programs, in addition to the cost of merely forming the corporation.

[¶112] WHAT IF INCORPORATION DOES NOT APPEAR TO BE WARRANTED?

If an analysis of the relevant facts indicates that incorporation should not be pursued because of insufficient income or minimal exposure to personal liability, you should so advise your client. The worst thing that can happen is to advise your client to incorporate when he shouldn't. He will not be very happy if he incurs the expenses associated with incorporation only to discover that the whole procedure has accomplished nothing for him.

PART TWO

TAX CONSIDERATIONS

2

How to Analyze the Tax Aspects of Operating a Business in the Form of a Closely-Held Corporation

This chapter will explain what happens from a tax standpoint when a business is conducted through a corporation. A "closely-held" corporation for our purposes means a corporation that has only a few stockholders. The stockholders are usually the officers and directors as well. In some states the terms "close" corporation and "closely-held" corporation refer to a particular type of corporation that is governed by different state laws than other corporations. We are not using the term in the technical sense. In our discussion a closely-held corporation is just like General Motors except that it has only a few stockholders.

Income tax consequences often will dictate which form of doing business will be most advantageous from an economic viewpoint. Our discussion will be limited to analyzing businesses with one or several owners. The basic forms in which such a business may be conducted are:

- A sole proprietorship;
- A partnership; or
- A corporation.

[¶200] SOLE PROPRIETORSHIP AS A BUSINESS FORM

The simplest form of doing business is the sole proprietorship, which involves one person engaging in business activity.

> *Example:* Mr. X individually operates a business of manufacturing widgets which generates $100,000 per year. He is a sole proprietor. To establish his proprietorship, Mr. X merely had to set up business accounting books to keep track of his income and expenses. The fact that Mr. X is the only owner of the business does not mean that the business is small in an economic sense. There could be many employees. Also, Mr. X may have invested a lot of money in his business. However, because of the tax and limited liability benefits that are provided by incorporation, most large businesses prefer incorporation.

[¶200.1] How Is the Owner Taxed on the Income?

In our example, Mr. X personally reports items of income and expense, and the net result is included as income or loss on his personal tax return. If a business is generating a taxable loss, the owner may deduct the loss if he is not incorporated. Thus, in such a case, it may be advisable not to incorporate because a corporate loss is not normally deductible by a stockholder. However, a loss can be deducted on the personal tax return of the stockholder if the corporation makes a special election to be treated under the provisions of Subchapter S of the Internal Revenue Code. (A corporation may elect to have income and losses taxed to the shareholders. See Sections 1371–1379 of the Internal Revenue Code.)

[¶200.2] Disadvantage of a Sole Proprietorship

A sole proprietorship has no limited liability since it is not a separate legal entity from the owner. The owner's personal assets are not insulated from business liabilities.

The owner of a sole proprietorship is not considered to be an employee of the business. Instead, he is treated as being self-employed for income tax purposes. Thus, he is unable to take advantage of numerous fringe benefits which are available only to persons who come within the definition of an employee.

[¶201] PARTNERSHIP

Whenever two or more persons own a business, the business will be classified as a partnership. It is like a sole proprietorship except that it has more owners.

[¶201.1] How a Partnership is Treated for Tax Purposes

From an income tax standpoint, each of the partners is treated essentially the same as a sole proprietor. Instead of directly reporting income or loss on his own personal tax return, a partner reports his distributive share of partnership income or loss. The partnership itself has to file an informational income tax return. The partnership return reports how the income or loss is to be divided among the partners.

Normally, the partners will have a written partnership agreement that explains how profits and losses are to be divided. There is no requirement for a written agreement.

[¶201.2] Disadvantage of a Partnership

The partnership does not provide any protection for the general partners against personal responsibility for business liabilities. In fact, a partnership exposes the partners to even greater potential liability than a sole proprietorship. The partners are not only responsible for the consequences of their own acts, but also for the acts of their co-partners.

> *Example:* Jones and Smith are partners in a law practice. Jones gives a client improper advice and the client obtains a judgment against Jones in a malpractice suit. Smith never had anything to do with the matter. Jones is unable to pay the judgment, and the client can hold Smith responsible.

A limited partner is one who has no interest in the management of the partnership. His interest is limited to an investment in the partnership business. The potential liability of a limited partner for business debts will not exceed his investment in the partnership.

[¶201.3] Fringe Benefits for a Partnership

Partners treated as being self-employed cannot take advantage of incorporated employee fringe benefits. They can, however, adopt certain benefit programs that offer more tax benefits to the partners than similar programs for a sole proprietor.

An example of such a program is retirement benefits. A sole proprietor may set up a retirement plan which has tax benefits. He deposits certain amounts each year into a retirement trust, and these amounts are accumulated to be used for retirement. He is allowed to deduct the amounts deposited on his income tax return. The earnings on the funds placed in the trust are accumulated tax-free until he retires. The only problem is that the sole proprietor has to cover all of his full-time employees under such a plan and he cannot discriminate against them. For instance, if he deposits 15% of his total wages into the retirement trust, he must also put 15% of their total wages into the trust.

However, a partnership may set up a retirement plan that excludes certain non-partners. As long as such a plan covers 70% of the full-time employees, the plan still gets the favorable tax treatment described above. There are other restrictions on eligibility which may be available, but these will be included in Chapter 8. In essence, the partnership retirement plan can be like a corporation's plan. For a partnership to be able to set up such a plan, the plan must exclude any partner who owns more than 10% of the partnership.

[¶202] HOW A CORPORATION PROVIDES TAX BENEFITS AND HOW TO AVOID POTENTIAL PROBLEMS

In contrast to a sole proprietorship or a partnership, a corporation is a complete separate entity from its owners. This is beneficial both for income tax and liability purposes.

Once a business is incorporated, all future income generated by the business will be income to the corporation. From that point on, the individual owners will receive taxable income only to the extent that the corporation pays them:

1. *Compensation* for services rendered as an employee;

2. *Dividends* as a stockholder; or

3. Cash or other property to *redeem* their stock.

Dividends have an undesirable tax impact. Both the corporation and the shareholder pay income tax on the amount distributed as a dividend.

Example: Corporation X has $100 of taxable income which it plans to distribute to the stockholders as a dividend. Of the original $100, $83.20 may be paid in taxes.

Reason: The corporation pays income tax of $46. If the remaining $54 is distributed to shareholders as a dividend, they include the $54 in their taxable income as unearned income. Dividends can be subject to Federal income tax at the rate of 70%. This means a potential additional tax of $37.80. Of the original $100 earned by the corporation, only $16.20 ends up in the pocket of the owners. If the $54 were retained by the corporation, it could be used for business purposes or invested without any additional current tax.

[¶202.1] A Corporation Provides Flexibility

Limit Personal Taxable Income: One significant advantage to operating in the corporate form is that the owner can limit his personal taxable income. He can establish a salary for himself. Income in addition to his salary can be:

1. Accumulated in the corporation; or
2. Used to provide various fringe benefits.

Earnings may be accumulated in the corporation. Each fiscal (taxable) year, the corporation will pay income tax and the remaining income can be used for business purposes or may be invested. Business purposes include such things as plant expansion or research and development. Investments include deposits in bank accounts or purchase of stocks or bonds. If a corporation invests in stock of another company, it is possible to exclude from its income 85% of any dividend income it receives.

$100,000 Can Be Accumulated Each Year by a Corporation with Favorable Tax Consequences: By law, a corporation pays federal income tax at the rate of 17% on the first $25,000 of taxable income, 20% on the next $25,000, 30% on the next $25,000, 40% on the next $25,000 and 46% on all taxable income over $100,000. In many instances, the first $100,000 of the corporation's taxable income can be accumulated at a lower after-tax cost than if the same income were taxable to the owners.

CORPORATE TAX CHART

Taxable Income	Effective Tax Rate
$ 25,000	17.00%
30,000	17.50
35,000	17.86
40,000	18.13
45,000	18.33
50,000	18.50
55,000	19.54
60,000	20.42

Taxable Income	Effective Tax Rate
65,000	21.15
70,000	21.79
75,000	22.33
80,000	23.44
85,000	24.41
90,000	25.28
95,000	26.05
100,000	26.75
105,000	27.67
110,000	28.50
115,000	29.26
120,000	29.96
125,000	30.60
130,000	31.19
135,000	31.74
140,000	32.25
145,000	32.72
150,000	33.17

CAVEAT: There are several important potential problems and benefits that relate to the accumulation of earnings, the source of earnings, and the investment of corporate funds.

[¶202.2] How to Justify Accumulated Earnings of More Than $150,000

Earnings may be accumulated in the corporation at a lower after-tax cost than if the earnings were distributed as compensation or dividends. Reference is made to Sections 531–536 of the Internal Revenue Code for limitations as to how much can be accumulated. An accumulation of earnings must be considered reasonable: Basically, if earnings are being accumulated for "reasonable business needs," no difficulty arises. "Reasonable business needs" include such things as:

- Business expansion,
- Research and development,
- Reserves for potential liabilities,

- Payment of business debt,
- Working capital for such things as inventories, and
- Loans to suppliers.

CAVEAT: Income may not be accumulated to avoid paying dividends. Dividends may not be deducted by the corporation, and they are taxed to the stockholders.

If earnings are accumulated beyond the reasonable needs of the business in order to avoid declaring dividends, the Internal Revenue Service may attempt to impose the *Accumulated Earnings Tax* on the unreasonable accumulated earnings. Due to the credit which the tax code allows, a corporation may accumulate $150,000 without having any penalty tax imposed.

If a corporation wants to accumulate more than $150,000 in earnings, it should keep detailed records of the business needs. For example, if a corporation plans to build a new building, corporate minutes should be prepared to reflect plans for expansion. Such minutes should include a description of the type of expansion as well as the place where the expanded facilities will be located.

Corporate records must be retained for several years as they may be the only evidence available to substantiate the reasons for accumulated earnings.

[¶202.3] The Accumulated Earnings Penalty Tax

If a corporation accumulates earning and profits instead of distributing them as taxable dividends, it runs the risk of a penalty tax under Code §531. The tax is imposed on the current year's "accumulated taxable income" at the rate of 27½% on the first $100,000 of accumulated taxable income and 38½% on any additional amount. This tax is in addition to the regular corporate tax.

A corporation may accumulate income without incurring the penalty tax if the accumulations remain below the accumulated earnings tax credit. All corporations are entitled to an automatic $150,000 credit, but members of a controlled group must split one credit among them. If accumulations exceed $150,000, it becomes necessary to show that the accumulation is for "reasonably anticipated needs of the business" (§537).

Checklist of Cases: Below, you will find a list of cases in which courts held that the accumulations were reasonable.

Accumulations were justified where they were for:

☐   (1) A definite plan of expansion even though temporarily postponed because of high costs and lack of funds (*Korrick's, Inc.,* TC Memo 1953-96).

☐   (2) Acquiring the stock of another corporation in the same field and constructing new buildings (*Hedberg-Freidheim Contracting Co.,* CA-8, 251 F.2d 839, 1953).

☐   (3) Converting a photo-finishing business to color processing where the conversion was a necessary move to keep up with competitors (*Fotocrafters, Inc.,* TC Memo 1960-254).

☐   (4) Advances and loans to a stockholder to enable him to buy land and make it available to a realty corporation (*House Beautiful Homes, Inc.,* TC Memo 1967-51).

☐   (5) A reserve for a pending lawsuit (*Casey,* CA-2, 267 F.2d 26, 1959; *Wean, Engineering Company, Inc.,* TC Memo 1943-348).

☐   (6) A reserve due to the threat of strikes in the industry (*Smokeless Fuel Company,* TC Memo 1943-425).

☐   (7) Financing and expanding oil drilling operations. It was taxpayer's custom never to borrow for these purposes (*Solar Oil Corp.,* DC Kan., 12/3/59).

☐   (8) Purchase of new machinery for virtually forced entry into new fields (*Wean Engineering Company, Inc.,* TC Memo 1943-348).

☐   (9) Expanding auto dealer's facilities (according to agreement with auto manufacturer) and to meet present and future operating costs (*F.E. Watkins Motor Company, Inc.,* 31 TC 288, 1958, *acq.; Breitfeller Sales, Inc.,* 28 TC 1164, 1957, *acq.*).

☐ (10) A reserve for converting small groceries into supermarkets, for carrying an inventory necessary to meet its future expanded business needs (*A.H. Phillips, Inc.*, TC Memo 1951-318).

☐ (11) Replacement of old machinery with new equipment bought for cash, even though credit is easily available (*Mohawk Paper Mills*, DC N.Y., 267 F. Supp. 365, 1967).

☐ (12) The hazards in a business subject to risks of weather (*Millane Nurseries & Tree Experts, Inc.*, TC Memo 1942-65).

☐ (13) Financing payments for watch movements (which it imported) within eight days after receiving delivery. Time of deliveries was not known and the corporation had trouble with bank financing (*Gsell and Co., Inc.*, CA-2, 294 F.2d 321, 1971).

☐ (14) A reserve of amounts that would have been spent on key-man insurance if it had bought such insurance (*Branford-Robinson Printing Co.*, DC Ct., 12/19/57).

☐ (15) The need for substantial amounts of working capital without definite plans (*Penn Needle Art Co.*, TC Memo 1958-99).

☐ (16) Payment of a mortgage on a subsidiary's valuable land, even where the subsidiary is not operating.

☐ (17) Reserves due to the honest expectation of major national depression (*Heyward*, DC N.C., 9/1/66).

☐ (18) The purchase of new equipment for a subsidiary by parent corporation (*Inland Terminals*, DC Md., 10/3/73).

☐ (19) Finance various ventures and maintain upkeep of buildings (*Starks Building Co.*, TC Memo 1973-256).

☐ (20) Repairs of railroad cars; maintenance of railways and equipment, the office building, and truck operation; and insurance reserves (*Sandersville Railroad Co.*, DC Ga., 385 F. Supp. 59, 1974).

☐ (21) The purchase of additional automatic equipment for a laboratory that is needed in the near future (*North Valley Metabolic Laboratories*, TC Memo 1975-79).

☐ (22) Purchase of undeveloped land of real estate developer engaged in the business of purchasing unimproved land and erecting stores and apartments (*Dahlem Foundation*, CA-6, 405 F.2d 993, 1969).

☐ (23) Needs of motel venture (*Montgomery Co.*, 54 TC 986, 1970).

☐ (24) Purchase of real estate, since a definite plan was in existence for several years (*Delaware Trucking Co.*, TC Memo 1973-29).

Accumulations for the following purposes may indicate unreasonable accumulations (Reg. §1.537-2(c)):

☐ (1) Loans to shareholders or the expenditure of funds of the corporation for the personal benefit of the shareholders (see *KOMA, Inc.*, CA-10, 189 F.2d 390, 1951; *United Business Corp. of America*, CA-2, 62 F.2d 754, 1933; *Regensburg*, CA-2, 144 F.2d 41, 1944).

On the other hand, if the loans are short-term, interest-bearing obligations and amply secured so that their repayment is a certainty, they become liquid assets; but under §531, the liquidity must still be justified (*Corporate Investment Co.*, 40 BTA 1156, 1939, *nonacq.*). Where there were large stockholders' loans but the corporations themselves were indebted to the banks in similar amounts, the loans to stockholders had no net effect on the corporation's liquidity position since the stockholders' loans were not from surplus but from borrowed money; hence the surtax wasn't imposed (*Walkup Drayage & Warehouse Co.*, TC Memo 1945-241).

☐ (2) Loans having no reasonable relation to the conduct of the business made to relatives or friends of shareholders or to other persons.

☐ (3) Loans to another corporation, the business of which is not that of the taxpayer corporation, if the capital stock of such other corporation is owned, directly or indirectly, by the shareholder or shareholders of the taxpayer corporation and such shareholder or shareholders are in control of both corporations (*Factories Investment Corp.*, 39 TC 908, 1963).

☐ (4) Investments in properties that are unrelated to the activities of the business or the taxpayer corporation (*Nodell Motors*, TC Memo 1967-209).

If investments are liquid; e.g., government bonds or notes, so that the funds can be readily realized when needed, the sole question is whether a business need exists for such liquidity. If the investments are permanent or not readily realizable, it must be shown that they are related to the taxpayer's business. What is related to the taxpayer's business is not restricted to the historical past. Expansion aims or obsolescence may require a conversion of the business to new end products; the necessity of such a conversion would justify earnings retained to meet the cost (*Dill Mfg. Co.*, 39 BTA 1023, 1939). On the other hand, the courts have held that a cold storage company went too far afield when it went into the construction business (*Perry & Co.*, CA-9, 120 F.2d 123, 1941).

The rules are stricter when the new business is not directly acquired by the taxpayer but is operated through another corporation. A new business of another corporation will be regarded as the taxpayer's business only if the other corporation is merely the taxpayer's instrument by ownership of all of the stock. Whether such ownership involves the improper accumulation of surplus depends upon the circumstances of each case (*Crawford County Printing & Publishing Co.*, 17 TC 1404, 1952, acq., *Lannom Mfg. Co.*, TC Memo 1952-42; *Kimbell Milling Co.*, TC Memo 1952-61). The acquisition must be made within a reasonable period after the accumulation of surplus. Investments should be related to the business of the corporate taxpayers; otherwise, §531 will probably be invoked.

☐ (5) Retention of earnings and profits to provide against unrealistic hazards or tort claims (*Turnbull, Inc.*, CA-5, 373 F.2d 87, 1967).

☐ (6) Accumulation to enable the corporation to redeem the stock of the two controlling shareholders who held 80% of the stock (*Pelton Steel Casting Company*, CA-7, 251 F.2d 278, 1958).

☐   (7) Partnership ventures and other non-corporate matters where actual working needs were well taken care of by cash flow. The expansion planned didn't take place. There was no declaration of dividends. The corporation was always in a desirable liquid position (*Goodall,* CA-8, 391 F.2d 775, 1968).

☐   (8) Investments were unrelated to the business. Diversification plans were vague, and there was no evidence of any future investment in another company. Company failed to prove its intention of lessening the income taxes of its merger shareholders (*Atlantic Commerce & Shipping Co., Inc.,* CA-2, 500 F.2d 937, 1974).

☐   (9) Contemplated construction of new plant was never carried out (*Roth Properties Co.,* CA-6, 511 F.2d 527, 1975).

☐   (10) Plans to refurbish buildings of a leasing business were vague (*Atlantic Properties, Inc.,* CA-1, 519 F.2d 1233, 1975).

[¶202.4] How to Prove Reasonable Compensation

A problem related to excess accumulation of earnings involves the deduction from gross income that a corporation is entitled to take for compensation paid to stockholders. If a payment exceeds a reasonable amount, the income tax consequences to the corporation and the stockholder may be detrimental.

Problem: The maximum income tax rate on earned income (compensation for services rendered) is 50%. The maximum marginal tax rate on dividend income is 70%. Thus, the owner of a closely-held corporation would normally try to handle payments to himself as compensation instead of dividends.

The corporation should also handle excess earning payments as compensation. In arriving at its taxable income, a corporation is allowed a deduction for compensation paid to employees for services rendered. It is not entitled to a deduction for dividends that are paid to shareholders. In a closely-held corporation the shareholders initially control how payments to them are designated. Therefore, payments would be called compensation in order to reduce the corporation's taxable income and accumulated earnings.

However, IRS May Not Agree with Shareholder

A problem arises when a shareholder receives higher compensation for his services than a person performing similar services for a corporation which he does not control. The Internal Revenue Service may attempt to classify a portion of the payment as a dividend.

Suggested Solution: Since the corporation may only deduct a "reasonable" amount of compensation, the following can be done to avoid potential dividend classification if it appears that a potential problem exists or may exist in the future:

☐ The corporate records should state the nature and extent of the duties of the shareholder-employee.

☐ Corporate records also should state why such services are so valuable to corporation.

☐ The shareholder should keep a record of compensation paid to other employees in similar businesses. He can obtain this information from business acquaintances or from financial statements of publicly held corporations.

☐ The shareholder-employee of a one-person corporation should enter into a binding contract with the corporation whereby he agrees to return to the corporation any amounts of compensation he receives which the IRS treats as a dividend. If a deduction is disallowed for any portion of his compensation, he reimburses the corporation, and he is entitled to a personal deduction in arriving at his taxable income of the year in which the reimbursement is made. The net effect of such an agreement is to put both parties in the same position as if the excess payment had never been made.

CAVEAT: If there is more than one shareholder, the advantage of the personal deduction must be balanced against the fact that the shareholder who is required to make the reimbursement does not receive the entire benefit of the reimbursement. He shares it with the other stockholders.

[¶202.5] How to Avoid the Penalty

It is possible for income to be accumulated in a corporation and be taxed at lower rates than an individual. Sometimes taxpayers attempt to minimize current overall taxes by incorporating personal service businesses or investment activities.

The business activity may produce unearned income that can be taxed at a maximum rate of 70%. If the individual reported the income, he can be taxed at a maximum rate of 70%. A corporation might be able to accumulate such income at an effective rate of 17%.

What Is a Personal Holding Company? With certain exceptions, a "personal holding company" means any corporation that meets an income test *and* ownership test.

INCOME TEST

> *At least 60%* of its adjusted ordinary gross income for the taxable year must be *personal holding company income*, and

OWNERSHIP TEST

> At any time during the last half of the taxable year *more than 50% in value* of its stock must be owned, directly or indirectly, *by or for not more than five (5) individuals*.

How to Apply the Income Test

"Ordinary gross income" means gross income less:

- All gains from the sale or other disposition of capital assets, and
- All gains from the sale of property used in the trade or business.

To arrive at the "adjusted ordinary gross income," the ordinary gross income is further reduced by deducting:

□ depreciation,

□ property taxes,

41

☐ certain types of interest, and

☐ rent paid by the corporation in connection with generating mineral royalty income and rental income.

Once the adjusted gross income is determined, it is necessary to find out whether at least 60% of such income constitutes *personal holding company income. Personal holding company income* is that portion of the adjusted ordinary gross income which consists of:

1. *Dividends.*

2. *Interest.*

3. *Annuities.*

4. *Rents,* unless such rental income constitutes 50% or more of the adjusted ordinary gross income *and* the amount of dividends paid during or attibutable to the taxable year equals or exceeds the amount by which the non-rental personal holding company income exceeds 10% of the corporation's ordinary gross income.

Observation: If 10% or less of a corporation's ordinary gross income constitutes non-rent personal holding company income (such as dividends or interest) then the corporation will not be classified as a personal holding company.

Example: Assume that Corporation X has interest income equal to 10% of its ordinary gross income and that it has rental income equal to 50% of its adjusted ordinary gross income.

Comment: Remember that a corporation must have at least 60% personal holding company income to be classified as a personal holding company. In the above example, the rental income is excluded from personal holding income because it equals 50% of adjusted ordinary gross income. Thus, the 60% test is not met.

If the rental had been less than 50%, the rent would have been personal holding company income, but the total personal holding company income would have been less than 60% of the total income.

5. *Mineral, oil and gas royalties,* unless: they constitute 50% or more of the adjusted ordinary gross income; other personal holding company income is not more than 10% of ordinary gross income; *and* certain trade or business expenses equal or exceed 15% of the adjusted ordinary gross income.

6. *Copyright royalties* with certain exceptions to prevent publishing companies from being classified as personal holding companies.

7. *Film rents* received with respect to an interest in a film if that interest was acquired before substantial completion of production of the film *unless* such rents constitute 50% or more of ordinary gross income.

8. If a corporation's other personal holding company income is more than 10% of its ordinary gross income, then personal holding company income also includes *amounts received as compensation for the use of tangible property* of the corporation. This rule applies only when 25% or more in value of the outstanding stock is owned by or for an individual who is entitled to the use of the property.

9. Amounts received under personal *service contracts* pursuant to which the corporation is to furnish personal services if some person other than the corporation has the right to designate the individual who is to perform the service or if the individual is named in the contract. These amounts are personal holding company income only if at some time during the taxable year 25% or more in value of the outstanding stock is owned, directly or indirectly, by or for the individual who performs, or may be designated as the one to perform, such services.

10. Amounts includible in taxable income of the corporation as beneficiary of a trust or estate under the income tax provisions of the Internal Revenue Code relating to trusts and estates.

The above explanation of personal holding company income is intended to alert the advisor to potential problem areas, but it is not meant to be a comprehensive analysis of this area of corporate tax law. If it appears that a personal holding company income situation might exist, direct reference should be made to the Internal Revenue Code and the Regulations thereunder.

To prevent avoidance of tax by corporate accumulations of income, Congress added the provisions to the Internal Revenue Code relating to "personal holding companies" (Sections 541–547 of the Internal Revenue Code). It is important to avoid having a corporation classified as a personal holding company if it plans to accumulate income. Any undistributed personal holding company income is subject to a 70% tax in addition to the normal corporate income tax.

> *Example:* Mr. Jones sets up a corporation to provide consulting services. The corporation enters into a contract under which the corporation agrees with Mr. Smith that it will provide the services of Mr. Jones for one year for a fee of $50,000. The corporation pays Mr. Jones a salary of $30,000 and accumulates $20,000. The corporation pays a Federal income tax of approximately $3,400. In addition, the corporation would have to pay a personal holding company tax equal to 70% of the undistributed personal holding company income or $11,620. Of the $20,000 retained by the company, all but $4,980 must be paid out in taxes.

Although only a few manufacturing concerns may be faced with a personal holding company problem, the penalties are sufficiently severe to warrant a discussion of the subject.

How to Define Ownership in a Personal Holding Company

Even if a corporation satisfies the personal holding company *income* provisions of the Internal Revenue Code, the corporation still may not be classified as a personal holding company. *REMEMBER:* A corporation is not a personal holding company unless more than 50% in value of its stock is owned directly or indirectly by or for not more than five individuals.

Constructive Ownership Rules

In applying the stock ownership test, the Internal Revenue Code provides specific rules for determining constructive ownership of a corporation stock—i.e., certain related persons will be treated as owning stock of other related persons (Section 544 of the IRC).

For example, stock owned, directly or indirectly, by or for a corporation, a partnership, or an estate or trust shall be considered as being owned proportionately by its shareholders, partners, or beneficiaries.

Also, an individual will be considered as owning the stock owned, directly or indirectly by or for his partner or by or for his *spouse, ancestors, lineal descendants, brothers and sisters.* The Code contains more explicit rules which should be reviewed if problems appear.

Escape Hatch

Even if a corporation is classified as a personal holding company, it is important to remember that the penalty tax is imposed only on *undistributed* personal holding company income. For instance, if a corporation is formed for purposes of taking advantage of employee fringe benefits and the owners do not intend to accumulate income, then no problem exists.

Non-Allowance of Inter-Corporation Dividend Deduction

If a corporation is not a personal holding company and it does accumulate income, the income may be used to purchase property for use in the business or it may be invested. If the earnings are invested in the stock of another corporation, dividends paid on such are entitled to favorable income tax treatment. Basically, a corporation is entitled to deduct from its gross income an amount equal to 85% of the dividends it receives from a domestic corporation which is also subject to income tax. This 85% deduction is not allowed in computing the accumulated earnings tax or the personal holding company tax.

Example: Corporation X owns stock in a publicly traded corporation and receives a dividend of $5,000 during the taxable year. Of the $5,000 dividend, only $750 is includible in the taxable income of Corporation X. However, the full $5,000 would be treated as personal holding company income for purposes of the penalty tax.

[¶202.6] What Happens if the Corporation Has a Loss

Although most business would not consider the possibility of incorporating for tax purposes if they were generating losses, it is important to understand the tax implications of losses. The shareholders are separate taxpayers from the corporation. They cannot offset a corporate loss against other income unless the corporation has made a Subchapter S election. Instead, the corporation must wait and offset the loss against future corporate income.

If a previously profitable corporation incurs a loss, the loss may be carried back of offset prior income. This will entitle the corporation to a refund of some or all of the taxes paid for the prior year (Section 172 of the Internal Revenue Code).

CAVEAT: Check state law as corporate losses are not necessarily carried forward or backward for purposes of state income taxes.

3

Subchapter S Corporations

In Chapter 2 the tax treatment of a corporation was based on the concept that the corporation was a completely separate entity from its shareholders for income tax purposes. A corporation is always a separate entity for purposes of limited liability (assuming that the corporation has been properly created and is not a "front"). However, given certain circumstances, a corporation may make an election to have its income or loss passed through to its shareholders in proportion to their respective stock ownership (Sections 1371 through 1379 of the IRC). If a corporation makes such an election, it is commonly referred to as a Subchapter S Corporation.

Sometimes a business will consider incorporation for non-tax reasons. However, the tax consequences of operating in the corporate form might be disadvantageous—for instance, if the business is generating a loss that the owners can deduct on their personal tax returns.

Congress decided that if a small business wanted to incorporate for business purposes, the possible adverse tax consequences of operating as a corporation should not act as a deterrent. Subchapter S of the Internal Revenue Code was enacted to provide relief.

If a corporation elects to be subject to corporate income tax under the provisions of Subchapter S of the Code, and if all the shareholders consent to such election, the corporate income tax is eliminated. The shareholders report the income or loss individually.

[¶300] ADVANTAGES OF MAKING SUBCHAPTER S ELECTION

There are several advantages that may be realized by causing the corporation to make a Subchapter S election.

A. Shareholders Deduct Corporate Losses. If a business anticipates generating a loss for a limited period of time, incorporation normally would deprive the owners of a deduction for such loss. However, by electing to be governed under Subchapter S, the owners may obtain the tax benefits of a personal deduction for corporate losses and still have the non-tax advantage of limited liability.

B. Shareholders Avoid Double Tax. Another advantage to making a Subchapter S election is that it avoids the "double tax" that currently results when a regular corporation is required to declare dividends to its stockholders. This advantage is clearly shown in two situations:

☐ When the corporation's earnings are too great to be paid out as reasonable compensation to the shareholder-employees, or

☐ When earnings are in excess of those which may be accumulated for the reasonable needs of the corporation.

A regular corporation would be faced with the necessity of declaring a dividend or facing the possibility of the accumulated earnings tax.

Example: If the shareholders and the corporation were subject to the maximum marginal tax rates, $1.00 of corporate income would amount to less than $.17 in the hands of the shareholders after corporate taxes and individual income taxes had been paid.

Reason: The corporation pays a tax of $.46. If the remaining $.54 is paid as a dividend and the stockholder pays tax at the 70% rate, his tax will be $.38. Total tax on the $1.00 would be approximately $.84.

On the other hand, if the corporation makes a Subchapter S election, the same $1.00 of corporate income would be worth $.30 to the shareholders as the $1.00 is treated as a dividend to the stockholder and he pays tax at the 70% rate.

Although neither prospect in the above example is particularly pleasing to the taxpayer, the Subchapter S election obviously results in a benefit.

C. Spread Income Among Family Members. A further advantage that may make a Subchapter S election attractive is the fact that the corporate income may be spread among various family members to minimize the total income tax for the family unit.

Example: Mr. Smith owns a business which generates $100,000 worth of taxable income per year. Mr. Smith has two grown children who are in a low income tax bracket. Suppose he gives 20% of the stock in a Subchapter S corporation to each of his children. Each child would report $20,000 of income. Mr. Smith's taxable income from the business would be reduced to $60,000. If Mr. Smith were going to provide financial assistance to his children anyway, the gift of Subchapter S stock has obvious tax advantages.

CAVEAT: This aspect of the Subchapter S corporation should not be abused. The Internal Revenue Service will reallocate income if it determines that a parent is diverting income from himself to his children by paying himself an unreasonably low salary.

Example: Suppose that in the above example Mr. Smith only paid himself a salary of $10,000. Persons in similar positions in other companies receive a salary of $60,000. The IRS might argue that Mr. Smith should have received a $60,000 salary. This would decrease the corporate profits to $50,000. Mr. Smith's children would be deemed to receive only $10,000. Mr. Smith would be deemed to receive $80,000 ($50,000 additional salary plus $30,000 profit).

D. Tax Rates for the Corporation and the Shareholders. If the corporation's shareholders are in a lower income tax bracket than the corporation, the total current income tax will be reduced. In this situation, the Subchapter S election also offers two advantages if funds are to be accumulated for business:

- *First,* since the total current tax is lower, more funds are available to be used in the business; and
- *Second,* the shareholders can loan the funds to the corporation and they can recover funds from the corporation in the future without paying additional tax.

If a non-Subchapter S corporation accumulates income, the accumulated funds are locked in; i.e., the shareholders would have to report additional income if the accumulated funds were subsequently distributed.

CAVEAT: Subchapter S Corporation Is NOT a Partnership. It is quite often stated that a Subchapter S election causes a corporation to be treated as a partnership from a tax standpoint. Such statements are clearly incorrect because many differences exist between partnerships and Subchapter S corporations.

A Subchapter S corporation is a corporation. A good example of the distinction between the two entities is the availability of tax-preferred fringe benefits that are permitted for shareholder-employees of a Subchapter S corporation that are not permitted for members of a partnership. For example, a medical reimbursement plan or group term life insurance is available for the benefit of shareholder-employees of a Subchapter S corporation. These tax-preferred programs are not available to partners of a partnership. It should be noted that pension and profit-sharing plans for Subchapter S corporations are more limited than for regular corporations.

FURTHER CAVEAT: Only "Small Business Corporations" as Defined in the Internal Revenue Code, Are Eligible to Make a Subchapter S Election. This, though, can be very misleading because "small" in the definition relates only to the number of shareholders. "Small" in no way has anything to do with the financial size of the corporation. As a matter of fact, some of the most financially successful corporations are forced to make a Subchapter S election because of such factors as the potential accumulated earnings tax.

[¶301] What Is the "Small Business Corporation"?

The Code defines a "small business corporation" as a *domestic corporation* which:

☐ Is not a member of an affiliated group;

☐ Does not have more than 15 shareholders (with certain exceptions to be mentioned later);

☐ Does not have a shareholder who is not an individual (again with certain exceptions to be discussed later);

☐ Does not have a non-resident alien as a shareholder; and

☐ Does not have more than one class of stock.

This definition appears to be fairly straightforward. However, there are many potential pitfalls in coming within the definition; so a fairly detailed analysis of the various eligibility requirements is necessary.

[¶301.1] Permissible Shareholders

As stated above, the corporation may not have more than 15 shareholders.

Joint Ownership. A problem sometimes arises in identifying the actual shareholders in situations involving joint ownership. Normally, the persons who have to include the dividends of the corporation in their gross income are the persons who are considered to be the shareholders of the corporation. The Code specifically provides that a husband, a wife and their estates shall be treated as one shareholder.

A corporation may not elect Subchapter S treatment if any of its stock is owned by a partnership because the partnership is treated as the owner (not the individual partners), and a partnership is not a permissible stockholder.

In order to make a Subchapter S election, all of the shareholders must be:

- Individuals,
- Estates, or
- Certain trusts.

Trusts. A trust may be a shareholder in certain circumstances. If the grantor is treated as the owner of the trust, the grantor is treated as the shareholder. If the grantor trust continues in existence after the grantor's death, he is treated as the owner for 60 days thereafter. If the entire trust corpus is included in the grantor's estate, the 60-day period is extended to a 2-year period. Also, a trust may be a shareholder if it is created to exercise voting power. Finally, if stock is transferred to a trust pursuant to the terms of a will, it may be a shareholder, but only for a period of 60 days following the stock transfer.

The exception which permits certain trusts to be eligible shareholders was added to the Code to be effective after December 31, 1976. The new rule recognizes the fact that a trust which is established for the primary benefit of its creator should not be a disqualified shareholder.

CAVEAT: Revocable Living Trusts as Shareholders. The new rule raises a very dangerous problem for the unwary taxpayer in situations involving revocable living trusts. Such trusts are often established for the purpose of avoiding probate proceedings upon the death of the grantor, and normally the trust may be revoked at any time during the life of the grantor or the joint lives of the grantors.

Upon the death of a grantor, all or a portion of the trust quite often becomes irrevocable. At the expiration of the grace period, the grantor would no longer be treated as the owner of the trust. Thus, the trust becomes an ineligible shareholder, and the Subchapter S election may be terminated unintentionally. Though it is permissible to have a so-called "grantor" trust as a shareholder of a Subchapter S corporation, it may not be desirable.

No Non-resident Aliens. The requirement that a corporation may not have a non-resident alien as a shareholder is self-explanatory. The reason for this requirement is that the government permits the corporation to elect not to be subject to corporate income tax because the individual shareholders will be taxed on the income. Congress imposed this restriction on stock ownership because non-resident aliens may not have to pay U.S. taxes in the same manner as resident aliens and U.S. citizens.

[¶301.2] Corporation May Have Only One Class of Stock

The requirement that a corporation will not be eligible to make a Subchapter S election unless it has only one class of stock was designed to avoid problems that might arise in allocating corporate income and loss among shareholders who own stock with different rights and privileges.

However, the Internal Revenue Service has often taken the position that two classes of stock exist even when the corporation appears to have only one class of stock. This problem arose primarily in the area where debt obligations were treated as a second class of stock unless they were owned by the shareholders in the same proportion as their stock. After a series of adverse court decisions, the Service has abandoned this avenue of attack on Subchapter S corporations. It is still important to remember that nothing should be done to create any question as to whether more than one class of stock is issued and outstanding.

[¶302] How to Make a Proper Subchapter S Election

Once it has been determined that it is advantageous to make a Subchapter S election and that the corporation is eligible to make the election, there are still certain potential problems that can prevent the corporation from making an effective election. Also, the election may be negated by inadvertent actions of the shareholders.

[¶302.1] Form 2553

In order to make an election to be governed by the provisions of Subchapter S, a corporation must file a Form 2553 with the IRS. The form must be filed within the taxable year preceding the taxable year for which the election is to be effective or within the first 75 days of such year. The first month of the corporation's taxable year does not begin until it:

- □ has shareholders,
- □ acquires assets, or
- □ begins doing business [Treasury Regulation § 1.1372-2(b)].

CAVEAT: If the election is not made in a timely manner, but is made prior to the end of the taxable year, it will be effective for the following year.

[¶302.2] Shareholder Consent

The corporation makes the election to be treated under the provisions of Subchapter S. It is necessary for all of the persons who are shareholders of the corporation on the day of the corporation's election to consent to the election. The consent by the shareholders should be filed before the last day prescribed for making the election.

Unlike the rules relating to the election, a late filing of a consent by a shareholder may be allowed if reasonable cause is shown for the delay in filing [Treasury Regulations Section 1.1372-3(a)].

[¶302.3] Spouse's Consent

A problem that often arises in connection with obtaining the consent of shareholders involves obtaining the consent of spouses who have a property interest in the stock. For instance, in a community property state, a husband and wife both must sign the consent to the Subchapter S election if the stock constitutes community property. This is true even if the stock is nominally held in the name of only one spouse.

[¶302.4] New Shareholders

If a Subchapter S corporation obtains a new shareholder or if an estate becomes a shareholder, the Subchapter S election may terminate. It will terminate, however, only if the new shareholder or the representative of the estate affirmatively refuses to consent to the Subchapter S election. A new shareholder has 60 days after he acquires the stock to refuse to consent. The representative of an estate must refuse to consent within 60 days after he qualifies as the estate's representative, or 60 days after the last day of the taxable year in which the former shareholder died, whichever is earlier [Section 1372 (e) (1) of the Internal Revenue Code].

[¶303] HOW A CORPORATION CAN CEASE TO BE A SUBCHAPTER S CORPORATION

After a corporation has made an effective election to be governed by the provisions of Subchapter S, and after the shareholders have consented to the election, there are still hidden pitfalls that may cause the election to be terminated.

☐ *Foreign Income*

There is a limitation placed on the amount of foreign income that a corporation can receive without having its Subchapter S status automatically terminated. If a corporation derives more than 80% of its gross receipts from sources outside the United States, the Subchapter S election is terminated [Section 1372 (e) (4) of the IRC].

☐ *Passive Income*

There are also limitations on the amount of passive investment income that a corporation can generate without having the Subchapter S election terminated. If more than 20% of a corporation's gross receipts (not gross *income*) are royalties, rents, dividends, interest, annuities or gains from the sale of stock or securities, the Subchapter S election will terminate [Section 1372 (e) (5) of the IRC].

□ *Ineligible Shareholders*

One of the most obvious ways to have the election terminated is for the corporation to obtain a shareholder who is not permitted to be a shareholder of a small business corporation. This method of terminating the election is so obvious that it hardly appears worth mentioning. However, it can happen inadvertently with potentially disastrous results.

> *Example:* Suppose a shareholder is a trustee of a grantor trust. As pointed out above, such a trustee is a permissible shareholder. However, if the trustor dies and the representative of his estate is unaware that he was a shareholder of a Subchapter S corporation, a problem can arise. The corporation's election will be terminated unless the shares are transferred out of the trust within the requisite time.

In addition to inadvertent revocation, a Subchapter S election may be voluntarily revoked if all of the persons who are shareholders on the day of the revocation consent to the revocation. In order to be effective, the revocation must be made before the close of the first month of the corporation's taxable year [Section 1372 (e) (2) of the IRC].

In any of the above instances of termination of Subchapter S status, the termination shall be effective as of the beginning of the taxable year in which the termination takes place.

In light of the relative ease with which a Subchapter S election may be terminated by having the corporation cease to qualify as a small business corporation, it is difficult to explain the strict timing requirements for a voluntary revocation of the election. *NOTE:* The IRS may ignore a transfer of stock to a nominal disqualifying shareholder if the purpose of the transfer is to artificially terminate the Subchapter S election.

CAVEAT: It is important to note that once a Subchapter S

election is terminated a corporation normally may not make a new election until the fifth year beginning after the year for which the termination or revocation is effective. However, a new election may be made if the Internal Revenue Service consents to such new election [Section 1372 (f) of the IRC].

[¶304] INCOME TAX CONSEQUENCES OF SUBCHAPTER S CORPORATIONS

It is important to understand how a corporation can come within the definition of a small business corporation and how it can make a valid election to be governed under the provisions of Subchapter S. It is also essential to understand how a Subchapter S corporation is treated for income tax purposes.

As mentioned previously, a Subchapter S corporation is not subject to Federal income tax except on certain capital gains. This aspect of taxation is relatively straightforward. However, the actual mechanics involved in determining the income tax consequences to the shareholder merit some attention.

Undistributed Taxable Income

The income of a Subchapter S corporation is taxed directly to its shareholders. This is true whether the income is actually distributed to the shareholders or is accumulated by the corporation. Amounts accumulated by the corporation are called "undistributed taxable income." Each shareholder must include in his income the amount he would have received as a dividend. (The total amount treated as dividends may not exceed the corporation's earnings and profits if an amount equal to the corporation's undistributed taxable income for the corporation's taxable year had been distributed to its shareholders on a pro rata basis.) A person must actually be a shareholder on the last day of the corporation's taxable year to be taxed on his portion of the corporation's undistributed taxable income. This aspect of the income tax treatment of shareholders can present tax planning opportunities such as splitting income among various family members at the year's end. It can also cause severe problems for people who purchase stock in a Subchapter S corporation without being aware of the rule. The term "undistributed taxable income" means taxable income with the following adjustments:

No deduction may be taken for:

- □ net operating losses incurred in other years, or
- □ dividends received from other corporations, or
- □ certain other minor items.

However, the following items may be deducted:

- □ taxes imposed at the corporate level (tax on the corporation's net capital gains including any minimum tax), and
- □ any cash distributions deemed to be made from the corporation's current earnings and profits.

A shareholder's portion of undistributed taxable income is treated as if the income had been distributed to him and he reinvested such income in the corporation. Thus, he is able to increase the basis of his stock in an amount equal to his portion of the undistributed taxable income.

Example: Smith owns 100% of the stock of a Subchapter S corporation. When the corporation was set up, Smith contributed $10,000 in cash to get the business going. His initial basis in the stock is $10,000.

Result: Subchapter S corporation accumulates $1,000 of income; Mr. Smith has to pay tax on the $1,000. However, the basis in his stock would be increased to $11,000.

Comment: Except for net-long-term capital gain and certain items of tax preference which may be passed through to the shareholders, actual and constructive dividends are reported as ordinary income by the shareholders.

Undistributed Taxable Income Paid to Shareholders

The Internal Revenue Code contains a provision to avoid the imposition of additional tax on the shareholders when previously taxed income is later distributed.

A Subchapter S corporation may distribute to any shareholder all or a portion of his share of the corporation's undistributed taxable income for prior taxable years and such distribution shall not be considered a dividend.

With respect to the corporation, such a distribution does not reduce its earnings and profits. With respect to the shareholder, it decreases the basis of his stock, and any distribution in excess of his basis is treated as capital gain [Section 1374 of the IRC].

In order to determine a shareholder's "net share of undistributed taxable income," it is necessary to reduce his portion of undistributed taxable income for all prior years by two amounts. First, it is reduced by the amount of the losses passed through to him in all prior years; then, it is further reduced by any amounts previously treated as not being a dividend because of the relief provisions that are now being discussed.

CAVEAT: Non-dividend treatment applies only to cash distributions. Distributions of other property may result in dividend income to the shareholder if the corporation had earnings and profits which were generated prior to the time the Subchapter S election was made [Treasury Regulations §1.1375.4 (b)].

The Right to Non-Dividend Treatment Is Non-Transferable

One other limitation is placed on the right to receive a distribution which will not be treated as a dividend. The right is non-transferable. Earlier it was mentioned that a shareholder could make year-end transfers of stock to spread the Subchapter S income among family members. In determining whether to make such transfer, it is extremely important to analyze what effect the transfer will have on the ability to receive further distributions of previously taxed income without having the distributions treated as dividends. The transferor of shares does not lose any of his share of previously taxed income. The problem is that future distributions made to the new shareholders will not receive the benefit of non-dividend treatment. A shareholder's right to non-dividend treatment does not continue once the Subchapter S election is no longer in effect. However, a cash distribution is treated as a distribution of the preceding year's undistributed taxable income if it is made with 2½ months after the close of the previous year. Such a distribution will be eligible for non-dividend treatment even if the Subchapter S election is not in effect at the time of the actual distribution [Section 1375 F of the IRC].

Capital Gains

As stated above, most income generated by a Subchapter S corporation is aggregated and taxed to the shareholders as dividend income. A Subchapter S corporation's net capital gain (less the taxes imposed on the corporation as a result of the gain) is treated as long-term capital gain to the shareholders to the extent that the corporation has taxable income for the year. If the distributions are out of current earnings and profits, each shareholder is entitled to treat his dividend distribution (actual or constructive) as including his pro rata share of the net capital gain.

A Subchapter S corporation normally pays no income tax. In some instances, however, capital gains may be subject to tax at the corporate level. If a Subchapter S corporation has a net capital gain which exceeds $25,000 and which exceeds 50% of the corporation's taxable income, and if the corporation's taxable income exceeds $25,000, a tax is imposed on the corporation. The tax is equal to the lower of the following two amounts:

- 30% of the excess of the net capital gain over $25,000, or
- the tax that would be imposed by determining the normal corporate income tax on the taxable income without taking a deduction for dividends received or for a net operating loss.

The capital gains tax applies only if the corporation has not been a Subchapter S corporation for the preceding three years or if it has not been a Subchapter S corporation during its entire existence. As was mentioned previously, if the corporation pays tax as a result of its capital gain, the capital gain to the shareholders is reduced by the capital gains tax and the minimum tax on capital gain tax preferences [Section 1375 (a) (3) of the IRC].

[¶305] HOW TO ASSURE AN ORDINARY LOSS DEDUCTION IF THE BUSINESS GOES BAD

One of the features of a Subchapter S corporation that may make the election desirable is the fact that corporate losses are passed through to the individual shareholders. If a Subchapter S sustains a net operating loss, each person who was a shareholder of the corporation at any time during the year may personally deduct a pro rata share of such loss. He deducts the loss for the calendar year in which, or with which, the taxable year of the corporation ends. The loss is treated as a deduction attributable to a trade or business. Any loss that is in excess of the shareholder's other taxable income may be carried back three years and forward five years [Section 1374 (d) (1) of the IRC].

In order to allocate the net operating loss, it is necessary to compute the *daily* net operating loss of the corporation. Such loss is then allocated on a pro rata basis among the shareholders on that day. The "daily net operating loss" is the total net operating loss divided by the number of days in the corporation's taxable year.

The loss that a shareholder may take is limited to the adjusted basis of his stock plus the adjusted basis of any amount the corporation owes to him. A shareholder's basis in the stock and indebtedness are reduced by his portion of the corporation's net operating loss. The basis cannot be reduced below zero. A shareholder does not obtain any tax benefit to the extent that his share of the corporation's loss exceeds his basis in the two items mentioned above.

If it is determined that the corporation will have a loss that exceeds the shareholders' basis in the stock or indebtedness, the stockholders can contribute additional property to enable them to take advantage of the loss deduction.

The shareholders are not entitled to a deduction with respect to capital losses incurred by a Subchapter S corporation. The capital loss may be applied against capital gains and the balance may be carried forward for five years to offset further gains. Any portion of the loss that cannot be utilized for either of these purposes is lost.

4

Professional Corporations

One type of closely-held corporation that merits separate consideration is the professional corporation. Because of the high income of some self-employed professionals, tremendous tax savings often can be achieved by incorporating a successful professional practice.

[¶400] HOW TO KNOW WHEN INCORPORATION IS INDICATED

A common misconception is that a professional has to make a certain fixed sum of income before incorporation is appropriate. In simple economic terms a professional should incorporate if he has the financial means to take advantage of corporate fringe benefits that would result in overall tax savings. In many instances, the personal spending habits of a professional or his spouse are a more important factor than the income from his practice.

By becoming familiar with the factors relating to professional corporations, you will be able to provide your professional clients with valuable assistance in planning. Chapter 8 will describe the specific fringe benefits that are available to professional employees of a professional corporation. These benefits are unavailable to self-employed, unincorporated, professionals. This chapter will present the steps involved in the establishment of a professional corporation.

It should be noted that the mechanics for forming a professional corporation constitute one area in which the income tax laws force a business to conduct its affairs in an artificial manner merely to achieve income tax advantages. For instance, it seems completely unfair and illogical to require a one-physician medical practice with no employees, other than the physician, to go through the expense and complications of establishing and maintaining a corporation in order to take advantage of such benefits as a profit-sharing plan. Philosophical objections to the requirement that a professional person must incorporate to obtain maximum tax benefits are not important from a practical standpoint. The requirement does exist, and it is necessary to be able to advise a professional as to the proper procedure to follow in order to incorporate his practice.

The mechanics of forming a professional corporation are prescribed by state law and will vary from state to state. However, the basic elements are similar. The following discussion will be based on the laws of the State of California.

[¶401] WHAT IS A PROFESSIONAL CORPORATION?

A professional corporation is the same as any other corporation, with one basic exception. That exception is that the shareholders must practice a profession that requires a license. The various State Boards which control the activities and practices of professionals do not permit the practice of medicine, dentistry, law, accounting, etc. by a corporation unless specific certification requirements are met.

Once a professional person sets up a corporation, it is necessary to apply to the governing Board for a certificate which will permit the corporation to conduct the relevant professional practice.

CAVEAT: Until such a certificate is obtained, it is unlawful and unethical to conduct business through the corporation. However, once the certificate has been issued, the practice can be transferred to the corporation in the same manner as any non-professional business is transferred to a corporation.

> *Comment:* Normally the issuance of stock to shareholders of a professional corporation is exempt from laws relating to obtaining permits, etc.

> *Reason:* Such exemption is based on the fact that only licensed professionals may be shareholders and thus the likelihood of misleading prospective shareholders is minimal.

[¶402] CONDUCT OF BUSINESS

After the corporation has been formed and the practice has been transferred, the most important fact to remember is that the corporation must be operated as a corporation and *ALL CORPORATE FORMALITIES SHOULD BE OBSERVED.*

The Internal Revenue Service has acknowledged the validity of conducting professional practices in the corporate form. However, it may attempt to disallow corporate fringe benefits if the corporation is a mere "sham."

CAVEAT: If no appropriate corporate minutes are kept, if the professional co-mingles corporate and personal assets, or if he treats the corporate bank account as his personal account, the IRS can eliminate all of the benefits for which the corporation was formed. This point cannot be emphasized enough since professionals frequently do not pay attention to details where business matters are involved.

The Professional Must Establish a Salary

One of the procedural necessities to be followed is the establishment of a salary for the professional employee. This can be one of the most significant practical stumbling blocks encountered in effectively setting up the corporation. The professional is quite often accustomed to taking a "draw" and then scraping up the money to pay taxes on an emergency-type basis when quarterly taxes are due. It is sometimes difficult for him to adjust to the fact that monthly withholding of taxes is essential for responsible financial planning.

[¶403] POSSIBLE LIMITED LIABILITY

The primary motivation for a professional person to incorporate his practice normally relates to the tax benefits. However, the limitation of personal liability is also an important factor. In a professional partnership, if one partner commits malpractice, all partners are jointly and severally liable for any damage caused by the malpractice. In the case of a professional corporation, on the other hand, the individual shareholders who did not participate in the act of malpractice would be liable only to the extent of their investment in the corporation.

> *Example:* Dr. Smith and Dr. Jones are equal shareholders in Smith & Jones, A Medical Corporation. Dr. Smith commits an act of malpractice on a patient.

> *Result:* Dr. Jones is not personally liable for payment of damages to the patient if Dr. Smith is unable to pay.

> *Comment:* If the practice had been a partnership, Dr. Jones would be personally responsible along with Dr. Smith.

Because of this ability to insulate against responsibility for damages caused by a fellow stockholder, the governing Board may require that a corporation obtain certain minimum levels of malpractice insurance. Or, in the alternative, they might require that the stockholders be jointly and severally liable for acts of malpractice committed by other stockholders up to certain minimum levels in the absence of insurance.

[¶404] PARTNERSHIP CONSISTING OF UNINCORPORATED AND INCORPORATED PROFESSIONALS

In situations where one is advising a professional partnership, it is not unusual that a large number of partners cannot reach agreement as to whether the partnership should be incorporated. The reasons for disagreement may include ignorance or personal ethical considerations. Also, the personal financial circumstances of a particular partner may make him unable to take advantage of the benefits attributable to incorporation. In the event of disagreement, a solution may be to have the partners make their decision on an individual basis. Those partners who favor incorporation do incorporate. They transfer their partnership interests to their new individual corporations. Such an approach offers a great deal of flexibility in terms of deciding what type of fringe benefits might be best suited to each partner.

Example #1: Doctors A, B and C engaged in the practice of medicine and each earns $80,000 per year. Dr. A is 55 years old and has relatively modest personal financial needs; so he is in a position to take advantage of the maximum fringe benefits. Dr. B is 45 years old with children in college and is spending all of his income. Dr. C is 35 and wants to take advantage of a profit sharing plan but is not able to set aside as much as Dr. A.

Comment: They should not incorporate because of the differences in objectives.

Suggestion: Dr. A and Dr. C should incorporate separately and each one can take advantage of whatever fringe benefits he feels are desirable. Dr. B should remain unincorporated until his personal financial situation improves.

CAVEAT: A potential problem arises if a corporate partner has a different taxable year than the partnership. A partner's income from a partnership is determined at the end of the partnership's taxable year. The amount of such income is included in the partner's gross income for the partner's taxable year in which the partnership's year ends.

Example #2: Partnership ABC has three equal partners and one of them is a corporate partner, A Corp. The taxable year for A Corp. is from July 1 to June 30. The partnership is on a calendar year. As of December

31st, the partnership determines the distributive share of A Corp. in the partnership income. The amount so determined is the gross income of A Corp. for its taxable year from the preceding July 1 to the following June 30.

Result: If the partnership has income of $90,000 for its taxable year ending December 31, 1978, A Corp.'s gross income for its year from July 1, 1978 to June 30, 1979 is $30,000 (⅓ of the $90,000). Income earned by the partnership from January 1, 1979 to June 30, 1979 would not be income to A Corp. for its fiscal year ending June 30, 1979.

How Does This Cause a Problem?

Suppose that ABC partnership was formed on July 1, 1978, and that A Corp. incorporated on July 1, 1978. The partnership made monthly distributions of $5,000 to A Corp. for the next 12 months. A Corp. received $60,000 during its taxable year. Suppose further that A Corp. paid Dr. A a salary of $4,000 per month.

At the end of the year A Corp. planned to make a contribution to a profit-sharing plan for Dr. A. A Corp. cannot contribute to a profit-sharing plan because it has no profit.

Why?

Remember, A Corp. only had gross income of $30,000 for its entire taxable year. That was its share of partnership profit. It paid out a salary of $48,000 to Dr. A; so it had a net loss of $18,000.

CAVEAT: Always remember that receipt of cash does not necessarily result in income.

Do not use the idea of multiple corporate partners to discriminate against non-professional employees unless you want to fight the IRS. For instance, Dr. A should not try to avoid covering his nurse under his pension and profit sharing plan by claiming she is an employee of the ABC partnership.

Although the professional Boards of some states have taken the position that the above-described arrangement would be unethical, such a conclusion is erroneous. The conclusion is based upon the theory that the public might be misled as to which persons are actually responsible for the conduct of the professional practice. The conclusion ignores the fact that the public can be equally informed in the case of (1) a group practice which includes corporate and individual partners or (2) a group practice which is incorporated in its entirety. As a practical matter, a partnership consisting of some individuals and some corporations offers more protection to the public than a completely incorporated professional practice.

[¶405] LIQUIDATION

What happens if the owner or owners want to liquidate the corporation? Problems may arise in the liquidation of any corporation. However, in the liquidation of a professional corporation, they are more likely to occur.

What About Goodwill?

Perhaps the most important potential problem relates to the fact that the practice that was incorporated may have had goodwill. No problem with goodwill would have existed at the time the practice was converted into a corporation if the incorporation was tax-free under Section 351. However, in a routine corporate liquidation, the shareholders recognize gain to the extent the fair market value of property received by them exceeds the basis of their stock.

One Month Liquidation

Thus, if goodwill does exist, the professional stockholder could recognize gain upon the liquidation of his corporation even if he receives no tangible assets. If it appears that this potential problem is present, it may be avoided by the use of a one-month liquidation under Section 333.

> *Example:* Dr. A and Dr. B had an existing medical practical that was incorporated. They were in practice for several years prior to incorporation and were well established in the community. They determined that they could sell their practice for a price in excess of the

value of the tangible assets because a number of existing patients would remain after they left. Therefore, if Dr. A and Dr. B decided to liquidate, the IRS could place a value on goodwill. If the Service did this, the doctors would recognize gain on the value of the goodwill.

Section 333 of the IRC can provide relief. In order to qualify for one-month liquidation:

☐ The liquidation must be made pursuant to a plan of liquidation.

☐ The transfer of assets must be in complete cancellation or redemption of all of the stock.

☐ The *transfer* of all of the property under the liquidation must occur within *any one calendar month*.

If the above conditions are met, the gain will be limited to (1) the amount equal to the corporation's current or accumulated earnings plus (2) the value of any stock or securities or money transferred to the stockholder in the liquidation. This limitation applies regardless of the value of the assets received by the stockholders. Most professional corporations do not accumulate earnings; so the one-month liquidation can be advantageous.

To proceed with a one-month liquidation, it is essential to understand the provisions of Section 333. A failure to comply strictly with its requirements will result in the loss of its benefits.

CAVEAT: A common mistake is the thought that the liquidation has to be accomplished within one month after it is commenced. Any one calendar month is sufficient.

5

Tax-Saving Strategies in Setting Up the Closely-Held Corporation

We have seen that a corporation offers many potential advantages to business owners. It can reduce the overall income tax imposed on business income by allocating income between the corporation and the business owners and by using different taxable years for the corporation and the owners. It can also provide limited liability. In addition to these advantages, there are numerous fringe benefit programs that can be established to create significant further tax savings to the owners of an incorporated business. The procedures for setting up such programs will be discussed in Chapter 8.

Once it has been decided that incorporation is desirable, what should you do? There are many areas relating to the incorporation process that can give rise to disastrous and irreversible tax consequences. The following discussion will explain what happens from a tax standpoint when a corporation is set up.

[¶500] TAX CONSEQUENCES OF TRANSFERRING PROPERTY TO A CORPORATION

First, examine the tax consequences of transferring property to a corporation. A transfer of property to a newly-formed corporation could result in taxable income to the owner of the property.

Example: Mr. Smith owns a piece of property which is worth $50,000. He paid $25,000 for it. Suppose he transfers the property to a corporation in exchange for $25,000 worth of stock and a promissory note for $25,000.

Result: Mr. Smith may have a taxable gain of $25,000.

Comment: Unless the incorporation qualifies for tax-free treatment, the IRS says the transaction is the same as if Mr. Smith sold the property. The fact that he received stock and a promissory note instead of cash does not make any difference to the IRS.

[¶501] DECIDING WHETHER TO USE A TAX-FREE OR TAXABLE INCORPORATION

A transfer may be made to a corporation in a completely tax-free manner if the transaction complies with the rules stated in Section 351 of the Internal Revenue Code. The rules in Section 351 are designed to insure that the transfer to the corporation is not actually a sale. The Code also requires that the ownership of the corporation is substantially the same as the ownership of the transferred property. There are a number of factors to consider in making a decision as to whether the incorporation should be taxable or tax-free. (NOTE: It is not always desirable to have a tax-free incorporation.)

For instance, the corporation may determine that it would be beneficial to get a depreciation deduction on the transferred property—i.e., the potential tax savings to the corporation (by getting a depreciation deduction) might be greater than the tax paid by the property owner if he transferred the property to the corporation. In our previous example, if Mr. Smith had a taxable gain of $25,000, the corporation could depreciate the property as if it had paid $50,000 for it. If the transfer had been tax-free, the corporation would only be able to depreciate it on a cost of $25,000.

On the other hand, if the transferred property was not the type that could be depreciated, a tax-free incorporation would be advantageous. Using the tax-free approach, Mr. Smith would have no taxable gain and the corporation would be treated as if it had paid $25,000 for the property.

[¶501.1] How Does a Tax-Free Incorporation Work?

In a tax-free incorporation, no taxable income or loss is recognized by the transferor, and the corporation's basis in the transferred assets is the same as the transferor's basis. ("Basis" essentially means the cost of the property for purposes of determining whether a person has gain or loss if the property is sold.) Also, the transferor's basis in the stock he receives for the transfer of the assets is the same as his basis in the transferred assets.

> *Example of a Non-recognition of gain problem:* Mr. Smith has a parcel of unimproved real property which is currently worth $50,000, but he only paid $25,000 for it 10 years ago. He now wants to transfer the property to his new corporation, but he does not want to have to recognize capital gain.

> *Solution:* If the corporation issues stock to him in exchange for the transfer of the property under a Section 351 incorporation, he does not have to recognize a capital gain at the time of the transfer. Mr. Smith has a tax basis (cost) of $25,000 for his newly issued stock (the cost of his property). The corporation has a basis of $25,000 for the parcel of real property (also Mr. Smith's cost basis for the transferred property). Now, if Mr. Smith were to sell his stock to someone for $50,000 cash, he would have to recognize a gain of $25,000. Likewise, if the corporation were to sell the property

for $50,000 cash, it would also have to recognize a gain of $25,000.

Comment: Note that the government has not lost its tax on the capital gain; it has merely postponed the time when the tax will be imposed until the stock is sold or the property is sold. The government is accommodating the businessman by deciding not to let income taxes be an obstacle to incorporating a business if (1) the ownership of the incorporated business is substantially the same as the ownership of the property prior to its transfer to the corporation and (2) if the transferor is not cashing out of his investment in the property.

[¶501.2] What Happens in a Taxable Incorporation?

If the incorporation is taxable, the basis of the assets in the hands of the corporation is equal to the fair market value of the assets on the date of transfer. The basis of the transferor's stock is also equal to that value. In addition, the transferor will have to recognize gain or loss on the transfer if the fair market value of the property is higher or lower than its cost basis to the transferor.

Example: Mr. Smith transfers his property (current value $50,000 and original cost $25,000) to a corporation in a taxable transaction. Thus, Mr. Smith has a taxable gain of $25,000 and the corporation would be treated as having paid $50,000 for the property. *A subsequent sale of the property by the corporation for $50,000 would not result in any taxable gain to the corporation.*

[¶501.3] Other Factors to Consider in Deciding Whether Incorporation Should Be Taxable or Tax-Free

Personal Income Tax Situation of Transferor

To determine whether the incorporation should be taxable or tax-free, it is necessary to consider the personal income tax circumstances of the transferor.

For instance, if a loss would be recognized by a transferor in a taxable incorporation, it must be determined whether the transferor can take advantage of the loss. An individual is permitted to deduct capital losses from capital gains that result from sales or exchanges of capital assets in the same year. Any unused capital loss may be carried over indefinitely to future years with the loss retaining its original character as short-term or long-term. Long-term capital loss only offsets other income on a 2 for 1 basis. It takes $2 of long-term loss to offset $1 of ordinary income.

If it is advantageous to have a loss recognized upon incorporation, consideration must be given to the ownership of the stock. A loss is not deductible if more than 50% of the stock is to be held by the transferor or a certain member of his family [Sec. 267 of the IRC].

CAVEAT: If any of the property to be transferred is depreciable, and if certain family members will own at least 80% in value of the outstanding stock, it is important to have the transfer meet the requirements for tax-free incorporation. If the transfer does *not* meet these requirements, any gain will be taxed as ordinary income instead of capital gain [Sec. 1239 of the IRC].

If it is important to have the incorporation taxable for purposes such as giving the corporation a stepped-up basis, the ordinary income tax treatment (except for possible recapture of depreciation) will be avoided if less than 80% of the capital is contributed by non-related persons.

CAVEAT: Recapture of depreciation means that the IRS may treat a portion of that taxable gain as ordinary income if the taxpayer has taken a deduction for depreciation in prior years.

For purposes of Section 1239, it is important to note that the measure of control in this regard is not measured by the number of shares owned, but by the *value of the shares.*

CAVEAT: If restrictions are imposed on the stock that is to be held by parties who are unrelated to the transferor, what appears to be a favorable result may present difficulties.

Example: In *Revenue Ruling* 69-33, 1969-1 C.B. 203, Mr. Martin owned 80% of the corporation's outstanding shares of stock. The remaining 20% of the shares were owned by a key employee, but they were subject to restrictions on sale. The Revenue Service held that Martin owned more than 80% in value of the corporation's shares because the restrictions on the key employee's stock made it worth less than Martin's. Thus, Mr. Martin's shares are taxed as ordinary income instead of capital gain.

Suggestion: Use a trust for children. Although Treasury Regulations provide otherwise, judicial support in the Fourth and Tenth Circuits has been given to permit the trustee of an irrevocable trust for the benefit of the transferor's minor children to hold 21% of the value of the stock to avoid the problem of ordinary income.

[¶502] HOW TO MAKE THE INCORPORATION TAX-FREE

If it is determined that a tax-free incorporation is advisable, the next steps are:

☐ Property must be transferred to the corporation *solely* in exchange for stock or securities in the corporation, *and*

☐ Immediately after the exchange, the transferring persons must be in control of the corporation [Section 351 of the IRC].

[¶502.1] What Is "Property"

The term "property" includes cash and other personal property and real property, but it does not include services. It also includes the bad debt reserve of a prior existing business. Even though a partnership may have received a tax benefit from its bad debt reserve, the unused portion of the bad debt reserve does not have to be treated as income in a tax-free incorporation. The transferor or transferors in a Section 351 incorporation may be individuals, estates, trusts, partnerships, associations, companies or other corporations. A creditor may even transfer his claim against a prior entity to the new corporation in return for stock. See *Suberling Rubber Co. v. Commissioner* (CCA-6, 1948) 169 F.2d 595.

[¶502.2] What Is a Security

A critical requirement of Section 351 is that the transfer of property must be made in exchange solely for stock or securities. Although this is a strict requirement, the term "stock or securities" is not clearly defined by the Code. The meaning of "stock" is fairly straightforward. However, determining whether an instrument is a "security" is sometimes difficult. As a general rule, securities are considered long-term obligations [*Jonn W. Harrison*, 24 TC 46, aff'd. (CCA-8, 1956), 235 F.2d 587]. A short-term note is *not* regarded as a security [*Pinellas Ice and Cold Storage Co. v. Commissioner* (1933), 287 U.S. 462].

Courts have ruled that notes of five years or less do *not* qualify as securities [reference *Lloyd-Smith v. Commissioner* (CCA-2, 1941), 116 F.2d 642, cert. den.]. They have ruled that a bond, debenture or script of ten years or more does constitute securities. [See *Helvering v. Watts* (1935), 296 U.S. 387].

The time period is one factor which the courts consider in determining whether a certificate qualifies as a security. The courts also evaluate:

☐ The nature of the debt,

☐ The degree of a participation and continuing interest in the business, and

☐ The extent of proprietary interest compared with the similarity of the certificate or note to a cash payment.

Basically, the requirement that a security be something other than a short-term note was added to prevent the transferor from cashing out on his investments in a tax-free manner.

A transferor who desires *not* to come within the requirements of Section 351 does not want notes or other evidence of indebtedness to be classified as securities.

Making the obligations short-term will not ensure that the incorporation will be taxable. The IRS and the Courts will determine the true nature of the obligations.

Example: If a corporation is under-capitalized (not enough property transferred for stock), the IRS might consider a short-term note as an investment in the business and classify it as a security.

If the decision is made that a taxable incorporation will be beneficial, the corporation should not be undercapitalized. No general rule has been developed to determine what constitutes adequate capitalization. However, the Code does provide five factors to consider in determining whether a debtor-creditor or a corporation-shareholder relationship exists [Section 385(b) of the IRC]. These five factors are:

☐ Whether there is a written unconditional promise to pay a sum of money on demand or on a specified date and to pay a fixed rate of interest;

☐ Whether there is a subordination to, or preference over, any indebtedness of the corporation;

☐ The ratio of debt to equity of the corporation;

☐ Whether there is convertibility into the stock of the corporation; and

☐ The relationship between holdings of stock in the corporation and holdings of the interest in question.

CAVEAT: The stock or securities must not be distributed to the shareholders in different proportions than the value of the property transferred by the shareholders. If they are, the Regulations indicate that in appropriate cases "the transaction may be treated as if the stock and securities had been received in proportion and then some of such stock or securities had been used to make gifts, . . . or pay compensation, . . . or to satisfy obligations of the transferor of any kind" [Treasury Regulations Section 1.351-1 (b) (1)]. A disproportionate issuance of stock will not cause the exchange itself to be taxable. However, the collateral transaction may create tax liability.

Example: Suppose that Mr. Jones and Mr. Smith are forming a new corporation. They plan to transfer equal amounts of property. Suppose also that Mr. Jones had performed some services for Mr. Smith for which he had never been paid. Instead of paying Mr. Jones cash, both men agree that Mr. Jones will receive 60% of the stock and Mr. Smith will receive only 40%.

Result: The fair market value of the additional 10% of the stock received by Mr. Jones is compensation to him. Also, since Mr. Smith had an obligation to pay Mr. Jones for the prior services, he could recognize capital gain. Mr. Smith would have to recognize gain if the value of the property he transferred to the corporation was greater than his cost basis for the transferred property.

[¶503] WHAT IF PROPERTY OTHER THAN STOCK OR SECURITIES IS TRANSFERRED TO THE SHAREHOLDER?

To the extent a shareholder receives property other than stock or securities, the shareholder may recognize gain up to the amount of the fair market value of such other property. Other property received is commonly referred to as "boot." Whether the gain is recognized as capital gain or ordinary income depends on the type of property that is transferred to the corporation.

Example: Mr. Carr transfers property worth $50,000 to his new corporation in exchange for a $10,000 demand note and $40,000 worth of stock. Let's assume that Mr. Carr originally paid $20,000 for the property. Since the demand note is not "stock or securities," Mr. Carr will recognize a $10,000 gain.

Reason: Mr. Carr would have a gain of $30,000 if he had sold the property. The demand note for $10,000 is essentially the same as cash. For this reason, of the $30,000 gain, $10,000 is taxable.

Comment: The tax basis that a shareholder obtains in the stock that is issued to him in exchange for the transfer of property is normally equal to his cost for the transferred property. The cost basis is *decreased* by money and the fair market value of other property received by the transferor. The basis is then *increased* by any gain recognized on the exchange [Section 358 (a) (1) of the IRC].

In the above example, Mr. Carr's basis in his stock would still be $20,000 after adjustments. His original basis would be reduced by the amount of the note ($10,000). It then would be increased by the amount of gain recognized ($10,000). The basis to the corporation of the property it acquired in the transaction is the basis in the hands of the transferor, *increased* by any gain recognized by the transferor. In our example, the corporation's basis in the transferred property would be $30,000.

[¶503.1] Transferors Must Be in Control Immediately After the Exchange

A tax-free incorporation is possible only if the person (or persons) transferring property to the corporation is in control of the corporation immediately after the exchange. The phrase, "immediately after the exchange," does not necessarily require simultaneous exchanges by two or more persons. Instead, it refers to a situation where the rights of the parties have been previously defined and the execution of the agreement proceeds with an expedition consistent with orderly procedure [Treasury Regulations Section 1.351-1 (a) (1)].

CAVEAT: "Control" is defined as (1) the ownership of at least 80% of the total combined voting power of all classes of stock entitled to vote, and (2) at least 80% of the total number of shares of all other classes of stock of the corporation.

To determine if the required control is present, the entire transaction must be analyzed. For instance, the transaction would not be tax-free if the contract for a later sale of stock exists at the time of the original exchange, and if the control requirement would not be met if the contemplated sale took place at the time of the exchange. This is true even if the stock is initially issued to the individuals who contributed the assets to the corporation.

Example: Matthews and Frame each transfer property of equal value to BW Corporation solely in exchange for 100% of the stock which consists of 100 shares of voting stock. They each own 50 shares of the stock. However, Frame has an agreement to sell 4 shares of his stock to each of 10 other persons immediately after the incorporation. If the 10 other persons had been stockholders at the time of the incorporation, the control test would not have been met. Thus, there is no tax-free incorporation.

Suggestion: If a later sale of the initial stock is contemplated, be sure that the later sale is an independent step. If it is part of a preconceived plan, it will prevent a business owner from meeting the control requirement.

[¶504] BUSINESS PURPOSE TEST

In determining whether the incorporation is taxable or tax-free, the IRS will also apply a "business purpose test." If the incorporation is merely one step in an overall plan which is designed only for purposes of tax avoidance, the incorporation will be taxable. The fact that a corporation assumes liabilities of the transferor does not make the exchange taxable. However, if the IRS determines that there is no business purpose behind the exchange or it appears that the *principal* purpose behind the exchange is tax avoidance, a problem arises. The total amount of the liability assumed by the corporation is considered as money received by the transferor and is taxed accordingly. Even if an exchange qualifies as a Section 351 incorporation, tax liability can occur. If the liabilities assumed by the corporation and liabilities to which the transferred property is subject exceed the total adjusted basis of the transferred property, the assumed liabilities which exceed the value of the assets are considered ordinary income or capital gain. Any such taxable excess is computed with reference to the liabilities and property of *each* transferor without regard to the adjusted basis and liabilities of other transferors [Section 357 of the IRC, Rev. Rule 66-142, 1966.1 CB 66].

[¶505] TAXABLE INCORPORATION

Sometimes it may be desirable for a corporation to obtain a stepped-up basis with respect to some assets while having the remainder of the transaction qualify as a tax-free incorporation. In such cases, the specific assets could be sold to the corporation at a later date so that the basis to the corporation would be the purchase price.

CAVEAT: If the sale takes place at or about the same time as the organization of the corporation or is made pursuant to a previous understanding, the IRS might attempt to treat the sale as a transfer to the corporation under an overall plan of incorporation. This treatment would cause the transferor to recognize gain on the transfer of all of the assets to the extent of the sales proceeds. This could produce a disastrous result if the incorporation involved the transfer of goodwill of a going business. The benefit obtained from the step-up in basis for the particular assets would be decreased by the tax imposed on the amount of gain attributable to the goodwill and other assets.

To avoid this problem, separate the transfer of the specific assets from the organization of the corporation by a significant interval of time (i.e., several months). This will support the argument that the two transactions are not parts of one plan. [See *Enola C. Hartley*, 467, 038 P-H Memo T.C.] The future sale should not be required by a written agreement executed before the organization of the corporation.

[¶506] WATCH OUT FOR RECAPTURE OF DEPRECIATION

The tax advantages which accompany a stepped-up basis for property transferred to the corporation in a taxable incorporation can be substantially reduced or eliminated because of potential recapture of depreciation. (Recapture of depreciation means that the IRS will treat gain that results from having taken depreciation as ordinary income.)

Example: Suppose Mr. Smith has a piece of equipment

which cost him $10,000 five years ago. He took depreciation of $1,000 per year so that its depreciated cost basis is $5,000. Suppose that the equipment is now worth $8,000.

Result: If he transfers it to a corporation in a taxable incorporation, his $3,000 gain would be ordinary income.

Comment: The recapture rules prevent the taxpayer from taking advantage of an unwarranted benefit. In the previous example, Mr. Smith was allowed to write off $5,000 as past depreciation. However, if the property is valued at $8,000, he should have deducted only $2,000. By recapturing $3,000, the IRS gives him depreciation of only $2,000.

NOTE: Any gain attributable to depreciable personal property will be taxed as ordinary income to the extent of depreciation taken after 1961 [Sec. 1245 of the IRC].

[¶506.1] Real Property

With respect to real property, there is recapture of depreciation to the extent of certain accelerated depreciation taken after 1963. There is recapture in full of any depreciation in excess of straight line depreciation for periods after 1969 on the sale of all real estate except residential rental housing [Section 1250 of the IRC]. However, if the incorporation is to be held tax-free, then there is no immediate recapture of depreciation. The transferor's basis and recapture potential for the property are carried over to the corporate transferee [Sections 1245 (b) (3) and 1250 (b) (3) of the IRC].

[¶507] INVESTMENT TAX CREDIT

In addition to recapture of depreciation, the transfer of certain property to a corporation could mean recapture of all, or a part of, any investment tax credit which was taken for the property. This occurs when there is an *early disposition of Section 38 property.* Generally speaking, "Section 38 property" means depreciable or amortizable property having a useful life of three years or more. The rule applies to the transfer of property in a taxable or nontaxable incorporation regardless of whether gain or loss occurs as a result of the transaction [Treasury Regulation Section 1.47-2]. Whether the entire credit or only a portion of the credit is recaptured depends on how long the property was held by the transferor at the time of the exchange [Treasury Regulation Section 1.47-1].

NOTE: If the incorporation merely represents a change in the form of conducting a going business, there is no recapture of the investment tax credit if the following conditions are met:

☐ The Section 38 property is retained as Section 38 property in the same trade or business;

☐ The transferor of the Section 38 property retains a substantial interest in such trade or business;

☐ Substantially all of the assets necessary to operate such trade or business are transferred to the transferee to whom such Section 38 property is transferred; and

☐ The basis of such Section 38 property in the hands of the transferee is determined in whole or in part by reference to the basis of such Section 38 property in the hands of the transferor.

[¶507.1] What Is Section 38 Property?

As defined, Section 38 is depreciable or amortizable personal property having a useful life of 3 years or more, and it includes:

☐ Tangible personal property;

☐ Elevators and escalators;

☐ Other tangible personal property (not including a building or its components) but only if such property:

    1. Is used as an integral part of manufacturing, production, or extractions of furnishing transportation,

communications, electrical energy, gas, water, or sewage disposal service; or

2. Constitutes a research facility used in connection with any of the activities referred to in 1; or

3. Constitutes a facility used in connection with any of the activities referred to in 1, for the bulk storage of tangible commodities.

[¶507.2] What Is Early Disposition?

Early disposition occurs when Section 38 property is disposed of or ceases to be Section 38 property before the end of its estimated useful life. The question of when property "ceases to be" Section 38 property can be a little tricky. For instance, property ceases to be Section 38 property in the following situations:

☐ Sale by a shareholder of stock in a Subchapter S corporation;

☐ Conversion of the property to personal use;

☐ Sale by a partner of his partnership interest;

☐ Contribution of the property to a partnership or corporation, unless a mere change in the form of operating the trade or business is involved.

NOTE: If possible, defer the transfer of any property to a corporation until recapture is minimized or eliminated. Often even a short delay can result in substantial savings depending on how long the property has been held by the transferor. If delay is not feasible, then the impact of recapture of investment tax credit must be considered as an additional cost of incorporation.

[¶508] HOW TO INCORPORATE AN EXISTING BUSINESS

Now that the problems that are encountered in the most simple type of incorporation (a new business) have been solved, it appears appropriate to analyze the incorporation of going business. When considering the incorporation of an existing business, it is necessary to consider certain problems that are not usually involved in the incorporation process. Some of these problems are:

- Goodwill;
- Inventory;
- Installment obligations; and
- Liabilities in excess of the basis of the property transferred.

[¶508.1] Goodwill

The earnings record and balance sheets of a business must be analyzed. Determine whether the business has experienced an investment return that is in excess of the normal rate of return for similar businesses. If so, this is evidence that the business has an asset usually designated as goodwill.

Example: Mr. Smith operates a business that manufactures a product. The business has a net worth of $100,000 and it generates a net annual income to him of $150,000. Mr. Smith could hire someone to take his place if he paid him a salary of $50,000 per year. Is there goodwill? There certainly is.

Reason: If Mr. Smith sold his assets and paid his business debts, he would receive $100,000. However, if he hired someone to take his place and keep the business going, he would make $100,000 *per year.* If he wanted to sell the business to an investor who was looking for a 20% pre-tax return on his investment, he could sell the business for $500,000 which is $400,000 more than the value of the tangible assets.

Comment: Goodwill arises when a business generates more than a reasonable return on the investment in tangible assets.

Possible Taxable Gain

Since goodwill enhances the value of the stock received by the incorporators, it will result in taxable gain if the transfer to the corporation is a taxable transaction. This point should be considered carefully because most businessmen do not think about goodwill or they do not realize that it exists. If the IRS determines that goodwill was present upon incorporation, it may be too late at that time to do anything to avoid any adverse tax consequences.

The importance of proper analysis also is emphasized by another fact. If the transaction is taxable, the value of any goodwill purportedly transferred may be taxable as ordinary income if the gain recognized on the incorporation is attributable to depreciable property and Section 1239 (ownership by family members) applies.

CAVEAT: When the incorporation is taxable, the results may prove to be disastrous if there is a substantial amount of goodwill.

Additional Problem with Depreciable Assets

The presence of goodwill can have adverse tax effects even if the boot (property other than stock or securities) received on the transaction is limited to the appreciation in value of the depreciable assets. In such a situation, the carryover basis of the depreciable assets in the hands of the corporation would not be stepped-up by the full amount of the recognized gain. Instead, the corporation would increase the zero basis of the goodwill by part of the gain and the depreciable assets by part of the gain. The allocation of the stepped-up basis would be made according to the respective fair market value of the goodwill and the depreciable assets. This would tend to minimize an otherwise advantageous step-up in basis for the depreciable assets. In fact, the presence of such goodwill could actually change a decision to effect a taxable incorporation for purposes of stepping-up the basis of depreciable assets. The additional depreciation available to the corporation as a result of the transaction may not be sufficient to compensate for the immediate tax liability incurred.

NOTE: If the potential problem of goodwill exists (and is recognized) at the time of incorporation, consideration should be given to transferring the depreciable assets at a future date and not having such transfer be part of the overall plan of incorporation. However, if a simultaneous transfer of all of the assets of a going business is the only practical course of action, the boot received by the transferors should be allocated in writing to the desired assets at the time of incorporation.

[¶508.2] Inventory

The transfer of inventory in a taxable incorporation will result in ordinary income to the extent that the boot received is attributable to it. However, there would be a compensating step-up in basis for the inventory in the hands of the corporation which may or may not be advantageous in a particular case. This would depend upon the applicable individual and corporate income tax rates.

[¶508.3] Installment Obligations

A problem can arise if a business uses the installment sale method in reporting its business income. The business would recognize the entire profit on part sales at the time of the transfer to a corporation in a wholly taxable transaction. However, if the transaction is nontaxable because of compliance with the provisions of Section 351, then no gain or loss will be recognized [Treasury Regulation Section 1.453-9(c) (2)]. If gain is recognized in a Section 351 transaction only to the extent of cash or other property received, the amount of partially recognized gain would be allocated to the installment obligations and the other assets transferred to the controlled corporation. In such a situation the amount allocated to the installment obligations would be ordinary income.

Related Problem—Payment of Business Debts

An existing business that is on the cash method of accounting can incur a problem with respect to unpaid debts which it has at the time of the incorporation. If the debts are assumed by the corporation, they obviously would not be deductible by the transferor [reference *Arthur L. Kniffen*, 39 TC 553, Acq.] because the transferor would not be paying them. It is quite likely that they would not be deductible when paid by the corporation because they were not the corporation's expenses. Instead, the corporation might have to capitalize the unpaid debts which it assumed from the transferor. The failure of the old business to pay the debts may result in the loss of any tax benefit.

Suggestion

In the case of the incorporation of a cash method business, it is advisable to have the old business retain sufficient funds to discharge its unpaid expenses so the deduction is not lost.

[¶508.4] Liabilities in Excess of Basis

In connection with the transfer of assets and liabilities from a sole proprietorship or partnership to a corporation, a problem can arise if excess liabilities are transferred. The transaction results in taxable gain to the transferor to the extent that the amount of liabilities assumed (whether mortgages or accounts payable) exceeds the adjusted basis of the assets transferred [Section 357 (c) of the IRC]. Any gain recognized as excess basis is taxed as ordinary income or capital gain determined by allocating the gain among the transferred assets according to their fair market values. The reason for the taxation is that unless the transferor remains personally responsible to discharge the liability it is no different than having someone else pay his debts.

NOTE: For purposes of the tax calculation, accounts receivable of a cash basis taxpayer have a zero adjusted basis. At the same time, accounts payable may be included at their face value. This position of the Revenue Service has been rejected [*Focht v.*

Commissioner, 68 TC 223 (1977)]. However, it may be desirable to retain sufficient funds within the old business to enable it to discharge its own obligations and avoid the transfer of excess liabilities. This action also avoids any question of deductibility of expenses.

[¶509] HOW TO INCORPORATE A PARTNERSHIP

Special rules apply to the incorporation of a partnership. It is not as simple as incorporating a sole proprietorship.

[¶509.1] What Happens When a Partnership Interest Is Transferred to a Corporation

Income Tax Basis to Partner

When an unincorporated partnership is liquidated, the basis of the property received by a partner is the adjusted basis of his interest in the partnership, reduced by any money received [Section 732 (b) of the IRC]. This basis is first allocated to inventory and certain receivables in an amount equal to the respective bases of the partnership.

The basis of stock received by a transferring partner upon incorporation will be equal to the former basis of his partnership interest. This is relevant whether the partnership property is transferred to the corporation before or after the partnership is liquidated.

Income Tax Basis to Corporation

The basis of the assets of the corporation will be the basis of the assets of the partnership if the transfer to the corporation is made prior to the liquidation of the partnership.

If the transfer to the corporation occurs after the former partnership has been liquidated, the corporation's basis will be equal to the total basis of the assets of the former partner.

Normally the Result Is the Same

The basis of the assets to the corporation generally will be the same in either situation. However, if a partnership interest was transferred during the term of the partnership by sale or upon the death of a former partner, the basis could be different. In the case of such transfers, the partnership may elect to adjust the basis of the partnership assets so the basis of the assets to the corporation would be the same whether the transfer to the corporation is made before or after liquidation of the partnership [Section 743 of the IRC]. An analysis of the partnership records is essential to determine whether an election to adjust the basis of partnership assets has been made. Regardless of the procedure followed to effect the incorporation of a partnership, normally there is not a reallocation of total basis among capital and non-capital assets. The partnership usually takes the non-capital assets at the partnership basis.

[¶509.2] Timing Is Critical

Timing is another important point to consider in the incorporation of a partnership. A partner must include his share of partnership income for his taxable year with which, or during which, the partnership's taxable year ends. Thus, if a partnership is on a fiscal year other than the calendar year, a partner can be faced with a bunching of income in the year of incorporation. The income profit is excessive because the transferring partner must include in his gross income his share of the partnership income up through the date of transfer in addition to any compensation he receives from the corporation.

> *Example:* Suppose that the XYZ partnership is on a June 30th fiscal year and that it plans to incorporate and retain the same fiscal year. The income of an individual partner for the calendar year in which the transfer is made will include his share of the partnership income for the period from the prior July 1 through June 30. It will also include any income he receives from the corporation from the date of incorporation through the end of the calendar year.

Result: The partner could have 18 months of income during the calendar year.

Suggestion: The impact of the bunching of income to the individual may be offset by establishing a relatively low salary for the balance of the calendar year. The corporation might also pre-fund certain tax-preferred fringe benefits such as pension or profit-sharing plans.

[¶509.3] Avoid Investment Tax Credit Recapture

The transfer of an established business to a corporation generally does not result in the recapture of any previously claimed investment tax credit.

[¶509.4] Be Sure to Comply with the Regulations

However, if the parameters of the Treasury Regulations are not followed in detail, all or a portion of such previous credit may have to be repaid. Specifically, it is important to remember two things:

☐ Substantially all of the property in the business is transferred to the corporation; and

☐ The transferors retain a substantial interest in the business.

CAVEAT: If a transferor receives both stock and boot in connection with the incorporation, his ownership in the business could be substantially reduced. If an interest in a business is reduced upon incorporation, the remaining interest owned by the transferor must be substantial in relation to the total interest of all owners. If the transferor's interest in the business remains the same, or has grown since the incorporation, then he is presumed to have retained a substantial interest in the business. The percentage of interest is insignificant.

[¶509.5] Completed Contract Method of Reporting

The liquidation of a partnership that reports its income on a completed contract basis may require the immediate accrual of all unreported income at the time of liquidation. The attorney for the business must interface with the accountant for the business review. Contingent or unsettled liabilities that exist at the time of the change-over should be looked at to determine whether they might be offset against future gains. Contingent or unsettled liabilities can only be deductible by the business entity that originally incurred the liability.

[¶510] HOW TO CONTRIBUTE ASSETS TO THE CORPORATION

Once the decision has been made to incorporate a business and the tax consequences of the process of incorporation have been analyzed, it remains necessary to determine which assets should be contributed to the capital of a corporation. Once assets have been transferred to a corporation, a taxable exchange will normally result if they are transferred out at a later date. The taxable transfer may take the form of a capital gain or loss, and/or may result in a dividend if the corporation has earnings and profits.

[¶510.1] General Rule

The general rule is to avoid the contribution of excessive amounts of cash or other assets. Retaining the excess assets outside the corporation might produce an overall tax saving. If such assets are needed in the business, they may be made available to the corporation in another manner. For instance, the stockholder could lease such assets to the corporation.

[¶510.2] No Excess Cash

Cash in excess of the reasonably anticipated operating needs of the business should not be contributed to the corporation.

Excess cash transferred out of the corporation is taxed to the shareholders. Unnecessary cash in the corporation might also prompt an IRS agent to attempt to assess the penalty tax on unreasonable accumulations of earnings. Excess cash puts a corporation in a potentially unjustified, highly capitalized position. If it appears that substantial earnings are being accumulated, a corporation should establish, document and take action on future business plans to avoid the penalty tax. Accumulations should not exceed the needs required for the established plans of the corporation.

[¶510.3] Don't Transfer Assets You Expect to Sell

Double Tax

If the owners of a business anticipate the sale of certain appreciated assets, such assets should not be transferred to the corporation. A sale of the assets after transfer could produce a tax at the corporate level and a second tax at the shareholder level. The tax at the shareholder level occurs only if the proceeds of the sale are distributed.

Possible Depreciation Recapture

If depreciable assets are involved, the gain on the sale could be recaptured as ordinary income. This will occur to the extent of certain depreciation deductions taken by the corporation. Under these circumstances, the advantages to be derived from a taxable exchange at the time of incorporation, to obtain a stepped-up basis for later depreciation, would probably more than offset the disadvantage resulting from the gain attributable to recaptured depreciation and taxed as ordinary income to the shareholder.

[¶510.4] Mortgaged Property

Two potential problems arise when mortgaged property is contributed to the capital of a corporation. As noted, Section 357 (c) provides for recognition of gain when a corporation assumes liabilities which exceed the adjusted basis of the assets transferred to the corporation.

Consideration must also be given to the transfer of depreciable property to a corporation that is owned by the transferor and certain family members. The transferor could be subject to an immediate tax at ordinary income tax rates on the amount by which the mortgage exceeds his basis. Below is an example of how Section 1239 may cause a tax difficulty:

> *Example:* The transferor bought an apartment house for $150,000 twenty years prior to incorporation. At the time it was contributed to his new corporation it was worth $320,000. The transferor had taken straight-line depreciation deductions of $60,000 over the years. This left him with an adjusted basis of $90,000. To obtain some tax-free cash he had refinanced the building and borrowed $250,000, placing a mortgage on the property as collateral. Selling the building would have resulted in a capital gains tax.

Tax Disaster

Upon the transfer to the corporation, the transferor had an immediate taxable gain of $160,000, the amount by which the mortgage exceeded his basis. Most of the gain was taxed as ordinary income because Section 1239 provides that when depreciable property is transferred to a controlled corporation the recognized gain is ordinary income. Since the bulk of the $160,000 gain was attributable to the depreciable building and only a small portion to the non-depreciable land, the gain was all primarily ordinary income.

[¶510.5] Two Methods for Avoiding a Problem When Borrowing Against Appreciated Property

There are two ways to avoid the problem presented when a person wants to obtain cash by borrowing against a piece of property that has appreciated in value and also wants to transfer the appreciated property to a corporation.

First, the person may transfer the property to the corporation and have the corporation take out the loan. The corporation could then transfer cash to the transferor as a return of capital since the corporation would presumably have little or no earnings and profits.

NOTE: If the property were acquired less than three years prior to the distribution of cash to the transferor, the collapsible corporation rules [Section 341 of the IRC] might apply and the transferror would be treated as having received ordinary income. [See para. 510.6 for a discussion of collapsible corporations.]

The second method of avoiding the problems associated with borrowing money against appreciated property is to avoid the control rule imposed by Section 1239. One possibility is to have an adult son or daughter own at least 21% of the stock of the corporation. Only stock owned by the transferor's spouse, minor children or grandchildren is attributed to the transferor for purposes of the control requirement.

[¶510.6] How to Avoid the Problem of a Collapsible Corporation

The collapsible corporation rules were enacted to prevent a taxpayer from converting ordinary income into capital gains by having the corporation liquidated or by having the corporate stock sold before the corporation could realize a substantial part of the taxable income that would otherwise result from the sale of certain property [Section 341 of the IRC].

A "collapsible" corporation is one which is formed principally for the:

☐ Manufacture, construction, or production of property; or

☐ Purchase of property that would be inventory, i.e., property held by the corporation primarily for sale to customers in the ordinary course of business, unrealized receivables or fees, trade and business property and which property is held for less than three years; or

☐ Holding of stock in a corporation formed or availed of to do the preceding acts.

Secondly, a "collapsible" corporation is one which is formed for the:

☐ Sale or exchange of stock by its shareholders on a distribution to its shareholders before the corporation realizes a substantial part of the taxable income to be derived from such property; and

☐ Realization by such shareholders of gain attributable to such property.

A shareholder who owns more than 5% of the stock of a "collapsible" corporation will receive ordinary income treatment on any gain resulting from the sale or exchange of such stock or from the partial or complete liquidation of the corporation.

Here is a rundown on some of the moves that can be taken to avoid collapsibility and to get capital gain treatment.

☐ *Stock Ownership Not High Enough:* The rules do not apply if after commencement of construction you do not own more than 5% of the value of the corporation's stock. This defense by itself should exempt most shareholders of a widely held corporation.

☐ *Gain Attributable to Noncollapsible Property:* If at least 30% of the recognized gain is attributable to noncollapsible property, collapsible status may be avoided [Section 341 (d) (2)]. This rule is most useful because collapsibility may be avoided where the corporation has more than one property and a substantial amount of income is realized from one of them. Here are two examples of how this works:

Example 1: A corporation owning two commercial buildings on separate tracts is collapsed at a time when $80,000 out of a possible $200,000 total rental income is realized from one building and nothing (out of a possible $300,000) is received on the other which was just completed. If 40% constitutes a "substantial" realization of income, the first building constitutes a noncollapsible asset. And if a sale of the stock yields a gain of $475,000, with $175,000 (after expenses) attributable to the non-collapsible asset, then the 30% rule is satisfied.

Example 2: If, however, the two buildings in example (1) were physically connected on a single tract and were rented to a single commercial tenant, they might constitute an integrated property so that with only 16% of the total income recognized ($80,000/$500,000) the entire property would probably be deemed "collapsible," and the 30% rule would have no application.

Note: IRS has held that the land and the improvements thereon are a single property so that in most cases involving land and buildings, the 30% rule would not help [Rev. Rul. 68-476, CB 1968-2, 139].

☐ *Right Timing:* The rules do not apply if gain is realized by the shareholder after the expiration of three years following the completion of construction of the property.

Note: While routine repairs would not constitute "construction" for purposes of Section 341 [Rev. Rul. 63-114, CB 1963-1, 74], substantial improvements would prolong the completion of the activity and thus the running of the three-year waiting period.

☐ *Sale of Assets:* Where the corporation is thought to be collapsible, it may be best to have the corporation sell its assets and then liquidate. If the corporation is in fact collapsible, the corporation will presumably pay a capital gain tax on the sale, and you will have to pay a capital gain tax on the liquidation on the amount that's left.

☐ *Tax-Free Reorganization:* The adverse results of a collapsible situation can also be avoided by a tax-free reorganization, since the collapsible rules do not extend to transactions in which there is no recognized gain.

☐ *Multiple Entities:* When you intend to develop more than one property, it may be advantageous to incorporate each property separately. In this way, the favorable three-year rule can be applied on an individual basis. What's more, if an unfavorable determination is made with regard to one property, it will not infect other properties. However, a single corporation may be preferable where you want to keep the gain above the 30% limit so as to come within this exception.

☐ *Subchapter S Election:* If a potentially collapsible corporation has an office building or other Section 1231 asset as its principal asset, electing Subchapter S treatment may avoid Section 341 consequences. If the corporation sells the assets and distributes the proceeds to the shareholders in liquidation, the gain on the sale passes through to the shareholders as a long-term capital gain.

☐ *Using Two Holding Companies to Avoid Collapsible Rules:* You can't avoid the collapsible rules by using a corporation (other than the corporation manufacturing, constructing, producing or purchasing collapsible assets) to hold the stock of a collapsible corporation. Section 341 provides that such a holding company is also a collapsible corporation. However, since the Section only speaks of one such holding company, it might be possible to avoid it by the use of two holding companies—the first holding company holds the stock of the collapsible corporation, and the second holding company holds the stock of the first holding company. Note that where the collapsible rules have been applied to the liquidated subsidiary they won't be again applied upon liquidation of the parent [Rev. Rul. 56-50, CB 1956-1, 174].

[¶511] LEASES TO THE CORPORATION

It is frequently desirable to have certain business assets retained by the incorporators in their capacity as individuals so they can be leased to the corporation or assigned on a royalty basis. As a result, additional corporate earnings may be paid to the business owners without the double tax which accompanies dividend distributions. Certain assets lend themselves to this type of treatment. For example:

• patents;
• copyrights; and

• real property on which the office or plant of the business is located.

The retention of income-producing assets by the incorporators may have the desirable effect of spreading the aggregate income of the business among separate taxpayers. It also can avoid any later spin-off or split-up complications.

> *Example:* Mr. Smith owns a piece of real property on which his business is located. He also has two children for whom he provides some support. They have a relatively low income and Mr. Smith has a high income.
>
> Suppose Mr. Smith gives a portion of the real property to his children. If the children lease the property to the corporation, the children receive rental income on which they pay taxes. Mr. Smith does not pay taxes.

[¶512] ASSETS GENERATING TAX-EXEMPT INCOME

In the event the business holds any assets that produce tax-exempt income, such as state or municipal securities, such assets should not be transferred to the corporation. While the interest received by the corporation would be exempt from taxation, a later distribution of the income probably would be taxed as a dividend to the stockholders.

[¶513] MISCELLANEOUS CONSIDERATIONS

The following four paragraphs are items that should be considered when organizing a corporation. You may use all of them, or none of them, but you should be aware of them.

[¶513.1] Reporting on Installment Basis

If a business is reporting income on the installment basis and you contemplate incorporation prior to the payment of outstanding obligations, the unreported profit on installment sales would have to be reported on the final return. The exception would be if the transfer to the corporation is tax-free.

> *Suggestion:* If a taxable incorporation is desired, perhaps the incorporation could be delayed until collection of installment sales has been completed.

The disadvantage of paying additional tax on unreported profit in a taxable incorporation should be measured against the advantage of obtaining a stepped-up basis for purposes of depreciation.

[¶513.2] How to Handle Operating Losses

Section 172 of the Internal Revenue Code provides, in general, that operating losses of a business may be carried back three years [Section 172 (b) (1) (A) (i)] and the unused portion of such losses may be carried forward to each of the next seven years, following the loss year [Section 172 (b) (1) (B)].

> *Example:* If a business operated at a profit of $5,000 a year for each of five years and then incurred a loss of $10,000, the loss could be used to offset the preceding two years' income and the taxpayer would receive a refund. If the loss was larger than the total income for the preceding three years, the excess could be used to reduce taxable income for the next seven years.

Special rules apply for deductions that may be taken in determining the existence of a net operating loss for both corporate and non-corporate taxpayers. If an existing business is to be incorporated, the advantages of a loss carryover may not be retained.

CAVEAT: It is significant to determine whether the business to be incorporated has generated a net operating loss in excess of the amount that can be offset against prior income. If so, the excess is of no value if it cannot be carried forward beyond the date of incorporation. In most instances, the deductions of one taxpayer may not be used to offset the income of another taxpayer. By applying the same rule, any losses of the new corporation cannot be carried back to offset the income of the prior noncorporate business [*Wisconsin Central Railroad Co. v. United States* (C+Cl., 1961), 296 F.2d 750].

If such a loss period is involved, the tax savings anticipated by operating as a corporation should be balanced against the cost of losing the ability to carry the loss over to the corporation.

> *Suggestion:* It may be advantageous to keep the partnership or proprietorship in existence until the advantage of the loss has been fully utilized.

[¶513.3] The Effect of Using Multiple Corporations

Frequently, the use of more than one corporation can result in tax savings. Establishing more than one corporation is simple when a natural division of the business activity exists. Spreading the income over multiple corporate entities lessens the impact of the graduated income tax rates. Each separate corporation is entitled to an accumulated earnings surtax credit [Section 535 (c) of the IRC] for purposes of determining whether the corporation has an unreasonable accumulation of earnings.

There must be a bona fide basis for the division of the business. If not, the IRS may disregard the formal structure and allocate the income, deductions, credits and other items to properly reflect the taxable income of the entire business [Sections 61, 269 (a) (1) and 482 of the IRC]. If the corporations are related, they are not permitted to apply the under-46% rates to more than one of each of the $25,000 income brackets. Also, the accumulated earnings surtax credit must be shared by the whole group. The tax credit is to be divided equally among the controlled corporations, or to be allocated in such a manner as the group elects [Sections 1561-1564 of the IRC].

How to Define a Controlled Group: These restrictions are applicable to the division of an existing business into multiple corporations only in instances when:

☐ Five or fewer persons (individuals, estates or trusts) own at least 80% of the voting stock or the value of the corporation, and

☐ The same five or fewer persons own more than 50% of the voting stock or value of each corporation, considering a particular person's stock only to the extent that it is owned identically with regard to each corporation [Section 1563 (a) (2) of the IRC].

How to Define "owned identically with regard to each corporation": This term means that each stockholder is considered to own a percentage of the group that is equal to the lowest percentage he owns in any one corporation. The rules for determining whether a controlled group of corporations exists can best be illustrated by example:

Example: Suppose that the stock of the following corporations is owned in the percentages set forth below:

	CORP. A	CORP. B	CORP. C
Smith	30	20	10
Jones	0	15	0
Black	0	0	45
White	15	40	10
Green	5	25	0
Brown	25	0	15
Grey	25	0	20

Corporations A, B, and C do not constitute a controlled group.

Reason: because the same five or fewer shareholders do not own at least 80% of the stock of each corporation.

Corporations A and B also do not meet the definition to constitute a controlled group.

Reason: although Smith, White, Green, Brown and Grey own at least 80% of each corporation, the identical ownership percentage that they all have in Corporation A and B is only 40%.

Corporations A and C are a controlled group.

Reason: Smith, White, Green, Brown and Grey own at least 80% of each corporation; *and* considering identical ownership in each corporation, the same five shareholders own more than 50% of each corporation.

Comment: In determining whether the ownership percentage requirements are met, it is important to consider the special attribution rules relating to stock owned, directly or indirectly, by or for a partnership. Section 1563 (e)(2) of the Internal Revenue Code provides that stock owned directly or indirectly by or for a partnership shall be considered as owned by any partner who owns 50% or more of the partnership in proportion to his partnership interest.

How to Make Use of Flexibility: Long term advantages can result from establishing multiple corporations. With a proper division, flexibility exists in that the stock of one corporation can be sold without affecting the other corporations. On the other hand, an eventual sale of part of the assets of a single corporation could result in a tax at both the corporate and shareholder levels. Additionally, complications such as recapture of depreciation, or the investment tax credit, could arise [Sections 47, 1245 and 1250 of the IRC].

Be Alert for Possible Drawbacks: There are certain advantages that may result from dividing a business into separate corporations. There are also disadvantages that may result. For instance, such a division can preclude offsetting the losses of one entity against the profits of another. This disadvantage is eliminated if the corporations file consolidated income tax returns. However, there must be an existent common parent corporation, or there is no basis for filing the consolidated returns [Sections 1501 and 1504 (a) of the IRC]. It should be further noted that a Subchapter S corporation cannot be a member of an affiliated group of corporations for purposes of filing a consolidated tax return.

Note: If a corporation has made an election to be taxed under the provisions of Subchapter S of the Code, the losses of a particular corporation will pass through to the shareholders and offset their individual income [Sections 1371-1378 of the IRC].

In addition to dividing a business into separate corporate entities, some advantages may result from having a partnership as one of the entities. A corporation could lease assets to a partnership and thus allow the partnership to obtain the advantages of renting business assets that would not be available if the assets were purchased [*Interior Securities Corp.*, 38 T.C. 330, but see *Richard Cooper*, 61 T.C. 599]. If this approach is utilized, it is important to analyze the sources of the corporation's income to insure that the corporation does not become a personal holding company. A personal holding company is subject to the 70% additional tax on undistributed personal holding company income. The receipt of sufficient rent can actually contribute to avoiding personal holding company status while the receipt of compensation from shareholders for the use of corporate property has the opposite effect [Sections 543 (a) (2) (A) and (b) (3) of the IRC].

Don't Abuse the Use of Multiple Entities

A general caution should be advanced with respect to the use of related entities. Under Section 482 of the Code, the IRS may distribute, apportion or allocate gross income, deductions, credits or allowances among the various entities if it determines that such an allocation is necessary to prevent tax evasion or to clearly reflect the income of each entity. The IRS has the authority to determine actual taxable income if the taxable income of a controlled taxpayer differs from what it would have been if the taxpayer had been uncontrolled and was dealing at arm's-length with another uncontrolled taxpayer.

Keep Detailed Records

In order to satisfy the IRS, careful handling of the business affairs of related corporations is essential. If the relationship between the controlled entities is an arm's-length relationship and if the corporate books clearly and accurately reflect the income and expenses of each, an attempt by the IRS to reallocate income will be rejected [reference *South Texas Rice Warehouse Co.*, 43 TC 540]. The IRS is not justified in reallocating income merely because the requisite control of the various entities exists. Reallocation is authorized only if there is an unwarranted shifting of income from one controlled entity to another.

Controlled corporations should maintain records to indicate what standards were used in establishing the prices to be paid for goods and services passing between controlled entities. Evidence of transactions with outside interests should be maintained as a measure of arm's-length dealings. Generally, controlled corporations should not expect to obtain tax advantages from dealing with each other if those tax advantage do not exist in dealing with third parties. However, each situation has to be analyzed to be sure that a controlled group of entities is maximizing the benefits that are available.

[¶513.4] Consider Available Elections at Time of Incorporation

When a new corporation is established, there are a number of elections which are available. The various elections can have significant tax implications.

□ Taxable Year

A new corporation may elect any taxable year when filing its first return. It is not necessary to obtain prior approval of the Commissioner of Internal Revenue.

□ Method of Accounting

It may also elect any permissible method of accounting [Treasury Regulation Section 1.446-1 (e) (1)]. However, if the corporation wishes to report its inventory on the last-in, first-out (LIFO) basis, it must elect to do so in a statement that is filed with its income tax return for the year in which the method is first used. The LIFO method can save taxes in periods of inflation since it reduces ending inventory valuations. The higher priced inventory which is acquired last is deemed to be sold first. This increases the cost-of-goods sold and thus decreases taxable income.

CAVEAT: Even though an existing business is using the LIFO method, if the business is incorporated, a new and timely election must be made [*Textile Apron Co.*, 21 T.C. 147, Acq.].

□ *Subchapter S*

The possible advantages of this election were discussed in Chapter 3.

It is important that a corporation consider the consequences of its various initial elections. If the corporation wants to change fiscal years or accounting methods, it may be necessary to obtain the consent of the Commissioner of Internal Revenue.

□ *Short Taxable Year*

Taxes may be saved if the first taxable year of the corporation is brought to an end at the close of the month in which its taxable income approaches or reaches the amount at which the 46% tax is imposed ($100,000). This is a one-shot tax advantage, but it should not be overlooked as a planning possibility. It is also important to remember that it is not necessary to annualize the income generated in the short taxable period [Treasury Regulation Section 1.443-1 (a) (a)]. The Regulations provide for an apportionment of the full surtax exemption among the component members of a controlled group of corporations for certain short taxable periods. Under some state franchise tax statutes, an initial taxable period of less than twelve months may require a double prepayment of the franchise tax. In such instances this disadvantage must be considered in selecting the initial taxable year. Franchise taxes are imposed on corporations for the privilege of doing business.

[¶513.5] How to Treat Expenses Incurred in Organizing the Corporation [Section 248 of the IRC]

Organizational expenses may be treated as deferred expenses. They may be deducted pro-rated over a fixed period of 60 months or more. The period selected must begin with the month in which the corporation began business. The election must be made in a statement which is attached to the corporation's income tax return for the taxable year in which it begins its business. The corporation can deduct only those expenses that are incurred before the end of the taxable year in which the corporation commences its business operations.

CAVEAT: In order to deduct organizational expenses, an express election is necessary. In one case a corporation mistakenly elected to deduct its organizational expenses as business expenses under Section 162 of the Code. When the deduction was disallowed, the corporation could not take advantage of deductions authorized by Section 248 because it was held that the corporation made a binding election not to claim the benefits of Section 248 when it claimed the deduction as an ordinary business expense [*Bay Sound Transportation Co. v. United States* (DC Tex., 1967), 410 F.2d 505].

Organizational expenses must be directly related to the creation of the corporation, and must be of a character that is chargeable to the capital account of the corporation.

Qualifying expenditures include [Treasury Regulation Section 1.248-1 (b) (2)]:

☐ Legal and accounting fees paid in connection with organizing the corporation, and

☐ Fees paid to the state of incorporation.

Qualifying expenditures *do not* include [Treasury Regulation Section 1.248-1 (b) (3)]:

☐ Expenses incurred in issuing stock (commissions, professional fees and printing costs), or

☐ Expenditures connected with transferring assets to the corporation.

Expenses incurred in connection with the reorganization of a corporation are not deductible unless they are related to the creation of a new corporation which is being formed as a part of the reorganization.

6

Estate and Gift Tax Planning

It is important to analyze the tax implications which accompany the transfer of stock in a corporation. These tax implications are important whether the transfers are made during the shareholder's life or upon his death.

In many instances, the stock of a closely-held corporation may constitute a major asset of the shareholder's estate. In such cases it may be advisable for the shareholder to reduce the value of his estate by making lifetime transfers of stock. For the purpose of this chapter, it will be assumed that the stock of a corporation initially was owned by one person with a family.

Income taxes and estate taxes for the owner of a closely-held corporation should be minimized. Estate taxes may be due upon the death of the business owner or upon the death of *his spouse*. Too often, people overlook the fact that the death of the owner's spouse may create liability for death taxes. For example, in a community property state, a wife may own one-half of stock which is listed only in the husband's estate.

Example: Mr. Smith owns 100% of the stock of XYZ Corporation. The stock has a value of $500,000. He has other assets which also have a value of $500,000. All of the assets are in his name alone, but he lives in a community property state and the source of the assets constituted community property of Mr. Smith and his wife. The total estate value of Mr. and Mrs. Smith is $1,000,000. Thus Mrs. Smith has a gross estate of $500,000. This will create a substantial estate tax. The need to pay substantial sums of money for estate taxes could have a tremendously adverse effect on XYZ Corporation, particularly if the other assets are not liquid.

There are provisions of the Internal Revenue Code which permit estate taxes to be paid in installments which might provide some relief. Depending upon the state of residence, tax laws must be considered to determine what happens when the spouse dies as well as when the owner dies.

Income taxes are familiar to taxpayers because they are encountered on a quarterly or yearly basis. Estate taxes are not normally considered unless the client has had occasion to be involved in the settlement of an estate. If the impact of death is ignored, financial chaos can occur. Upon death there is a potential immediate need for cash to pay estate taxes. And there are possible delays and complications involved with probate proceedings. In the absence of proper planning, an estate with a value of $500,000 easily could result in death taxes and costs of administration in excess of $100,000.

[¶600] THE PURPOSE OF ESTATE PLANNING

The ultimate objective of estate planning is to see that the maximum amount of a person's assets is retained by his beneficiaries with the least amount of complications. In estates which involve closely-held corporations, proper planning includes taking steps to:

• minimize taxes,

• insure continuity of the business,

• minimize expenses of administration, and

• facilitate transfer of the business ownership.

There are simple methods of avoiding many of the problems associated with premature death. A business owner can:

- give some of his stock to his ultimate beneficiaries during his lifetime to reduce the value of his taxable estate;
- establish a living trust to avoid the costs and time delays involved in probate proceedings;
- take steps that will be beneficial in establishing the value of the business at the time of his death, and
- enter an agreement relating to the disposition of his stock.

Procrastination often occurs in the area of estate planning. There is a natural instinct to avoid consideration of the consequences that flow from death. An advisor has a responsibility to make a client aware of what can happen upon his death or his spouse's death.

[¶601] HOW TO MINIMIZE ESTATE AND/OR GIFT TAXES

The net value of a person's assets is determined at the time of death. If the value (after allowable deductions) exceeds $147,333 ($161,563 in 1980 and $175,625 in 1981 and later years), his estate will be subject to a Federal estate tax. There may also be a State inheritance tax or estate tax. Under Federal law (and under some State laws), the taxable estate is composed of the value of certain gifts made during a decedent's life and the value of the assets actually owned by the decedent at the date of his death.

The general rule is that the value of any gift which is in excess of $3,000 per donee, per year, is taken into account in determining the Federal estate tax. If taxable gifts are made within three years of the decedent's death, the value of the property as of the date of death is added to the value of the decedent's estate. The Federal estate tax is then computed on that total value. If the decedent paid gift tax on such gifts during his lifetime, a credit is subtracted from the estate tax [Sections 2001 and 2010 of the IRC]. The net effect of these rules is to aggregate all transfers, whether made during his lifetime or at death, for the purpose of determining the total transfer tax.

> *Example:* Suppose Mr. Smith dies in 1981. At the time of death he has a total separate property estate of $1,000,000. Four years prior to his death he gave his son $30,000 in *property*. Two years later he gave his son other *property* which was worth $10,000. The first property is worth $60,000 at the date of Mr. Smith's death, and the second property is worth $30,000. Assume that upon his death he left his entire estate to his wife. The taxable transfers for Federal purposes would be determined as follows:

> *Gift of First Property.* No gift tax, but the value of the property at the date of gift ($30,000) less the annual exclusion ($3,000) is added to the value of Mr. Smith's gross estate.

> *Gift of $10,000 property.* No gift tax, but $30,000 is added to the value of Mr. Smith's gross estate. Since the gift was made within 3 years of the date of death, you use the value at date of death.

> *Gross Estate.* The actual estate of Mr. Smith is $1,000,000. However, for purposes of determining the Federal estate tax, his gross estate would be valued at $1,057,000.

[¶601.1] Gift Program

Before TRA '76, most lifetime gifts were excluded from a decedent's estate. Also, the gift tax was imposed at a lower rate than the estate tax. Now the gift tax and estate tax rates are identical. However, there are still certain tax advantages that may result from lifetime transfers of stock in a closely-held corporation.

According to Section 2503 (c) of the IRC, a person may make outright gifts in amounts of $3,000, or less, per year to as many different persons as he wishes ($6,000 per year in the case of gifts by a husband and wife). Such gifts will not be added to the value of the assets he owns at the date of his death to determine the Federal estate tax. Thus, the owner of a closely-held business and his spouse can give shares of stock with a total value of $6,000 or less to each of their children (and grandchildren and spouses of children) each year, and the value of such gifts will not be subject to any Federal gift tax or estate tax.

Advantages of Stock Transfer

If the owner of a business transfers stock to his ultimate beneficiaries more than three years before his death, any increase in value of such stock after the gift is made will not be included in determining the Federal estate tax [Section 2035 of the IRC].

> *Example:* If stock worth $100,000 is transferred to the owner's son and the owner dies five years later when the value of the same stock is $200,000, only $97,000 would be added to the value of the owner's assets at the date of his death for purposes of determining his taxable estate. ($100,000 value at date of gift less $3,000 annual exclusion). If the father had died within three years from the date of the gift, the value of the stock at the date of the father's death ($200,000) would be brought back in determining the taxable estate. If he had not made the gift at all, the full amount of $200,000 also would be included in his gross estate.

One of the most common deterrents to making lifetime gifts is that potential donors do not want to give away assets. They normally feel that they might need at some later date to maintain their own desired standard of living. Stock in a closely-held corporation is an asset that may be given away without creating financial restrictions.

First, such stock normally is not an income-producing asset. Dividends are not normally declared because of the income tax disadvantages. Also, as long as the original owner of the stock maintains control of the corporation, he can determine, within limits, his own compensation. As a pratical matter, a parent has an exceptional degree of control in connection with this latter item. He can exert pressure on his children to not create any problems with his operation of the business, or they will not be treated favorably in his ultimate estate plan.

If all of a stockholder's children are involved in the business, a gift program is a simple method of transferring the ownership of a closely-held business to the original stockholder's ultimate beneficiaries. But if a business owner has several children and not all of the children are involved in the business, potential problems exist.

Normally, a child who is active in the operation of a corporation would not want to have interference from his brothers or sisters who are not interested in the business. Also, he would not want them to be in a position to inhibit his conduct of the business by outvoting him in corporate decisions. By the same token, most children who are not interested in the operation of a closely-held business do not want to inherit the stock. A very practical solution to this potential problem exists:

> *Example:* Suppose that a business owner has an estate worth $2,000,000. $1,000,000 of the estate is attributable to the stock of a closely-held corporation. Only one of the four children is interested in the business. Assume, further, that two of the children are daughters who are married. Each daughter has two daughters, none of whom are interested in the father's business.
>
> A solution is that the father and mother can make total gifts of $6,000 or less per year of the stock to each of the children and grandchildren.
>
> *The value of such gifts will not be subjected to Federal gift tax or estate tax.*

Agreement of Heirs Prior to Stockholder's Death

To avoid potential problems with respect to control of the business operations by the children who are not interested in the business, the children should enter into an agreement as to the disposition of the stock after the death of their parents. The child who is involved in the business should agree for the corporation to redeem the stock of the other children at a price pre-determined by an appropriate formula. With a legal agreement, the children who are not involved in the business can be cashed-out of the business and the child interested in the business can pursue his desired objectives without interference.

Flexibility of Agreement

An agreement among the heirs should be flexible to accommodate the potential situation in which the corporation may not have the cash available to make an immediate redemption of the stock of the non-involved children. The pre-determined formula may establish the redeemed price, but the agreement could provide for a pay-out over a period of years. The use of such a gift program to maximize tax-free transfers to beneficiaries who may not ever be interested in the corporation can obviously result in tax savings without any practical disadvantages.

CAVEAT: As long as the original owner of the business does not contemplate the sale of the corporation, the above-mentioned tax planning has no particular disadvantages. However, if the business is sold, the value of the stock transferred to the owner's children would be placed beyond the reach of the owner.

Establishing the Dollar Value of the Gift Program

One of the problems associated with closely-held corporations is the determination of the value of the corporate stock for estate or gift tax purposes. A gift program can be helpful in establishing value for two reasons:

First, when the gifts are made, gift tax returns may be filed with the Internal Revenue Service even if no gift tax will be due. If the Service disagrees with the method of valuation for gift-tax purposes, the disagreement may be resolved during the donor's life. This procedure is advantageous because the owner of the business is still living. Presumably, he has an intimate knowledge of his own business which should be helpful in negotiating with the IRS to arrive at the proper value of the corporate stock.

Second, a gift program provides an agreement between the children with respect to redemption upon the death of both parents. The children can have adverse economic interests. If the stock is valued too high, the children who are not in the business would be receiving an advantage over the child or the children who retained their stock. If it is valued too low, the opposite result would occur. When children who do not want to be in the business agree to have their stock redeemed at a formula price, it is evidence that the formula price represents the fair market value of the stock.

[¶602] INCOME TAX PROBLEMS IN REDEMPTIONS

There may have to be some adjustments because of certain other valuation factors that are peculiar to closely-held corporations. If the owner of a closely-held corporation dies without a sufficiently liquid estate to pay death taxes and expenses involved in settling his estate, a significant tax problem may be presented to his estate or his heirs. It is possible that the estate will need the corporation to redeem some of the decedent's stock to raise cash to pay taxes and expenses. This is an area in which extreme caution must be exercised. Improper advice on corporate redemptions may lead to disastrous tax consequences.

Dividend Distribution

Normally, when a corporation makes a distribution to a shareholder (and an estate is a shareholder), the distribution is treated as a dividend to the extent that the corporation has any current or accumulated earnings and profits [Section 301 of the IRC].

Exceptions to Dividend Distribution

There are two exceptions which can allow a redemption of stock from the estate to avoid dividend treatment.

First, there is no dividend if the payment from the corporation is for a complete redemption of all stock owned by the estate.

The payment will be treated as being made for the exchange of the stock [Section 302 of the IRC]. Also, dividend treatment will not result if the redemption of the decedent's stock is substantially disproportionate.

A third exception applies when the value of the stock constitutes a large portion of the decedent's estate [Section 303 of the IRC]. In that event, a redemption will be allowed to raise necessary funds for taxes and expenses of administration. No dividend results.

[¶602.1] Procedure for Complete Redemption

The application of the attribution rules (where certain related persons or entities are deemed to own stock which is actually owned by someone else) can cause problems. These rules make a complete redemption from an estate virtually impossible where the stock of a closely-held corporation is held by certain family members or where certain family members are beneficiaries of the estate.

> *Example:* If an estate owns stock in a corporation, the estate is also deemed to own all of the stock owned by the beneficiaries of the estate. In such a situation, a complete redemption may not occur even if all of the stock actually owned by the estate is redeemed. If some of the beneficiaries own stock, the attribution rules provide that the estate will be deemed to own such stock and a complete redemption is impossible.

A Living Stockholder Can Avoid Redemption Problems

Relief is possible if the attribution rules prevent a complete redemption from a living shareholder. The shareholder can have the transaction treated as a complete termination of his interest if he follows the proper procedure. There will be a complete redemption if, after the redemption:

☐ he has no interest in the corporation (including an interest as an officer, director or employee), other than an interest as a creditor;

☐ he does not acquire any such interest (other than stock acquired by bequest or inheritance) within ten years from the date of the redemption distribution; and

☐ he files with the Internal Revenue Service an agreement to notify the Service of any acquisition of a prohibited interest in the corporation [Section 302 (c) (2) of the IRC].

An Estate Cannot Avoid Redemption Problems

The IRS takes the position that the representative of an estate does not have the opportunity to prevent the application of the attribution rules. However, there is case law which permits an estate to file the necessary waivers of interest. This apparently insurmountable problem can be solved in some instances. If the redemption is delayed until the stock has been distributed to the beneficiaries, the beneficiaries can comply with the requirements that will permit a complete redemption. If there are beneficiaries who have no continuing interest in the corporation, they can redeem their stock. They can also loan the redemption proceeds to the estate for purposes of paying taxes and expenses.

Special Problems of Two or More Stockholders

If a closely-held corporation is owned by two or more persons, particular care must be given to an attempted complete redemption of a deceased stockholder's stock. If other stockholders are beneficiaries of the decedent's estate, a disaster may occur:

Example: Two unrelated persons own the stock of a corporation, and they each share the hobby of fishing. If one stockholder dies and leaves his fishing equipment to the other stockholder, the surviving stockholder is a beneficiary of the estate. The representative of the decedent's estate causes all of the decedent's stock to be redeemed in what he thinks is a complete redemption.

If the corporation had earnings and profits, the proceeds of the redemption would be treated as a dividend to the extent of the earnings and profits.

The stock of the surviving stockholder would be attributed to the estate because the surviving stockholder was a beneficiary of the decedent's estate. He got the fishing equipment. In such a situation a complete redemption would not have occurred because the stock of the survivor is attributed to the decedent's estate.

[¶602.2] Redemption to Pay Taxes and Expenses of Administration

In the event that a complete redemption is impossible or impractical, it is still possible to redeem a portion of a decedent's stock and not have the redemption distribution treated as a dividend. This happens if the value of the stock constitutes a large portion of the decedent's estate.

Section 303 of the Internal Revenue Code provides that if the value of a decedent's stock in a closely-held corporation constitutes more than 50% of the value of his adjusted gross estate a redemption will not be taxed as a dividend. However, non-dividend treatment applies only to the extent that the amount of the distribution does not exceed:

☐ death taxes;

☐ funeral expenses; and

☐ costs of administration.

For a redemption to qualify under Section 303, it is also necessary that the redemption be made from shareholders whose interest in the estate would be reduced by the payment of the above-mentioned taxes and expenses. Also, the redemption treatment applies only to the extent that the interest of the beneficiaries would be reduced by the redemption.

Example: Mr. Smith is unmarried and has a gross estate valued at $800,000. The principal asset is 100% of the stock of XYZ Corporation which is valued at $450,000. Mr. Smith leaves his non-business assets to his sister and his stock equally to his two nephews. He further provides that his nephews are to pay estate taxes, funeral expenses and costs of administration.

According to Section 303, the redemption would not be treated as a dividend to the extent stock is redeemed to pay taxes and expenses.

However, if Mr. Smith left the stock to his nephews and the residue to his sister with the provision that taxes and expenses were to be paid out of the residue, Section 303 redemption would not be available.

The nephews' interest in the estate would not be reduced by any redemption since they were not responsible for paying taxes and administration expenses.

CAVEAT: Even if Payment Is Not a Dividend, There Could Be a Big Capital Gain

Before TRA '76, if either of the above-discussed redemptions could be effected, normally little or no income tax would be generated as a result of the redemption. The basis of the stock (or any other assets) owned by a decedent received a new tax basis for the estate or beneficiaries equal to the value of the stock as of the date of death. If stock were redeemed at a value which was close to the value for estate tax purposes, no significant capital gain would have been involved.

Example: Mr. Jones invested $10,000 in a corporation in 1977. He dies in 1980 when the value of the stock is $100,000. Under prior law, the estate would have received a stepped-up basis equal to the value of the stock at the date of Mr. Smith's death.

Result: A redemption for $100,000 would have resulted in no taxable gain.

Comment: No more stepped-up basis. TRA '76, however, has changed the tax consequences of a redemption of stock upon the death of the owner of a closely-held corporation, even if problems of dividend treatment are successfully avoided.

Important note: The 1976 Tax Reform Act made significant

changes which will be discussed below. However, the Revenue Act of 1978 postponed the effective date of the carry-over basis provisions of the new law so that the basis of property acquired from a decedent dying before January 1, 1980, will be covered by prior law. It is possible that the basis provisions of the new law discussed below may be revised prior to January 1, 1980, or it may be completely repealed. In any event, remember that they do not apply to property acquired from a person dying prior to January 1, 1980.

Decedent's Basis Carried Over for Assets Acquired by the Decedent After 1979

The problem relates to the fact that a beneficiary of an estate will obtain an income tax basis equal to the cost basis of the decedent for assets acquired by the decedent after 1979. The basis is then increased by the amount of death taxes attributable to the appreciation in value of the property. If the value of the property at the date of death is greater than the decedent's cost, a capital gain will result if the property is sold.

Partial Step-Up for Assets Acquired Before 1977

With respect to assets acquired by the decedent prior to 1977, the tax basis to the beneficiaries will be determined by one of two possible methods:

Method I: For marketable bonds or securities, the fair market value as of December 31, 1976, would be the basis that would be carried over to the beneficiaries.

Method II: If the assets did *not* have an ascertainable fair market value as of December 31, 1976, then the basis to the beneficiaries will be determined by using a formula.

Method III: For tangible personal property it will only be necessary to determine the value of the property at the decedent's death. Appreciation after 1976 will be assumed to have accrued at approximately 8% per year.

The formula assumes that appreciation in value occurred at a uniform rate from the date of acquisition until the date of death. Under this formula, the assumed value as of December 31, 1976, will be the cost basis to the estate or the beneficiaries.

Suggestion: Consider an Installment Redemption

As a result of the changes in the income tax treatment of redemptions upon death, it is essential to consider the income tax consequences that will result from a redemption of stock even if the distribution is not treated as a dividend. If a substantial capital gain would be realized by the beneficiaries of a deceased stockholder, it may be desirable to have the redemption made on an installment basis [Section 453 of the IRC]. In this way, the gain could be reported over a number of years.

> *Example:* Mr. Smith owned 50% of ABC Corporation at the time of his death. His cost basis was $10,000. The fair market value at the date of his death was $200,000. The corporation could pay $50,000 in one year (must not exceed 30% of the selling price in the first year) and pay the balance in 60 equal installments. Thus the beneficiaries would recognize the gain over a five-year period.

In almost all instances, the installment method of reporting gain will result in tax savings.

CAVEAT: The 30% limitation applies to not only the down payment, but also to other payments of principal in the year of the sale.

Looking at a redemption from the corporation's point of view, it should be noted that a corporation may transfer appreciated assets to redeem its stock. It may do so without realizing taxable gain if the decedent owned at least 10% of the corporation's outstanding stock continuously for the twelve-month period preceding his death [Section 311 (d) of the IRC].

The above discussion has dealt with the situation in which stock would be redeemed from the estate of a deceased stockholder or from his beneficiaries. Another way of handling the disposition of stock in the event of death is by the use of a buy-sell agreement if the corporation has more than one stockholder.

[¶603] INSURE CONTINUITY OF INTEREST IN BUSINESS— CROSS-PURCHASE AGREEMENTS

Under a typical cross-purchase agreement, the existing stockholders agree that their respective estates will be required to sell all of their stock to the surviving stockholders. The agreement also provides that the surviving stockholders will be required to purchase such stock. Such an agreement minimizes the chances of conflict within the corporate management and provides some assurance that the business will continue to operate smoothly.

A cross-purchase agreement avoids the potential dividend problem. The parties are the individuals and no distributions are made from the corporation. In some states, a corporation may not redeem stock unless it has sufficiently retained earnings. (This requirement is imposed primarily for the protection of creditors of the corporation.) This potential problem is also not present in the case of a buy-sell agreement among the shareholders.

Another advantage that results from the use of a cross-purchase agreement is that the surviving shareholder or shareholders obtain a stepped-up basis for the stock they acquire. In many instances involving closely-held corporations, this advantage is illusory. It is true that an acquiring shareholder gets a basis for the stock which is equal to the price he pays for it. However, under a cross-purchase agreement, he has to pay for it rather than have the corporation pay for it. The identical result could be reached in the case of a corporate redemption if the surviving stockholders contributed capital to the corporation which in turn used the contributed capital to redeem the stock of the deceased stockholder.

Example: Smith and Jones each own 50% of the stock of S & J, Inc., for which they each paid $10,000. They have a cross-purchase agreement that provides that the value of the corporation is $200,000 and that the survivor will purchase the decedent's stock for $100,000. Smith dies. Jones pays Smith's estate $100,000 for his stock. Now Jones has a basis of $110,000 for his 100% of S & J, Inc. (His original $10,000 investment plus the $100,000 he paid Smith's estate.) If the corporation had redeemed Smith's stock, Jones would only have a basis equal to the cost of his stock, i.e. $10,000.

Illusion

It appears that Jones has the advantage with a cross-purchase situation because his basis for determining gain is $110,000. It is only $10,000 under the redemption approach. In either event, he owns 100% of S & J, Inc. Why isn't the stepped-up basis an advantage? In the redemption situation, the total value of S & J, Inc. is only $100,000 because the corporation paid $100,000 of its $200,000 value to Smith's estate. In the case of the cross-purchase, the value of S & J, Inc. remains at $200,000 because Jones paid the $100,000 to Smith's estate. If Jones were to sell S & J, Inc. or liquidate it, he would have a $90,000 capital gain.

The reason Jones gets a stepped-up basis in the cross-purchase arrangement is that he pays for it with cash—i.e., if Jones contributed the $100,000 to the capital of S & J, Inc., he would have a basis of $110,000. S & J, Inc. would then redeem Smith's stock for $100,000. Under this latter situation all parties would be in the identical position as if the cross-purchase had taken place.

Funds Must Be Available to Effect Cross-Purchase

Although the use of a cross-purchase agreement is often desirable, there is at least one potential problem that should not be overlooked.

The agreement is beneficial only if the surviving stockholders are financially able to fulfill their obligation to purchase the stock.

Life Insurance

The obligation could be funded through the use of cross-owned life insurance policies. In our example, Jones could have owned life insurance on Smith's life and Smith could have owned life insurance on Jones's life. Then, when either one died, funds would be available for the buy-out.

Installment Purchase

If the proceeds of such policies are insufficient for a complete purchase, or if no life insurance is used, the cash problem may be solved by having the surviving stockholders purchase the stock on an installment basis. The installment purchase can be advantageous to the surviving stockholders from a cash-flow standpoint. It can be beneficial to the beneficiaries of the deceased stockholder if a significant capital gain is involved. The beneficiaries can spread the gain over several years.

How Should Stock Be Valued?

Corporate redemptions or cross-purchase agreements require one critical determination: an agreed value of the corporation.

If a binding redemption agreement or buy-sell agreement is in effect and if it restricts the rights of the stockholders to sell their stock during their life (or death), the agreed value of the corporation will determine the value for estate tax purposes. Normally, unrelated stockholders have adverse economic interests. Therefore, it is essential that they attempt to establish a value that accurately reflects the worth of the corporation. If an accurate value is not determined, they will be gambling as to who benefits the most from the death of the first stockholder.

> *Example:* Smith and Jones agree that S & J, Inc. is worth $200,000. If, in fact, S & J, Inc. should be valued at $300,000, the estate of the first shareholder to die would receive $50,000 less than it should. By the same token, the surviving shareholder would receive a

windfall of $50,000. The estate would only receive $100,000 when it should have received $150,000.

There are many approaches which may be taken in valuing the stock of a closely-held corporation.

□ Book Value

Perhaps the most straightforward method is to base the value on the adjusted book value of the corporation. This is basically the excess of the value of the corporation's assets over its liabilities. Although this is a relatively simple way to determine value, it is not normally an accurate measure of the actual worth of the business. If the corporation is a going concern, the ability of the corporation to earn money is normally more important than the value of its assets.

□ Book Value Plus

One method to determine the value of a business is to capitalize the excess earnings and add that figure to the book value of the assets.

Example: Let's suppose the book value of a corporation is $1,000,000 and the corporation has an average taxable income of $500,000. In such a case, the value of the business would probably be in excess of $1,000,000.

Defining Excess Earnings

Excess earnings are the amount the corporation earns in excess of a reasonable return on the value of its assets. For instance, assume that 10% is a reasonable rate of return. Reasonable earnings on $1,000,000 of assets would be $100,000 per year. In the above example, the corporation had an annual income of $500,000; so the excess earnings were $400,000.

Capitalization of Excess Earnings

In order to capitalize earnings, we must determine how much capital it would take to earn $400,000 worth of annual income at some assumed rate of return. While we used 10% to determine a reasonable rate of return on the corporation's assets, it is more realistic to assume a higher rate of return for capitalizing excess earnings. The reasoning is that if someone buys the corporation based on excess earnings there is certainly some risk involved because there is no assurance that the excess earnings will continue in the future. The capitalization rate is relative to the amount of risk associated with the business. If we assume that an investor would want a 20% return on his investment, the $400,000 would be equal to a value of $2,000,000. (If an investor paid $2,000,000, $400,000 would represent a 20% annual return on his investment.)

By adding the capitalized excess earnings ($2,000,000) to the book value of the corporation ($1,000,000), we arrive at a total value of $3,000,000.

□ *Look at Publicly Traded Stock*

If publicly-held corporations exist in the same industry as the closely-held corporation, see what price they are selling for in relation to their earnings. The ratio of the price to the earnings of the public corporation can be applied to the earnings of the closely-held corporation. Obviously, there are many factors that may make such an approach to valuation unsatisfactory. In a closely-held corporation, the owners can control the amount of the corporation's income by declaring bonuses to themselves or by having the corporation pay certain expenses that might otherwise be considered as personal expenses.

CAVEAT: Before following any approach that is based on corporate earnings, it is absolutely essential to determine whether the earnings reflected on the corporate financial statements fairly represent the earnings that would be reported on the financial statement if the corporation were a publicly-held corporation. If the earnings are distorted, appropriate adjustments should be made.

□ *Reference to Prior Sales of the Corporation's Stock*

Prior sales of stock of a closely-held corporation can be a valuable guide in determining the worth of the corporation.

However, in order to be of importance, any such sales must have been made in arm's-length transactions. Also, they are a valid guide only if such sales occurred relatively close to the validation date.

☐ Consider the Value of Key Employees

In many cases, the value of a closely-held corporation may be attributable to the efforts of one person. In such instances, the value of the corporation while the key person is involved in the business may be much greater than if the key person dies or becomes disabled. This factor should definitely be considered in estimating the value of a closely-held corporation for purposes of estate and inheritance taxes.

☐ Examine the Possibility of Minority Discount

A minority interest in a closely-held corporation is not as valuable as a majority interest. The disposition of corporate earnings can be determined by the owner of the majority interest. In most states the owner of a controlling interest can determine whether or not dividends will be paid. Thus, the owner of a minority interest may have an asset which produces no income.

☐ Possible Professional Appraisals

Professional appraisals may be obtained to determine the value of a corporation. However, they are quite expensive. Since the professional appraisers will have to consider the same factors as the non-professional, the employment of a professional may not be warranted. If it is critical that the value be established by an independent party, the use of a professional appraiser may be advisable.

Note: Don't Undervalue Stock to Save Estate Tax

At this point it appears advisable to point out one tactic that is often erroneously used in connection with valuing a business. This chapter emphasizes that a binding buy-sell or redemption agreement can establish the value of stock for purposes of computing death taxes. Some advisors will recommend that an artificially low value be placed on the corporate stock to minimize estate taxes. Such advice completely ignores the fact that by reducing the value of the stock for death tax purposes the stockholder is also reducing the amount his beneficiaries will receive for his stock. As long as the estate tax rate is less than 100%, such an arrangement does not make sense from an economic standpoint.

> *Example:* X and Y each own 50% of the stock of XYZ Corporation, and they enter into a binding agreement which values the stock of XYZ Corporation at $200,000. In fact, XYZ Corporation is worth $300,000, but they thought they would lower the value to save estate taxes. X then dies. X's taxable estate is $50,000 lower, but his estate loses $50,000. If they received the proper amount initially, the estate would be $50,000 ahead. It is true that the taxable estate would be $50,000 greater. However, since the estate tax is not 100%, it is advantageous to the estate to use the true value of the stock.

Without going into an extensive analysis of all the factors to be considered in valuing a closely-held business, suffice it to say that valuation is extremely important.

[¶604] FACILITATING TRANSFER OF STOCK AND MINIMIZING ADMINISTRATION EXPENSES UPON DEATH

Minimizing estate taxes upon the death of a stockholder of a closely-held corporation is possibly the most important estate planning consideration. However, a second matter to be looked into is the availability of methods to facilitate the transfer of the stock to an owner's beneficiaries upon his death.

Living Trust

A revocable living trust could be established by the stockholder. He could transfer his stock to the trustee. [Reference Chapter 3 relating to Subchapter S corporations; if the corporation has elected to be taxed under the provisions of Subchapter S, only certain trusts may be shareholders.]

Establishing a Living Trust

The mechanics of establishing and maintaining a living trust to hold stock in a closely-held corporation are extremely simple in most instances. The benefits which flow from the use of such a trust may be quite significant. State law will have to be analyzed to determine the proper manner to set up a living trust. In many states, a person may establish a revocable living trust and appoint himself as trustee. During the person's lifetime, he can retain the right to alter, amend or revoke the trust. Upon his death, the disposition of the trust assets can be made in the same manner as he would have disposed of them by a Will if the trust had not been established.

The Advantage of a Living Trust

The critical difference between testamentary disposition (Will) of stock and disposition by means of a trust is that, in the latter case, no probate administration of the stock is necessary. Since a probate proceeding (court proceeding) provides no benefit to the decedent or his beneficiaries, in most cases it is desirable to avoid probate. In addition to usually providing no affirmative benefit, *probate has two significant disadvantages:*

☐ first, there is a time delay during which the stock may not be dealt with unless court approval is obtained; and

☐ second, most states award statutory attorney's fees and executors' commissions as compensation for handling the probate proceedings for the decedent's estate.

A probate proceeding is not necessary to have the stock transferred to the beneficiaries. Therefore, it seems to make little economic sense to pay an attorney and/or an executor to handle a needless court proceeding.

Many attorneys tend to discourage clients from establishing a living trust. They point out a number of *apparent* disadvantages, such as:

- additional attorneys' fees for preparing the trust and transferring assets to the trustee;
- additional expenses for administering the trust;
- complicated record keeping;
- trustee's fees; or
- the possibility that a named successor trustee might balk at taking over the trust upon the death of the creator of the trust.

The apparent disadvantages are completely without merit. If the asset to be placed in a living trust is stock in a closely-held corporation, each of the above objections does not apply.

Cost of a Living Trust

Once it has been determined how a business owner desires to dispose of his stock, the cost of implementing that desire by means of a living trust *should not* exceed the cost of providing for the disposition of the stock by means of a Will. However, an attorney can make this objection a reality. He can charge an excessively high fee for establishing a living trust. (In this way he can compensate himself for the fee he will not receive for handling the probate proceeding.)

Transfer of Stock Is Extremely Simple

The transfer of the stock to the trustee simply involves the cancellation of one share certificate and the preparation of a new certificate in the owner's name as trustee of his trust. If the corporation does not declare dividends, this is the *only* step that needs to be taken to effectively avoid probate.

Administration Fees of a Living Trust

If the owner acts as his own trustee (and there is no reason for anyone else to be the trustee), there are no expenses of administration or trustee's fees.

Establish a Successor Trustee

No annual record-keeping is required with respect to a non-income producing trust asset. Thus, there is no validity to the argument that difficulty might arise in having a successor trustee take over the trust upon the death of the business owner. The person who would have otherwise been appointed as executor of the owner's probate estate should probably be named as the successor trustee. He should be advised of the fact that he has been so named. In many instances, the owner ought to name his surviving spouse or other adult beneficiary as successor trustee.

Even if a closely-held corporation declares dividends, the income tax consequences to the owner of the trust will be exactly the same as if the trust had not been established. If the creator of a trust retains the right to alter, amend or revoke it, he will be treated as the owner of any income generated by the trust assets. He will include such income in his personal gross income [Section 671 of the IRC].

Establishing a living trust is not complicated. It is foolish for a business owner to pay a fee to outsiders (attorneys and possibly executors) to have them handle a potentially complex court proceeding. Probate proceedings merely complicate what can otherwise be a simple transfer of assets to a decedent's ultimate beneficiaries.

PART THREE

FIXING
THE CAPITAL STRUCTURE

7

How to Determine the Proper Capital Structure for the Closely-Held Corporation

A corporation cannot conduct business without cash or other assets. In exchange for the transfer of assets into a corporation, shares of stock or other securities may be issued. These documents are legal evidence of corporate ownership. A corporation may also provide the transferors of assets with documents that represent an indebtedness of the corporation to those persons.

There are many different types of corporate securities and debt. Those most frequently used in connection with closely-held corporations are:

- common stock
- preferred stock
- convertible preferred stock
- promissory notes or debentures

[¶700] FACTORS TO CONSIDER IN SETTING UP THE CAPITAL STRUCTURE

When determining the proper method of setting up the capital structure for a closely-held corporation, primary considerations include the:

☐ *Income tax consequences* which will result from future distributions of corporate earnings or capital;

☐ *Degree of risk* that the transferors are willing to take in the success of the business;

☐ *Restrictions imposed* on the type of capitalization which can be used and yet allow the corporation to make an election under Subchapter S or have the transfer be tax-free under Section 351; and

☐ *Potential income tax consequences* to the corporation, resulting from obtaining a stepped-up income tax basis for depreciable property.

☐ Dividing Company Earnings

One investor or class of investors may be given a preference in or disproportionate share of earnings by using preferred stock or by using two classes of stock. The use of preferred stock is perhaps the most common way of giving one class of investors a priority in earnings. If the investors are in a position to demand a share in earnings in addition to their preferred dividend, this may be done either (1) by making the preferred participating as to further dividends or (2) by giving them common in addition to their preferred. The first route presents problems, however, if the preferred is to be callable as it normally should be, because then it should also be made convertible if the holders are to share in the growth of the company (as they bargained for), and if it's convertible for an extended period there will be serious problems in working out fair conversion rates. Hence, the second route is apt to be favored.

Where the situation calls for one class of investor receiving a disproportionate share of earnings, as distinguished from priority in the earnings, a two-class stock set-up will usually be called for. For example, a two-class stock arrangement might be used where investor A is willing to put in $55,000 and is willing to settle for 45% of the earnings provided he is given 55% of the voting control of the business and B is willing to put in $45,000 provided he gets 55% of the earnings and is willing to wield only 45% of the vote.

Where two classes of stock are used, care must be exercised to make sure they are properly labelled. Where the two classes share dividends on a percentage basis, for example, it might be incorrect to designate the class getting the larger percentage as "common." Differentiate by calling it Class A. The other class could be designated common.

□ Dividing Company Assets

Some investors may demand priority or preferential participation in the distribution of assets on premature liquidation. For example, suppose one group of investors makes two-thirds of the cash or tangible investment for one-third of the shares, and the so-called talent gets two-thirds of the shares for only one-third of the tangible investment, and let's say the respective investments are $100,000 and $50,000. If the corporation were to liquidate at a time when the assets were worth $150,000, the "talent" would come out with $50,000 more than they went in with, this at the expense of the "money" investors. The "money" investors would come out even only if liquidation occurred at a time when the asset value had doubled. Two classes of shares bearing different participation rights in the distribution of assets, as distinguished from a preference in distribution, might be used to assure an equitable result. Thus, Class A might be given $2 for every $1 to be distributed to Class B until the original investments were repaid, with provision for equal distribution of assets thereafter.

CAVEAT: In addition to establishing the proper form of the capital structure, it is critical that the substance of the capital structure be consistent with the form. In other words, if a document is classified as a debt, be sure that it is not really an equity investment.

[¶701] HOW TO ESTABLISH DEBT OR EQUITY

Before the means of capital structure of a corporation is established, it is important to understand the difference between debt and equity capital for income tax purposes.

Debt gives its owner a right to be repaid his investment with interest. The owner is entitled to be paid regardless of the success or failure of the business venture. The return on an *equity* investment is dependent upon the success of the business.

If a corporation pays a portion of its future earnings to a person who owns capital stock as a return on his investment, the payment will ordinarily be treated as a dividend.

[¶701.1] Tax Effects of Corporate Dividends

Corporation

The corporation is not allowed to deduct the payment of a dividend in determining its taxable income.

Stockholder

The stockholder must include the amount in his gross income as unearned income (could be subject to a marginal income tax rate of up to 70%).

The net effect of a dividend distribution is that it has been subjected to double income taxation (once at the corporate level and once at the shareholder level).

[¶701.2] Tax Effects of Corporate Interest Payments

Corporation

If a person holds a debt instrument and the corporation pays interest, the interest is deductible by the corporation.

Debt Holder

Interest is included in the gross income of the person to whom payment is made as unearned income. Thus payment of interest is not subject to double taxation.

[¶701.3] Repayment of Original Investment

Another significant difference between equity and debt arises upon the repayment of the original investment. If a distribution is made to the holder of an equity interest in a corporation, it normally will be treated as a dividend to the investor. This is so even though the payment is called a return of investment. It can only be a dividend, however, if the corporation has either current or accumulated earnings and profits. If the corporation has neither current nor accumulated earnings and profits, the repayment would be a return of capital.

However, if the investor holds a note or a bond, the principal amount of the obligation may be paid by the corporation without any tax consequences to the individual.

[¶702] MINIMUM CAPITALIZATION

There are tax advantages which accompany debt-financing. As a result of the tax advantage it is quite often advantageous to maximize the corporation's debt instruments and to minimize its equity capital. If these tax advantages are utilized, the corporation is commonly said to be "thinly capitalized."

CAVEAT: It is extremely important to realize that if a corporation is too thinly capitalized serious tax consequences can occur. The Internal Revenue Service takes the position that the substance of a transaction takes precedence over the form of the transaction.

[¶702.1] How to Define Interest or Repayment of Principal As a Dividend

The IRS can restructure the apparent debt-equity situation to reflect the true nature of the capitalization—i.e., they could find that insufficient equity capital has been contributed to the corporation. If this occurs, the apparent debt of the corporation may be reclassified as equity, and the interest payments can be treated as dividends. The corporation is denied the deduction for what initially appeared to be an interest payment.

Repayment of Principal

Another possible tax consequence of such an action by the IRS is that repayment of the principal of the supposed loan could result in dividend income to the individual. Again, it is a dividend only to the extent the corporation has accumulated earnings and profits.

[¶702.2] Personal Liability Can Result from Thin Capitalization

A non-tax consequence that may occur if a corporation is too thinly capitalized is that creditors of the corporation might be able to "pierce the corporate veil." They may be able to ignore the corporation, and hold the corporate stockholders personally responsible for corporate liabilities.

[¶702.3] How to Make Debt Obligations Stand Up

No definitive rules have been established for determining when a corporation will be considered to be too thinly capitalized.

Definition According to the Courts

However, the courts have listed the following factors to be considered in determining whether investments are debt or equity:

- ☐ The name given the certificate;
- ☐ The presence of a maturity date;
- ☐ The source of payments;
- ☐ The right to enforce the payment of principal and interest;
- ☐ Participation in corporate management by the holders of the certificates;
- ☐ Relative status compared to the corporation's creditors;

☐ The intent of the parties;

☐ Identity of interest between creditors and stockholders;

☐ Capitalization in terms of apparent ratio between debt and equity;

☐ Whether payments of interest are only from sources that would otherwise be dividends;

☐ The probability that the corporation could have obtained the loans from outside sources.

If these facts indicate that a particular item should be treated as debt or equity, the courts will classify the investment accordingly.

Definition According to the Internal Revenue Code

Section 385 of the Code authorizes the Treasury to issue Regulations to define the terms under which an interest in a corporation is to be classified as stock or indebtedness. The factors to be considered include the following:

☐ Whether there is a written unconditional promise to pay on demand, or on a specified date, a predetermined sum of money in return for an adequate consideration in money or money's worth, and to pay a fixed rate of interest;

☐ Whether there is subordination to, or preference over, any indebtedness of the corporation;

☐ The ratio of debt to equity of the corporation;

☐ Whether there is convertibility into the stock of the corporation;

☐ The relationship between holdings of stock in the corporation and holdings of the interest in question.

[¶703] POTENTIAL PROBLEM FOR SUBCHAPTER S CORPORATIONS

A thin incorporation can also cause problems in connection with a corporation's right to make a Subchapter S election. A corporation is not eligible to elect to be treated under Subchapter S unless it has only one class of stock. If purported debts owed to stockholders are treated as additional stock, the corporation might be deemed to have more than one class of stock outstanding. Thus, the corporation would be ineligible to make the election. The Regulations provide that obligations purporting to represent debt, but which are actually equity, will usually be a second class of stock unless (1) the debt is owned solely by owners of the actual stock issued, and (2) it is owned in substantially the same ratio as their actual stock ownership. If there is a difference in the proportionate ownership of stock and debt, the IRS will determine whether more than one class of stock is outstanding.

Basically, there are two separate tests to be applied.

First, there is the question of whether the purported debt is really a debt or whether it is a disguised equity interest. *Second,* if it is determined by the traditional thin-capitalization rules to be equity rather than debt, there is the question of whether the equity interest is a second class of stock. Although the IRS follows this approach, certain cases have held that actual debt may not be reclassified as equity for purposes of Subchapter S status.

[¶704] FORMS OF CAPITALIZATION

There are many different types of stock and securities that may be used in establishing the capital structure of a corporation (bonds, convertible debentures, subordinated debentures, etc.). However, in most closely-held corporations, the investment in the business is represented by common stock, preferred stock or promissory notes or some combination thereof.

[¶704.1] Common Stock

Common stock represents the most simple and straightforward evidence of an equity investment. The owners of common stock normally have voting rights that enable them to control the management of the corporation's affairs. However, the proprietary rights are limited to sharing in what remains of the corporate assets upon liquidation after all claims against the corporation have been satisfied. Payment of claims includes the payment of owners of any preferred stock.

The owners of common stock assume the most risk in connection with their financial commitment to the corporation's ultimate success. If the corporation is successful, however, they will obtain a larger financial reward than the owners of other types of corporate investments.

> *Example:* ABC Corporation has three stockholders, A, B and C, who invest $5,000, $10,000 and $25,000 respectively in exchange for a proportionate number of shares of common stock. The corporation commenced business, and in 5 years a Mr. Y bought all of the stock for $120,000. The purchase price would be payable as follows:
>
> $15,000 to A
> $30,000 to B
> $75,000 to C

It is possible to have different classes of common stock with different voting rights or financial priorities, but this is unusual in a closely-held corporation.

Ordinary Loss: Section 1244 Plan

When a closely-held corporation that is going to issue common stock is being formed, the corporation should take advantage of provisions of Section 1244 of the Code. This section permits a qualifying individual investor to deduct as an ordinary loss any loss up to $50,000 per year ($100,000 on a joint return) which results from the sale, exchange or worthlessness of "Section 1244 stock."

How to Define Section 1244 Stock

"Section 1244 stock" is common stock in a domestic corporation if:

☐ the corporation is a small business corporation at the time such stock is issued;

☐ such stock was issued by the corporation for money or other property (other than stock and securities); and

☐ the corporation, during the period of its 5 most recent taxable years ending before the date the loss on such stock was sustained, derived more than 50% of its aggregate gross receipts from sources other than royalties, rents, dividends, interest, annuities, and sales or exchanges of stock or securities.

How to Define a Small Business Corporation

A corporation is treated as a small business corporation if the aggregate amount of money and other property received by the corporation as a contribution to capital or paid-in surplus does not exceed $1,000,000.

Note: The requirements that must be met are determined as of the date the stock is issued. Subsequent changes will not result in the loss of the potential benefits.

How Many Shares Will Be Authorized and Issued

The ownership of a corporation is determined by the number of shares issued. If two people owned a corporation equally, they could each own one share or they could each own one million shares. The number of shares that a corporation is authorized to issue merely establishes a limit on the total shares that may be issued without obtaining further authorization from the state of incorporation. The primary concern in this area is to authorize and issue enough shares to provide flexibility for future planning—i.e., if the business owner wants to make gifts of stock or bring in future stockholders, enough stock should be issued to permit him to make gifts. Also, enough stock should be authorized but unissued to permit him to issue stock to a new investor. Some states impose a fee based on the number of authorized shares of stock. In such situations, you would normally authorize the maximum number of shares which would subject the corporation to the lowest fee.

[¶704.2] Preferred Stock

Preferred stock is a preferred equity investment in the corporation. The owners of such stock have preference over the owners of common stock with respect to rights upon liquidation of the corporation. They also normally have preferred rights with respect to the payment of dividends. Usually, preferred stock is issued at some stated par value with a provision that dividends will be paid at a certain fixed rate, or a provision that no dividends will be paid to owners of common stock before certain minimum dividends are paid to the owners of preferred stock. If the corporation is liquidated, or if the preferred stock is redeemed, the owner normally is entitled to receive only the stated par value plus any accumulated unpaid dividends that might be payable to him.

> *Example:* Suppose that ABC Corporation has two classes of stock, common and preferred. Mr. A buys $5,000 worth of common stock. Mr. B buys $10,000 worth of common stock. Mr. C buys 250 shares of preferred stock valued at $100 per share.
>
> Will dividends be cumulative? The preferred stock provides for the payment of an annual dividend of $8 per share. Note: Mr. C is guaranteed an $8 dividend each year out of corporate profits before any distributions can be made to the holders of the common stock. The preferred is *cumulative*—i.e., if the corporation is unable to pay the dividend in any year, the dividend carries over and is paid in a later year or when the stock is redeemed. However, unlike Mr. A and Mr. B, Mr. C is not entitled to any more than a return of his investment plus accumulated dividends in the event the corporation is dissolved.
>
> If ABC Corporation liquidates and has assets for distribution in the amount of $115,000 and all preferred dividends have been paid, Mr. C will receive $25,000. Mr. A will receive $30,000 and Mr. B will receive $60,000.

Should the Shareholders Be Given
Conditional Voting Rights?

Preferred stock is a less risky investment than common, but the potential for gain if the business is successful is limited.

Quite often, the holders of preferred stock are not entitled to vote on matters affecting the management of corporate affairs. However, in the event the corporation is in arrears on the payment of dividends to preferred stockholders, the shares can give the stockholders conditional voting rights. This allows them to have a voice in the management of the corporation until dividend payments become current.

Income Tax Disadvantage

Issuance of preferred stock is not usually a very desirable form of corporate investment in the context of a closely-held corporation because of the normal desire to avoid the payment of dividends. Preferred stock is similar to a debt investment as it does not participate in the appreciation in value of the corporation's net worth. However, the dividends are not deductible by the corporation. From a tax standpoint, it is desirable to have debt investment since the payments of interest are deductible by the corporation.

Preferred Stock May Be Useful for
Estate Planning

There is one particular situation in which the issuance of preferred stock may offer advantages in connection with the estate planning for the owner of a closely-held corporation. It is specifically advantageous for an owner who has children who are involved in the business.

Under current estate and gift tax laws, the value of lifetime gifts is returned to the donor's estate at the time of his death for purposes of determining the total estate tax. However, the lifetime gifts are valued as of the date of the gift if the donor survives for a period of three years. If an individual owns 100% of the common stock of a corporation, he could cause the corporation to be recapitalized on a tax-free basis. He could cause the corporation to issue him preferred stock with voting control in exchange for almost all of his common stock. The balance of the common stock could then be given to his children.

> *Example:* Suppose Mr. Smith owns 100% of the common stock of X Corporation, which is worth $200,000. In a reorganization, Mr. Smith exchanges his common stock for $10,000 of common stock and $190,000 worth of preferred stock which will pay a 6% dividend. Mr. Smith then gives the common stock to his children. The common stock would have a low value at the time of the gift. This would be the value at which the stock would be returned into Mr. Smith's estate. Any appreciation in the net worth of the corporation after the gift would be effectively removed from his estate if he survives three years. The value of the preferred stock would remain at approximately $190,000.

What Dividend Rate They Should Bear

Note: The estate tax savings must be weighed against the potential income tax disadvantages which accompany the payment of dividends. Also, it is important to know that, in order for a recapitalization to qualify as a tax-free reorganization under Section 368 of the Code, three things must be present:

- ☐ The readjustment of the corporate structure must be made for a business purpose;
- ☐ The business enterprise must continue under the modified corporate form; and
- ☐ There must be a continuity of interest on the part of the owner of the enterprise prior to the reorganization.

These requirements would be satisfied in the above example. We assumed the children were involved in the business, and transferring stock to the future managers of a business constitutes a valid business purpose.

CAVEAT: If a corporation has earnings and profits, preferred stock issuance could result in a dividend.
How can two classes of stock be used to give one group of

investors a disproportionate share of the earnings, or a larger share of the company's assets upon liquidation? It is a problem if a corporation has earnings and profits but does not want to distribute them as dividends due to the adverse tax consequences. A solution can be to distribute a dividend of preferred stock to its common stockholders. The preferred stock could then be sold to a third party and the corporation could redeem the stock from the third party.

CAVEAT: Apparent Result

Common stockholders end up with cash the same as if they had received a dividend. However, the payment would result in a capital gain instead of ordinary income. Also, the control and equity investment of the common stockholders would remain unchanged.

It Doesn't Work—Section 306 Stock

Generally speaking, "Section 306 stock" is stock received by a common stockholder as a tax-free dividend from a corporation that has earnings and profits. Section 306 provides that if such stock is disposed of other than by redemption, the amount received by the stockholder will be treated as ordinary income, up to the amount that would have been taxed as a dividend if the corporation had distributed cash to the stockholder in an amount equal to the value of the preferred stock.

Preferred stock should not be distributed to existing stockholders without considering the possible impact of Section 306.

Section 306 does not apply to preferred stock issued as part of the original organization of the corporation.

[¶704.3] If Preferred Shares Are Used, Should They Be Convertible into Common?

A speculative aspect may be added to preferred stock by giving the preferred stockholder a right to convert some or all of the preferred stock into common stock at some future time. Normally, the conversion ratio is established at an increasing value, for future purposes. This prevents the preferred stockholders from obtaining a disproportionately large benefit at the expense of the corporation.

> *Example:* X Corporation has common stock which has a value of $10 per share. X Corporation also has $100 par value convertible preferred stock which is convertible into 10 shares of common stock for a period of one year, into 9 shares for the next year, and into 8 shares for the next year. At the end of the third year, the conversion privilege expires. Assume that the value of the common stock increased from $10 to $15 per share over the 3 year period. If the conversion rate remained at 10 to 1, the preferred shareholder would realize a gain of $50. He could convert his $100 preferred stock into 10 shares of common stock. At the conversion ratio of 8 to 1, the preferred shareholder would have a potential gain of only $20.

[¶704.4] Debt Instruments

Debt instruments do not actually represent part of a corporation's capital structure. However, in the context of setting up a closely-held corporation, debt instruments should be considered at the time assets are transferred to the corporation. The owners of a business do not want to over capitalize a newly formed corporation. There are potentially adverse tax consequences that accompany a future transfer of property from the corporation to a stockholder. Over-capitalization can be avoided if the corporation issues some capital stock and some debt instruments in exchange for the transfer of assets to the corporation.

> *Example:* If assets with a fair market value of $50,000 are transferred to a newly-formed corporation, the corporation could issue stock in exchange for $25,000 worth of the assets and give the transferor a promissory note for $25,000.

CAVEAT: The Internal Revenue Service will examine the transaction closely to determine whether the note represents a true debt of the corporation. This is important when interest payments are deducted and when the principal is repaid.

Section 351

If a tax-free Section 351 incorporation is desired, it is critical that the note also constitutes a "security." To qualify for tax-free treatment, the transfer to the corporation must be made solely in exchange for stock or securities. If a taxable incorporation is desired, the issuance of a short-term demand note in exchange for the transfer of a portion of the assets will cause the incorporation to be taxable.

If a new corporation needs a substantial amount of cash for operating purposes, arrangements should be made to have the corporation borrow the funds. This is relevant even if the business which is being newly incorporated has a relatively large sum of cash at the time of the transfer to the corporation. The corporation could borrow the funds from some outside sources. The owner or owners could personally guarantee the corporate promissory note. After the incorporation has been completed, the stockholders could personally lend funds to pay off the debt and issue themselves demand promissory notes. This procedure avoids the difficulty of having excess cash in the corporation which cannot be withdrawn by the stockholders without a potential dividend problem. It also enables the corporation to qualify as "tax-free" since the demand notes to the stockholders were not given in exchange for the transfer of assets to the corporation.

> *Example:* Mr. Jones has a business of manufacturing auto parts. The value of his equipment and other assets is $50,000. He also has $50,000 of cash in the business bank account. Problems can occur if he transfers everything to the corporation in exchange for stock: (1) If he decides he wants to take some cash out of the business there may be a dividend. (2) If he takes $50,000 worth of stock and a demand promissory note of $50,000, the corporation will not be tax-free.
>
> *Suggestion:* The problem is solved if he exchanges the equipment for stock and borrows $50,000 from a bank. The corporation is tax-free, and he does not have his $50,000 of cash absorbed in the business. But what about the interest he has to pay the bank? After a few months, Mr. Jones loans the corporation the $50,000 he

had in the business bank account. The corporation then pays off the bank loan.

CAVEAT: If it is determined that this approach might be desirable, make sure that the transfer of assets to the corporation and the subsequent loan to the corporation by the stockholders are separate transactions. Otherwise, the IRS might apply the step-transaction theory. Under this theory, if various transactions can be viewed as individual steps of an overall larger transaction, the IRS will aggregate the transactions and treat them as if they occurred at the same time.

[¶704.5] Stock Options

To capitalize a closely-held corporation, stock options may be available to purchase the corporation's stock. The options may be given by the corporation or by the stockholders. Options are important because of the advantages that can be obtained by the option holder. It is imperative to understand the consequences of giving options as difficulties generally relate to possible violations of securities laws and unforseen tax results.

Options May Be Classified As Securities

Many business owners who are planning to incorporate a business are not aware that to offer someone an option to buy stock is to offer that person a security. An option to buy stock which is given in exchange for service or other consideration may be a security for purposes of the securities laws of many states.

To avoid potential problems, business owners must not offer options to purchase corporate stock unless the options are not in violation of any state or federal law. If options are improperly granted, it is possible that a person who exercises the option may have the right to completely rescind the purchase of stock. He may also be entitled to damages against the original stock owners or the corporation.

Income Tax Consequences

The income tax consequences which result from the purchase of an option or its subsequent exercise are fairly complex.

Normally, when a person is granted an option to purchase

stock in a closely-held corporation, he will immediately recognize income. Due to the IRC, this is true even if the apparent value of the stock exceeds the price at which the option holder may purchase the stock.

However, an option holder recognizes income upon the grant of the option only if:

☐ The option itself has a readily ascertainable market value, *and*

☐ If that value exceeds the option price.

If these two facts exist, he will recognize ordinary income to the extent that the fair market value of the option exceeds what he paid for it. His cost basis for the stock when the option is exercised is equal to the price he pays for the stock plus the amount of gain recognized on the grant of the option. In such a case, he would not recognize any further gain until the stock is sold. At that time he would recognize capital gain if the sales price exceeded his cost basis.

Options Normally Have No Readily Ascertainable Value

It is virtually impossible for an option-to-purchase closely-held stock to have a "readily ascertainable market value" due to the definition of that term in the Regulations.

Example: The apparent value of stock is $10 per share. If a person is given the option to buy the stock for $5 per share over a five-year period, it seems that the option would have a value of $5. For income tax purposes, the option does not have a readily ascertainable market value.

CAVEAT: In most cases, for the option to have an ascertainable value, the option itself must be traded on an exchange. Thus, the individual, in this example, recognizes no gain as a result of obtaining the option because it does not have a readily ascertainable value.

Assume that the option holder exercises his option after three years. At that time the value of the stock has risen from $10 to $30 per share. He pays the option price of $5 per share and receives the stock. At the time the option is exercised the individual recognizes a gain of $25 per share, and the gain is taxed as ordinary income.

Note: The individual has to recognize ordinary income and all he has done is to *buy* the stock. The stock has not been sold, and *he may not be able to sell the stock if it is subject to restrictions.*

Suggestion to Avoid Tax Problem—Promissory Note

To avoid the problem and to achieve the same economic result without the adverse tax consequences, have the corporation sell stock in exchange for a promissory note.

In the previous example, the option holder could have purchased the stock for $5 per share. Instead of paying cash, he could give the corporation a promissory note for the purchase price. His basis for the stock would have been $10 per share ($5 purchase price plus $5 bargain element of the purchase). Any subsequent increase in value would result in capital gain. The capital gain would be recognized only when the stock is sold.

A Recourse Note

If the stock option is exercised as a promissory note, it is important that the promissory note be a recourse note. CAVEAT: A recourse note is one which provides that the creditor may attach any of the promisor's assets in the event the note is not paid. If it is necessary for the corporation to recover the shares due to non-payment of the note, the Internal Revenue Service will treat the transaction in the same manner as the grant of an option. In addition to the requirement of a recourse note, it is unlawful in some states for a corporation to issue stock in exchange for a promissory note unless the payment of the note is adequately secured by assets other than the shares themselves.

If a key employee is required to recognize ordinary income as a result of exercising an option to purchase stock, the corporation is entitled to a deduction in the same amount. Thus, depending upon the relative marginal tax brackets of the individual and the corporation, it may be possible for the tax disadvantages accompanying a stock option arrangement to be mitigated. The corporation can pass the tax benefit of its unexpected deduction onto the employee in the form of a bonus. The bonus in turn would be additional compensation to the employee.

> *Example:* Assume that an employee exercises his option to purchase stock for $5 a share when the value of the stock is $30. He has a $25 gain and the corporation gets a corresponding deduction. Since the corporation was originally prepared to sell him the stock for $5, the $25 deduction is an unexpected benefit. It would result in a tax-savings to the corporation of approximately $12. The corporation can give the employee a cash bonus of $12 using the government's money. The bonus would be further income to the employee. However, the corporation would obtain a corresponding deduction for the cash bonus which would result in an additional tax savings of about $6. This savings could also be passed on to the employee.
>
> If the corporation is in the 50% combined Federal and state tax bracket, the corporation can afford to give the employee a cash bonus equal to the value of its unexpected deduction without any reduction in its capital.
>
> The corporation would pay $25 as a cash bonus but would receive a deduction of $50 (the $25 bonus plus the $25 that the employee had to report as income because of the option). The tax savings from the $50 deduction would be $25, or the amount of the cash bonus.
>
> If the employee has income of $50, and is in the 50% marginal tax bracket, he at least has received enough cash to pay his taxes. Without the bonus he would have had taxable income of $25 with no cash.

CAVEAT: Compensation Must Be Reasonable

A corporation may deduct only reasonable compensation.

Options Granted by Stockholders

Options granted by stockholders may be advantageous in that the terms of the option may be more flexible than if the corporation gives the option. This flexibility may also create a substantial tax problem. As noted in the preceding paragraph, if the employee recognizes income on the exercise of a corporation-granted option, the corporation gets a corresponding deduction.

If the option is given by a stockholder, he does *not* get a deduction.

CAVEAT: A deduction is allowed only to the taxpayer for whom services were performed, i.e., the corporation.

If the stockholder grants the option the corporation cannot take a deduction because it did not transfer the stock to the employee. No one is entitled to a deduction even though the employee recognizes ordinary income.

[¶704.6] Restricted Stock

A matter closely related to stock options is restricted stock. Restricted stock involves the transfer of stock to a person who renders service to the corporation, but restrictions are placed on his ability to freely dispose of the stock. Often the restrictions include the possibility that the person will forfeit all or part of the stock unless he remains with the corporation for a certain period of time or satisfies certain other requirements. Again, the tax consequences of such a program are best illustrated by an example:

> *Example:* Assume that a corporation issues stock to a key employee. The value of the stock is $10 per share. However, in the event the employee leaves the corporation before five years of additional employment, he must forfeit the stock and return it to the corporation. Let's suppose that the employee is still with the corporation at the end of the five year period and that the value of the stock is $30 per share at that time. The employee does not recognize any income in the year when he receives the stock. He recognizes income in the year when the stock is no longer subject to a sub-

stantial risk of forfeiture—at the expiration of the five year period. The amount recognized as ordinary income at that time is the difference between what was paid for the stock and the fair market value of stock [Section 83 of the IRC]. In this case, it is $30 per share since the employee paid nothing for the stock.

Suggestion: The adverse income tax consequences related to restricted stock may be avoided if the employee makes an irrevocable election to include in his gross income the difference between what he pays for the stock and the fair market value of the stock for the year in which he receives the stock.

In order to make an election, the person performing the service must file a statement with the Internal Revenue Service officer with whom he files his return within 30 days after the property has been transferred to him. A copy of the statement is to be attached to his own personal income tax return and a copy is to be provided to the person for whom the services are rendered. The statement shall be signed by the person making the election and shall indicate that it is being made under Section 83 (b) of the Code and shall contain the following information:

(1) The name, address and taxpayer identification number of the taxpayer;

(2) a description of each property with respect to which the election is being made;

(3) the date or dates on which the property is transferred and the taxable year for which such election is made;

(4) the nature of restriction or restrictions to which the property is subject;

(5) The fair market value at the time of transfer for each property with respect to which the election is being made;

(6) the amount, if any, paid for such property;

(7) a statement to the effect that copies have been furnished to the Internal Revenue Officer and the person for whom the services were rendered.

If such an election is made [Section 83(b)] , future appreciation in the value of the stock would be converted from ordinary
income into capital gain. The fair market value is determined
without regard to any restrictions other than restrictions which,
by their terms, will never lapse. Since the possible forfeiture of
the stock will be eliminated at the end of five years, that restriction may not be considered in determining the fair market value
of the stock. The employee would have to report $10 per share as
compensation income.

In the previous example, the employee might lose the entire
amount of stock initially received. However, the value of the
stock is not reduced for purposes of determining his gross income
if he makes the election under Section 83 (b). If the stock is
actually forfeited, the employee is not entitled to any income tax
deduction. Any employee who receives restricted stock must
analyze and accept the possibility of the forfeiture provisions.
Otherwise, he may make an election which results in potential
income tax advantages but which also is an economic disaster.

> *Example:* An employee elects to include $10 per share
> in his gross income for the year in which he receives the
> stock in order to convert potential future appreciation
> in value into capital gain. If he leaves the corporation
> before the expiration of the five-year period, he has to
> return the stock. However, he will have paid tax at
> ordinary income tax rates on the value of the stock.
> These are the dictates of the current law.

[¶705] WHERE ARE VOTING AND OTHER CONTROLS TO REST?

In considering how to set up the capital structure of a corporation, the matter of voting rights is very important. The stockholders of a corporation are the persons who have the ultimate
authority in the corporation's operation.

The most simple situation involves a corporation with only
one class of voting common stock. Each share of stock represents
one vote. A majority of shares of stock controls the decisions of
the corporations. At the other end of the spectrum is a corpora-

tion which has various classes of common stock. Each class may have different voting rights, and the corporation may also have preferred stock with certain voting rights.

Should Voting Rights Be Set Up to Give Minority Interests Representation?

Cumulative voting rights may be desirable in order to ensure that minority stockholders will have representation on the Board of Directors. Cumulative voting rights mean that each share of stock is given a number of votes equal to the number of directors to be elected. A stockholder's votes may be cast for the election of each director or they may be pooled and be cast in favor of one director.

> *Example:* X Corporation has three shareholders (A, B, and C) who each own 1000 shares of common stock. X Corporation has three people on the Board of Directors. A and B have the same business philosophies, but C doesn't. If the directors were elected by a majority vote without cumulative voting privileges, A and B could elect the entire Board. C would not be represented. However, if the shares had cumulative voting rights, C could assure himself of a spot on the Board of Directors. Each shareholder would have a total of 3,000 votes for purposes of electing all of the directors. In order to be elected as a director, a person would have to receive a vote of a majority of the outstanding shares (at least 1,501). A and B could use 1,501 of their votes to elect the first two directors. If C used none of his votes for the first two directors, C could elect himself as the third director by casting all of his 3,000 votes for himself. A and B could cast 2,998 in favor of someone else, but that would not be enough. The various combinations of voting rights are virtually endless.

CAVEAT: Voting rights must be given careful consideration at the outset or unnecessary impasses may occur.

PART FOUR

MAPPING OUT
EMPLOYEE BENEFIT PLANS

8

How to Help Executives Make the Most of Fringe Benefits

In some cases, the availability of employee fringe benefits is the motivating factor for incorporation. This section discusses the advantages of various benefit plans along with other money-saving fringe benefit opportunities.

Qualified Retirement Plans

One of the most significant benefits available to the owners of a financially successful business is the ability to participate in a qualified retirement plan or plans such as pension or profit-sharing plans. If a corporation adopts a qualified retirement plan, contributions to a trust are made on behalf of participating employees. These contributions may be invested and the earnings are accumulated for the benefit of the participants until retirement or other termination of employment. At that time the balance in a participant's account is distributed to him.

The corporation is entitled to a current income tax deduction for the contribution to the retirement trust. However, the participating employees do not have to include their share of the contribution as income. Participants don't have any taxable income until they receive a distribution of their benefit. The income that is earned on trust investments is not subject to income tax, so the income accumulates tax-free. If a participating employee dies prior to receiving his share of the trust assets, his designated beneficiaries will receive distribution and the value of his interest in the trust may not be included in his gross estate for purposes of determining the Federal estate tax. In order to get the favorable estate tax treatment, the distribution of the entire balance may not be made within one calendar year.

Plans Cannot Discriminate, but There Can Be Flexibility

A common misconception among business owners is that they cannot establish a qualified retirement plan unless they cover all of their employees. The requirement with respect to coverage is that in determining who is going to participate in such a plan, the contributions or benefits provided under the plan may not discriminate in favor of employees who are officers, stockholders or who are highly compensated. This does not mean that all employees must participate.

The Code provides two tests for determining whether a plan is engaging in the prohibited discrimination. One of the tests is objective and the other is subjective.

First, there is no discrimination if the plan benefits 70% or more of all employees (part-time employees and employees who have not met certain minimum service requirements may be ignored). Also, if 70% of all employees are eligible to participate, and if 80% of the eligible employees actually do participate under the plan, then there is no prohibited discrimination. If the percentage requirements are not met, the plan can still qualify if it covers a classification of employees, and does not result in discrimination in favor of highly compensated employees who are officers or shareholders. For instance, it is possible to have a plan that covers only *salaried* employees.

Under the percentage test it is possible to cover as few as 56% of the full-time work force and still have a qualified plan. Under the subjective test it is possible to cover as few as two employees out of a work force of hundreds. If one low-paid employee who is not an officer or shareholder is a participant, and if the sole shareholder is the other participant, the plan does not discriminate in favor of the shareholder.

As a practical matter, qualified retirement plans should be submitted to the IRS for approval. The corporation receives a letter indicating that the plan meets all the requirements of the Code. If there is any question as to whether possible discrimination exists, the matter can be resolved at the outset.

If a business has union employees, these employees may be specifically excluded from the corporation's retirement plans *if* retirement benefits for the union employees have been the subject of good faith bargaining. This exists even if the only non-union employees are highly compensated officers or shareholders.

Part-time employees (generally those who work less than 1,000 hours per year) and employees who have not completed a minimum length of service, may be excluded from coverage without causing any prohibited discrimination.

Once the business owner has excluded any and all of the employees under the application of the rules stated above, he can further tailor the plan to weigh the benefits in his direction with certain other permissible steps.

Graduated Vesting Schedule

After an employee becomes a participant in a retirement plan, he will be entitled to have a contribution made on his behalf. However, he is not entitled to receive the full balance of the contributions made for his benefit if his employment is terminated. The plan may provide that a participant must be employed for a certain period of time before he is entitled to the full amount that is allocated to him under the plan. This is the concept commonly referred to as graduated vesting. For example, the plan could indicate that if an employee left after one year he would be entitled to only 10% of his account balance. If he left after two years he would receive 20%.

In a closely-held corporation with few employees, an extended vesting schedule is subject to limitations. The IRS will permit a vesting schedule which gives participants no vested interest until 4 years of employment, 40% after 4 years of employment, and gradual increases thereafter until a participant is 100% vested after 11 years. In some cases it is possible to have no vesting for 5 years and to delay full vesting until the expiration of 15 years of service. Another statutory vesting schedule permits no vesting for 10 years, after which a participant is fully vested.

The portion of a former participant's account that is not vested is forfeited. The forfeited amount is either allocated to the accounts of the other participants or is used to reduce the corporation's next contribution to the plan. It depends on whether the plan is a profit-sharing plan or a pension plan. If a corporation has made an election under Subchapter S, no portion of the forfeitures may be allocated for the benefit of a "shareholder-employee."

CAVEAT: The vesting schedule to be applied must be the same for all participants. However, this should not be a problem for the owner of the business since he will presumably continue to be an employee. If he (the owner) decides to quit, the retirement plan can be terminated. If a plan is terminated, all participants become fully vested.

If a qualified retirement plan includes a graduated vesting schedule, there is a maximum waiting period before an otherwise eligible full-time employee can become a participant. The maximum wait is 6 months after he has completed one year of service with the corporation. The most simple way to meet this requirement is to admit all full-time employees as participants on the last day of the corporation's taxable year *if* they have been employed for at least 6 months at that time. If a plan does not provide for graduated vesting, then the required waiting period may be extended. Participation does not have to commence prior to the expiration of 6 months after an employee has completed 3 years of service with the corporation.

Integration with Social Security

Another way to favor the more highly paid participants is to integrate social security with the qualified retirement plans. What does this mean? A benefit may be provided under the plan for participants based on their compensation in excess of the social security wage base for each year. No such benefit has to be provided for participants who earn less than the social security wage base. The way social security integration works is different for profit-sharing plans than it is for pension plans. The details will be presented later in this chapter when a specific description of the various types of retirement plans is considered.

What Type of Plans Are Available

The most common types of qualified retirement plans which are adopted by closely-held corporations are profit-sharing plans, money-purchase pension plans and defined benefit plans. Other types of qualified retirement plans include stock bonus plans and employee stock ownership plans (commonly referred to as ESOP's).

[¶800] PROFIT-SHARING PLANS

The most straight-forward type of plan is a profit-sharing plan. A corporation adopts a plan and establishes a trust to which it makes contributions out of its current or accumulated earnings and profits. The amount of the contribution may vary from year to year. Management of the corporation has discretion with respect to the amount of the contribution. A maximum contribution of 15% of the compensation paid to all the participating employees during the fiscal year of the trust is deductible by the corporation. Normally, the trust is on the same fiscal year as the corporation. In the event that a corporation does not make the maximum deductible contribution in a particular year, the underpayment may be carried over to subsequent years. It may be added to the 15% deduction in the succeeding year except that the deduction may never exceed 25% (accrued) of the compensation paid to participating employees.

If the plan is not integrated with social security, the contribution must be allocated to the accounts of the participants based on each participant's pro rata share of total compensation.

If the plan is integrated with social security, an amount equal to 7% of each participant's compensation in excess of the social security wage base for the year is allocated to the account of each such participant. The balance of the corporation's contribution is allocated on a pro rata basis in accordance with each participant's share of total compensation.

Example: Suppose a corporation has four employees. They earn total annual compensation as follows:

"A" earns $85,000
"B" earns $15,000
"C" earns $15,000
"D" earns $10,000

Total compensation is $125,000 and the corporation makes the maximum deductible contribution of $18,750 (15% of $125,000).

Assume that covered compensation for purposes of social security is $18,000.

"A" earned $67,000 in excess of the social security limit. 7% of such excess, or $4,690, is allocated to his account from the $18,750 contribution. The balance of the contribution, or $14,060 is allocated on a pro rata basis. Since "A" earned 85/125 of the total compensation, his account is credited with 85/125 of the balance of the contribution. This means he receives an additional allocation of $8,921.

Under the integrated plan, "A" has $13,611 allocated to his account. This is equal to a little more than 16% of his compensation. "B," "C" and "D" have less than 14% of their compensation allocated to their account.

If a closely-held corporation has elected to be taxed under the provisions of Subchapter S of the Code, then the annual contribution on behalf of the owner may be limited. The contribution of a "shareholder-employee" is limited to the lesser of 15% of his compensation or $7,500. Also, the percentage limitation is applied on only the first $100,000 of compensation. Thus, if the owner of a Subchapter S corporation receives compensation in excess of $100,000, the corporation will have to contribute at least

7½% of the other participants' compensation in order for the owner to obtain the maximum allowable contribution for himself.

> *Example:* Mr. Bell owns 100% of the stock of Bell Corporation. Bell Corp, is a Subchapter S corporation. Mr. Bell has a salary of $200,000 per year. The maximum contribution that can be made to the corporation's profit-sharing plan on behalf of Mr. Bell is the lesser of $7,500 or 15% of his compensation. $7,500 constitutes only 3.75% of Mr. Bell's compensation. If Bell Corp. was not a Subchapter S corporation, the contribution for all employees could be limited to 3.75% of their compensation. However, since Bell Corp. is a Subchapter S corporation, consideration may be given only to the first $100,000 of Mr. Bell's compensation. $7,500 equals 7.5% of the first $100,000 of Mr. Bell's compensation. Thus, the corporation would have to contribute 7.5% of the compensation of non-owner employees to the pofit-sharing plan if it is going to contribute the maximum allowable amount for Mr. Bell.

Voluntary Contributions

In addition to the contribution by the corporation, a plan may permit voluntary contributions. An employee may contribute from his own funds an amount equal to 10% of the compensation he earns while the plan is in effect. He gets no income tax deduction for such a contribution. However, the earnings on it will accumulate, tax-free until the participant terminates his employment.

Who Should Be the Trustee

As previously indicated, the profit-sharing contributions are made to a profit-sharing trust. The trustee of the trust may be a bank or a trust company, or the trustee may be the owner of the business. How does one make a decision as to the appropriate trustee? The cost of a corporate trustee must be weighed against the potential liability of an individual trustee. If imprudent investment of trust assets occurs, the trustee may be liable to plan participants. Also, there are administrative duties which are the responsibility of the trustee.

If a corporate trustee is appointed, the corporate management may retain the right to direct the investment decisions relative to the trust funds. The Employee Retirement Income Security Act of 1974 places fairly comprehensive responsibility on any person who has the authority to deal with the investment of retirement funds or to otherwise affect their operation. Thus, whether the stockholder of a closely-held corporation or an independent trust company acts as trustee, the business owner must review trust investments. The owner may be responsible to "plan participants" for any investment losses that result from his lack of prudence, even if the owner of the business is not the trustee.

What Can Trust Funds Be Invested In?

Once cash has been contributed to a profit-sharing trust, the trustee or the corporation management has wide latitude in determining appropriate trust investments. For instance, the trustee can buy publicly traded stocks or bonds or deposit the funds in savings accounts in bank or savings and loan associations.

Because the trust earnings accumulate tax-free and because the trustee may be financially responsible to plan participants for trust losses, it is normally advisable to adopt a fairly conservative investment policy. For instance, an 8% return on a deposit in a savings account by a qualified retirement trust could be equivalent to a 16% return on an investment that did not receive the tax advantages attributable to the qualified retirement trust.

If the trustee wants to be free from investment responsibility, the plan may provide for individual investment accounts. Under such a plan, each participant may direct the manner in which his or her account shall be invested.

Limitation on Life Insurance

The reason for permitting tax-favored treatment for retirement plans is that such plans will ease the burden on government for taking care of retired employees. Therefore, certain investments which do not provide retirement benefits are not permitted. For instance, life insurance may not be bought in an unlimited amount. It may be purchased only if the death benefit to a participant is "incidental" to the retirement benefit.

No Self-Dealing

Care should be taken to be sure that no transactions occur between a profit-sharing trust and any "parties-in-interest." Such transactions are strictly prohibited by the Code and can result in substantial penalties to the plan and to the party-in-interest who is involved. "Parties-in-interest" include: the corporation, the stockholders, the officers, the plan participants, the relatives of such individuals; or in short, virtually any person connected with the retirement plan.

The retirement trust may not loan money to the corporation for *any* reason. It is also a violation of the law for the trust to buy property from, or sell property to, the corporation or any other party-in-interest. There are certain limited exceptions to the prohibited transaction rules. However, the general rule is that any dealings between the trust and the corporation, or the individuals involved in the management of the corporation, should be avoided.

Loans to Participants May Be Made

CAVEAT: One important exception to the prohibition of self-dealing is that the trust may make loans to participants.

The loans must be made available to all participants in a manner which does not result in discrimination in favor of stockholders, etc. Loans are permitted if they bear a reasonable rate of interest and if the repayment of the loan is adequately secured.

It is erroneous to state that loans to participants may not exceed the value of their vested interest in their account. The error stems from the fact that a pledge of a participant's vested interest in his account is only one of many ways to secure the repayment of the loan. For instance, he could pledge other assets, such as his house, as adequate security.

CAVEAT: All the trust funds cannot be loaned to members

of the group in whose favor discrimination is prohibited. Loans must be available to the rank and file employees. Although loans to participants may be desirable, it is important to note that a plan does not have to make such loans available.

Before leaving the area of loans to participants, a potentially significant planning device should be mentioned. A qualified retirement trust may not directly loan money to the corporation that set up the trust. However, it may loan money to a participant under the guidelines discussed above. The participant can, in turn, loan the money to the corporation. This technique does indirectly what cannot be done directly, but there is no reason why it should not be permitted. If a loan to a participant is adequately secured, the manner in which the participant spends the proceeds of the loan is irrelevant. If the participant defaults on the loan, the plan forecloses on the security. If the corporation defaults on the loan from the participant, the profit-sharing trust would not be affected.

If the owner of a closely-held corporation has a large portion of the profit-sharing contribution alllocated to his account, and if the corporation has a temporary cash flow shortage, this technique may be employed to allow the corporation to make a tax-deductible contribution that would be otherwise impossible. As with any other tax-planning device, care should be taken to see that its potential benefits are not abused.

Consider the Cost of Maintaining the Plan

Before the owner of a closely-held business should establish a profit-sharing plan or any other type of employee benefit plan, he must analyze the cost of the plan. He must consider the cost of providing benefits for his other employees before he can determine whether such a program makes economic sense. Obviously, if the costs of the plan exceed the tax benefits to the owner, then the plan should not be instituted. The tax advantages relating to the contribution and the trust earnings have already been described. In addition, there are tax considerations which are involved in the distribution of a participant's benefits.

When Are Benefits Distributed to Participants?

When a participant in a profit-sharing plan or other qualified retirement plan terminates his employment with the corporation, he is entitled to an amount equal to his vested benefit under the terms of the plan. The non-vested portion of his account will be reallocated among the remaining participants in the plan. The fact that he has a vested interest in his profit-sharing account does not mean that he is entitled to an immediate distribution of his benefit. The corporation may delay distributing his benefit until he attains normal retirement age (usually age 65). It may use his vested interest to purchase an annuity contract that will pay the employee a certain amount per month for the rest of his life with the first payment starting on the date of his normal retirement. The corporation might also direct that the payment be made in yearly installments. If a participant is married, he or she must receive what is called a qualified joint and survivor annuity unless he or she elects otherwise. Instead of exploring this concept here, reference is made to the sample plans in the next chapter for treatment of this technical point.

If the payment to a terminated participant is delayed, the value of his account must continue to accrue interest on its portion of trust earnings until actual distribution is made. Normally, distribution is made immediately if a participant is fully vested. If he is not fully vested, distribution may be delayed for one year. The different treatment relates to a technical requirement that must be met if a participant who is not fully vested leaves the corporation and is re-employed before he incurs what is called a "one-year break in service." However, it is very important to remember that the corporation can delay distribution until normal retirement date and can determine the method in which his benefit will be paid.

The corporation's control in this area can be critical. Suppose that an employee leaves the corporation and plans to use the funds credited to his profit-sharing account to form a competitive corporation. The owner of a closely-held corporation does not want to establish a plan that would enable key employees to establish a competing business. This is particularly true if the tax consequences which occur when a participant receives a distribution from a qualified plan are very favorable.

Tax Treatment of Annuity Payments

If an employee receives distribution in the form of an annuity, he will include the annuity payments in his gross income as he receives them. Presumably, a retired employee will be in a lower income tax bracket after retirement. The net tax impact of the retirement plan for such a participant may be summarized as follows:

- The contributions for his benefit are not subjected to income tax at the time they are made to the trust;
- The full amount of contribution accumulates income without having any income tax imposed; and
- The ultimate distribution of his portion of the trust fund will probably be taxed at lower levels than if the profit-sharing contributions had been paid to him as a bonus while he was working.

To fully appreciate the potential magnitude of the above-described tax benefits, a calculation should be made using the client's actual projected income, contributions, and investment rate of return. By way of example, a profit-sharing contribution will almost double in eight years if the investment return is 8%.

Tax Treatment of Lump-Sum Payment

If a participant receives a lump sum distribution of his retirement benefit, the taxable portion attributable to his length of service prior to 1974 may be taxed as long-term capital gain. However, the Employee Retirement Income Security Act of 1974 added a new favorable averaging method for determining the tax payable by someone who receives a lump sum distribution of his retirement plan benefit upon the termination of his employment. A participant may elect to have the capital gain portion of a distribution taxed under the new income averaging rule. The term "lump sum" has a defined meaning. It includes only a distribution upon an employee's separation from service (unless he is over the age of 59½ years) after he has been a participant in the plan for at least 5 years. Thus, if distribution is made as a result of the termination of a qualified retirement plan or if the participant has not been a participant for 5 years, a distribution of the entire balance in his account simply would be added to his other income and taxed as ordinary income.

If a lump sum distribution is made, the taxable portion is equal to the total distribution less the amount of voluntary contributions made by the participant. If any employer securities were a part of the distribution, any appreciation in value of such securities would also be excluded from the taxable portion. In order to determine the tax, the total distribution is divided by 10 and a tax on that amount is figured by using the tax table for a single individual. The tax calculated for a single individual is then multiplied by 10 to determine the total tax that is imposed on the lump sum distribution. A former participant's other income during the year of the distribution is disregarded. Therefore, the so-called 10 year averaging is often more advantageous than capital gain treatment. In situations which involve large distributions, it should be noted that benefits payable under the provisions of a qualified retirement plan are considered to be earned income. Thus, they are subject to the rules which limit the maximum marginal tax rate on earned income to 50%.

[¶801] MONEY-PURCHASE (DEFINED CONTRIBUTION) PENSION PLAN

A money-purchase pension plan is very similar to a profit-sharing plan. It is also quite easy to administer. To best understand how a money-purchase pension plan operates is to think of it as a profit-sharing plan with three basic differences:

Fixed Contribution

☐ First, the percentage of each participants' compensation that will be contributed each year is established at the time the plan is established. It is not something that may be changed from year to year.

Larger Contribution Is Permitted

☐ Next, the amount of the contribution is not limited to 15% of the participants' total compensation. Instead, the practical limit is 25% of such compensation. The reason for limiting the contribution to 25% of compensation will be explored in connection with covering the situation in which a corporation adopts more than one type of pension plan.

Forfeitures Are Treated Differently

☐ The final difference relates to the treatment of forfeitures under a money-purchase pension plan. Forfeitures are not allocated among remaining participants. Instead, they are retained by the pension trust to reduce the next contribution that will be required by the corporation.

There is a basic conceptual difference between a profit-sharing plan and a pension plan. Under a profit-sharing plan, a participant is not being guaranteed any particular retirement benefit. However, in the case of a pension plan, he is being promised some type of retirement income. By requiring a fixed rate of annual contribution and by treating forfeitures as part of the contribution, the IRS has concluded that a money-purchase pension plan provides a participant with a definitely determinable benefit. This conclusion is not actually correct since a participant's retirement benefit will be affected by the investment experience of the pension trust fund. It is the uncertainty that relates to the success or failure of trust investment that led to the name "money-purchase" pension plan; i.e., the benefit to which a participant entitled is equal to whatever amount of monthly pension can be purchased with the money in a participant's account at the time of his retirement.

CAVEAT: The distribution of benefits at retirement or other termination of service does not have to be in the form of a monthly pension, but can be a lump sum distribution or a distribution in installments over a period of years.

Combination of Profit-Sharing Plan and Money-Purchase Pension Plan

The income tax treatment on distributions to a former participant from a money-purchase pension plan is the same as distributions under a profit-sharing plan.

In determining the maximum permissible contribution for the benefit of a participant, all defined contribution plans are aggregated. The total "annual-addition" to a participant's account or account for all such plans may not exceed the lesser of 25% of his covered compensation or $25,000. The dollar limitation is to be changed from year-to-year based on changes which occur in the cost-of-living index after 1974. For the year 1979, the dollar limit is $32,700. A participant's voluntary contributions which are in excess of 6% of his compensation are added to the employer contributions for purposes of limiting the amount of permissible annual additions to the account of a participant.

If a business owner wants to provide for the maximum permissible contribution under a defined contribution plan, the corporation could adopt a money-purchase pension plan with the maximum contribution formula. However, such a plan requires the corporation to make the fixed percentage contribution each year, whether or not the corporation is profitable.

A different approach to permit the maximum contribution with more flexibility is to have the corporation adopt a money-purchase pension plan and a profit-sharing plan. The money-purchase plan can require a contribution equal to 10% of covered compensation. The profit-sharing plan could have a contribution of anything between 0% and 15%. Under this approach the corporation is obligated only to make the smaller contribution. However, it may make a total contribution equal to 25% of compensation by making a 15% contribution to the profit-sharing plan.

[¶802] DEFINED BENEFIT PENSION PLAN

The third common type of qualified retirement plan is the defined benefit pension plan. As in the case of a profit-sharing plan or a money-purchase plan, a defined benefit has the same requirements with respect to such matters as nondiscrimination and vesting. However, the determination of the amount of retirement benefits is completely different. As the name suggests, a participant in a denied benefit pension plan is promised a specific amount of retirement benefit. Normally the benefit is expressed in terms of a monthly benefit payable at his normal retirement age. The amount of the benefit usually is equal to a certain percent of the monthly compensation each participant earns prior to retirement. For instance, a plan might provide that a participant will receive a retirement benefit equal to 25% of his average monthly compensation over the five-year period preceding his retirement.

The amount of the defined benefit may not exceed the lesser of 100% of his average annual compensation or $75,000. The absolute dollar figure is subject to change based on changes in the cost-of-living index and is equal to $98,100 for the year 1979. A defined benefit pension plan may also be integrated with social security by providing a higher percentage benefit for those participants earning more than the social security wage base than for those who earn less than that amount.

How to Determine the Required Annual Contribution

A defined benefit pension plan provides what the retirement benefit will be. It does not provide how much has to be contributed to the plan each year. In order to determine the annual contribution which must be made each year so the plan can provide the promised benefits, an actuary must be hired. The actuary informs the corporation how much should be contributed each year to have sufficient funds available at retirement to pay the required pension.

A fixed pension at normal retirement age requires that a certain sum of money be available at that time for each participant. The actuary has to make assumptions with respect to such things as:

• The projected earnings on the trust funds;

• The anticipated forfeitures (which are retained by the

trust instead of being allocated to the account of other participants); and

• Variations in compensation paid to participants.

The corporation is entitled to deduct whatever contribution the actuary determines is necessary to enable the pension plan to meet its eventual liability to retired participants. If the trust funds experience favorable investment performance (rate of return higher than the actuary predicts), subsequent annual contributions will be lower than originally anticipated. If the fund does *not* perform up to expectations, the required contributions will be higher in subsequent years.

As in the case of a money-purchase pension plan, the corporation is committing itself to an annual contribution whether or not it has profits. The amount of the contribution is not discretionary. Furthermore, the amount of the required contribution is subject to some factors which are completely beyond the control of corporate management.

Age of the Participants Is an Important Factor

One extremely important factor to note when a business owner is contemplating setting up a defined benefit pension plan is the employee's age. The age of a participant may affect his benefit as much as or more than the amount of his compensation.

> *Example:* Two employees each earn $20,000 per year. The pension plan provides a retirement equal to 25% of average compensation. They will each be entitled to a retirement pension of $5,000 per year. Assume that one employee is 30 years old and the other is 55 years old. The annual contribution for the benefit of the older employee has to be considerably higher than the one for the benefit of the younger employee.

The fact that benefits under a defined benefit pension plan are related to age make this type of plan advantageous in cases where the owners of a business are older than the other employees.

Abuses can occur under this type of plan if all the owners are relatively older. Thus, limitations are placed on the maximum benefits which may be paid to employees who have had less than 10 years of service with the corporation at the time of their retirement. The limitations apply when a participant has less than 10 years of service with the corporation, *not* 10 years on participation under the plan.

Potential Loophole

A 60-year-old business owner whose business had been incorporated more than 5 years could establish a defined benefit pension plan. The plan could provide him with a maximum pension benefit, and that benefit could be funded over a period of only 5 years.

Consider the Cost of Administering a Defined Benefit Plan

Although a defined benefit pension plan can provide extremely valuable benefits in appropriate situations, the administrative complexities and costs are considerably greater than those involved in the operation of a defined contribution plan.

The Plan Needs an Actuary

As noted, it is necessary to hire an actuary to determine the amount of the required annual contribution to a defined benefit pension plan. Employment of an actuary is not necessary in the case of a profit-sharing plan or a money-purchase pension plan. The contribution under those plans is merely a fixed percentage of each participant's compensation.

The Employee Retirement Income Security Act of 1974 has established certain procedures which are designed to ensure that participants in defined benefit pension plans will actually receive the benefits. For instance, the Act sets forth the method to determine the minimum amount a corporation must contribute each year so that the plan will be able to pay the promised pension benefits. Each qualified defined benefit pension plan must maintain what is referred to as a funding standard account. This account determines whether or not the plan is meeting the minimum funding requirements to insure that benefits can be paid. If the corporation does not make sufficient contributions to meet the minimum funding requirements, it will be subject to an excise tax on the amount of under-funding. The minimum funding requirements may be waived if a corporation cannot meet the minimum standard without incurring substantial business hardship. However, it is extremely difficult to qualify for such a waiver.

The Plan Must Be Insured with the Pension Benefit Guaranty Corporation

In addition to imposing more stringent rules on the amount of required contributions, the Act also established a federal agency called the Pension Benefit Guaranty Corporation ("PBGC"). This corporation insures that participants in defined benefit pension plans and the beneficiaries of such participants will receive promised benefits even if the plan is terminated. The PBGC charges pension plans an annual premium equal to $1.00 times the number of plan participants. If the premium is not paid on time, a civil penalty of 100% is charged to the plan. The plan termination insurance guarantees the payment of any vested rights that a participant has under a pension plan. However, the guaranteed benefits will not exceed the actuarial equivalent of the lesser of two amounts:

☐ 100% of a former participant's average wages over his 5 highest-paid years of participation;

☐ $750 per month.

If a corporation chooses to terminate a defined benefit pension plan, it must notify the PBGC at least 10 days before the date of the proposed termination. No distributions should be made to any participants until the PBGC has determined that the pension assets are sufficient to pay all insured benefit obligations. In the event the assets are not sufficient, the PBGC will provide the difference. However, the corporation is responsible for reimbursing the PBGC for insurance benefits paid to plan participants upon termination of the plan. The extent of the corporation's liability to the PBGC cannot exceed 30% of the corporation's net worth. However, the potential liability for an under-funded plan can be substantial.

> *Example:* A corporation sets up a defined benefit pension plan. During the period of time the plan was in existence, the corporation paid $50,000 less than was required. The company now wants to terminate the plan for economic reasons.
>
> The participants will be protected by the PBGC. The PBGC can recover the $50,000 of under-funding from the corporation unless the $50,000 exceeds 30% of the corporation's net worth. If the $50,000 exceeds 30% of the corporation's net worth, then the liability to the PBGC will be equal to 30% of the corporation's net worth.

In addition to reports which must be filed on behalf of profit-sharing plans and money-purchase pension plans, an actuarial report must be filed by a defined benefit pension plan. This report is necessary for the plan's first year and for each third plan year thereafter.

[¶803] COMBINATION OF PLANS— BENEFITS CAN BE INCREASED

Suppose that the owner of a business is highly compensated and that he has few other employees who would have to be included in the corporation's qualified retirement plan. The owner's retirement plan benefits could be maximized by the adoption of a money-purchase pension plan and a defined benefit pension plan. For instance, the corporation could establish a money-purchase plan with a required contribution of 25%. It could, in addition, set up a defined benefit plan which provides a benefit equal to 40% of what would otherwise have been the maximum permissible defined benefit. The defined benefit plan could provide a retirement pension benefit in an amount equal to 40% of each participant's average compensation.

On the other hand, the corporation could adopt a defined benefit plan which provides the maximum retirement pension equal to 100% of a participant's average annual covered compensation during employment. The corporation could also adopt a money-purchase pension plan. The additional plan could require an annual contribution equal to 40% of what would have been the maximum allowable contribution if the money purchase plan was the only plan that had been established. Thus, a money-purchase plan could provide for an annual contribution equal to 10% of each participant's covered compensation. The 10% figure is arrived at by taking 40% of the normal 25% limitation.

The tax law permits a combination of plans as long as the total of the percentages of the maximum permissible contribution or benefit under either plan does not exceed 140%. For example, a corporation could have a defined benefit plan with a retirement benefit equal to 70% of average compensation and a money-purchase plan with a contribution equal to 17½% (70% of 25%) of current compensation. Using the method of adopting two pension plans in order to maximize the total available tax-deferred retirement benefit may be desirable. However, the corporation is making a commitment to make definite future contributions. The above described approach will not work if a profit-sharing plan and a defined benefit pension plan are combined. The Code specifically limits the corporation's total deduction for contributions made pursuant to the provisions of a pension plan and profit-sharing plan. The overall limitation is 25% of the covered compensation of all participants. The combination of two such plans might require a larger contribution. In such a case, the excess over 25% of the participants' compensation would not be deductible by the corporation.

[¶804] MULTIPLE CORPORATIONS USUALLY WON'T INCREASE PERMISSIBLE BENEFITS

If two or more corporations are commonly controlled, all defined benefit plans of a corporation are aggregated and treated as one plan and all defined contribution plans are aggregated and treated as one plan.

Corporations are commonly controlled if 5 or fewer persons own more than 50% of each corporation. As indicated, only the lowest percentage held by each stockholder can be counted by the corporations for purposes of the percentage test. These rules are designed to prevent corporations from avoiding the limitations.

Example 1: Dr. Smith and Dr. Jones are both making $25,000 from their medical corporation, S & J, A Medical Corporation. They establish a money-purchase pension plan. The contribution for each doctor is limited to $32,700.

The doctors want to increase their pension contributions. They set up another equally owned corporation, J & S, A Medical Corporation. They take a salary of $125,000 from each corporation. They also set up a money-purchase pension plan in each corporation. Can they contribute $32,700 for themselves under each plan? No. The new corporation gets no deduction for the contribution to the pension plan on behalf of the doctors. Both corporations are treated as one for the purposes of pension limitations.

Example 2: Suppose Dr. Smith and Dr. Jones take another approach. Dr. Smith sets up Smith, M.D., Inc., in which he owns all the stock. Dr. Jones sets up Jones, M.D., Inc., in which he owns all the stock. Smith, M.D., Inc. employs Dr. Smith and Dr. Jones at a salary of $125,000 each. Jones, M.D., Inc. employs Dr. Smith and Dr. Jones at $125,000 each. Both corporations establish a 25% money-purchase pension plan. Each doctor has $32,700 contributed to the plans on his behalf from each corporation. Each corporation can deduct the full contribution for the doctors because the corporations are not commonly controlled. Dr. Smith owns no stock in Dr. Jones' corporation. Dr. Jones owns no stock in Dr. Smith's corporation. Under the 50% control test, each doctor owns 0%.

[¶805] HOW TO HELP DECIDE BETWEEN A PENSION AND PROFIT-SHARING PLAN FOR THE CLOSELY-HELD CORPORATION

Here is a checklist summarizing the salient features of both pension and profit-sharing plans to help you in your choice:

Profit Sharing	Pension
1. Generally favors younger employees.	1. Generally favors older employees.
2. Need not provide retirement benefits.	2. Must provide retirement benefits
3. Contributions can be made only from profits (includes accumulated earnings).	3. Contributions must be made for loss years as well as for profitable ones.
4. Definite contribution formula not necessary; contributions need only be "recurring and substantial."	4. Must have a definite contribution formula which will provide for definitely determinable benefits.
5. Contributions cannot exceed 15% of year's payroll.	5. No maximum limit on contributions as long as they are actuarially justifiable and reasonable, and benefits do not exceed ERISA limits.
6. Forfeitures may be allocated by a fixed formula in favor of remaining participants.	6. Forfeitures may be used to decrease future cost to employer.
7. No more than 50% of a participant's account may be invested in life insurance.	7. May be completely funded by investment in life insurance.

Profit Sharing	Pension
8. Life insurance on the lives of key employees as well as "incidental" life insurance is allowed.	8. May provide insurance protection of 100 times the employee's monthly pension as a death benefit.
9. May provide layoff and accident and health benefits as "incidental" benefits.	9. May not provide benefit not usually included in a pension plan (e.g., layoff benefits, sickness, accident, hospitalization, or medical reimbursement).
10. Distributions may be made after a fixed number of years (e.g., two) sufficient to indicate that a deferred compensation plan was contemplated.	10. Distributions may be made upon retirement, disability, death or other termination of employment.

[¶806] ESOT or ESOP

Although stock bonus plans and Employee Stock Ownership Plans (ESOP) are not normally established by closely-held corporations, each may provide advantages in certain situations. Both of these plans are similar to profit-sharing plans. As opposed to profit-sharing plans, the contributions are *not* necessarily geared to profits, and the benefits are distributable in stock of the employer corporation. Recently, there has been a considerable amount of material written about ESOP's and their apparent benefits. However, most of the benefits attributable to ESOP's are available through the use of other types of qualified retirement plans.

The contribution to an ESOP may be made in cash or in company stock. If the contribution is made in stock, the stock must be accurately valued in order to determine the amount of the corporation's deduction. In the case of a closely-held corporation, the determination of value may be extremely difficult. If the valuation can be made, the contribution of stock does reduce the need for a cash contribution. Under an ESOP, company stock must be purchased at some point because the retirement benefits must be made in the form of corporate stock. Under an ESOP, a corporation normally would give a retired participant the right to sell his stock to the corporation. The price for the stock would be based on some formula (presumably the same formula to be used in valuing the stock for purposes of determining the amount of the deduction for contributions). However, the corporation cannot require the former participant to sell his stock. Thus, before the owner of a closely-held corporation should establish an ESOP, he must understand that shares of stock will actually be transferred to participating employees.

An ESOP is advantageous if a shareholder wants to dispose of some of his stock. However, the stock may not be sold to the ESOP at more than fair market value. A requirement for all qualified retirement plans is that they must be established and maintained exclusively for the benefit of the corporation's employees or their beneficiaries. Thus, extreme caution must be exercised to avoid having the IRS take the position that an ESOP has been established primarily as a vehicle to provide a market for the stock of shareholders in a closely-held corporation instead of being established for the benefit of plan participants.

Some writers have incorrectly indicated that an ESOP can be used in connection with borrowing money in a manner that enables the corporation to repay the principal of the loan with tax-deductible dollars. Careful analysis shows that the tax deduction is attributed to the annual contribution to the ESOP, not to the repayment of the loan.

> *Example:* A corporation establishes an ESOP. The ESOP borrows $1,000,000 from a bank to buy $1,000,000 worth of the corporation's stock from the corporation. Obviously, the corporation receives an immediate $1,000,000. The corporation guarantees the loan. The loan is to be repaid at the rate of $100,000 per year plus interest over the next 10 years.
>
> Each year the corporation contributes $100,000 to

the ESOP. The ESOP then repays $100,000 of the principal of the loan from the bank. The apparent result is that the loan is repaid with tax deductible dollars. *However, the role of the ESOP is illusory.*

Suppose the corporation has an ESOP to which it contributes $100,000 per year. Instead of using the ESOP to borrow money, the corporation borrows $1,000,000 on its own. Each year, the corporation pays off $100,000 of principal of the loan. It also contributes $100,000 worth of its stock to the ESOP, for which it gets a $100,000 deduction without paying out any cash. From a tax standpoint, the corporation is in exactly the same position as it would have been if the ESOP had borrowed the money.

If the owners' of a business want to spread stock ownership among employees in order to enable them to share in the economic growth of the company, then an ESOP may be a desirable vehicle for achieving such a result.

[¶807] HOW TO PROVIDE FOR MEDICAL REIMBURSEMENT PLANS; SALARY CONTINUATION PROGRAMS; GROUP LIFE INSURANCE; AND EMPLOYEE DEATH BENEFITS PAYMENTS

Qualified retirement plans, formed primarily to enable the business owner to shelter his income from tax, are usually the most important fringe benefit for employees of a closely-held corporation. However, other tax-favored fringe benefits may be provided for owner-employees of corporations and may be available even if the corporation was established for non-tax purposes such as limitation of liability. Examples of such benefits include:

- medical reimbursement plans,
- salary continuation programs,
- group term life insurance, and
- employee death benefit payments.

A number of expenses are incurred by business owners

whether or not their business is incorporated. If the corporation can pay the expense and obtain a tax deduction in cases when no deduction is available to the individual if paid by the individual, it appears foolish not to provide the fringe benefit. The type of benefits referred to above are presently exempt from the requirement that they must be offered on a basis that does not discriminate in favor of the business owners. Thus, it is not uncommon to find such plans covering only those persons in whose favor discrimination may not be made in the area of qualified retirement plans. *Fringe benefits are available to persons in their capacity as employees.* If the benefits are only made available to stockholders, the IRS may take the position that the benefits are being made to stockholders in their capacity as stockholders—and the IRS will treat the payments as dividends. Thus, in defining eligible employees, the plan should not refer to coverage of stockholders, even if that is the intent of the plan. A different classification should be used, such as "officer-employees," even if the stockholders are the only persons who come within the definition of "officer-employees." Another way to minimize the chance of having the IRS assert dividend treatment is to cover certain key employees who are not stockholders.

[¶807.1] Medical Reimbursement Plan

A medical reimbursement plan is simply a plan whereby the corporation agrees to reimburse covered employees for any incurred medical expenses. The net effect of such a plan from an income tax standpoint is that it removes the restriction imposed on medical deductions that may be taken by individuals. Medical expenses are deductible only to the extent that they exceed 3% of an individual's adjusted gross income (or the adjusted gross income of a husband and wife, if a joint return is filed).

The financial benefit of a medical reimbursement plan cannot be over-emphasized since the owner will incur the same medical expenses regardless of a medical plan.

> *Example:* A corporation had only enough income to pay its owner his normal salary. The owner has medical expenses. The owner should have a portion of what would otherwise be designated as salary treated as medical reimbursement. The total amount he receives

from the corporation will be the same whether the payment is called compensation or medical reimbursement.

If defined as medical reimbursement, the amount received as payment for medical expenses will not be included in the owner's taxable income.

The medical expenses may be reimbursed by a corporation, or they may be paid directly on an employee's behalf. Permissible medical expenses may include charges for psychiatric or optometric care and charges for orthodontia and normal dentistry. Covered medical expenses also may include charges incurred on behalf of an employee's dependents and premiums paid for medical insurance. If medical expenses are covered by insurance, they may not be reimbursed by the corporation.

CAVEAT: For taxable years beginning after December 31, 1979, amounts received by a "highly compensated employee" from a medical reimbursement plan may be included in his current income unless the plan is nondiscriminatory. To be qualified, the plan must:

☐ not discriminate in favor of highly paid individuals, i.e. persons who are among the employer's five highest paid officers, are shareholders who own more than 10% in value of the employer's stock, or are among the highest paid 25% of all employees other than officers or shareholders.

☐ benefit 70% or more of all employees, or 80% of all the employees who are eligible to benefit under the plan if 70% of all employees are eligible to benefit under the plan.

These requirements are similar to those currently imposed on qualified pension and profit sharing plans.

[¶807.2] Disability Insurance—Salary Continuation Plan

Another benefit available to corporate employees is a program which enables a corporation to obtain disability insurance for key employees and deduct the premiums. If an individual purchases disability insurance, the cost of the premiums is not deductible. If the corporation pays the premiums, they are an expense deductible by the corporation. The payment of benefits to the employee in the case of disability is treated as taxable income to him to the extent the benefits exceed certain minimum levels. If premium payments are not deductible, benefit payments are not considered to be taxable income. Most persons do not anticipate that they will become disabled. Thus, the most common approach is to have the corporation provide disability insurance.

Closely-held corporations have a good reason to adopt a salary-continuation plan for stockholder-employees. As previously indicated, a problem with closely-held corporations is the question of deductibility of payments made to owner-employees. If such payments are determined to be unreasonably high, a corporation may be deemed to have made a dividend distribution. The dividend would be equal to the amount by which the payment exceeds the value of the services rendered to the corporation. If a stockholder becomes disabled and is unable to render services to the corporation, it is difficult to justify compensation. Thus, any such payment could be treated as a dividend by the IRS. However, if a stockholder enters into an agreement with his corporation that in consideration for the performance of services the corporation will continue making payments to him in the event of disability, the dividend treatment is avoided. Such disability payments are deductible by the corporation. The promise-to-pay in the event of disability constituted compensation to the stockholder-employee during the time that he was actually performing services for the corporation.

If a corporation maintains disability insurance to fund its potential liability under a wage continuation plan, the premiums for such insurance are deductible by the corporation. As stated, the employee reports disability payments as ordinary income when they are received.

[¶807.3] Life Insurance

Ordinary Life Insurance

Another advantage that is available to corporate employees but is not available for self-employed persons involves certain life insurance premiums.

If a corporation purchases ordinary life insurance on the life of a key employee and names the corporation as the beneficiary, the premium payments are not deductible. However, if the corporation's taxable income is under $50,000, there may still be an advantage. The after-tax cost of the premiums often will be considerably less if the corporation pays the premiums than if the employee pays the premiums with after-tax personal income. If someone other than the corporation is the beneficiary, then the employee must include the amount of the premiums paid as additional compensation.

> *Example:* Suppose Mr. Smith's corporation, Smith Corp., has taxable income of $20,000. Mr. Smith received a salary of $80,000 for the year. Mr. Smith owns 100% of the stock of Smith Corp. He wants to buy $100,000 of ordinary life insurance and the premium is $5,000. Let's assume that Mr. Smith is in a 50% tax bracket and the corporation is in a 25% bracket.
>
> For Mr. Smith to have $5,000 after taxes to pay the premium, the corporation would have to pay him a $10,000 bonus. He would pay $5,000 in tax and have $5,000 for the premium. The corporation's tax would be reduced by $2,500 because it gets a tax deduction for the bonus. The IRS gains $2,500 on the transaction.
>
> If the corporation paid the $5,000 premium and was named as the beneficiary, the taxes would be less. The corporation would not get a deduction, so its tax would be $2,500 higher than if it had declared a $10,000 bonus. However, Mr. Smith's personal tax would be $5,000 lower. The net income tax savings would be $2,500.

Group Term Life Insurance

The above rules apply to the purchase of ordinary life insurance. However, if a corporation purchases group term life insurance, the premiums are deductible as a business expense. The employee does not have to include the premiums in his personal income to the extent that the face amount of the insurance benefit does not exceed $50,000. In many instances it is advantageous to purchase policies for key employees which have face values in excess of $50,000. Even though the cost of the excess coverage is taxed to the employee, the cost is not equal to the premiums paid for the additional insurance. The amount of income which must be reported is determined by a table contained in Treasury Regulations. The amount determined is normally considerably less than the actual cost. The monthly amounts to be included in an employee's income for each $1,000 of excess coverage are as follows:

5-YEAR AGE BRACKET	MONTHLY COST PER $1,000 OF FACE VALUE
Under 30	$ .08
30 to 34	.10
35 to 39	.14
40 to 44	.23
45 to 49	.40
50 to 54	.68
54 to 59	1.10
60 to 64	1.63

The net effect of the Regulations is to permit the corporation to deduct the entire premium cost of group term coverage but to require that the employee include only a portion of such cost as additional income.

As in the case of other insurance policies, an employee can prevent the proceeds of the policy from being included in his gross estate for estate tax purposes by irrevocably transferring all of his "incidents of ownership" under the policy to someone else. If an employee attempts to assign his incidents of ownership, state law must be reviewed to determine if an assignment is permissible. Also, it is possible that the Service may attempt to tax the proceeds in the employee's estate as a gift in contemplation of death.

There are numerous methods in which insurance may be used to maximize benefits to the corporate stockholders. The services of a competent insurance agent will maximize the options available to the corporation.

[¶807.4] Employee Death Benefit

Another form of employee fringe benefit to be considered is the employee death benefit. The first $5,000 paid to the beneficiaries or estate of a deceased employee are excluded from taxable income if the payment is made "by reason of the death of the employee." However, such payments are not excludable from income if the deceased employee had a nonforfeitable right to receive such amounts while living.

PART FIVE

DRAFTING
THE LEGAL DOCUMENTS

9

Step-by-Step Guide
to Drafting
the Legal Documents

So far, this book has described the factors to be considered in determining whether incorporation of a closely-held business would be advantageous to the owners. It has described the various benefits that can be provided to the owners in their capacity as employees. This section outlines the procedural steps to establish and maintain a corporation. It also examines the proper method of documenting programs to take advantage of the benefits available to owners of an incorporated business.

You can use this section to save time and money. Complete sample forms are included with an explanation of each form. These sample forms are copies of forms actually used in practice and may be adopted for your clients by making only minor changes. Everything necessary to set up the plans and get them approved by the IRS is contained in this chapter. By using the forms, a client is provided the same beneficial information as attorneys and accountants who specialize in this area.

CAVEAT: Although the forms included have been approved by the appropriate governmental agencies, it is essential that an attorney have the final responsibility for determining that a specific program complies with the applicable law.

The documents you will find in this section are as follows:

- Corporate Formation Data Sheet
- Articles of Incorporation
- Bylaw Drafting Checklist
- Sample Form of Corporate Minutes
- Medical Reimbursement Plan
- Wage Continuation Plan
- Employment Contract
- Cross-Purchase Agreement
- Employees' Profit Sharing Plan and Trust Agreement
- Employees' Pension Trust
- Notice to Employees After Plans Have Been Adopted
- Forms 5301 and 5302
- Form 2848
- Cover Letter to IRS
- Summary Plan Description
- Form EBS-1
- Form 5500-C

[¶900] CORPORATE FORMATION DATA SHEET

A worksheet for gathering the information you will need to set up the corporation is prepared for your convenience.

CORPORATE FORMATION DATA SHEET

1. Proposed names of corporation. You should have your client give you several names, as the first choice might not be available.

_____

_____

_____

_____

2. Names of proposed stockholders.

3. Names of first directors.

4. Names of officers.

    President

    Vice President

    Secretary

    Chief Financial Officer (Treasurer)

5. Address of business.

6. Bank.

7. What is to be transferred to the corporation?

8. How many shares of stock are to be authorized?

9. How many shares of stock are to be issued?

10. What will be the fiscal year?

11. Time designated for annual meeting of shareholders and directors. This should be near the end of the fiscal year of the proposed corporation.

12. Will Subchapter S election be made?

13. What salaries will be paid to the key employees?

[¶901] HOW TO CREATE THE CORPORATION

The exact procedure to be followed in establishing a corporation is a matter governed by state law. In California, for example, a corporation is created by filing Articles of Incorporation with the California Secretary of State.

Articles of Incorporation

The Articles of Incorporation simply describe the following checklist:

☐ what type of activities the corporation will be entitled to engage in;

☐ how many shares the corporation will be permitted to issue; and

☐ the names of the original directors of the corporation.

In most jurisdictions, a corporation is formed by filing related papers with the secretary of state or other state officer. Following is a list of the appropriate state officers:

State	Filing
Alabama	Secretary of State Montgomery, Alabama 36100
Alaska	Commissioner of Commerce Juneau, Alaska 99801
Arizona	Corporation Commission Phoenix, Arizona 85000
Arkansas	Secretary of State Little Rock, Arkansas 72200
California	Secretary of State Sacramento, California 95801
Colorado	Secretary of State Denver, Colorado 80200
Connecticut	Secretary of State Hartford, Connecticut 06100
Delaware	Secretary of State Dover, Delaware 19901

State	Filing
District of Columbia	Office of Supt. of Corporations Washington, D.C. 20000
Florida	Secretary of State Tallahassee, Florida 32301
Georgia	Secretary of State Atlanta, Georgia 30300
Hawaii	State Treasurer Honolulu, Hawaii 96800
Idaho	Secretary of State Boise, Idaho 83700
Illinois	Secretary of State Springfield, Illinois 62700
Indiana	Secretary of State Indianapolis, Indiana 46200
Iowa	Secretary of State Des Moines, Iowa 50300
Kansas	Secretary of State Topeka, Kansas 66600
Kentucky	Secretary of State Frankfort, Kentucky 40601
Louisiana	Secretary of State Baton Rouge, Louisiana 70800
Maine	Secretary of State Augusta, Maine 04301
Maryland	State Dept. of Assessments and Taxation
Massachusetts	Secretary of the Commonwealth Boston, Massachusetts 02100
Michigan	Department of Treasury Corporation Division Lansing, Michigan 48904
Minnesota	Secretary of State St. Paul, Minnesota 55100
Mississippi	Secretary of State Jackson, Mississippi 39200
Missouri	Secretary of State Jefferson City, Missouri 65101

State	Filing
Montana	Secretary of State Helena, Montana 59601
Nebraska	Secretary of State Lincoln, Nebraska 68500
Nevada	Secretary of State Carson City, Nevada 89701
New Hampshire	Secretary of State Concord, New Hampshire 03300
New Jersey	Secretary of State Trenton, New Jersey 08600
New Mexico	State Corporation Commission Santa Fe, New Mexico 87501
New York	Secretary of State Albany, New York, 12200
North Carolina	Secretary of State Raleigh, North Carolina 27600
North Dakota	Secretary of State Bismarck, North Dakota 58501
Ohio	Secretary of State Columbus, Ohio 43200
Oklahoma	Secretary of State Oklahoma City, Oklahoma 73100
Oregon	Corporation Commissioner Salem, Oregon 97301
Pennsylvania	Department of State Harrisburg, Pennsylvania 17101
Rhode Island	Secretary of State Providence, Rhode Island 02900
South Carolina	Secretary of State Columbia, South Carolina 29200
South Dakota	Secretary of State Pierre, South Dakota 57501
Tennessee	Secretary of State Nashville, Tennessee 37200
Texas	Secretary of State Austin, Texas 78700
Utah	Secretary of State Salt Lake City, Utah 84100

State	Filing
Vermont	Secretary of State Montpelier, Vermont 05601
Virginia	State Corporation Commission Richmond, Virginia 23200
Washington	Secretary of State Olympia, Washington 98501
West Virginia	Secretary of State Charleston, West Virginia 25300
Wisconsin	Secretary of State Madison, Wisconsin 53700
Wyoming	Secretary of State Cheyenne, Wyoming 82001

The following form is a sample of the Article of Incorporation for the State of California. Be sure to check your own statute books for changes required in your state. Once these Articles have been properly filed, the corporation is formally in existence.

ARTICLES OF INCORPORATION
OF
BIG BUCKS, INC.

(A California Corporation)

I

The name of this corporation is BIG BUCKS, INC.

II

Corporate
Purpose

The purpose of this corporation is to engage in any lawful act or activity for which a corporation may be organized under the General Corporation Law of California other than the banking business, the trust company business or the practice of a profession permitted to be incorporated by the California Corporations Code.

III

Agent for
Service of
Process

The name and address in this state of the corporation's initial agent for service of process is:

Herbert Bucksup
445 South Figueroa Street
34th Floor
Los Angeles, California 90071

IV

Authorize
Type and
Number of
Shares

This corporation is authorized to issue one class of shares which shall be designated as "common" shares. The total number of such shares which this corporation is authorized to issue is One Hundred Thousand (100,000).

V

Initial   The first directors of the corporation shall be
Directors   HERBERT BUCKSUP, BETTY BUCKSUP and
FLO CASH.
DATED: February 1, 1978.

_____

Herbert Bucksup

_____

Betty Bucksup

_____

Flo Cash

We, the undersigned, declare that we are the persons who executed the above Articles of Incorporation, and such instrument is our act and deed.

_____

Herbert Bucksup

_____

Betty Bucksup

_____

Flo Cash

[¶902] BYLAW DRAFTING CHECKLIST

The bylaws contain the rules which state how the corporation will be operated from a procedural standpoint. For instance, the bylaws provide:

- ☐ a definition of the officers the corporation will have (President, Vice President, etc.);
- ☐ how the officers and directors are to be elected;
- ☐ when and where meetings of directors will be held;
- ☐ meeting of stockholders;
- ☐ voting rights;
- ☐ who is authorized to sign checks; and
- ☐ the proper method of maintaining corporate books and records.

The following bylaw drafting checklist will be of assistance. It is followed by a sample set of bylaws for a typical California closely-held corporation. The bylaws (see pages 213 to 245) will explain in detail just how the corporate business is to be conducted.

☐ *Corporate Offices.* The bylaws will generally spell out the location of the principal office of the corporation. It is in the principal office of the corporation that the shareholders will be entitled to inspect the books and records of the corporation, unless otherwise provided in the bylaws of the corporation. Similarly, the principal office of the corporation will generally be designated as the place to send certain notices and demands.

Where the principal office of the corporation is spelled out in the bylaws, provision (not inconsistent with the requirements of the statute under which the corporation is being incorporated) should be made for changing the designation of the corporate office. This will be particularly important where a temporary address, like the office of the corporation's counsel, is being used or the corporation's offices are actually rented in an office building.

In many states, the location of the corporation's principal office must be spelled out in the certificate of incorporation.

Where it is, similar provisions should be made for an amendment without requiring the formalities required in other amendments if such provision is not inconsistent with local law.

☐ *Time of the Shareholders Meeting.* Most states require an annual meeting of the shareholders. The time (date and hour) of this meeting, or a procedure whereby it will be determined, should be spelled out in the bylaws. It should not be so rigidly fixed as to prevent flexibility. An approach used by many corporations, large and small alike, is to fix a date for a shareholders meeting and to provide that the date will govern, unless another date is set by the directors or designated officers.

☐ *Location of the Shareholders Meeting.* The bylaws will generally designate the corporate office as the place where the shareholders meeting will be held, unless otherwise ordered by the directors.

☐ *Voting Requirements.* The bylaws will generally spell out voting requirements where greater than majority voting requirements are authorized by the certificate of incorporation. It is important to avoid conflicts between the voting requirements spelled out in the bylaws, the articles of incorporation, and the law of the state where the corporation is incorporated. The articles and bylaws may prescribe rules in most jurisdictions whereby greater than majority votes are required for the election of directors and other corporate activities. Case law has struck down certain bylaw provisions which require unanimity of corporate action as being contrary to the general scheme authorized by the state for the conduct of corporate affairs.

☐ *Voting Procedure.* The bylaws should spell out appropriate voting procedure. In drafting the bylaws, you should be careful not to establish an elaborate procedure for a small corporation, because the effect will be that the shareholders will ignore the procedure established by the laws in many instances.

☐ *Notice Requirements.* The bylaws should contain a provision with respect to notice of shareholders meetings. The notice provision must be within the restrictions imposed by the corporate statute. In some states the state corporate statutes require publication in addition to personal service and mailing of notice. A requirement that notice be published in a particular manner can be written into the bylaws.

Often in small corporations, the notice requirement is waived by having the shareholder sign a waiver.

☐ *Proxy Requirements.* The bylaws will generally spell out certain rules with respect to voting by proxy—i.e., the proxy must be in writing and signed, and the duration may be specified. In many states proxies must be in writing to be enforceable. In some states the acceptability of a telegram is expressly recognized.

Death or incapacity of the shareholder may cause a revocation of the proxy.

☐ *Special Meetings of Shareholders.* The bylaws should designate who is authorized to call a special meeting of the shareholders. Generally, this authority will be vested, by statute, in the board of directors and other persons designated by the certificate or bylaws. The bylaws provision will often indicate that the president or other corporate officer can call a special meeting. In many states the holder of a prescribed percentage of the stock can call a shareholder's meeting. The mechanics will vary. However, the usual method is to require that the desired proportion request that the president call the meeting.

☐ *Shareholder Consent.* The bylaws should contain provision for shareholder action by shareholder consent. In a small close corporation, the bylaws may make suitable provision for corporate action by consent. Generally, where the corporate statute recognizes corporation action by consent, there must be unanimous consent. In some states corporate action by consent is limited to certain actions like voluntary dissolution, sale or lease of corporate property, reduction of capital and amendment of articles of incorporation.

☐ *Quorum Requirements at Shareholders' Meetings.* Unless the certificate of incorporation or the bylaws increases the requirement, it is customary to require the holders of at least a majority of the shares eligible to vote to be present, either in person or by proxy, to constitute a quorum. This number may be increased where such an increase is authorized by statute. In some states the quorum will be fixed by the bylaws or the articles of incorporation. Varying the quorum requirement may constitute an important method of establishing corporate control.

Where a quorum is designated to be a particular proportion of the stock, the bylaws should specify that it is the issued and outstanding stock or the stock entitled to vote. Similarly, the bylaws should specifically refer to shares rather than stockholders. (*State v. Price*, 21 Ohio 114).

☐ *Number of Directors.* The bylaws should either spell out the number of directors or provide machinery whereby the number of directors will be determined. In most states there must be at least three directors. However, in some states there may be less than three directors if all the shares are beneficially held by less than three individuals. In these states where all the shares are beneficially held by one person, there need be only one director.

☐ *Qualifications of Directors.* A few states prescribe residence qualifications for directors. Other states merely prescribe that at least one director must be a resident of the state of incorporation. A common provision also provides that at least one or a majority of directors must be citizens of the United States. Other states require that directors be of full age or 21.

☐ *Term of Office of Directors.* Generally, directors are elected for a term of office prescribed in the bylaws. In the absence of a bylaw provision, presumably directors would be elected for a one-year term. Directors will be elected for a longer term where classification of directors is authorized by the bylaws.

☐ *Cumulative Voting in the Election of Directors.* In some states cumulative voting for the election of directors is dealt with on a mandatory basis in either the constitution or the corporate statutes. However, in a great majority of states the issue of cumulative voting is left to be dealt with in the corporate certificate of incorporation or the bylaws.

☐ *Filling Vacancies on the Board of Directors.* The bylaws should specify a procedure for filling vacancies on the board of directors. Generally, the corporate statutes provide a procedure which can either be adopted by the corporation or altered by the bylaws.

☐ *Removal of Directors.* The bylaws should specify a procedure for the removal of directors. Generally, removal of directors can be separated into two categories—removal for cause and removal without cause. In many states directors may be removed by the shareholders with or without cause. However, provision should be made to protect directors who have been elected through cumulative voting or by reason of class voting.

☐ *Directors' Meetings.* The bylaws may provide for the time and place of directors' meetings.

A common bylaw provision calls for a meeting of the board of directors immediately following the annual meeting of the shareholders and at such other times as may be designated by the board or other individual designated in the bylaws. Unless there is a provision to the contrary in the bylaws or the certificate of incorporation, it may be necessary to have the meetings of the board of directors at the principal place of business of the corporation or in the state of incorporation of the corporation. Here it is wise to write sufficient flexibility into the bylaws to permit the effective operation of the corporation's business while protecting the interests of the shareholders. In some instances the interests of minority shareholders in a close corporation will be protected if the meeting is held at the corporation's office or in the city in which the corporation's office is located. This protection may be important where the shareholders reside close to the corporation's office. The statutes of must jurisdictions permit wide variation.

☐ *Notice of Directors' Meetings.* In most jurisdictions, the corporate statute does not spell out details as to the notice which must be given to directors prior to directors meetings. This matter is left to the bylaws. Where the bylaws specify the time and place of the meeting, it would appear that no notice is required. Of course, notice is required where there is a special meeting of the board of directors. Where the notice procedure is being dispensed with, it is wise to have the directors sign waivers of notice.

☐ *Quorum at Directors' Meetings.* Most states leave the determination of quorum requirements for board action to the bylaws or the article of incorporation. In many states a majority of the board constitutes a quorum unless the articles of incorporation or the bylaws specify a greater number.

☐ *Voting Requirements for Director Action.* In the absence of a bylaw provision to the contrary, director action usually requires a majority of the directors present and voting. However, in many states a provision in the bylaws calling for greater than majority vote for director action will be upheld.

☐ *Indemnification.* Indemnification of directors, officers and other employees of the corporation may be governed by charter, bylaws, contractual or statutory provisions.

☐ *Officers.* The bylaws should spell out and identify the officers. Here's a checklist of corporate titles often used:

    ☐ Chairman of the Board
    ☐ President
    ☐ Vice President
    ☐ Secretary
    ☐ Recording Secretary
    ☐ Treasurer
    ☐ Chief Financial Officer

Generally, the president, secretary, and treasurer are the only officers required. In some states there is a prohibition against one officer holding more than one position. For example, in some states the president cannot also be the secretary.

☐ *Selection of Officers.* Generally, the bylaws will provide for the selection of officers of the corporation by the directors.

☐ *Removal of Officers.* The bylaws will generally contain a provision specifying the procedure for the removal of officers. In most states officers can be removed by the board with or without cause. Even where this provision is not required by statute, it will usually be included in the bylaws. Removal of an officer by the board of directors without cause will not prejudice an officer's right to recover damages for breach of an employment contract in most jurisdictions.

☐ *Bonds for Corporate Officers.* In some statutes the secretary and treasurer will be required to give a surety bond in the amount required by the bylaws.

☐ *Duties of Officers.* Many lawyers recommend the inclusion of a general statement of the duties expected of each officer. The nature of these duties will, of course, vary from business to business. Where the duties are specified in the bylaws, you should be careful to see to it that they are kept up to date. An officer's duties may have changed, but the description in the bylaws can be easily overlooked. Where a provision of this type is not kept up to date, it may subsequently cause considerable trouble.

☐ *Capital Stock.* The bylaws should spell out the various forms of capital stock to be issued, although the details as to the types and classes of stock will also be elaborated on in the certificate of incorporation or charter of the corporation.

☐ *Stock Transfer.* The bylaws will spell out provisions for the transfer of stock. Where a buy-sell agreement or other form of restriction on the transfer of stock is in force, the bylaw provision must conform with the terms of the agreement between the shareholders. However, where all shareholders are not parties to the agreement, the bylaws should have a provision spelling out the details and prescribing rules for the transfer of stock.

☐ *Annual Reports.* The bylaws will generally provide for reports to the shareholders. Generally, reports are available quarterly, although practice varies widely. Corporations subject to the requirements of the SEC and those listed on the major stock exchanges must comply with the requirements of these agencies with respect to annual reports. Many large publicly traded corporations have bylaw provisions calling for post-meeting reports to the shareholders.

☐ *Fiscal Year.* The bylaws or a resolution of the board should pin down the corporation's fiscal year. Tax and other business considerations will be important here.

☐   *Accounting Practices.* Bylaws will often contain provision as to accounting practices and the selection of accountants. Generally, the selection of accountants will be subject to the approval of the shareholders.

☐   *Inspection of Books and Records.* The shareholders of the corporation are entitled to inspect the books and records of the corporation. However, this right can be restricted by the bylaws of the corporation in many instances so long as the restrictions are reasonable. The right to inspect corporate books and records is available only for corporate purposes. Where it appears that a shareholder is not desirous of inspecting the corporation books and records for a corporate purpose, he may be refused the right to inspect them in many jurisdictions.

BYLAWS OF
BIG BUCKS, INC.
(A California Corporation)

TABLE OF CONTENTS
TO
BYLAWS

TABLE OF CONTENTS TO BYLAWS (*Continued*)

BYLAWS
OF
BIG BUCKS, INC.

(A California Corporation)

ARTICLE I

OFFICES

Section 1.01 Principal Offices. The Board of Directors shall fix the location of the principal executive office of the corporation at any place within or outside the State of California. If the principal executive office is located outside this state, and the corporation has one or more business offices in this state, the Board of Directors shall fix and designate a principal business office in the State of California.

Section 1.02 Other Offices. The officers or the Board of Directors may at any time establish branch or subordinate offices at any place or places where the corporation is qualified to do business, and may change the location of any office of the corporation.

ARTICLE II

MEETINGS OF SHAREHOLDERS

Section 2.01 Place of Meetings. Meetings of shareholders shall be held at any place within or outside the State of California designated by the Board of Directors upon proper notice. In the absence of any such designation, shareholders' meetings shall be held at the principal executive office of the corporation.

Section 2.02 Annual Meetings. Unless held at a time and date designated each year by the Board of Directors in accordance with applicable law, an annual meeting of shareholders shall be held on the last Monday of January of each year at 5:00 o'clock P.M., provided, however, that should such day fall upon a legal holiday, then the annual meeting of shareholders shall be held at the same time and place on the next day thereafter ensuing which is a full business day. At the annual meeting, Directors shall be elected and any other proper business may be transacted.

Section 2.03 Special Meetings. (a) A special meeting of the shareholders may be called at any time by the Board of Directors, or by the Chairman of the Board, or by the President, or by one or more shareholders holding shares which, in the aggregate, entitle them to cast not less than ten percent (10%) of the votes at any such meeting.

(b) If a special meeting is called by any person or persons other than the Board of Directors, the request shall be in writing, specifying the time of such meeting and the general nature of the business proposed to be transacted, and shall be delivered personally or sent by registered mail or by telegraphic or other facsimile transmission to the Chairman of the Board, the President, any Vice President, or the Secretary of the corporation. The officer receiving the request shall cause notice to be promptly given to the shareholders entitled to vote, in accordance with the provisions of Sections 2.01, 2.04 and 2.05 of this Article II, that a meeting will be held at the time requested by the person or persons calling the meeting, not less than thirty-five (35) nor more than sixty (60) days after the receipt of the request. If the notice is not given within twenty (20) days after receipt of the request, the person or persons requesting the meeting may give the notice. Nothing contained in this Section 2.03 shall be construed as limiting, fixing or affecting the time when a meeting of shareholders called by action of the Board of Directors may be held.

Section 2.04 Notice of Shareholders' Meetings. (a) All notices of meetings of shareholders shall be sent or otherwise given in accordance with Section 2.05 not less than ten (10) nor more than sixty (60) days before the date of the meeting being noticed. The notice shall specify the place, date and hour of the meeting and (i) in the case of a special meeting, the general nature of the business to be transacted, or (ii) in the case of the annual meeting, those matters which the Board of Directors, or the other person or persons calling the meeting, at the time of giving the notice, intend to present for action by the shareholders. The notice of any meeting at which Directors are to be elected shall include the names of any nominees which, at the time of the notice, management intends to present for election.

(b) If action is proposed to be taken at any meeting for approval of (i) a contract or transaction in which a Director has a direct or indirect financial interest, as contemplated by Section 310 of the Corporations Code of California (herein the "Code"), (ii) an amendment of the Articles of Incorporation, pursuant to Section 902 of the Code, (iii) a reorganization of the corporation, pursuant to Section 1201 of such Code,

(iv) a voluntary dissolution of the corporation, pursuant to Section 1900 of such Code, or (v) a distribution in dissolution other than in accordance with the rights of outstanding preferred shares pursuant to Section 2007 of such Code, the notice shall also state the general nature of such proposal.

Section 2.05 Manner of Giving Notice; Affidavit of Notice. (a) Notice of any meeting of shareholders shall be given either personally or by first class mail or telegraphic or other written communication, charges prepaid, addressed to each shareholder at the address of such shareholder appearing on the books of the corporation or more recently given by the shareholder to the corporation for the purpose of notice. If no such address appears on the corporation's books or has been so given, notice shall be deemed to have been properly given to such shareholder if sent by first class mail or telegraphic or other written communication to the corporation's principal executive office to the attention of such shareholder, or if published at least once in a newspaper of general circulation in the county where such office is located. Notice shall be deemed to have been given at the time when delivered personally or deposited in the mail or sent by telegram or other means of written communication.

(b) If any notice addressed to a shareholder at the address of such shareholder appearing on the books of the corporation is returned to the corporation by the United States Postal Service marked to indicate that the United States Postal Service is unable to deliver the notice to the shareholder at such address, all future notices or reports shall be deemed to have been duly given without further mailing if the same shall be available to the shareholder upon written demand of the shareholder at the principal executive office of the corporation for a period of one (1) year from the date of the giving of such notice.

(c) An affidavit of the mailing or other means of giving any notice of any shareholders' meeting shall be executed by the Secretary, Assistant Secretary or any transfer agent of the corporation giving such notice, and shall be filed and maintained in the minute book of the corporation.

Section 2.06 Quorum. The presence in person or by proxy of the holders of a majority of the shares entitled to vote at the subject meeting of shareholders shall constitute a quorum for the transaction of business. The shareholders present at a duly called or held meeting at which a quorum is present may continue to transact business until adjournment, notwithstanding the withdrawal of enough shareholders to leave less than a quorum, if any action taken (other than adjournment) is approved by at least a majority of the shares required to constitute a quorum.

Section 2.07 Adjourned Meeting and Notice Thereof. (a) Any shareholders' meeting, annual or special, whether or not a quorum is present, may be adjourned from time to time by the vote of a majority of the shares represented at such meeting, either in person or by proxy, but in the absence of a quorum, no other business may be transacted at such meeting, except as provided in Section 2.06.

(b) When any meeting of shareholders, either annual or special, is adjourned to another time or place, notice need not be given of the adjourned meeting if the time and place thereof are announced at the meeting at which the adjournment is taken, unless a new record date for the adjourned meeting is fixed, or unless the adjournment is for more than forty-five (45) days from the date set for the original meeting, in which case the Board of Directors shall set a new record date. Notice of any such adjourned meeting, if required, shall be given to each shareholder of record entitled to vote at the adjourned meeting in accordance with the provisions of Sections 2.04 and 2.05. At any adjourned meeting the corporation may transact any business which might have been transacted at the original meeting.

Section 2.08 Voting. (a) The shareholders entitled to vote at any meeting of shareholders shall be determined in accordance with the provisions of Section 2.11, subject to the provisions of Section 702 to 704, inclusive, of the Code (relating to voting shares held by a fiduciary, in the name of a corporation or in joint ownership). Such vote may be by voice vote or by ballot; provided, however, that all elections for Directors must be by ballot upon demand by a shareholder at such election made before the voting begins. Any shareholder entitled to vote on any matter (other than the election of directors) may vote part of the shares in favor of the proposal and refrain from voting the remaining shares or vote them against the proposal, but if the shareholder fails to specify the number of shares such shareholder is voting affirmatively, it will be conclusively presumed that the shareholder's approving vote is with respect to all shares such shareholder is entitled to vote. If a quorum is present, the affirmative vote of a majority of the shares represented at the meeting and entitled to vote on any matter (other than the election of Directors) shall be the act of the shareholders, unless the vote of a greater number or voting by classes is required by the Code or the Articles of Incorporation.

(b) At a shareholders' meeting involving the election of Directors, no shareholder shall be entitled to cumulate votes (i.e., cast for any candidate a number of votes greater than the number of the shareholder's shares) unless the names of such candidates have been placed in nomination prior to commencement of the voting and a shareholder has given notice to the meeting, prior to commencement of the voting, of the shareholder's intention to cumulate his votes. If any shareholder has given such notice, then every shareholder entitled to vote may cumulate his votes for candidates in nomination and give any candidate up to a number of votes equal to the number of Directors to be elected multiplied by the number of votes to which such shareholder's shares are entitled, or distribute the total number of his votes as so calculated among any or all of the candidates. The candidates receiving the highest numbers of votes, up to the number of Directors to be elected, shall be elected.

Section 2.09 Waiver of Notice or Consent by Absent Shareholders. (a) The transactions of any meeting of shareholders, either annual or special, however called and noticed, and wherever held, shall be as valid as though had at a meeting duly held after regular call and notice, if a quorum be present either in person or by proxy, and if, either before or after the meeting, each person entitled to vote but not present in person or by proxy, signs a written waiver of notice, a consent to the holding of the meeting, or an approval of the minutes thereof. The waiver of notice, consent or approval need not specify either the business to be transacted or the purpose of any annual or special meeting of shareholders, except that if action is taken or proposed to be taken for approval of any of those matters specified in Section 2.04(b), the waiver of notice shall state the general nature of such proposal. All such waivers, consents and approvals shall be filed with the corporate records or made a part of the minutes of the meeting.

(b) Attendance of a person at a meeting shall constitute a waiver of notice of and presence at such meeting unless such person objects at the beginning of the meeting to the transaction of any business because the meeting is not lawfully called or convened, except that attendance at a meeting is not a waiver of any right to object to the consideration of matters required by the Code to be included in the notice of the meeting but not so included if such objection is expressly made at the meeting.

Section 2.10 Shareholder Action by Written Consent Without a Meeting. (a) Any action which may be taken at any annual or special meeting of shareholders, other than the election of Directors, may be taken without a meeting and without prior notice, if a consent or consents in writing, setting forth the action so taken, are signed by the holders of outstanding shares representing not less than the minimum number of votes that would be necessary to authorize or take such action at a meeting at which all shares entitled to vote thereon were present and voted. In the case of election of Directors, such consents shall be effective only if signed by the holders of all outstanding shares entitled to vote for the election of Directors; provided, however, that a Director may be elected at any time to fill a vacancy not filled by the current Directors by the written consent of the shareholders pursuant to Section 3.04 of these Bylaws.

(b) All such consents shall be filed with the Secretary of the corporation and shall be maintained in the corporate records. Any shareholder giving a written consent, or the shareholder's proxyholders, or a transferee of the shares or a personal representative of the shareholder or their respective proxyholders, may revoke the consent by a writing received by the Secretary of the corporation prior to the time that written consents respecting the number of shares required to authorize the proposed action have been filed with the Secretary, but may not do so thereafter. Such revocation is effective upon receipt by the Secretary.

(c) If the consents of all shareholders entitled to vote have not been solicited in writing, and if the unanimous written consent of all such shareholders shall not have been received, the Secretary shall give prompt notice of the corporate action approved by the shareholders without a meeting. This notice shall be given in the manner specified in Section 2.05 of this Article II. In the case of approval of (i) contracts or transactions in which a director has a direct or indirect financial interest, pursuant to Section 310 of the Code, (ii) indemnification of agents of the corporation, pursuant to Section 317 of the Code, (iii) a reorganization of the corporation, pursuant to Section 1201 of the Code, and (iv) a distribution in dissolution other than in accordance with the rights of outstanding preferred shares, pursuant to Section 2007 of the Code, the notice shall be given at least ten (10) days before the consummation of any action authorized by that approval.

Section 2.11 Record Date for Shareholder Notice, Voting, and Giving Consents. (a) For purposes of determining the shareholders entitled to notice of any meeting, to vote, or to give consent to corporate action without a meeting, the Board of Directors may fix, in advance, a record date which shall not be more than sixty (60) days nor less than ten (10) days prior to the date of any such meeting nor more than sixty (60) days prior to such action without a meeting, and in such case only shareholders of record at the close of business on the date so fixed are entitled to notice and to vote or to give consents, as the case may be, notwithstanding any transfer of any shares on the books of the corporation after the record date fixed as aforesaid, except as otherwise provided in the California General Corporation Law.

(b) If the Board of Directors does not so fix a record date:

(i) the record date for determining shareholders entitled to notice of, or to vote at, a meeting of shareholders shall be at the close of business on the business day next preceding the day on which notice is given or, if notice is waived, at the close of business on the business day next preceding the day on which the meeting is held; and

(ii) the record date for determining shareholders entitled to give consent to corporation action in writing without a meeting, (A) when no prior action by the Board has been taken, shall be the day on which the first written consent is given, or (B) when prior action of the Board has been taken, shall be at the close of business on the day on which the Board adopts the resolution relating thereto, or the sixtieth (60th) day prior to the date of such other action, whichever is later.

Section 2.12 Proxies. Every person entitled to vote for Directors or on any other matter shall have the right to do so either in person or by one or more agents authorized by a written proxy signed by such person and filed with the Secretary of the corporation. A proxy shall be deemed signed if the shareholder's name is placed on the proxy (whether by manual signature, typewriting, telegraphic transmission or otherwise) by the shareholder or the shareholder's attorney-in-fact. A validly executed proxy which does not state that it is irrevocable shall continue in full force and effect unless: (i) revoked by the person executing it, prior to the vote pursuant thereto, by a writing delivered to the corporation stating that the proxy is revoked, or by a subsequent proxy executed by the person executing the prior proxy and presented to the meeting, or by such person's attendance at the meeting and voting in person; or (ii) written notice of the death or incapacity of the maker of such proxy is received by the corporation before the vote pursuant thereto is counted; provided, however, that no such proxy shall be valid after the expiration of eleven (11) months from the date of such proxy, unless otherwise provided in the proxy. The revocability of a proxy that states on its face that it is irrevocable shall be governed by the provisions of Section 705(e) and (f) of the Code.

Section 2.13 Inspectors of Election. (a) Before any meeting of shareholders, the Board of Directors may appoint any persons other than nominees for office to act as inspectors of election at the meeting or its adjournment. If no inspectors of election are so appointed, the chairman of the meeting may, and on the request of any shareholder or a shareholder's proxy shall, appoint inspectors of election at the meeting. The number of inspectors shall be either one (1) or three (3). If inspectors are appointed at a meeting on the request of one or more shareholders or proxies, the holders of a majority of shares, or their proxies present at the meeting, shall determine whether one (1) or three (3) inspectors are to be appointed. If any person appointed as inspector fails to appear or fails or refuses to act, the chairman of the meeting may, and upon the request of any shareholder or a shareholder's proxy shall, appoint a person to fill the vacancy.

(b) The inspectors shall:

(i) determine the number of shares outstanding and the voting power of each, the shares represented at the meeting, the existence of a quorum, and the authenticity, validity and effect of proxies;

(ii) receive votes, ballots or consents;

(iii) hear and determine all challenges and questions in any way arising in connection with the right to vote;

(iv) count and tabulate all votes or consents;

(v) determine when the polls shall close;

(vi) determine the result; and

(vii) do any other acts that may be proper to conduct the election or vote with fairness to all shareholders.

ARTICLE III

DIRECTORS

Section 3.01 Powers. (a) Subject to the provisions of the Code and any limitations in the Articles of Incorporation and these Bylaws relating to action required to be approved by the shareholders or by the outstanding shares, the business and affairs of the corporation shall be managed and all corporate powers shall be exercised by or under the direction of the Board of Directors.

(b) Without prejudice to such general powers, but subject to the same limitations, it is hereby expressly declared that the Directors shall have the power and authority to:

(i) select and remove all officers, agents, and employees of the corporation, prescribe such powers and duties for them as are not inconsistent with law, the Articles of Incorporation or these Bylaws, fix their compensation, and require from them security for faithful service;

(ii) change the principal executive office or the principal business office in the State of California from one location to another; cause the corporation to be qualified to do business in any other state, territory, dependency, or foreign country and conduct business without or outside the State of California; designate any place within or without the State for the holding of any shareholders' meeting or meetings, including annual meetings; adopt, make and use a corporate seal, and prescribe the forms of certificates of stock, and alter the form of such seal and of such certificates;

(iii) authorize the issuance of shares of stock of the corporation from time to time, upon such terms as may be lawful, in consideration of money paid, labor done or services actually rendered, debts or securities cancelled or tangible or intangible property actually received; and

(iv) borrow money and incur indebtedness for the purposes of the corporation, and cause to be executed and delivered therefor, in the corporate name, promissory notes, bonds, debentures, deeds of trust, mortgages, pledges, hypothecations, or other evidences of debt and securities therefor.

Section 3.02 Number and Qualification of Directors. The authorized number of Directors shall be three (3) until changed by a duly-adopted amendment to the Articles of Incorporation or by an amendment to this bylaw adopted by the vote or written consent of holders of a majority of the outstanding shares entitled to vote; provided, however, in the event there are ever more than five (5) directors in this corporation, that an amendment reducing the fixed or minimum number of Directors to a number less than five (5) cannot be adopted if the votes cast against its adoption at a meeting, or the shares not consenting in the case of action by written consent, are equal to more than 16⅔% of the outstanding shares entitled to vote.

Section 3.03 Election and Term of Office of Directors. Directors shall be elected at each annual meeting of the shareholders to hold office until the next annual meeting. Each Director, including a Director elected to fill a vacancy, shall hold office until the expiration of the term for which elected and until a successor has been elected and qualified.

Section 3.04 Vacancies. (a) Vacancies in the Board of Directors may be filled by a majority of the remaining Directors, though less than a quorum, or by a sole remaining Director, except that a vacancy created by the removal of a Director by the vote or written consent of the shareholders or by court order may be filled only by the vote of a majority of the shares represented and voting at a duly held meeting at which a quorum is present (which shares voting affirmatively also constitute at least a majority of the required quorum), or by the unanimous written consent of all shares entitled to vote for the election of Directors. Each Director so elected shall hold office until the next annual meeting of the shareholders and until a successor has been elected and qualified.

(b) A vacancy or vacancies in the Board of Directors shall be deemed to exist in the case of the death, resignation or removal of any Director, or if the Board of Directors by resolution declares vacant the office of a Director who has been declared of unsound mind by an order of court or convicted of a felony, or if the authorized number of Directors is increased, or if the shareholders fail, at any meeting of shareholders at which any Director or Directors are elected, to elect the full authorized number of Directors to be voted for at that meeting.

(c) The shareholders may elect a Director or Directors at any time to fill any vacancy or vacancies not filled by the Directors, but any such election by written consent, other than to fill a vacancy created by removal, shall require the consent of a majority of the outstanding shares entitled to vote.

(d) Any Director may resign upon giving written notice to the Chairman of the Board, the President, the Secretary or the Board of Directors. A resignation shall be effective upon the giving of the notice, unless the notice specifies a later time for its effectiveness. If the resignation of a Director is effective at a future time, the Board of Directors may elect a successor to take office when the resignation becomes effective.

(e) No reduction of the authorized number of Directors shall have the effect of removing any Director prior to the expiration of his term of office.

Section 3.05 Place of Meetings and Telephonic Meetings. Regular meetings of the Board of Directors may be held without notice, at any time and at any place within or outside the State of California that may be designated by these Bylaws, or from time to time by resolution of the Board. In the absence of the designation of a place, regular meetings shall be held at the principal executive office of the corporation. Special meetings of the Board shall be held at any place that has been designated in the notice of the meeting or, if not stated in the notice, at the principal executive office of the corporation. Any meeting, regular or special, may be held by conference telephone or similar communications equipment, so long as all Directors participating in such meeting can hear one another, and all such Directors shall be deemed to be present in person at such meeting.

Section 3.06 Annual Meetings. Immediately following each annual meeting of shareholders, the Board of Directors shall hold a regular meeting for purposes of organization, any desired election of officers and the transaction of other business. Notice of such meeting shall not be required.

Section 3.07 Other Regular Meetings. Other regular meetings of the Board of Directors may be held without call at such time as shall from time to time be fixed by the Board of Directors. Such regular meetings may be held without notice.

Section 3.08 Special Meetings. (a) Special meetings of the Board of Directors for any purpose or purposes may be called at any time by the Chairman of the Board, the President, any Vice President, the Secretary or any two (2) Directors.

(b) Notice of the time and place of special meetings shall be delivered personally or by telephone to each Director or sent by first-class mail or telegram, charges pre-paid, addressed to each Director at his or her address as it is shown upon the records of the corporation. In case such notice is mailed, it shall be deposited in the United States mail at least four (4) days prior to the time of the holding of the meeting. In case such notice is delivered personally, or by telephone or telegram, it shall be delivered personally or by telephone or to the telegraph company at least forty-eight (48) hours prior to the time of the holding of the meeting. Any oral notice given personally or by telephone may be communicated to either the Director or to a person at the office of the Director who the person giving the notice has reason to believe will promptly communicate it to the Director. The notice need not specify the purpose of the meeting nor the place if the meeting is to be held at the principal executive office of the corporation.

Section 3.09 Quorum. A majority of the authorized number of Directors shall constitute a quorum for the transaction of business, except to adjourn as hereinafter provided. Every act or decision done or made by a majority of the Directors present at a meeting duly held at which a quorum is present shall be regarded as the act of the Board of Directors, subject to the provisions of Section 310 of the Code (regarding approval of contracts or transactions in which a Director has a direct or indirect material financial interest), Section 311 (regarding appointment of committees), and Section 317 (e) (regarding indemnification of directors). A meeting at which a quorum is initially present may continue to transact business notwithstanding the withdrawal of Directors, if any action taken is approved by at least a majority of the required quorum for such meeting.

Section 3.10 Waiver of Notice. The transactions of any meeting of the Board of Directors, however called and noticed or wherever held, shall be as valid as though had at a meeting duly held after regular call and notice if a quorum is present and if, either before or after the meeting, each of the Directors not present signs a written waiver of notice, thereof. The waiver of notice or consent need not specify the purpose of the meeting. All such waivers, consents and approvals shall be filed with the corporate records or made a part of the minutes of the meeting. Notice of a meeting shall also be deemed given to any Director who attends the meeting without protesting, prior thereto or at its commencement, the lack of notice to such Director.

Section 3.11 Adjournment. A majority of the Directors present, whether or not constituting a quorum, may adjourn any meeting to another time and place.

Section 3.12 Notice of Adjournment. Notice of the time and place of holding an adjourned meeting need not be given, unless the meeting is adjourned for more than twenty-four (24) hours, in which case notice of such time and place shall be given prior to the time of the adjourned meeting, to the Directors who were not present at the time of the adjournment.

Section 3.13 Action Without Meeting. Any action required or permitted to be taken by the Board of Directors may be taken without a meeting, if all members of the Board shall individually or collectively consent in writing to such action. Such action by written consent shall have the same force and effect as a unanimous vote of the Board of Directors. Such written consent or consents shall be filed with the minutes of the proceedings of the Board.

Section 3.14 Fees and Compensation of Directors. Directors and members of committees may receive such compensation, if any, for their services, and such reimbursement of expenses, as may be fixed or determined by resolution of the Board of Directors. Nothing herein contained shall be construed to preclude any Director from serving the corporation in any other capacity as an officer, agent, employee, or otherwise, and receiving compensation for such services.

ARTICLE IV

COMMITTEES

Section 4.01 Committees of Directors. The Board of Directors may, by resolution adopted by a majority of the authorized number of Directors, designate one or more committees, each consisting of two (2) or more Directors, to serve at the pleasure of the Board. The Board may designate one or more Directors as alternate members of any committee who may replace any absent member or members at any meeting of the committee. The appointment of members or alternate members of a committee requires the vote of a majority of the authorized number of Directors. Any such committee, to the extent provided in the resolution of the Board, shall have all the authority of the Board, except with respect to:

(a) the approval of any action which, under the Code, also requires shareholders' approval or approval of the outstanding shares;

(b) the filling of vacancies on the Board of Directors or in any committee;

(c) the fixing of compensation of the Directors for serving on the Board or on any committee;

(d) the amendment or repeal of bylaws or the adoption of new bylaws;

(e) the amendment or repeal of any resolution of the Board of Directors which by its express terms is not so amendable or repealable;

(f) a distribution to the shareholders of the corporation (as defined in Section 166 of the Code), except at a rate or in a periodic amount or within a price range determined by the Board of Directors; or

(g) the appointment of any other committees of the Board of Directors or the members thereof.

Section 4.02 Meetings and Action of Committees. Meetings and action of committees shall be governed by, and held and taken in accordance with, the provisions of Article III of these Bylaws, Section 3.05 (place of meetings and telephonic meetings), Section 3.07 (regular meetings), Section 3.08 (special meetings and notice), Section 3.09 (quorum), Section 3.10 (waiver of notice), Section 3.11 (adjournment), Section 3.12 (notice of adjournment) and Section 3.13 (action without meeting), with such changes in the context of those sections as are necessary to substitute the committee and its members for the Board of Directors and its members, except that the time of regular meetings of committees may be determined by resolution of the Board of Directors as well as the committee, special meetings of committees may also be called by resolution of the Board of Directors and notice of special meetings of committees shall also be given to all alternate members, who shall have the right to attend all meetings of the committee. The Board of Directors may adopt rules for the government of any committee not inconsistent with the provisions of these Bylaws.

ARTICLE V

OFFICERS

Section 5.01 Officers. The officers of the corporation shall be a Chairman of the Board or a President, or both, a Secretary, and a Chief Financial Officer. The corporation may also have, at the discretion of the Board of Directors, one or more Vice Presidents, a Treasurer, one or more Assistant Secretaries, one or more Assistant Treasurers, and such other officers as may be appointed in accordance with the provisions of Section 5.03 of this Article V. Any number of offices may be held by the same person.

Section 5.02 Election of Officers. The officers of the corporation, except such officers as may be appointed in accordance with the provisions of Section 5.03 or Section 5.05 of this Article V, shall be chosen by the Board of Directors, and each shall serve at the pleasure of the Board, subject to the rights, if any, of an officer under any contract of employment.

Section 5.03 Subordinate Officers, Etc. The Board of Directors may appoint, and may empower the President to appoint, such other officers as the business of the corporation may require, each of whom shall hold office for such period, have such authority and perform such duties as are provided in the Bylaws or as the Board of Directors may from time to time determine.

Section 5.04 Removal and Resignation of Officers. (a) Subject to the rights, if any, of an officer under any contract of employment, any officer may be removed, either with or without cause, by the Board of Directors, at any regular or special meeting thereof, or, except in case of an officer chosen by the Board of Directors, by any officer upon whom such power of removal may be conferred by the Board of Directors.

(b) Any officer may resign at any time by giving written notice to the corporation. Any such resignation shall take effect upon the giving of such notice or at any later time specified therein; and, unless otherwise specified therein, the acceptance of such resignation shall not be necessary to make it effective. Any such resignation is without prejudice to the rights, if any, of the corporation under any contract to which the officer is a party.

Section 5.05 Vacancies in Offices. A vacancy in any office because of death, resignation, removal, disqualification or any other cause shall be filled in the manner prescribed in these Bylaws for regular appointments to such office.

Section 5.06 Chairman of the Board. The Chairman of the Board, if such an officer be elected, shall, if present, preside at all meetings of the Board of Directors and exercise and perform such other powers and duties as may be from time to time assigned to him by the Board of Directors or prescribed by the Bylaws.

Section 5.07 President. Subject to such supervisory powers, if any, as may be given by the Board of Directors to the Chairman of the Board, if there be such an officer, the President shall be the general manager and chief executive officer of the corporation and shall, subject to the control of the Board of Directors, have general supervision, direction and control of the business and the officers of the corporation. He shall preside at all meetings of the shareholders and, in the absence of the Chairman of the Board, or if there be none, at all meetings of the Board of Directors. He shall have the general powers and duties of management usually vested in the office of President of a corporation, and shall have such other powers and duties as may be prescribed by the Board of Directors or the Bylaws.

Section 5.08 Vice Presidents. In the absence or disability of the President, the Vice Presidents, if any, in order of their rank as fixed by the Board of Directors, or, if not ranked, a Vice President designated by the Board of Directors, shall perform all the duties of the President, and when so acting shall have all the powers of, and be subject to all the restrictions upon, the President. The Vice Presidents shall have such other powers and perform such other duties as from time to time may be prescribed for them respectively by the Board of Directors or the Bylaws, the President, or the Chairman of the Board if there is no President.

Section 5.09 Secretary. (a) The Secretary shall keep or cause to be kept at the principal executive office, or such other place as the Board of Directors may designate, a book of minutes of all meetings and actions of Directors, committees of Directors and shareholders, with the time and place of holding, whether regular or special, and, if special, how authorized, the notice thereof given, the names of those present at Directors' and committee meetings, the number of shares present or represented at shareholder's meetings, and the proceedings thereof.

(b) The Secretary shall keep or cause to be kept at the principal executive office or at the office of the corporation's transfer agent or registrar, as determined by resolution of the Board of Directors, a share register, or a duplicate share register, showing the names of all shareholders and their addresses, the number and classes of shares held by each, the number and date of certificates issued for the same, and the number and date of cancellation of every certificate surrendered for cancellation.

(c) The Secretary shall give, or cause to be given, notice of all meetings of the shareholders and of the Board of Directors required by the Bylaws or by law to be given, and shall keep the seal of the corporation, if one be adopted, in safe custody, and shall have such other powers and perform such other duties as may be prescribed by the Board of Directors or by the Bylaws.

Section 5.10 Chief Financial Officer. (a) The Chief Financial Officer shall keep and maintain, or cause to be kept and maintained, adequate and correct books and records of accounts of the properties and business transactions of the corporation, including accounts of its assets, liabilities, receipts, disbursements, gains, losses, capital, retained earnings and shares. The books of account shall be open at all reasonable times to inspection by any Director.

(b) The Chief Financial Officer shall cause to be deposited all moneys and other valuables in the name and to the credit of the corporation with such depositaries as may be designated by the Board of Directors. He shall cause the funds of the corporation to be disbursed as he may be properly directed from time to time, shall render to the President and Directors, whenever they request it, an account of all of his transactions as Chief Financial Officer and of the financial condition of the corporation, and shall have other powers and perform such other duties as may be prescribed by the Board of Directors or the Bylaws.

ARTICLE VI

INDEMNIFICATION OF DIRECTORS, OFFICERS,

EMPLOYEES, AND OTHER AGENTS

Section 6.01 Agents, Proceedings and Expenses. For the purposes of this Article, "agent" means any person who is or was a Director, officer, employee, or other agent of this corporation, or is or was serving at the request of this corporation as a Director, officer, employee, or agent of another foreign or domestic corporation, partnership, joint venture, trust or other enterprise, or was a director, officer, employee, or agent of a foreign or domestic corporation which was a predecessor corporation of this corporation or of another enterprise at the request of such predecessor corporation; "proceeding" means any threatened, pending or completed action or proceeding, whether civil, criminal, administrative, or investigative; and "expenses" includes, without limitation, attorneys' fees and any expenses of establishing a right to indemnification under Section 6.04 or Section 6.05(c) of this Article VI.

Section 6.02 Actions Other Than by the Corporation. This corporation shall indemnify any person who was or is a party, or is threatened to be made a party, to any proceeding (other than an action by or in the right of this corporation to procure a judgment in its favor) by reason of the fact that such person is or was an agent of this corporation, against expenses, judgments, fines, settlements and other amounts actually and reasonably incurred in connection with such proceeding, if that person acted in good faith and in a manner that person reasonably believed to be in the best interests of this corporation, and, in the case of a criminal proceeding, had no reasonable cause to believe the conduct of that person was unlawful. The termination of any proceeding by judgment, order, settlement, conviction, or upon a plea of *nolo contendere* or its equivalent shall not, of itself, create a presumption that the person did not act in good faith and in a manner which the person reasonably believed to be in the best interests of this corporation or that the person had reasonable cause to believe that the person's conduct was unlawful.

Section 6.03 Actions by the Corporation. This corporation shall indemnify any person who was or is a party, or is threatened to be made a party, to any threatened, pending or completed action by or in the right of this corporation to procure a judgment in its favor by reason of the fact that that person is or was an agent of this corporation, against expenses actually and reasonably incurred by that person in connection with the defense or settlement of that action if that person acted in good faith, in a manner that person believed to be in the best interests of this corporation, and with such care, including reasonable inquiry, as an ordinarily prudent person in a like position would use under similar circumstances. No indemnification shall be made under this Section 6.03:

(a) in respect of any claim, issue or matter as to which that person shall have been adjudged to be liable to this corporation in the performance of that person's duty to this corporation, unless and only to the extent that the court in which that proceeding is or was pending shall determine upon application that, in view of all the circumstances of the case, that person is fairly and reasonably entitled to indemnity for the expenses which the court shall determine;

(b) of amounts paid in settling or otherwise disposing of a threatened or pending action, with or without court approval; or

(c) of expenses incurred in defending a threatened or pending action which is settled or otherwise disposed of without court approval.

Section 6.04 Successful Defense by Agent. To the extent that an agent of this corporation has been successful on the merits in defense of any proceeding referred to in Section 6.02 or Section 6.03 of this Article VI, or in defense of any claim, issue, or matter therein, the agent shall be indemnified against expenses actually and reasonably incurred by the agent in connection therewith.

Section 6.05 Required Approval. Except as provided in Section 6.04 of this Article, any indemnification under this Article shall be made by this corporation only if authorized in the specific case upon a determination that indemnification of the agent is proper in the circumstances because the agent has met the applicable standard of conduct set forth in Section 6.02 or Section 6.03 of this Article VI, by:

(a) a majority vote of a quorum consisting of Directors who are not parties to the proceeding;

(b) approval by the affirmative vote of a majority of the shares of this corporation represented and voting at a duly held meeting at which a quorum is present (which shares voting affirmatively also constitute at least a majority of the required quorum), or by the written consent of holders of a majority of the outstanding shares entitled to vote (for this purpose, the shares owned by the person to be indemnified shall not be entitled to vote thereon); or

(c) the court in which the proceeding is or was pending, upon application made by this corporation or the agent or the attorney or other person rendering services in connection with the defense, whether or not such application by the agent, attorney, or other person is opposed by this corporation.

Section 6.06 Advance of Expenses. Expenses incurred in defending any proceeding may be advanced by this corporation before the final disposition of the proceeding upon receipt of an undertaking by or on behalf of the agent to repay the amount of the advance unless it shall be determined ultimately that the agent is entitled to be indemnified as authorized in this Article VI.

Section 6.07 Other Contractual Rights. Nothing contained in this Article VI shall affect any right to indemnification to which persons other than Directors and officers of this corporation or any subsidiary hereof may be entitled by contract or otherwise.

Section 6.08 Limitations. No indemnification or advance shall be made under this Article VI, except as provided in Section 6.04 or Section 6.05(c), in any circumstance where it appears:

(a) that it would be inconsistent with a provision of the Articles, these Bylaws, a resolution of the shareholders, or an agreement in effect at the time of the accrual of the alleged cause of action asserted in the proceeding in which the expenses were incurred or other amounts were paid which prohibits or otherwise limits indemnification; or

(b) that it would be inconsistent with any condition expressly imposed by a court in approving a settlement.

Section 6.09 Insurance. This corporation may, upon a determination by the Board of Directors, purchase and maintain insurance on behalf of any agent of the corporation against any liability which might be asserted against or incurred by the agent in such capacity, or which might arise out of the agent's status as such, whether or not this corporation would have the power to indemnify the agent against that liability under the provisions of this Article VI.

Section 6.10 Fiduciaries of Corporate Employee Benefit Plan. This Article VI does not apply to any proceeding against any trustee, investment manager, or other fiduciary of an employee benefit plan in that person's capacity as such, even though that person may also be an agent of this corporation as defined in Section 6.01 of this Article VI. This corporation may, however, upon approval in accordance with Section 6.05, indemnify and purchase and maintain insurance on behalf of any fiduciary to the extent permitted by Section 207(f) of the Code.

Section 6.11 Amendment to California Law. In the event that California Law regarding indemnification of directors, officers, employees and other agents of corporations, as in effect at the time of adoption of these Bylaws, is subsequently amended to in any way increase the scope of permissible indemnification beyond that set forth herein, the indemnification authorized by this Article VI shall be deemed to be coextensive with that afforded by the California Law as so amended.

ARTICLE VII

CORPORATE LOANS AND GUARANTEES

TO DIRECTORS, OFFICERS AND EMPLOYEES

Section 7.01 Limitation on Corporate Loans and Guarantees. Except as provided in Section 7.02 of this Article VII this corporation shall not make any loan of money or property to, or guarantee any obligation of

(a) any Director or officer of the corporation or of its parent or any subsidiary, or

(b) any person, upon the security of shares of this corporation or of its parent, unless the loan or guaranty is otherwise adequately secured,

except by the vote of the holders of a majority of the shares of all classes, regardless of limitations or restrictions on voting rights, other than shares held by the benefited Director, officer or person.

Section 7.02 Permissible Corporate Loans and Guarantees. This corporation may lend money to, or guarantee any obligation of, or otherwise assist, any officer or other employee of this corporation or of any subsidiary, including any officer or employee who is also a Director, pursuant to an employee benefit plan (including, without limitation, any stock purchase or stock option plan) available to executives or other employees, whenever the Board determines that such loan or guaranty may reasonably be expected to benefit the corporation. If such plan includes officers or Directors, it shall be approved or ratified by the affirmative vote of the holders of a majority of the shares of this corporation entitled to vote, by written consent, or represented at a duly held meeting at which a quorum is present, after disclosure of the right under such plan to include officers or Directors thereunder. Such loan or guaranty or other assistance may be with or without interest and may be unsecured or secured in such manner as the Board shall approve, including, without limitation, a pledge of shares of the corporation. This corporation may advance money to a Director or officer of the corporation or of its parent or any subsidiary for expenses reasonably anticipated to be incurred in the performance of the duties of such Director or officer, provided that in the absence of such advance such Director or officer would be entitled to be reimbursed for such expenses by such corporation, its parent or any subsidiary.

ARTICLE VIII

GENERAL CORPORATE MATTERS

Section 8.01 Record Date for Purposes Other Than Notice and Voting. (a) For purposes of determining the shareholders entitled to receive payment of any dividend or other distribution or allotment of any rights or entitled to exercise any rights in respect of any other lawful action (other than for the purposes prescribed by Section 2.11 of Article II of these Bylaws), the Board of Directors may fix, in advance, a record date, which shall not be more than sixty (60) days prior to any such action, and in such case only shareholders of record at the close of business on the date so fixed are entitled to receive the dividend, distribution or allotment of rights or to exercise the rights, as the case may be, notwithstanding any transfer of any shares on the books of the corporation after the record date fixed as aforesaid, except as otherwise provided in the California General Corporation Law.

(b) If the Board of Directors does not so fix a record date, the record date for determining shareholders for any such purpose shall be at the close of business on the day on which the Board adopts the resolution relating thereto, or the sixtieth (60th) day prior to the date of such action, whichever is later.

Section 8.02 Checks, Drafts, Evidences of Indebtedness. All checks, drafts or other orders for payment of money, notes or other evidences of indebtedness, issued in the name of or payable to the corporation, shall be signed or endorsed by such person or persons and in such manner as, from time to time, shall be determined by resolution of the Board of Directors.

Section 8.03 Corporate Contracts and Instruments; How Executed. The Board of Directors, except as otherwise provided in these Bylaws, may authorize any officer or officers, agent or agents, to enter into any contract or execute any instrument in the name of and on behalf of the corporation, and such authority may be general or confined to specific instances; and, unless so authorized or ratified by the Board of Directors or within the agency power of an officer, no officer, agent or employee shall have any power or authority to bind the corporation by any contract or engagement or to pledge its credit or to render it liable for any purpose or to any amount.

Section 8.04 Certificates for Shares. A certificate or certificates for shares of the capital stock of the corporation shall be issued to each shareholder when any such shares are fully paid, and the Board of Directors may authorize the issuance of certificates for shares as partly paid provided that such certificates shall state the amount of the consideration to be paid therefor and the amount paid thereon. All such statements or references thereto appearing on the face of the certificate shall be conspicuous. All certificates shall be signed in the name of the corporation by the Chairman of the Board or Vice Chairman of the Board or the President or a Vice President and by the Chief Financial Officer or an Assistant Treasurer or the Secretary or any Assistant Secretary, certifying the number of shares and the class or series of shares owned by the shareholder. Any or all of the signatures on the certificate may be facsimile. In case any officer, transfer agent or registrar who has signed or whose facsimile signature has been placed upon a certificate shall have ceased to be such officer, transfer agent or registrar before such certificate is issued, it may be issued by the corporation with the same effect as if such person were an officer, transfer agent or registrar at the date of issue.

Section 8.05 Lost Certificates. Except as hereinafter provided in this Section 8.05, no new certificate for shares shall be issued in lieu of an old certificate unless the old certificate is surrendered to the corporation and cancelled at the same time as such issuance. The Board of Directors may, if any share certificate or certificate for any other security is lost, stolen or destroyed, authorize the issuance of a new certificate in lieu thereof, upon such terms and conditions as the Board may require, including provision for indemnification of the corporation secured by a bond or other adequate security sufficient to protect the corporation against any claim that may be made against it, including any expense or liability, on account of the alleged loss, theft or destruction of such certificate or the issuance of such new certificate.

Section 8.06 Representation of Shares of Other Corporations. The Chairman of the Board, the President, or any Vice President, or any other person authorized by resolution of the Board of Directors or by any of the foregoing designated officers, is authorized to vote on behalf of the corporation any and all shares of any other corporation or corporations, foreign or domestic, standing in the name of the corporation. The authority herein granted to said officers to vote or represent on behalf of the corporation any and all shares held by the corporation in any other corporation or corporations may be exercised by any such officer in person or by any person authorized to do so by proxy duly executed by said officer.

Section 8.07 Construction and Definitions. Unless the context requires otherwise, the general provisions, rules of construction, and definitions in the California General Corporation Law shall govern the construction of these Bylaws. Without limiting the generality of the foregoing, the singular number includes the plural, the plural number includes the singular, and the term "person" includes both a corporation and a natural person.

ARTICLE IX

RECORDS AND REPORTS

Section 9.01 Maintenance and Inspection of Share Register. (a) The corporation shall keep at its principal executive office, or at the office of its transfer agent or registrar, if one or the other has been appointed, and as determined by resolution of the Board of Directors, a record of its shareholders, giving the names and addresses of all shareholders and the number and class of shares held by each shareholder.

(b) A shareholder or shareholders of the corporation holding at least five percent (5%) in the aggregate, of the outstanding voting shares of the corporation may (i) inspect and copy the records of shareholders' names and addresses and shareholdings during usual business hours upon five (5) business days' prior written demand upon the corporation, and/or (ii) obtain from the transfer agent of the corporation, upon written demand and upon the tender of such transfer agent's usual charges for such list, a list of the names and addresses of the shareholders who are entitled to vote for the election of Directors, and their shareholdings as of the most recent record date for which such list has been compiled, or as of a date specified by the requesting shareholder or shareholders subsequent to the date of demand. Such list shall be made available to such shareholder or shareholders by the transfer agent on or before the later of the fifth (5th) business day after the demand is received or the date specified in the demand as the date as of which the list is to be compiled. The record of shareholders shall also be open to inspection upon the written demand of any shareholder or holder of a voting trust at any time during usual business hours, for a purpose reasonably related to such holder's interests as a shareholder or as the holder of a voting trust certificate. Any inspection and copying under this Section 9.01 may be made in person or by an agent or attorney of the shareholder or holder of a voting trust certificate making such demand.

Section 9.02 Maintenance and Inspection of Bylaws. The corporation shall keep at its principal executive office, or, if its principal executive office is not in the State of California, at its principal business office in such State, if any, the original or a copy of the Bylaws as amended to date, which shall be open to inspection by any shareholder upon the written demand of any such shareholder at all reasonable times during usual business hours. If the principal executive office of the corporation is outside this state and the corporation has no principal business office in this state, the Secretary shall, upon the written request of any shareholder, furnish to such shareholder a copy of the Bylaws as amended to date.

Section 9.03 Maintenance and Inspection of Other Corporate Records. The accounting books and records and minutes of proceedings of the shareholders and the Board of Directors and any committee or committees of the Board of Directors shall be kept at such place or places designated by the Board of Directors, or, in the absence of such designation, at the principal executive office of the corporation. The minutes shall be kept in written form and the accounting books and records shall be kept either in written form or in any other form capable of being converted into written form. Such minutes and accounting books and records shall be open to inspection upon the written demand of any shareholder or holder of a voting trust certificate, at any reasonable time during usual business hours, for a purpose reasonably related to such holder's interests as a shareholder or as the holder of a voting trust certificate. Such inspection may be made in person or by an agent or attorney, and shall include the right to copy and make extracts. The foregoing rights of inspection shall extend to the records of each subsidiary corporation of the corporation.

Section 9.04 Inspection by Directors. Every Director shall have the absolute right at any reasonable time to inspect all books, records and documents of every kind and the physical properties of the corporation and each of its subsidiary corporations. Such inspection by a Director may be made in person or by agent or attorney and the right of inspection includes the right to copy and make extracts.

Section 9.05 Annual Report to Shareholders. Until such time as there are one hundred (100) or more shareholders in this corporation, the annual report to shareholders referred to in Section 1501 of the California General Corporation Law is expressly dispensed with, but nothing herein shall be interpreted as prohibiting the Board of Directors from issuing such annual or other periodic reports to the shareholders of the corporation as they consider appropriate.

Section 9.06 Financial Statements. (a) A copy of any annual financial statement and any income statement of the corporation for each quarterly period of each fiscal year, and any accompanying balance sheet of the corporation as of the end of each such period, which have been prepared by the corporation shall be kept on file in the principal executive office of the corporation for twelve (12) months from their respective dates, and each such statement shall be exhibited at all reasonable times to any shareholder requesting an examination of any such statement or a copy thereof shall be mailed to any such shareholder.

(b) If a shareholder or shareholders holding at least five percent (5%), in the aggregate, of the outstanding shares of any class of stock of the corporation make a written request to the corporation for an income statement of the corporation for the three (3)-month, six (6)-month or nine (9)-month period of the current fiscal year having ended more than thirty (30) days prior to the date of the request, and a balance sheet of the corporation as of the end of such period, the Chief Financial Officer shall cause such statement to be prepared, if not already written form. Such minutes and accounting books and records shall be open to inspection upon the written demand of any shareholder or holder of a voting trust certificate, at any reasonable time during usual business hours, for a purpose reasonably related to such holder's interests as a shareholder or as the holder of a voting trust certificate. Such inspection may be made in person or by an agent or attorney, and shall include the right to copy and make extracts. The foregoing rights of inspection shall extend to the records of each subsidiary corporation of the corporation.

Section 9.07 Annual Statement of General Information. The corporation shall each year during the calendar month in which its Articles of Incorporation were originally filed with the California Secretary of State, or at any time during the immediately preceding five (5) calendar months, file with the Secretary of State of the State of California, on the prescribed form, a statement setting forth the authorized number of Directors, the names and complete business or residence addresses of all incumbent Directors, the names and complete business or residence addresses of the Chief Executive Officer, Secretary and Chief Financial Officer, the street address of its principal executive office or principal business office in this state (if any), and the general type of business constituting the principal business activity of the corporation, together with a designation of the agent of the corporation for the purpose of service of process, all in compliance with Section 1502 of the Code.

ARTICLE X

AMENDMENTS

Section 10.01 Amendment by Shareholders. New bylaws may be adopted or these Bylaws may be amended or repealed by the vote or written consent of holders of a majority of the outstanding shares entitled to vote; provided, however, that if the Articles of Incorporation of the corporation set forth the number of authorized Directors of the corporation, the authorized number of Directors may be changed only by an amendment of the Articles of Incorporation.

Section 10.02 Amendment by Directors. Subject to the rights of the shareholders as provided in Section 10.01 of this Article X, and Section 212 of the Code, to adopt, amend or repeal bylaws, bylaws may be adopted, amended or repealed by the Board of Directors.

CERTIFICATE OF SECRETARY

I, the undersigned, the duly elected and acting Secretary of BIG BUCKS, INC., A California Corporation, certify that the foregoing Bylaws, consisting of ten (10) Articles and 26 pages, are the true and correct Bylaws of said corporation adopted by the Board of Directors thereof on April 1, 1979.

IN WITNESS WHEREOF, I have hereunto subscribed my name, this 1st day of April, 1979.

_____
Secretary

[¶903] STEP-BY-STEP GUIDE TO DRAFTING THE CORPORATE MINUTES

Once the Articles of Incorporation have been filed, a meeting of the Board of Directors should be held to take additional action. The agenda of the first meeting should include:

- ☐ Adoption of the bylaws and a corporate seal;
- ☐ Adoption of a plan to take advantage of the provisions of Section 1244 of the Internal Revenue Code (ordinary loss treatment if the corporation ends up being a losing proposition);
- ☐ Authorization of the issuance of stock in exchange for the transfer of assets to the corporation;
- ☐ Authorization of the necessary acts required to obtain a permit from the State to issue stock or to otherwise ensure that the shares of stock are validly issued;
- ☐ Adoption of a corporate fiscal (taxable) year;
- ☐ Establishment of a corporate bank account;
- ☐ Authorization of the payment of expenses of incorporation; and
- ☐ Making an election to have such expenses deducted ratably over 60 months.

Normally, the Board of Directors should:

- ☐ Authorize the corporation to enter into employment contracts with key employees;
- ☐ Authorize the payment of an employee's death benefit; and
- ☐ Adopt a medical reimbursement plan and a wage continuation plan.

What Information Should Be Put Down and What Can Be Excluded

If the stockholders are going to enter into a redemption agreement with the corporation to cover situations in which the stockholders leave the corporation, such agreements should be approved. If the stockholders are going to enter into cross-purchase agreements with each other, these agreements should be executed at the outset even though they do not require the approval of the Board of Directors.

Sample Form of Initial Minutes

Below is a sample form of minutes of an organizational meeting of a Board of Directors (see pages 249 to 256). It is followed by sample forms that can establish the various programs referred to in the minutes.

ORGANIZATIONAL MEETING
OF THE BOARD OF DIRECTORS OF

BIG BUCKS, INC.

(A California Corporation)

A meeting of the members of the Board of Directors of Big Bucks, Inc., A California Corporation, was held at the principal office of the corporation at 5:00 P.M., on February 1, 1979, for the purpose of organizing the corporation. After their respective election, the President of the corporation acted as Chairman of the meeting and the Secretary of the corporation acted as secretary.

ARTICLES OF INCORPORATION

RESOLVED, that a copy of the Articles of Incorporation of this corporation as filed with the California Secretary of State on February 1, 1979, bearing said Secretary of State's filing number, be inserted in the Minute Book of this corporation, and that the contents of said Articles are hereby accepted and ratified by this Board of Directors.

ADOPTION OF BYLAWS

RESOLVED, that the Bylaws submitted to and reviewed by the Board of Directors of this corporation be, and they hereby are, adopted as the Bylaws for the regulation of the affairs of this corporation.

RESOLVED FURTHER, that the Secretary of this corporation certify said Bylaws as having been adopted as of the date of this Action, and insert said Bylaws in the Minute Book of this corporation.

ELECTION OF OFFICERS

RESOLVED, that the following persons are hereby elected to the offices set forth opposite their respective names:

Herbert Bucksup	—President
Herbert Bucksup	—Vice President
Betty Bucksup	—Secretary
Flo Cash	—Chief Financial Officer (Treasurer)

and that the above officers shall serve until their successors are duly elected and qualified.

CORPORATE MINUTE BOOK

RESOLVED, that this corporation shall maintain, as part of its corporate records, a book, entitled "Minute Book," which shall contain, without limitation, its Articles of Incorporation and amendments thereto, minutes of all meetings of its Directors, and minutes of all meetings of its shareholders, with the time and place of holding, whether regular or special, and, if special, how authorized, the notice thereof given, the names of those present at Directors' meetings, the number of shares present or represented at shareholders' meetings, and the proceedings thereof.

RESOLVED FURTHER, that the Secretary of the corporation is directed to procure such a Minute Book and such other books and records as may be required for the corporation.

ADOPTION OF SEAL

RESOLVED, that a corporate seal consisting of two concentric circles containing the name "Big Bucks, Inc.—California," and in the center of such circles the statement "Incorporated February 1, 1979," is adopted as the corporate seal of the corporation, and the Secretary is instructed to impress such Seal on the document recording this resolution opposite the place where this resolution appears.

(SEAL)

DESIGNATION OF PRINCIPAL EXECUTIVE OFFICE

RESOLVED, that 445 South Figueroa Street, Los Angeles, California, be, and the same hereby is, designated and fixed as the principal executive office for the transaction of business by this corporation.

ADOPTION OF STOCK CERTIFICATE

RESOLVED, that the share certificates representing common shares of this corporation shall be in substantially the same form as the form of share certificate attached to this document; that each such certificate shall bear the name of this corporation, the number of shares represented thereby, the name of the owner of such shares, and the date such shares were issued.

RESOLVED FURTHER, that such share certificates shall be consecutively numbered beginning with No. 1; shall be issued only when the signature of the Chairman or Vice Chairman of the Board, the President or a Vice President, and the signature of the Chief Financial Officer, or an Assistant Treasurer, the Secretary or any Assistant Secretary, are affixed thereto; and may also bear other wording related to the ownership, issuance, and transferability of the shares represented thereby.

ADOPTION OF 1244 STOCK PLAN

RESOLVED, that this corporation, having no portion of a prior stock offering outstanding and being a small business corporation, adopt the following plan in order to qualify in all respects under Section 1244 of the Internal Revenue Code of 1954, as amended, the Treasury Regulations issued pursuant thereto, Sections 18206-10 of the Revenue and Taxation Code of California, as amended, and the provisions of the California Administrative Code issued pursuant thereto:

(a) The maximum number of shares of common stock to be issued under this plan shall not exceed 25,000 shares, and the maximum aggregate value of consideration to be received from the proposed common shareholders in exchange therefor shall be $50,000.00.

(b) This plan shall expire not later than two (2) years from the date of this action, and all stock to be issued hereunder shall be issued within this period, provided that the Board may, in its discretion, terminate the plan at an earlier date;

(c) The shares to be issued to the proposed shareholders named in the resolutions adopted by this written consent are the shares to be issued under this plan; and

(d) No stock other than that sold and issued under this plan shall be offered or sold during the period of this plan.

RESOLVED FURTHER, that the officers of this corporation are hereby authorized and directed to do or cause to be done all acts required or appropriate to carry out the foregoing resolutions.

ISSUANCE OF COMMON STOCK

WHEREAS, this corporation is authorized in its Articles of Incorporation to issue an aggregate of one hundred thousand (100,000) shares of common stock;

WHEREAS, it is deemed to be in the best interests of this corporation to issue and sell 25,000 of its shares of common stock to the persons in the amounts and for the consideration set forth below:

Name	No. of Shares
Herbert Bucksup	12,500
Betty Bucksup	12,500

NOW, THEREFORE, BE IT RESOLVED, that each of the officers of this corporation is authorized and directed to issue and sell shares of common stock of this corporation to the persons and in the amounts set forth above, in consideration of the transfer of all the business assets subject to certain liabilities of Big Bucks Proprietorship.

RESOLVED FURTHER, that all such shares of stock shall be evidenced by a certificate or certificates which shall have placed prominently thereon a legend in accordance with the provisions of Section 25102(h) of the California Corporate Securities Law of 1968; and

RESOLVED FURTHER, that each of the officers of this corporation is authorized and directed to prepare and file, or cause to be prepared and filed, an appropriate Notice of Issuance of Securities, not later than ten (10) business days after receipt of consideration for the shares of stock pursuant to Section 25102(h) of the California Corporate Securities Law of 1968; and

RESOLVED FURTHER, that the Board of Directors hereby determines that the fair value of this corporation of the consideration for which said shares are to be issued is $50,000.00.

QUALIFICATION TO DO BUSINESS

RESOLVED, that the appropriate officers of this corporation be, and they hereby are, authorized, empowered and directed in the name and on behalf of this corporation to prepare or cause to be prepared, verified and filed, and to take any and all other actions they may deem necessary or advisable in order to obtain in the name of this corporation, any and all licenses and permits, tax and otherwise, as may be required for the conduct of the proposed business of this corporation by any federal, state, county, or municipal governmental statute, ordinance or regulation, and to transact business in compliance with the laws and regulations of any appropriate federal, state or municipal governmental authority, and that any such action previously taken by any officer of this corporation in this respect be, and it hereby is, approved, ratified, adopted and confirmed.

CORPORATE BANK ACCOUNT

RESOLVED, that this corporation establish in its name one or more deposit accounts with Big Bank, on such terms and conditions as may be agreed upon with such bank, and that the President and Secretary of this corporation be, and they hereby are, authorized to establish such account or accounts.

RESOLVED FURTHER, that the bank account authorization card, a copy of which is attached hereto, is by this reference incorporated herein and the resolutions contained therein are hereby adopted.

ADOPTION OF ACCOUNTING YEAR

RESOLVED, that the first accounting year of the corporation is hereby fixed from February 1, 1979, to the next succeeding January 31, and thereafter the accounting year of the corporation shall end on January 31 of each year.

FILING OF STATEMENT BY DOMESTIC CORPORATION

RESOLVED, that the appropriate officers of this corporation file with the California Secretary of State, as required by law, a statement of the names of the officers of this corporation, together with a statement of the location and address of the principal executive office of the corporation and the name and address of an agent selected for purposes of receiving service of process on this corporation.

PAYMENT OF EXPENSES OF INCORPORATION

WHEREAS, this corporation has incurred certain expenses and paid certain fees in connection with the incorporation and organization hereof; and

WHEREAS, the Chief Financial Officer of this corporation has presented to this Board a report of such expenses and fees, which has been reviewed by each member of this Board; and

WHEREAS, the members of this Board are informed and believe that said report accurately reflected all those costs reasonably incurred in connection with the incorporation and organization of this corporation;

NOW, THEREFORE, BE IT RESOLVED, that the Chief Financial Officer of this corporation is authorized and directed to pay all costs of incorporation and organization of this corporation, and to reimburse the persons advancing funds to this corporation for expenses and fees paid, as set forth in the report given to the members of this Board by the Chief Financial Officer.

MEDICAL REIMBURSEMENT PLAN

RESOLVED, that this corporation is hereby authorized to establish a direct payment medical plan known as the "Big Bucks Medical Reimbursement Plan," a copy of which is attached hereto pursuant to which the corporation shall reimburse certain employees and their immediate families for medical expenses which are not covered by any group hospitalization and/or major medical insurance policies.

RESOLVED FURTHER, that the appropriate officers of this corporation be, and they hereby are, authorized and directed to execute whatever documents are necessary to adopt said Direct Medical Reimbursement Plan.

WAGE CONTINUATION PLAN

RESOLVED, that this corporation is hereby authorized to establish a wage continuation plan in the form of the "Big Bucks, Inc. Wage Continuation Plan," a copy of which is attached hereto for the purpose of providing for a procedure whereby the corporation will make payments to certain employees which will constitute wages or payments in lieu of wages for a period during which such employees are absent from work on account of personal injury or sickness.

RESOLVED FURTHER, that the appropriate officers of this corporation be, and they hereby are, authorized to execute whatever documents are deemed necessary to institute and establish the foregoing plan.

EMPLOYMENT AGREEMENT

RESOLVED, that this corporation is hereby authorized to enter into an employment agreement with Herbert Bucksup in the form of the "Employment Agreement" attached hereto.

DEATH BENEFITS

RESOLVED, that upon the death of any officer-employee of this corporation, this corporation may pay to a designated beneficiary of such deceased employee or in the absence of such designation to his estate death benefits, in a single sum or otherwise, amounting to $5,000, unless such payment or payments shall render the corporation insolvent, or seriously impair its ability to meet its existing obligations as they become due.

DATED: February 1, 1979

_____

BETTY BUCKSUP, Secretary

ATTEST:

_____

HERBERT BUCKSUP

APPROVED:

_____

HERBERT BUCKSUP, Director

_____

BETTY BUCKSUP, Director

_____

FLO CASH, Director

[¶904] Medical Reimbursement Plan

The following medical plan (see pages 259 to 260) covers employees of the corporation who are also officers. The corporation picks up all of the medical expenses for such employees and their dependents. The payment is deductible by the corporation. The employee does not report the payment as income.

This particular plan provides for 100% of the expenses of covered employees. However, a plan could put a limit on the amount of expenses that will be reimbursed. It could also provide different levels of reimbursement for different classifications of employees.

Note that the plan may be amended or terminated at any time.

BIG BUCKS, INC.
MEDICAL REIMBURSEMENT PLAN

I
ESTABLISHMENT OF PLAN

Big Bucks, Inc., A California Corporation, hereinafter referred to as the "Corporation," hereby established a plan to be known as the "Big Bucks, Inc. MEDICAL REIMBURSEMENT PLAN," hereinafter referred to as the "Plan."

II
PURPOSE

The purpose of the Plan is to set forth a procedure whereby the Corporation will reimburse certain employees and their immediate families for medical expenses which are not covered by any group hospitalization and/or major medical insurance policies.

III
ELIGIBILITY

All corporate officer-employees and their dependents, as defined in Section 152 of the Internal Revenue Code of 1954, as amended, are covered under the Plan.

IV
BENEFITS

The Corporation shall pay to all corporate officer-employees and their dependents one-hundred percent (100%) of all medical expenses which are not covered by any group hospitalization and/or major medical insurance policies. For purposes of the Plan, the term "medical expense" means amounts incurred for the diagnosis, cure, mitigation, treatment or prevention of disease, or for the purpose of affecting any structure or function of the body. Such term is intended to include, but not by way of limitation, expenses incurred for psychiatric care and for care of eyes and teeth.

All benefits provided by the Plan will be paid on a monthly basis upon receipt of written proof, satisfactory to the Corporation, covering the occurrence, character and extent of the event for which a payment is to be made.

V

TERMINATION OF COVERAGE

Coverage of any officer-employee and his dependents (as defined in Section 152 of the Internal Revenue Code) shall terminate at the end of the month in which such employee ceases to be an employee. The coverage of an eligible employee's spouse shall terminate automatically upon the termination of marriage.

VI

TERMINATION OF PLAN

The Corporation may alter, amend, modify, suspend or terminate the Plan at any time.

IN WITNESS WHEREOF, the Corporation by its duly authorized officers has caused these presents to be executed on this 1st day of February 1979.

BIG BUCKS, INC.
(A California Corporation)

By _____
    HERBERT BUCKSUP, President

By _____
    BETTY BUCKSUP, Secretary

[¶905] WAGE CONTINUATION PLAN

The following Wage Continuation Plan (see pages 263 to 265) covers employees of the corporation who are also officers.

The corporation agrees to pay covered employees an amount equal to their full compensation in the event they become disabled. Under the terms of this plan, the payments continue for 12 months. The length of the payment period is discretionary with the company.

If a key employee of the corporation becomes disabled, the corporation may not generate enough operating income to meet its obligation under the plan. Therefore, it may be advisable for the corporation to buy disability insurance to fund all or part of its potential liability.

The plan does not provide disability benefits in certain situations. Also note that the corporation's obligation is reduced if the employee receives disability payments from certain other sources.

As in the case of the medical reimbursement plan, this plan may be amended or terminated at any time.

BIG BUCKS, INC.
WAGE CONTINUATION PLAN

I

ESTABLISHMENT OF THE PLAN

Big Bucks, Inc., a California Corporation, hereinafter referred to as the "Corporation," hereby establishes a plan to be known as the "Big Bucks, Inc. WAGE CONTINUATION PLAN," hereinafter referred to as the "Plan."

II

PURPOSE

The purpose of the Plan is to set forth a procedure whereby the Corporation will make payments to certain employees which will constitute wages or payments in lieu of wages for a period during which such employees are absent from work due to personal injuries or sickness.

III

ELIGIBILITY

All corporate officer-employees shall be covered by the Plan.

IV

BENEFITS

Subject to conditions and limitations hereinafter set forth, each covered employee shall receive disability benefits during periods of absence from his employment on account of disability due to sickness or accident and resulting in his total inability to perform the duties of his employment, in an amount equal to full compensation, beginning on the first day of such disability and continuing for a period not to exceed a total of twelve (12) months. Payment of benefits hereunder shall be made at the time any covered employee would have received compensation payments if he had not been absent from his employment.

V

CONDITIONS AND LIMITATIONS

The following conditions and limitations shall apply with respect to the payment of disability benefits under the Plan:

A. Disability payments shall not be payable:

    (1) For any period of disability due to willfully and intentionally self-inflicted injury, or to injury sustained in the perpetration by the employee of a felony;

    (2) For any period during which the employee performs any work for remuneration or profit;

    (3) For any period during which any employee would be disqualified for unemployment compensation benefits under the laws of the State of California, unless the disability commenced prior to such disqualification.

B. Disability payments otherwise required hereunder shall be reduced by an amount paid concurrently under any governmental or private retirement, pension or permanent disability benefit or allowance program to which the Corporation contributed on behalf of a covered employee.

C. In the event proof of disability is requested by the Corporation, disability payments shall be conditioned upon the covered employee furnishing the Corporation with satisfactory proof of disability within thirty (30) days after the commencement of the period of disability.

VI

TERMINATION OF COVERAGE

Coverage of any officer-employee shall terminate at the end of the month in which such employee terminates his employment with the Corporation. Such coverage shall terminate irrespective of the fact that employment may terminate during a period of disability for which payments are being made hereunder.

VII

TERMINATION OF PLAN

The Corporation may alter, amend, modify, suspend or terminate the Plan at any time.

IN WITNESS WHEREOF, the Corporation by its duly authorized officers has caused these presents to be executed this 1st day of February 1979.

BIG BUCKS, INC.
(A California Corporation)

By _____
    HERBERT BUCKSUP, President

By _____
    BETTY BUCKSUP, Secretary

[¶906] EMPLOYMENT CONTRACT

The purpose of the employment contract (see pages 269 to 271) is to formally state the financial arrangement between the corporation and key employees.

The following form provides flexibility by stating the fact that the employee may receive an annual bonus. It also contains a provision relating to repayment by the employee of payments to him if the IRS does not allow the corporation to deduct such payments. This is the provision which reduces the possibility that the IRS will attempt to treat a portion of a stockholder's compensation as a dividend.

An employment agreement is important even in a one-man corporation. In order to receive the benefits available to corporate employees, the business must be handled as a corporation.

EMPLOYMENT AGREEMENT

THIS AGREEMENT shall be effective as of the 1st day of February 1979, between Big Bucks, Inc., A California Corporation (hereinafter called "Employer"), and Herbert Bucksup (hereinafter called "Employee").

I

CONTRACT

Employer hereby employs and Employee hereby accepts employment upon the terms and conditions herein set forth.

II

TERM

Subject to the provisions for termination as hereinafter provided, the term of this Agreement shall be one (1) year; provided, however, that the Agreement shall be renewed automatically from year to year, upon the terms and conditions herein set forth provided the services of Employee are satisfactory.

III

SERVICES TO BE RENDERED

Employee is employed to serve as President and General Manager to render services for and on behalf of the Employer. If Employee is elected as a director of Employer, Employee agrees to serve in such capacity or capacities without additional compensation.

IV

FULL-TIME SERVICES

Employee shall be required to devote his full time to the business of Employer.

V

COMPENSATION

Employer shall pay Employee, as compensation for the services to be rendered, the following amounts:

A. A salary of $4,000 per month, payable on the last day of each month, commencing February 28, 1979.

B. An annual bonus in an amount to be determined in the sole discretion of the Board of Directors of Employer. In determining the amount of bonus, the Board of Directors will attempt to provide that the total annual compensation paid to the Employee will be equal to the reasonable value of the services rendered to the Employer by the Employee.

In the event that any part of any form of compensation paid by the Employer to the Employee shall be disallowed in whole or in part as a deductible expense of the Employer by the Internal Revenue Service, Employee shall reimburse the Employer for the expense for which a deduction was disallowed. Such reimbursement by the Employee shall be made within thirty (30) days after the Employer has notified the Employee of the amount of disallowed expense deduction.

In the event the full reimbursement is not made within said thirty (30) day period, the Employer shall have the right to withhold the unpaid balance or any portion thereof from future compensation payments. The reimbursement, if any, required hereunder may not be waived by the Employer.

VI

VACATION, LEAVES OF ABSENCE AND SICK LEAVE

1. Employee shall be entitled to such vacations as the Board of Directors shall from time to time establish. Employee shall be entitled to receive his regular salary during any such agreed period of absence.

2. In the event illness prevents Employee from discharging all of his duties, he may be allowed to continue to be employed in a limited capacity for a restricted period of time upon a vote of the Board of Directors. Such continued employment may be at a reduced rate of compensation if the Board of Directors so requires.

VII

AGREEMENT BINDING ALL ASSIGNS

This Agreement shall bind all parties, their respective heirs, executors, administrators and assigns, but nothing contained herein shall be construed as an authorization or right of any party to assign his rights or obligations hereunder.

VIII

ARBITRATION

If at any time during the continuance of this Agreement any disputes shall arise and the difference cannot be satisfactorily resolved within a period of sixty (60) days, it shall be determined and settled by arbitration to be held in Los Angeles, California, in accordance with the rules then obtaining of the American Arbitration Association. Any award rendered therein shall be final and binding on both parties hereto, and judgment may be entered thereon in the Superior Court of the State of California for the County of Los Angeles.

IX

APPLICABLE LAW

The provisions of this Agreement shall be governed and interpreted in accordance with the laws of the State of California.

IN WITNESS WHEREOF, the parties hereto have executed this Agreement the day and year first above written.

BIG BUCKS, INC.
(A California Corporation)

By _____
HERBERT BUCKSUP, President
"EMPLOYER"

_____
HERBERT BUCKSUP,
"EMPLOYEE"

[¶907] STOCK RESTRICTION (BUY-SELL) AGREEMENT

The following agreement is a cross-purchase agreement (see pages 275 to 280) between the stwo stockholders. The Agreement accomplishes a number of things:

☐ It provides how the stock should be valued;

☐ It sets the procedure to be followed if either stockholder wants to dispose of his stock voluntarily;

☐ In the event of the death of either stockholder, the survivor is required to purchase the stock of the deceased stockholder.

The Agreement also has provisions for a stockholder who becomes disabled or otherwise terminates his employment with the corporation.

By having stockholders enter into such an agreement at the outset, many future disputes may be avoided.

CROSS-PURCHASE AGREEMENT

This Stock Restriction Agreement is made and entered into as of this 1st day of February 1979, by and between HERBERT BUCKSUP and BETTY BUCKSUP;

WITNESSETH:

WHEREAS, Herbert Bucksup is the record and beneficial owner of 12,500 shares of the Common Stock, without par value, of Big Bucks, Inc., A California Corporation (hereinafter referred to as the "Company"), and Betty Bucksup is the record and beneficial owner of 12,500 shares of the Common Stock, without par value, of the Company; and

WHEREAS, the parties hereto are desirous of restricting the transfer of the Company's Common Stock and providing for the purchase of the Company's Common Stock under certain circumstances.

NOW, THEREFORE, in consideration of the premises and of the mutual covenants of the parties hereunto contained, it is hereby agreed as follows:

1. *Definitions of Terms.* For purposes of this agreement, the following terms are defined as follows:

(a) The *"Shareholders"* are Herbert Bucksup, Betty Bucksup, or their respective personal representatives following the death of either of them.

(b) The *"Fair Market Value"* of each share of the Company's Common Stock, without par value, is equal to the net book value of the Company as at the end of the month preceding the occurrence of the event which requires the computation of Fair Market Value divided by the total number of shares of Common Stock of the Company then outstanding, provided, however, that in computing the net book value of the Company any real property and buildings owned by the Company shall be valued according to an appraisal made by a qualified independent appraiser within 12 months before or 2 months after the date of the event which requires the computation of the Fair Market Value.

(c) The *"Optional Purchase Procedure"* shall be implemented and followed according to the procedures herein set forth after written notice of the implementation of the Optional Purchase Procedure is given to the remaining Shareholder as required hereby. Once commenced, the Optional Purchase Procedure shall be irrevocable except by agreement of the Shareholders. Such notice shall set forth the reasons that the Optional Purchase Procedure is invoked, the number of shares which may be purchased upon exercise thereof (the "Offered Shares") and the price, terms and conditions upon which the Offered Shares may be purchased. If the price upon which the Offered Shares may be purchased depends upon completion of an appraisal of the Company's land and buildings, such notice shall state that fact and shall be supplemented with the appraisal data and the amount of the price when the appraisal is completed, and such notice shall be considered final and effective upon the delivery of such supplement.

Upon receipt of the notice of commencement of the Optional Purchase Procedure, the remaining Shareholder shall be entitled to purchase the Offered Shares for the Fair Market Value, 10% of which shall be paid as a down payment and the balance of which shall be represented by a promissory note bearing interest at the rate of 7½% per annum with principal and interest payable in equal quarterly installments over the period of ten years commencing on the date of purchase. The right of the remaining Shareholder to purchase the Offered Shares shall continue for a period of ninety days after he receives the aforementioned notice. The remaining Shareholder may exercise his right to purchase the Offered Shares by giving written notice thereof to the selling Shareholder and tendering to him the appropriate down payment and pormissory note. In order for the Optional Purchase Procedure to be exercised, it shall be necessary for the remaining Shareholder to purchase all of the Offered Shares and not some lesser portion thereof. In the event the remaining Shareholder does not exercise his right to purchase under the "Optional Purchase Procedure" within the prescribed period, the offering Shareholder may dispose of the Offered Shares to a third party or parties upon whatever terms and conditions he deems appropriate.

(d) The *"Compulsory Purchase Procedure"* shall be implemented and followed according to the procedures herein set forth after written notice of the implementation of the Compulsory Purchase Procedure is given to the remaining Shareholder as required hereby. Such notice shall set forth the reasons that the Compulsory Purchase procedure is invoked, the number of shares which are to be purchased pursuant thereto (the "Purchased Shares") and the price, terms and conditions upon which the Purchased Shares are to be purchased. If the price upon which the Purchased Shares are to be purchased depends upon the completion of an appraisal of the Company's land and buildings, such notice shall state that fact and shall be supplemented with the appraisal data and the amount of the price when the appraisal is completed, and such notice shall be considered final and effective upon the delivery of such supplement.

Upon receipt of the notice of commencement of the Compulsory Purchase Procedure, the remaining Shareholder shall purchase all of the Purchased Shares for the Fair Market Value and such purchase shall be completed within 3 months after receiving such notice. Such purchase shall be on the terms set forth in the respective paragraph under which the Compulsory Purchase Procedure arises and shall be exercised by delivering to the selling Shareholder the appropriate down payment and promissory note.

2. *Voluntary Sale.* Should either of the Shareholders desire to sell, assign or otherwise transfer all or any number of the shares of Common Stock of the Company at any time owned by him, such Shareholder may give written notice of this desire to the remaining Shareholder. Such notice shall state the number of shares that such Shareholder desires to sell (the "Offered Shares") and shall commence the Optional Purchase Procedure pursuant to which the remaining Shareholder who receives such notice may purchase the Offered Shares. The price to be paid for the Offered Shares shall be the Fair Market Value, and 10% of such price shall be paid as a down payment, and the balance shall be represented by a promissory note bearing interest at the rate of 7½% per annum with principal and interest payable in equal quarterly installments over a period of ten years commencing on the date of purchase.

3. *Death of a Shareholder.* Should either of the Shareholders die, his estate shall give written notice of such death to the remaining Shareholder and such notice shall commence the Compulsory Purchase Procedure as of the date of such notice as to all of the shares of the Company's Common Stock owned by the deceased Shareholder on the date of his death (the "Purchased Shares"). The purchase price to be paid for the Purchased Shares shall be the Fair Market Value, and such price shall be paid 25% down at the time of purchase with the balance represented by a promissory note bearing interest at the rate of 7½% per annum with principal and interest payable in equal quarterly in-

stallments over a period of ten years commencing on the date of purchase.

4. *Disability of a Shareholder.* Should either of the Shareholders become permanently disabled, he shall give written notice of such disability to the remaining Shareholder and such notice shall commence the Optional Purchase Procedure as of the date of such notice as to all of the shares of the Company's Common Stock owned by the disabled Shareholder on the date of such disability (the "Offered Shares").

In the event that either of the Shareholders becomes so disabled that he is not able to perform his usual duties in the active conduct of the Company's business but said disabled Shareholder does not consider himself to be permanently disabled as contemplated by the provisions of this agreement, the remaining Shareholder may submit the questions of his disability to competent medical authority. In such event, each of the Shareholders shall appoint a Medical Doctor, and the two Medical Doctors so appointed shall appoint a third Medical Doctor, and all three of such Medical Doctors shall independently examine the allegedly disabled Shareholder and determine whether he is so disabled that he is not likely to be able to perform his usual duties in the active conduct of the Company's business for at least the 6 month period from the date of such examination. If, in the opinion of two of such Medical Doctors, the allegedly disabled Shareholder is so disabled, he shall be considered to be "permanently disabled" for purposes of this agreement and the Optional Purchase Procedure shall commence as of the date that the last of said Medical Doctors renders his written opinion in the matter.

5. *Termination of Employment.* In the event that the employment by the Company of either of the Shareholders is terminated for any reason whatsoever (except for the death or disability as contemplated by paragraphs 3 and 4 hereof) whether by the Company or voluntarily by the respective Shareholder, and whether or not for good cause, the Company shall give written notice of such termination to the remaining Shareholder on the date of termination or as soon thereafter as practicable, and such notice shall cause the Optional Purchase Procedure to be implemented as to all of the shares of the Company's Common Stock owned by the terminated Shareholder on the date of such termination (the "Offered Shares").

6. *Limitation on Other Transactions.* Each of the Shareholders agrees that he will not sell, assign or otherwise transfer, for a valuable consideration or otherwise, and that he will not pledge or hypothecate,

all or any number of the shares of Common Stock of the Company at any time owned by him, respectively, except with the written consent of the other Shareholder or pursuant to the provisions of this agreement. The right of each of the Shareholders to sell his shares of the Company's Common Stock is governed exclusively by this agreement.

7. *Certificate Legend.* Each and all of the stock certificates representing shares of the Common Stock of the Company which are owned by the Shareholders, or otherwise subject to this agreement, shall bear a legend in the following form: "The shares represented by this certificate may not be pledged, hypothecated, sold or transferred except in compliance with a Stock Restriction Agreement dated February 1, 1979, a copy of which is on file at the principal office of the Corporation."

8. *Miscellaneous Matters*

(a) Any notice or other communication required or permitted hereunder shall be sufficiently given if delivered personally or sent by registered or certified mail, postage prepaid and return receipt requested, to the address of the parties set forth at the end of this agreement or at such addresses as may have been provided in like manner in writing to all other parties hereto. Any notice which is sent by mail in accordance with this agreement shall not be considered to be received until it is actually delivered to the premises of the party to whom it is addressed.

(b) Should any one or more of the provisions hereof be determined to be illegal or unenforceable, all other provisions hereof shall be given effect separately therefrom and shall not be affected thereby.

(c) This agreement shall be binding upon and inure to the benefit of the respective parties hereto and their respective executors, administrators, personal representatives, heirs and legatees.

(d) In any action at law or in equity to enforce any of the provisions or rights under this agreement, the unsuccessful party to such litigation, as determined by the Court in a final judgment or decree, shall pay the successful party or parties all costs, expenses and reasonable attorneys' fees incurred therein by such party or parties (including without limitation such costs, expenses and fees on any appeals), and if such successful party shall recover judgment in any such action or proceeding such costs, expenses and attorneys' fees shall be included in as part of such judgment.

(e) It is the intention of the parties that the laws of California should govern the validity of this agreement, the construction of its terms and the interpretation of the rights and duties of the parties.

(f) This agreement shall terminate and be of no further force or effect following the effectiveness of any merger or consolidation to which the Company is not the surviving party, sale of substantially all of the Company's assets, complete liquidation of the Company, or issuance of the Company's Common Stock in any "public offering" within the contemplation of the Securities Act of 1933. Unless terminated sooner in accordance with the foregoing, this agreement shall terminate when one or the other of the Shareholders has purchased all of the other Shareholder's shares of the Company's Common Stock. Any such termination shall not limit or otherwise affect or terminate the rights and obligations or any of the Shareholders which have arisen or may arise pursuant to any Compulsory Purchase Procedure or Optional Purchase Procedure which has been commenced prior to any such termination.

(g) This agreement may be executed in separate counterparts which shall collectively and separately be considered one and the same agreement.

IN WITNESS WHEREOF, the parties hereto have executed this Stock Restriction Agreement as of the day and year first above written.

_____

HERBERT BUCKSUP

Address:

123 Easy Street
Beverly Hills, California

_____

BETTY BUCKSUP

Address:

567 Hard Way
Beverly Hills, California

If changes are made in the preceding forms to provide for differences in specific items which may vary from situation to situation, they may also be used in the majority of cases involving closely-held corporations. It is important to determine a reason for adopting each of the various programs. If a specific reason is designated, an intelligent decision can be made with respect to which programs should be adopted and what the programs should contain by way of coverage and the level of benefits.

[¶908] QUALIFIED RETIREMENT PLANS

One of the primary factors that makes incorporation of a closely-held business advantageous is the ability to provide substantial benefits to owner-employees through the adoption of qualified retirement plans. Once a business has been incorporated and has commenced operations, a qualified retirement plan may be adopted. If a plan is adopted prior to the end of the corporation's taxable year, the plan will be retroactive to the beginning of the taxable year. If a plan is established prior to the end of the taxable year, contributions can be made and any earnings on the contributions will begin to earn tax-deferred income from the date of contribution. If the owners do not contemplate making contributions prior to the end of the corporation's taxable year, the adoption of a qualified plan does not have to be immediate. Also, it is not necessary to receive the approval of the IRS prior to the end of the corporation's fiscal year. If the application to the IRS is made within the time permitted for filing the corporation's income tax returns (including any allowable extensions), no problems will be incurred. The corporation can make any amendments requested by the Service and such amendments will be retroactive to the beginning of the year in which the plan was adopted.

On pages 285–373 are forms that will enable a corporation to adopt a qualified retirement plan or plans. The specific provisions will have to be tailored to individual situations. Normally, the number of items to be changed will be relatively few. For example, if it has been determined that a corporation should adopt a profit-sharing plan and/or a pension plan, the only items that need to be determined to prepare the plan or plans from the following forms are:

☐ Who should be the trustee;

☐ The fiscal year of the plan (normally the same as the fiscal year for the corporation);

☐ Whether or not voluntary contributions by participants will be permitted (if two plans are adopted only one should permit voluntary contributions);

☐ Whether any employees are to be excluded (for example, union employees whose retirement benefits have been the subject of good faith bargaining);

☐ Whether the plan should be integrated with Social Security;

☐ The desired vesting schedule;

☐ Whether or not loans to participants will be permitted (if loans are to be allowed the plan must specifically authorize them in the manner stated in the forms); and

☐ Who should be on the administrative committee (normally the shareholders of directors).

All the other provisions in the sample forms are "boilerplate" language. It has been accepted by the IRS as properly complying with the provisions of the Internal Revenue Code and Regulations which state what a plan and trust must include in order to be a qualified pension or profit sharing plan. Except for the optional items listed above, the language contained in the forms must appear, or the plan will not be qualified. Most of the provisions are self-explanatory.

[¶908.1] How to Set Up Qualified Retirement Plans

The first form is a profit-sharing plan and trust (see pages 285 to 330). The second form is a money-purchase pension plan (see pages 331 to 373) that has been integrated with Social Security. If two plans are adopted, only one may use an allocation formula that integrates with Social Security.

A form for a defined benefit pension plan is not included

because the number of variables involved in different cases is extremely high, and a sample form would be of no practical use. Also, since an insurance company or actuaries are involved, in the administration of defined benefit pension plans, they normally provide forms to be used and obtain the IRS approval. It is important to note that the plan is a legal document and must be approved by an attorney.

[¶908.2] Profit-Sharing Plan and Trust

A profit-sharing plan (see pages 285 to 330) is flexible. The corporation may decide each year how much, if any, it will contribute to the plan. The annual deduction for contributions cannot exceed 15% of the compensation paid to participants with certain permissible carryovers. For instance, if a plan contributed only 10% of the participant's compensation for one year, it could use the additional 5% in a future year, i.e., it could contribute 20% the next year.

Remember that contributions to a profit-sharing plan may only be made out of current or accumulated profits.

Forfeitures which result from participants leaving before they have a fully vested interest in their accounts are reallocated among the remaining participants.

[¶908.3] Money-Purchase Pension Plan and Trust

A money-purchase pension plan (see pages 331 to 373 calls for an annual contribution equal to a specified percentage of participants' compensation. The fixed percentage may not exceed 25%.

Unlike a profit-sharing plan, the annual contribution is to be made whether or not the corporation has current or accumulated profits.

Forfeitures which result from participants leaving before they have a fully vested interest in their accounts reduce the company's required contribution. They are not reallocated among other participants as they are in the case of a profit-sharing plan.

BIG BUCKS, INC.

EMPLOYEES' PROFIT-SHARING PLAN
AND TRUST AGREEMENT

BIG BUCKS, INC.

EMPLOYEES' PROFIT-SHARING PLAN
AND TRUST AGREEMENT

TABLE OF CONTENTS

BIG BUCKS, INC.

EMPLOYEES' PROFIT-SHARING PLAN
AND TRUST AGREEMENT

WHEREAS, BIG BUCKS, INC., A California Corporation, desires to create a profit-sharing plan and trust for the exclusive benefit of its employees who qualify under the terms and conditions thereof;

NOW, THEREFORE, BIG BUCKS, INC., A California Corporation, hereby adopts a profit-sharing plan and trust, as follows:

ARTICLE I

DESIGNATION OF TRUST AND DEFINITIONS

1.1—Title.

This profit-sharing plan and trust shall be known as BIG BUCKS, INC., A California Corporation, EMPLOYEES' PROFIT-SHARING PLAN AND TRUST AGREEMENT. The Plan and Trust are designated and intended to qualify under the appropriate provisions of the Internal Revenue Code.

1.2—Definitions.

"Account" or "profit sharing account" means the account maintained by the Committee for each Participant as required by Article V.

"Anniversary Date" shall mean the last day of each fiscal year.

"Beneficiary" or "beneficiaries" means the person or persons last designated by a Participant as set forth in Section 2.3, or if there is no designated beneficiary, then to the Participant's surviving spouse, and if no surviving spouse, then equally to the surviving issue, and if none, then to the Participant's estate, or if there is no legal representative appointed to represent his estate within sixty (60) days after the Participant's death and his vested interest does not exceed Two Thousand Dollars ($2,000.00), to his heirs-at-law, under the laws of California then in force and effect.

"Committee" shall mean the Committee described in Article VII hereof.

"Company" shall mean BIG BUCKS, INC., A California Corporation.

"Compensation" shall mean the full regular basic salary and hourly wages, including overtime, bonuses, and commissions, but excluding health and welfare or any other payments before deductions authorized by the Employee or required by law to be withheld from the Employee by the Company.

"Employee" shall mean any person who is employed by the Company.

"Year of Service" for purposes of vesting and eligibility upon reemployment shall mean any twelve (12) month period during which an Employee has completed One Thousand (1,000) Hours of Service with the first twelve (12) month period to commence on the date of his employment. Year of Service for purposes of benefit accrual shall be the Plan Fiscal Year in which a Participant completes at least 1,000 Hours of Service, except that an Employee who first becomes a Participant pursuant to Section 2.1 shall be deemed to have completed a Year of Service as of the Anniversary Date upon which he becomes a Participant.

A "One Year Break in Service" shall be deemed to occur in each twelve (12) month period following the employment commencement date or any anniversary thereof during which the Employee has no more than 500 Hours of Service.

"Hour of Service" shall mean each hour for which (1) an employee is paid, or entitled to payment, for performance of duties for the Company, (2) an employee is paid, or entitled to payment, for nonperformance of duties, and (3) back pay, irrespective of mitigation of damages, is either awarded or agreed to by the Company. Hours shall not be credited under both (3) and (1) or (2). Hours for nonperformance of duties shall be credited in accordance with Department of Labor Regulations Section 2530.200b-2(b). Hours shall be credited to the applicable computation period in accordance with Department of Labor Regulations Section 2530.200b-2(c).

"Effective Date" shall mean February 1, 1979.

"Fiscal Year" shall mean each year beginning on the first day of February and ending on the last day of January.

"Net profits" shall mean the amount of Net Profit for the particular taxable year as calculated for Federal Income Tax purposes, before provisions for Federal Income Taxes and without deduction of the contributions to this trust for each year.

"Participant" shall mean an Employee of the Company who has been admitted to participation in the Plan and for whom a portion of the Company contributions is allocated.

"Plan" or "Trust" shall mean the Employees' Profit-Sharing Plan and Trust set forth in this Agreement and all subsequent amendments thereto.

"Trustees" shall mean that person or those persons appointed to be Trustees by the Board of Directors of the Company. The initial Trustee shall be HERBERT BUCKSUP.

"The Act" shall mean the Employee Retirement Income Security Act of 1974, or any future amendments thereto.

"Fiduciary" shall mean any person who exercises any discretionary authority or control respecting the management or disposition of trust assets or has any discretionary authority or responsibility in the administration of this Plan.

"Named Fiduciary" shall mean the fiduciary or fiduciaries who are named in the Plan and who jointly or severally shall have authority to control and manage the operation and administration of the Plan.

"Investment Manager" shall mean fiduciary as defined in Section 3(38) of the Act, which fiduciary has fully complied with the provisions of Section 3(38) of the Act and who has provided the Committee and the Trustee with written acknowledgment that he has done so and that he is a fiduciary with respect to this Plan.

ARTICLE II

PARTICIPATION

2.1—Commencement of Participation.

All employees of the Company shall commence participation on the Anniversary Date coinciding with or following the expiration of six (6) months from their date of employment.

2.2—Certification by Company.

Within thirty (30) days after each anniversary date of the Plan, the Company shall transmit to the Committee certified lists of the employees entitled to participate in the Plan as of any such anniversary date. Such certified lists shall be in such form and contain such information as the Committee may desire, and except in the case of a mistake, such certified lists shall not be questioned by the Committee.

2.3—Enrollment of Participant and Designation of Beneficiary.

Upon receipt of notification from the Committee that he is a Participant in the Plan, an Employee may designate, in writing, the beneficiary whom he desires to receive the benefits provided by the Plan in the event of his death, such designation to be filed on the form provided for that purpose by the Committee. A Participant may from time to time change his designated beneficiary hereunder without the consent of such beneficiary by filing such designation in writing with the Committee; and the Committee, the Company and the Trustees shall be authorized to rely upon the designation last filed with the Committee in acting in accordance with the terms of this Agreement.

2.4—Duration of Participation.

Participation of a Participant shall continue during his subsequent employment until the anniversary date coinciding with or preceding the actual termination of his employment for any reason, including retirement, at which time it shall terminate. A Participant may not voluntarily withdraw from participation or receive any distribution of his benefits from the Plan.

2.5—Retirement.

The normal retirement date shall be the anniversary date coinciding with or next preceding the date of a Participant's sixty-fifth (65th) birthday. While this Plan provides for the Participant's normal retirement date, such Participant may continue his employment after that time with approval of the Company.

2.6—Participation after Normal Retirement Date.

If, by mutual agreement between the Participant and the Company's Board of Directors, the Participant continues in the service of the Company beyond his normal retirement date, he shall continue to participate in the Plan during such continued employment.

2.7—Reparticipation by Former Participant.

A former Participant shall become a Participant immediately upon his return to employ, if, (1) such former Participant had a nonforfeitable right to all or a portion of his account balance derived from Company contributions at the time of his termination; or, (2) the former Participant's Years of Service before his termination exceed the number of consecutive one-year breaks in service after such termination. A former Participant who did not have a nonforfeitable right to any portion of his account balance derived from Company contributions at the time of his termination shall be considered a new Employee for eligibility purposes if the number of consecutive one-year breaks in service equals or exceeds the aggregate number of Years of Service before such break.

ARTICLE III
COMPANY CONTRIBUTIONS

3.1—Obligation.

Concurrently with the execution of this instrument, the Company has paid to the Trustee the sum of One Hundred Dollars ($100.00) on account of its initial contribution to the trust and, subject to its rights under Article X, will make additional contributions for each Fiscal Year in an amount determined as set forth in Section 3.3, said contributions to be held and administered by the Trustees, in trust, pursuant to the terms of this Agreement.

3.2—Payment.

All payments of contributions shall be made directly to the Trustees and may be made on any date or dates selected by the Company, provided that the total annual contributions for each fiscal year shall be paid within the time allowed by the pertinent provisions of the applicable Federal Tax Laws to obtain a tax deduction for that year. The Trustees shall have no duty to demand payment of a contribution, and shall not be responsible for the accuracy thereof.

3.3—Company Contribution Formula.

The profit-sharing contribution to be made by the Company each year shall be determined by the Board of Directors of said Company in its sole discretion; provided, however, that the contribution shall be made only out of current or accumulated net profits and shall be reflected in a resolution of the Board of Directors adopted prior to the end of the year to which the contribution is applicable. The total contribution shall not exceed fifteen percent (15%) of the remuneration paid to participating employees, plus carryover amounts if available for such fiscal year.

ARTICLE IV

PARTICIPANTS' CONTRIBUTIONS

4.1—Elective Contributions.

Subject to the provisions of paragraph 4.4 of this Article, each Participant may, in his sole discretion, contribute to the trust fund during each fiscal year, an amount which, at his election, may be an even percentage of his compensation but in an amount which shall not cause his total voluntary contributions under all qualified retirement plans to exceed ten percent (10%) of the compensation paid by the Company to him during the period of his participation.

4.2—Manner of Election and Payment.

Each employee who is a Participant hereunder and each employee who shall thereafter become a Participant hereunder shall indicate in writing to the Company the percentage of his compensation which he desires to contribute to the fund, and such percentage shall continue from year to year unless changed as hereinafter provided. Such amount so indicated shall be contributed by the Participant or deducted in equal installments so far as possible by the Company employing such Participant on each payday from the compensation paid to such Participant with respect to such period. In the event that the amount so deducted with respect to a Participant during the year is less or more than the amount designated by the Participant as his contribution under the terms of this Plan, the required adjustments shall be made in his last paycheck of the year.

4.3—Amending Contributions.

Each Participant shall have the right, during the thirty (30) day period ending either on June 30th or December 31st in any year, to increase or decrease within the limits theretofore mentioned and subject to the provisions set forth in paragraph 4.4 of this Article, the amount to be deducted as his contribution to the Fund. Such amendment shall be accomplished by filing with the Committee a written statement to that effect upon such form as shall be provided by the Committee. Such change shall remain in effect until a further change is made in accordance with this paragraph.

4.4—Amending Contributions
As Required by Company.

Notwithstanding anything to the contrary contained in any paragraph of this Article, if the Company shall be of the opinion that the contribution or contributions of any Participant or group of Participants will or might result in discrimination in favor of employees who are officers, shareholders, supervisors, or highly compensated employees, the Company shall have the right to cause such adjustments to be made in the future contribution or contributions of the Participant or Participants involved as will, in the opinion of the Company, avoid such discrimination. The decision of the Company in this regard shall be final.

4.5—Payment to Trustees.

All Participants' contributions or deductions by the Company of Participants' contributions in accordance with the terms and provisions of this Article shall be held in trust by the Company until paid over to the Trustee at such time or times as may be convenient to the Company but not less frequently than once every thirty (30) days.

ARTICLE V

ALLOCATION TO PARTICIPANTS' ACCOUNTS

5.1—Participant's Profit-Sharing Account.

At the commencement of this Trust, the Committee shall open a separate account for each Participant, and as of each Anniversary Date of this Plan, the Committee shall open a separate account for each new Participant who shall have then become eligible to participate in the Plan and Trust.

5.2—Participants' Contributions.

The contributions of a participating employee shall be credited to his account on each Anniversary Date.

5.3—Annual Contributions.

The Company's contribution and forfeitures for each Fiscal Year shall be allocated as of each Anniversary Date to the profit sharing account of all Participants who have completed a year of service for purposes of benefit accrual on such date in the proportion that the amount of compensation received by him during such Fiscal Year bears to the total amount of compensation received by all Participants during the Fiscal Year.

The annual additions to a Participant's account (including the additions to any other defined contribution plan to which the Company contributes for such Participant's benefit) during any Fiscal Year shall not exceed the lesser of $25,000 (subject to any annual cost-of-living increases permissible pursuant to the terms of the Act or corresponding provisions of subsequent revenue laws and/or regulations) or twenty-five percent (25%) of such Participant's compensation from the Company during such Fiscal Year.

The term "annual additions" means the sum of:

(a) The Company's contribution;
(b) forfeitures reallocated to such Participant's account pursuant to Section 5.4 of the Plan; and
(c) the lesser of:
  (i) one-half (½) of the Participant's contribution, or
  (ii) such Participant's contribution in excess of six percent (6%) of his compensation from the Company during the Fiscal Year.

Annual additions shall not include rollovers from a qualified plan or an individual retirement account. Any excess annual additions shall be placed in a suspense account and shall be treated as a forfeiture on the following Anniversary Date. The amount of the suspense account shall remain constant until such Anniversary Date.

5.4—Forfeitures.

Annually, as of each Anniversary Date, the forfeitures of the participating employees of the Company caused by a One Year Break in Service of each such Employee which occurs during the Plan Year ending on such Anniversary Date shall be allocated to the accounts of Participants, excluding Participants who became Participants on the Anniversary Date of such allocation, in the same manner as the Company's contribution.

5.5—Annual Revaluation.

Commencing with the Second Anniversary Date, the Committee shall revalue the account of each Participant so as to reflect any increase or decrease in the fair market value of the assets of the fund (including the income and earnings of, and expenditures from, the Fund) as of that Anniversary Date as compared with the value of the assets of the Fund as of the last preceding Anniversary Date, and such increase or decrease shall be allocated to the Participants in the proportion that the amount in the Participant's account bears to the total amount of all Participant's accounts of the Company as of the last preceding Anniversary Date. Neither the Company nor the Trustees nor any members of the Committee shall, in any manner or to any extent whatsoever, warrant, guarantee, or represent that the value of the Participant's account shall at any time equal or exceed the aggregate amount previously contributed thereto by the Company and the Participant.

5.6—Interim Revaluation.

The profit sharing account of a Participant whose participation is terminated on other than an Anniversary Date shall be valued currently for the purpose of distribution only in the event of a substantial change in the fair market value of trust assets. In such case, the Committee shall determine, as of the end of the calendar month in which the participation of an employee terminated, the fair market value of the net trust assets in order to determine the percentage of increase or decrease in the fair market value of such assets as of the preceding

Anniversary Date. The cumulative amount allocated as of the preceding Anniversary Date to the profit sharing account of such Participant shall, for the purpose of distribution only, be adjusted to reflect the increase or decrease, as the case may be, by multiplying such amount by the percentage so determined.

This interim revaluation shall not affect any amount to be forfeited under Section 6.4, and any increase or decrease so distributed or retained with respect to the profit sharing account to the former Participant shall merely increase or decrease unallocated assets for the purpose of the annual revaluation required by Section 5.5.

Interim revaluations shall be made in a uniform and nondiscriminatory manner.

ARTICLE VI

BENEFITS

6.1—Participants' Contributions.

Each Participant, or employee who was a Participant whose service as an employee of the Company is terminated for any reason, shall be entitled to receive the adjusted value of his contributions to the Plan as of the Anniversary Date preceding termination of service plus the amount of his cash contributions during the year of termination of services. Contributions by Participants shall not be subject to forfeiture and may be distributed at the direction of the Committee in the same manner as the benefits derived from the Company contributions as provided in Section 6.3.

In the event of an employee's or Participant's death prior to receiving all of the benefits attributable to his contributions, such unpaid benefits shall be paid to his beneficiaries, otherwise to his executor or administrator in accordance with Section 6.3.

6.2—Vesting of Company Contributions.

The interest of each Participant in the Company contributions account allocated to his benefit shall vest in accordance with the following provisions:

(a) If the employment of any Participant is terminated for any cause other than death, disability or retirement, such Participant shall have a nonforfeitable vested right in his Company contributions account determined as of the Anniversary Date coinciding with or next preceding the occurrence of a One Year Break in Service in accordance with the following schedule:

Years of Service with Company	Vested Interest
Less than 1 Year of Service	–0–
1 Year but less than 2 Years of Service	20%
2 Years but less than 3 Years of Service	40%
3 Years but less than 4 Years of Service	60%
4 Years but less than 5 Years of Service	80%
5 Years or more of Service	100%

In computing the period of service for the purpose of determining the percentage of nonforfeitable vested interest, a Participant's entire service with the Company shall be taken into account.

(b) One Hundred Percent (100%) on reaching his Normal Retirement Date, death, a judicial declaration of his incompetence, or a determination by the Committee, based upon competent medical evidence, that his employment is terminated because of his becoming totally and permanently, physically or mentally, incapacitated.

The vesting of a Participant's interest in whole or in part shall not preclude the allocations and evaluations provided for under Article V.

6.3—Distribution of Benefits.

The benefit distributable to a Participant upon the termination of his participation or to the beneficiary or beneficiaries of a Participant who dies shall be the adjusted value of the amount credited under Section 5.2 to his account; plus the amount allocated to his account under Section 5.3, adjusted if necessary in accordance with Section 5.6, multiplied by the percentage of vested interest determined in accordance with Section 6.2; provided, however, that distribution shall not be made until a terminated Participant has incurred a One Year Break in Service. When a Participant ceases to participate, the Committee shall, with reasonable promptness, determine in its discretion the method of distribution of the Participant's vested interest to commence not later than his Normal Retirement Date which it deems to be in the best interests of the Participant, and shall authorize the Trustees to distribute his interest in any of the following ways:

(a) A Participant who retires at his Normal Retirement Date shall be entitled to retirement income benefits in the form of a straight-life annuity.

In the event such Participant and his spouse have been married throughout a one (1) year period ending on the annuity starting date, payment of such annuity benefits shall be made in the form having the effect of a qualified joint and survivor annuity.

A qualified joint and survivor annuity required to be paid under this paragraph to a Participant and his spouse shall be a monthly amount which is reduced from but which will be actuarially equivalent to the monthly amount of the single life annuity to which such participant would be otherwise entitled, but such reduction shall not exceed the estimated actuarial costs associated with providing qualified joint and survivor annuities.

The term "qualified joint and survivor annuity" means an annuity for the life of the Participant with a survivor annuity for the life of his spouse which is not less than one-half (½) nor more than one hundred percent (100%) of the amount of the annuity payable during the joint lives of the Participant and his spouse.

In the event a Participant dies on or after the date his Normal Retirement Age is attained while still in active service of the Company, or separates from service on or after his Normal Retirement Age is attained and thereafter dies before beginning to receive benefits under the Plan, the Participant's benefits will be paid in the form of a qualified joint and survivor annuity unless the Participant otherwise elects within the election period specified in the following paragraph.

Each Participant shall have a reasonable period (not less than 90 days) before the annuity starting date during which he may elect in writing (after receiving a written explanation of the terms and conditions of the joint and survivor annuity and the effect of an election under this paragraph) not to take the joint and survivor annuity. The election period shall not end more than 90 days before commencement of benefits but must end before commencement of benefits. Any election made during the election period is revocable during the election period.

(b) In the event the Participant elects not to take a joint and survivor annuity upon retirement at his Normal Retirement Date or in the event any Participant is terminated for any cause other than death, disability or retirement; the Committee may direct the Trustee to distribute the benefits to which a Participant is entitled in any of the modes of settlement set forth below or any combination thereof, provided that each such mode shall have the same present value:

(1) A cash lump sum; provided, however, that the benefits of a Participant cannot be cashed without his written consent if the value of his accrued benefits is in excess of $1,750; or

(2) Substantially equal installments payable not less frequently than annually to commence not later than sixty (60) days subsequent to his retirement; provided, however, that the benefits to which the Participant is entitled must be

paid over a period not exceeding the life expectancy of the Participant determined at the date of his retirement; provided further, that in the event distribution is to be made in the form of installments, the Committee shall direct the Trustee to segregate in a separate account an amount equal to the lump sum value and to invest it in United States Government obligations or to deposit it in an interest-bearing savings account of any bank, or to deposit it in an interest-bearing savings account of a federal savings and loan association. Any interest received thereon shall be distributed with the final installment of benefits. In the event a Participant dies prior to complete distribution of his installments, his Beneficiary shall be entitled to the balance; or

(3) A life annuity, which may be a straight-life annuity or a joint and survivor annuity, with or without cash or installment refund, with or without a period certain, purchased from a legal reserve life insurance company. In the event a joint and survivor annuity is elected for the Participant, the present value of the annuity payable to the Participant must be more than fifty percent (50%) of the present value of the benefit payable to both the Participant and the joint annuitant; or

(4) Upon written request of the Participant or his Beneficiary, approved by the Committee, distribution of the lump sum value may be made in shares issued by a regulated investment company registered under the Investment Company Act of 1940 or shares of stock listed on a National Stock Exchange.

6.4—Non-Vested Interests.

If any Participant incurs a One-Year Break in Service prior to death or retirement, such portion of the cumulative amount previously allocated to his account as of the coinciding or next preceding Anniversary Date as is not vested shall be forfeited and allocated in the manner provided in Section 5.4.

6.5—Commencement of Benefits.

Notwithstanding anything contained herein to the contrary, unless a Participant otherwise elects, the payment of benefits hereunder to any Participant shall commence not later than the sixtieth (60th) day after the latest of the close of the plan year in which:

(a) The date on which such Participant attains the earlier of age sixty-five (65), or the normal retirement age specified under the Plan,

(b) such Participant terminates his service with the Company.

No distribution shall be made until a former Participant has incurred a One-Year Break in Service unless such former Participant is fully vested.

6.6—Loans to Participants.

The Committee is hereby specifically authorized to direct the Trustee to make loans to Participants or beneficiaries of this Plan. Such loans shall be available to all Participants and beneficiaries. Notwithstanding the foregoing, no loan shall be made pursuant to the provisions of this Section unless it bears a reasonable rate of interest and unless the repayment of such loan is adequately secured. Any such loan shall be repaid in full within five (5) years.

ARTICLE VII

THE COMMITTEE

7.1—Members.

The Board of Directors of the Company shall, by resolution, appoint a Committee of three (3) to be known as the Committee, who shall serve at the pleasure of the Company. Vacancies in the Committee arising by resignation, death, removal by the Company or otherwise, shall be filled by the Company as soon as is reasonably possible after the vacancy occurs, and until a new appointment is made, the remaining members or member of the Committee shall have full authority to act. The Company shall file written notice of the names of the members of the Committee with the Trustee, and as changes take place in membership, the names of the new members. The initial members of the Committee shall be HERBERT BUCKSUP, BETTY BUCKSUP and FLO CASH.

Except as otherwise provided for herein, the Committee is the Named Fiduciary and Administrator of the Plan provided for by the Act, and shall have the authority to control and manage the operation and administration of this Plan.

7.2—Committee Action.

The Committee shall choose a secretary who shall keep the minutes of the Committee's proceedings and all data, records and documents pertaining to the Committee's administration of the Plan. The Committee shall act by a majority of its members at the time in office, and such action may be taken either by a vote at a meeting or in writing without a meeting. The Committee may by such majority action authorize its Secretary or any one or more of its members to execute any document or documents on behalf of the Committee, in which event the Committee shall notify the Trustees in writing of such action and the name or names of those so designated. The Trustees thereafter shall accept and rely conclusively upon any direction or document executed by such Secretary, member or members as representing action by the Committee until the Committee shall file with the Trustees a written revocation of such designation.

A member of the Committee who is also a Participant hereunder shall not vote or act upon any matter relating solely to himself.

7.3—Rights and Duties.

The Committee, on behalf of the Participants and their beneficiaries, shall enforce the Plan in accordance with its terms, shall be charged with the general administration of the Plan, and shall have all the powers necessary to accomplish those purposes, including but not by way of limitation, the following:

(a) To determine all questions relating to the eligibility of employees to participate;

(b) To compute and certify to the Trustees the amounts and kind of benefits payable to Participants and their beneficiaries;

(c) To authorize all disbursements by the Trustees from the Trust;

(d) To maintain all the necessary records for the administration of the Plan other than those maintained by the Trustees;

(e) To interpret the provisions of the Plan and to make and publish such rules for the regulation of the Plan as are not inconsistent with the terms hereof;

(f) To direct the Trustees in writing from time to time to purchase, retain, sell, or lease any property, real or personal, which the Committee may designate;

(g) To approve or disapprove investment changes recommended by the Trustees;

(h) The terms and provisions of this Plan shall not be administered in such a manner as to cause discrimination in favor of those employees who are officers, shareholders, persons whose principal duties consist of supervising the work of other employees, or highly compensated employees.

7.4—Information.

To enable the Committee to perform its functions, the Company shall supply full and timely information to the Committee on all matters pertaining to the compensation of all Participants, their continuous regular employment, their retirement, death, or the cause for termination of employment, and such other pertinent facts as the Committee may require; and the Committee shall furnish the Trustees such information as may be pertinent to the Trustees' administration of the Plan.

7.5—Compensation, Indemnity,
    and Liability.

All expenses of the Committee shall be paid by the Company, and the Company shall furnish the Committee with such clerical and other assistance as is necessary in the performance of its duties.

The Company hereby indemnifies and saves harmless each member of the Committee against any and all expenses and liabilities arising out of his membership on the Committee, excepting only expenses and liabilities arising out of his own wilful misconduct or gross negligence.

ARTICLE VIII

THE TRUSTEES

8.1—Acceptance by Trustees.

The Trustees shall execute a written instrument acknowledging their acceptance to act as Trustees hereunder and agreeing to perform the obligations imposed by this Agreement.

8.2—Single Fund.

All contributions to the Trust and all income or other property derived therefrom shall be held and administered by the Trustees as a single Trust Fund except as otherwise provided in this Agreement.

8.3—Investments.

The Trustees are hereby granted full power and authority:

(a) To invest and reinvest the trust fund or any part thereof in any manner directed by the Committee. Without limiting the generality of the foregoing, the Trustees may invest in bonds, notes, mortgages, commercial paper, preferred stocks, common stocks, or other securities, rights, obligations or property, real or personal, including shares and certificates of participation issued by investment companies or investment trusts.

(b) To retain in cash or other property unproductive of income, without liability for interest, so much of the Trust assets as may be determined to be necessary and proper; to deposit cash in any bank and select any bank as custodian; and to cause securities or other property to be held in their own names as Trustees for the BIG BUCKS, INC., a California corporation, EMPLOYEES' PROFIT-SHARING PLAN AND TRUST. Action of a majority of the Trustees is required to dispose of trust property (including the transfer or endorsement of checks and other negotiable paper and the drawing of checks, or other withdrawals of funds from the bank account of the Trust) or to gain access to the safety deposit box of the Trust. The Trustees shall cause all securities and other documents constituting a part of the Trust Estate to be deposited immediately in the Trust's safety deposit box.

(c) To manage, control, sell, convey, exchange, partition, divide, subdivide, improve and repair; to grant options and sell upon deferred payments; to lease without limit as to term for any purpose; to compromise, arbitrate or otherwise adjust claims in favor of or against the trust; to institute, compromise and defend actions and proceedings and to take any other action necessary or desirable in connection with the administration of the trust.

(d) To vote any stock, bonds, or other securities of any corporation or other issuer at any time held in trust; otherwise to consent to or request any action on the part of any such corporation or other issuer; to give general or special proxies or powers of attorney, with or without power of substitution; to participate in any reorganization, recapitalization, consolidation, merger or similar transaction with respect to such securities in any voting trust, or with any protective or like committee, or with the Trustees, or with depositaries designated thereby, to exercise any subscription rights and conversion privileges; and generally to exercise any of the powers of an owner with respect to the stock or other securities or properties comprising the trust.

(e) Generally, to do all such acts, execute all such instruments, take all such proceedings, and exercise all such rights and privileges with relation to property constituting the trust fund as if the Trustees were absolute owner thereof.

(f) Before the Trustees may invest in the securities of the Company, a majority of the Trustees and a majority of the Board of Directors of the Company shall pass a resolution that the Company is in sound financial condition. All loans made by the Trust shall be adequately secured.

(g) All investments shall be made in accordance with the provisions of Section 2261 of the California Civil Code, and the Trustees have the responsibility to ensure that said Section is complied with.

8.4—Controversy or Disagreement.

If any controversy arises with respect to this trust, the Trustees may retain the funds or property involved without liability pending settlement of the controversy. The Trustees may take action as directed by the Committee or as they deem advisable, whether by legal proceedings, compromise, or otherwise. The Trustee shall be under no obligation to take any legal action of whatever nature unless indemnified or held harmless to their satisfaction, as often as they shall require, against loss, cost, liability and expense.

8.5—Joinder of Parties.

In any action or other judicial proceedings affecting the trust, it shall be necessary to join as parties only the Trustees, the Committee and the Company, and no Participant or other persons having an interest in the trust shall be entitled to any notice or service of process. Any judgment entered in such proceeding or action shall be binding upon all persons claiming under this trust.

8.6—Taxes.

If the whole or any part of the trust shall become liable for the payment of any estate, inheritance, income or other tax which the Trustees shall be required to pay, the Trustees shall have full power and authority to pay such tax out of any monies or other property in their hands for the account of the person whose interests hereunder are so liable. Prior to making any payment, the Trustees may require such releases or other documents from any lawful taxing authority as they shall deem necessary.

8.7—Employment of Counsel.

The Trustees may consult with legal counsel (who may be counsel for the Company) and shall be fully protected with respect to any action taken or omitted by them in good faith pursuant to the advice of such counsel.

8.8—Records.

The Trustees shall keep a full, accurate and detailed record of all transactions of the Trust which the Committee shall have the right to examine at any time during the Trustees' regular business hours. Within ninety (90) days following the close of the fiscal year of the Trust, the Trustees shall furnish the Committee with a statement of account. This account shall set forth all receipts, disbursements, and other transactions effected by the Trustees during said year and shall show the investments at the end of the year, including the cost of each item as carried on the books of the Trustees and the fair market value. The accounts of the Trustee shall be kept on an accrual basis of accounting. The Trustees shall provide each Participant with an annual statement of his account.

The Committee shall promptly notify the Trustees in writing of approval or disapproval of the account. The Committee's failure to disapprove the account within sixty (60) days after receipt shall be considered an approval. The Trustees may elect to have their account judicially settled.

The Trustees shall, in addition to the foregoing annual statement, render a comparable statement covering the period from the last annual statement to the date specified by the Committee, within ten (10) days after receipt of a request from the Committee for the purpose of making the interim evaluation in Section 5.6.

8.9—Notices and Directions.

Whenever a notice or direction is given to the Trustees, the instrument shall be signed in the name of the Committee as authorized in Section 7.2 or in the name of the Company by its Secretary, whichever is applicable, unless otherwise specifically authorized. The Trustees may act upon any such notice, resolution, order, certificate, opinion, telegram, letter or other document believed to be genuine and to have been signed by the proper party or parties and may act thereon without notice to any Participant.

8.10—Compensation and Indemnity.

The Company agrees to pay the Trustees for their services reasonable compensation as may from time to time be agreed upon, and to indemnify and save harmless the Trustees against all liabilities and costs, including specifically demands made by an individual claiming an interest hereunder, which they may incur in the lawful performance of their duties, including all actions taken at the direction of the Company or the Committee, whether or not such actions are authorized herein, except as to any liabilities arising from the Trustees' wilful misconduct or negligence or bad faith. If at any time any such amounts are not paid by the Company, the Trustees may pay the same from the trust assets in their possession.

The Trustees shall not be compelled to do any act under this Agreement or commence or defend any suit in respect thereof unless indemnified to their satisfaction, as often as they shall require, against lost, cost, liability and expense.

8.11—Duty of Care.

The Trustees shall use ordinary care and reasonable diligence in the exercise of powers and performance of duties hereunder. They shall not be liable for following the direction of the Company or the Committee or, in the absence of directions, for the omission of any act as to which direction is required or authorized, or for any mistake of judgment or other action taken or omitted by them in good faith, or for any loss, unless resulting from their own wilful misconduct or negligence. If at any time the Committee should fail to give directions to the Trustees, the Trustees may act, and shall be protected in acting without such directions, in such manner as in their discretion seems appropriate and advisable under the circumstances for carrying out the purposes of this Plan and Trust Agreement.

8.12—Third Persons.

A third person dealing with the Trustees shall not be required to make any inquiry whether the Committee has instructed the Trustees, or the Trustees are otherwise authorized, to take or omit any action, or to follow the application by the Trustees of any money or property which may be paid or delivered to the Trustees.

8.13—Investment Management.

Except as hereinafter provided, the Committee shall be the Named Fiduciary with respect to the investment, management and control of the Trust assets with full discretion in the exercise of such investment, management and control. The Committee, by appropriate action, may appoint an Investment Manager to direct the investment and management of such assets of the Trust.

(a) The Company may by resolution of its Board of Directors assume from the Committee and transfer to the Trustee or an Investment Manager the authority and duty to direct the investment and management of all or a portion of the Trust assets. A certified copy of any such Board resolution shall be delivered to the Trustee. Any tranfer of investment and management authority to the Trustee or to an Investment Manager may be revoked upon receipt by the Trustee of a notice to that effect by the Company through its Board of Directors. The appointment, selection and retention of a qualified Investment Manager shall be solely the responsibility of the Committee or the Company, as the case may be. The Trustee is authorized and entitled to rely upon the fact that said Investment Manager is at all times a qualified Investment Manager, as defined in Section 3(38) of the Act, until such time as the Trustee has received a written notice from the Company or Committee to the contrary, as well as to rely upon the fact that said Investment Manager is authorized to direct the investment and management of the assets of the aforesaid trust until such time as the Company or Committee, as the case may be, shall notify the Trustee in writing that another Investment Manager has been appointed in the place and stead of the Investment Manager named or, in the alternative, that the Investment Manager has been removed and the responsibility for the investment and management of the trust assets has been assumed by the Committee or has been transferred back to the Trustee, as the case may be.

(b) In the event the Committee is given full power and responsibility to direct the Trustee with respect to the investment and management of all or a portion of the assets of the Trust Fund, the Trustee shall not be liable nor responsible for losses or unfavorable results arising from the Trustee's compliance with proper directions of the Committee which are made in accordance with the terms of the Plan and Trust and which are not contrary to the provisions of any applicable Federal or State statute regulating such investment and management of the assets of an employee benefit trust. In the event that an Investment Manager has full authority and responsibility with respect to the investment and management of the trust assets, the Trustee shall not be liable nor responsible in any way for any losses or other unfavorable results arising from the Trustee's compliance with investment or management directions received by the Trustee from the Investment Manager. All directions concerning investments made by the Committee or the Investment Manager shall be signed by such person or persons, acting on behalf of the Committee or the Investment Manager, as the case may be, as may be fully authorized in writing; provided, however, that the transmission to the Trustee of such directions by photostatic teletransmission with duplicate or facsimile signature or signatures shall be considered a delivery in writing of the aforesaid directions until the Trustee is notified in writing by the Committee that the use of such devices with duplicate or facsimile signatures is no longer authorized. The Trustee shall be entitled to rely upon directions which it receives by such means if so authorized by the Committee and shall in no way be responsible for the consequences of any unauthorized use of such device which use was not, in fact, known by the Trustee at the time to be unauthorized. The Trustee shall be under no duty to question any directions of the Investment Manager nor to review any securities or other property of the Trust constituting assets thereof with respect to which an Investment Manager has investment responsibility, nor to make any suggestions to such Investment Manager in connection therewith. The Trustee shall, as promptly as possible, comply with any written directions given by the Committee or an Investment Manager hereunder and, where such directions are given by photostatic teletransmission with facsimile signature or signatures, the Trustee shall be entitled to presume that any directions so given are fully authorized. The Trustee shall not be liable, in any manner nor for any reason, for the making or retention of any investment pursuant to such directions of the Investment Manager, nor shall the Trustee be liable for its failure to invest any or all of the Trust Fund in the absence of such written directions. In any event, neither the Committee nor any Investment Manager referred to above shall direct the purchase, sale or retention of any assets of the Trust Fund if such directions are not in compliance with the applicable provisions of the Act and any Regulations or Rulings issued thereunder. No fiduciary shall permit the indicia of ownership of any of the Trust assets to be maintained at a location outside the jurisdiction of the District Courts of the United States, except as authorized by the Secretary of Labor.

(c) During such period or periods of time, if any, as the Committee or an Investment Manager is authorized to direct the investment and management of the trust assets, the Trustee shall have no obligation to determine the existence of any conversion, redemption, exchange, subscription or other right relating to any of said securities purchased of which notice was given prior to the purchase of such securities, and shall have no obligation to exercise any such right unless the Trustee is informed of the existence of the right and is instructed to exercise such right, in writing, by the Committee or the Investment Manager, as the case may be, within a reasonable time prior to the expiration of such right.

(d) During such period or periods of time, if any, as the Committee or an Investment Manager is authorized to direct the Trustee to purchase securities issued by any foreign government or agency thereof, or by any corporation domiciled outside of the United States, it shall be the responsibility of the Committee or Investment Manager, as the case may be, to advise the Trustee, in writing, with respect to any laws or Regulations of any foreign countries or any United States territories or possession which shall apply, in any manner whatsoever, to such securities including, but not limited to, receipt of dividends or interests by the Trustee from such securities; and the Company does hereby agree to forever hold the Trustee harmless and indemnify the Trustee against any losses which may occur with respect to the Trust Fund which are occasioned by the failure to give such written notification to the Trustee.

8.14—Insurance.

Notwithstanding any other provisions of this Plan and Trust Agreement, in the event the Committee directs that any monies constituting assets of the Trust Fund shall be invested in policies of life insurance or annuity policies, either on an individual or a group basis, the Committee shall select the insurance company or companies with respect to which such investments shall be made and shall further direct such insurance company or companies to notify the Committee of all premiums due or to become due, the respective amounts of any said premiums [which shall not exceed fifty percent (50%) of the contributions allocated to a Participant's account in the case of ordinary life insurance or twenty-five percent (25%) in the case of term life insurance] and the respective dates when the same are due, whereupon the Committee shall verify the names of the individual Participants if the policies or annuities involved relate to the lives of individual Participants in the Plan, and the Committee shall thereupon deliver to the Trustee such premium notices together with the Committee's verification, as aforesaid, and a written direction to pay such premiums, no less than five (5) bank working days prior to the date or dates any said premiums are due. In the event that the Committee does not strictly comply with the provisions of this Paragraph 8.14, time being of the essence thereof, the Trustee shall have no duty nor liability with respect to the payment of any of said premiums and shall be entitled to presume that the Committee has properly decided to permit such policies to lapse.

8.15—Method of Valuation.

Notwithstanding any other provisions contained in this Trust Agreement, the fair market value of assets in the trust shall be determined by the Trustee based upon such sources of information as it may deem reliable including, but not limited to, information report in (1) newspapers of general circulation, (2) standard financial periodicals or publications, (3) statistical and valuation services, (4) the records of securities exchanges, Investment Managers or brokerage firms or any combination thereof deemed by the Trustee to be reliable.

8.16—Fiduciary Responsibility.

Each of the fiduciaries under the Plan and Trust shall be solely responsible for its own acts or omissions. Except to the extent imposed by said Act, no fiduciary shall have the duty to question whether any other fiduciary is fulfilling all of the responsibilities imposed upon such other fiduciary by the Act, as the same may be amended from time to time, or by any Regulations or Rulings issued thereunder. No fiduciary shall have any liability for a breach of fiduciary responsibility or another fiduciary with respect to this Plan and Trust Agreement unless he participates knowingly in such breach, knowingly undertakes to conceal such breach, has actual knowledge of such breach and fails to take reasonable remedial action to remedy said breach or, through his negligence in performing his own specific fiduciary responsibilities which give rise to his status as a fiduciary, he has enabled such other fiduciary to commit a breach of the latter's fiduciary responsibilities.

8.17—Fiduciary Standard of Conduct.

Each fiduciary of the Plan shall discharge his duties solely in the interests of the Participants and their Beneficiaries. Each fiduciary of the Plan shall act with the care, skill, prudence, and diligence under the circumstances then prevailing that a prudent man acting in a like capacity and familiar with such matters would use in conducting an enterprise of like character and with like aims. Fiduciaries shall diversify Plan assets to minimize risk of large losses, unless under the circumstances it is clearly prudent not to do so.

8.18—Prohibited Transactions.

(a) Except as provided in subsection (c) of this Section 8.18, a fiduciary shall not cause the Plan to engage in a transaction if he knows or should know that such transaction constitutes a direct or indirect:

1. Sale or exchange, or leasing of any property between the Plan and a party-in-interest; or

2. Lending of money or extension of credit between the Plan and a party-in-interest; or

3. Furnishing of goods, services or facilities between the Plan and a party-in-interest; or

4. Transfer to, or use by or for the benefit of a party-in-interest, of any assets of the Plan; or

5. Acquisition, on behalf of the Plan, of any Employer security or Employer real property.

(b) Except as provided in subsection (c) of this Section 8.18, a fiduciary shall not:

1. Deal with the assets of the Plan to his own interest or for his own account; or

2. In his individual or any other capacity act in any transaction involving the Plan on behalf of a party or represent a party whose interests are adverse to the interests of the Plan or the interests of its Participants or Beneficiaries; or

3. Receive any consideration for his own personal account from any party dealing with such Plan in connection with a transaction involving the assets of the Plan.

(c) The prohibited transactions rules set forth in this Section 8.18 shall not prevent a plan fiduciary from:

1. Receiving benefits from the Plan as a Participant or Beneficiary so long as the benefits are consistent with the terms of the Plan as applied to all other Participants and Beneficiaries;

2. Receiving reasonable compensation for services to the Plan unless the fiduciary receives full-time pay from the Employer or Employee organization;

3. Receiving reimbursement for expenses incurred; or

4. Serving as an officer, employee, or agent, of a party-in-interest; or

5. Making payments to parties-in-interest for reasonable compensation for office space and legal, accounting and other services necessary to operate the plan; and

6. Taking other actions pursuant to specific instructions and authorizations in the Plan governing document so far as consistent with all other fiduciary rules of the Act.

(d) For purposes of this Section, the term "party-in-interest" shall include, but not by way of limitation, the following:

1. Any fiduciary or counsel of the Plan;

2. A person providing services to the Plan;

3. The Company; and

4. A relative of any individual described in subparagraphs (1) and (2) above.

8.19—Liability Insurance.

The following parties may purchase and maintain liability insurance under the following terms and conditions:

(a) The Plan administrator, as an authorized expense of the Plan, to cover liability or losses occurring by reason of the act or omission of a fiduciary provided such insurance permits recourse by the Insurer against the fiduciary in the case of a breach of a fiduciary obligation by such fiduciary;

(b) a fiduciary, to cover liability from and for his own account;

(c) the Employer, to cover potential liability of one or more persons who serve in a fiduciary capacity with regard to the Plan.

8.20—Prohibition Against Certain
Persons Holding Certain Positions.

No person who has been convicted of, or has been imprisoned as a result of his conviction of, robbery, bribery, extortion, embezzlement, fraud, grand larceny, burglary, arson, a felony violation of Federal or State law involving substances defined in Section 102(6) of the Comprehensive Drug Abuse Prevention and Control Act of 1970, murder, rape, kidnapping, perjury, assault with intent to kill, any crime described in Section 9(a)(1) of the Investment Company Act of 1940, a violation of any provision of the Employee Retirement Income Security Act of 1974, a violation of Section 302 of the Labor-Management Relations Act, 1947, a violation of Chapter 63 of Title 18, United States Code, a violation of Section 874, 1026, 1503, 1505, 1506, 1510, 1951, or 1954 of Title 18, United States Code, a violation of the Labor-Management Reporting and Disclosure Act of 1959, or conspiracy to commit any such crimes or attempt to commit any such crimes, or a crime in which any of the foregoing crimes is an element, shall serve or be permitted to serve:

(1) as an administrator, fiduciary, officer, trustee, custodian, counsel, agent, or employee of any employee benefit plan; or

(2) as a consultant to any employee benefit plan.

8.21—Bonding Requirements.

(a) Every fiduciary of the Plan and every person who handles funds or other property of the Plan shall be bonded, provided, however, that no bond shall be required of a fiduciary (or of any director, officer, or employee of such fiduciary) if such fiduciary:

(1) is a corporation organized and doing business under the laws of the United States or of any State;

(2) is authorized under such laws to exercise trust powers or to conduct an insurance business;

(3) is subject to supervision or examination by Federal or State authority; and

(4) has at all times combined capital and surplus in excess of such minimum amount as may be established by regulations issued by the Secretary of Labor, which amount shall be at least $1,000,000.

(b) The amount of such bond shall be fixed at the beginning of each Fiscal Year of the Plan. Such amount shall not be less than ten percent (10%) of the amount of funds handled. In no event shall such bond be less than $1,000 nor more than $500,000, except that the Secretary of Labor after due notice and opportunity for hearing to all interested parties, may prescribe an amount in excess of $500,000, subject to the ten percent (10%) limitation of the preceding sentence. Such bond shall provide protection to the Plan against loss by reason of acts of fraud or dishonesty on the part of the Plan official, directly or through connivance with others.

ARTICLE IX

RESIGNATION AND REMOVAL OF TRUSTEE

9.1—Method and Procedure.

Any Trustee may resign at any time by delivering to the Company a written notice of resignation, to take effect at a date specified therein, which shall not be less than thirty (30) days after the delivery thereof, unless such notice shall be waived.

Any Trustee may be removed by the Company by delivery of a written notice of removal, to take effect at a date specified therein, which shall not be less than thirty (30) days after delivery thereof, unless such notice shall be waived.

The Company, upon receipt of or giving notice of the resignation or removal of a Trustee, shall promptly appoint a successor Trustee. While a vacancy exists, the remaining Trustee may perform any act which the Trustees are authorized to perform.

Upon the appointment of a successor Trustee, all right, title and interest and such former Trustee in the assets of the trust and all rights and privileges under this Agreement theretofore vested in such Trustee shall vest in the successor Trustee, and thereupon all future liability of such Trustee shall terminate; provided, however, that the Trustee shall execute, acknowledge, and deliver all documents and written instruments which are necessary to transfer and convey the right, title and interest in the trust assets, and all rights and privileges to the successor Trustee.

In the event of the resignation or removal of the initial Trustee, the successor Trustee or Trustees may be one or more individuals and/or bank or trust company qualified and authorized to do business in the State of California.

ARTICLE X

AMENDMENT AND TERMINATION

10.1—Amendments.

The Company shall have the right to amend this Trust from time to time, and to amend or cancel any amendments. Such amendments shall be stated in an instrument in writing executed by the Company, and this Agreement shall be amended in the manner and at the time therein set forth, and all Participants should be bound thereby; provided, however:

(a) No amendments shall cause any of the assets of the Trust to be used for or diverted to purposes other than for the exclusive benefit of Participants or their beneficiaries;

(b) No amendment shall have any retroactive effect so as to deprive any Participant of any benefit already vested, except that such changes, if any, as may be required to permit the Plan to meet the requirements of the Internal Revenue Code, or of the corresponding provisions of any subsequent revenue law, may be made to assure the deductibility for tax purposes of any contributions;

(c) No amendment shall create or effect any discrimination in favor of Participants who are officers, shareholders, or whose principal duties consist of supervising the work of other employees, or highly compensated employees; and

(d) no amendment shall increase the duties or liabilities of the Trustees without their written consent.

10.2—Discontinuance of Plan.

This Trust is irrevocable, and it is the expectation of the Company that this Plan and the payment of contributions hereunder shall be continued indefinitely, but continuance of the Plan is not assumed as a contractual obligation of the Company, and the right is reserved at any time to reduce or discontinue contributions hereunder. In the event of complete discontinuance of contributions, each Participant shall have a vested and non-forfeitable interest in his profit-sharing account to the extent of one hundred percent (100%).

The Company may terminate this Plan at any time upon fifteen (15) days written notice to the Trustees. Upon termination or partial termination of the Plan, the entire interest of each of the affected Participants shall vest and become nonforfeitable to the extent of one hundred percent (100%) immediately. The Trustees shall, with reasonable promptness, liquidate all assets remaining in the Trust. Upon the liquidation of all assets, the Committee shall make, after deducting estimated expense for liquidation and distribution, the allocations required under Article V, where applicable, with the same effect as though the date of completion of liquidation were an anniversary date of the Plan. Following these allocations, the Trustee shall promptly, after receipt of appropriate instructions from the Committee, distribute in accordance with Section 6.3 to each former Participant a benefit equal to the amount credited to his account as of the date of completion of liquidation.

ARTICLE XI

EMPLOYEE RIGHTS

11.1—General Rights of Participants and Beneficiaries.

The Plan is established and Trust Assets are held for the exclusive purpose of providing benefits for such Employees and their Beneficiaries as have qualified to participate under the terms of the Company's Plan. Such benefits may be payable upon retirement, death, disability or termination of employment with the Company, subject to the specific provisions of the Plan.

Every Participant and Beneficiary receiving benefits under the Plan is entitled to receive, on a regular basis, a current, comprehensible and detailed written account of his personal benefit status and of the relevant terms of the Plan which provides these benefits.

11.2—Regular Reports and Disclosure Requirements.

Every Participant covered under the Plan and every Beneficiary receiving benefits under the Plan shall receive a summary plan description, summary of the latest annual report of the Plan, or such other information as may be required to be furnished by law, under any of the following circumstances:

(a) When the Plan is established, or any material modification or amendment is proposed or adopted;

(b) Within ninety (90) days after he becomes a Participant or begins to receive benefits under the Plan;

(c) Within two hundred and ten (210) days after the close of the Plan's Fiscal Year.

11.3—Information Generally Available.

The Committee shall make copies of the Plan description and the latest annual report and any bargaining agreement, trust agreement, contract or other instruments under which the Plan was established or is operated available for examination by any Plan Participant or Beneficiary in the principal office of the Committee and such other locations as may be necessary to make such information reasonably accessible to all interested parties, and subject to a reasonable charge to defray the costs of furnishing such copies, the Plan Committee shall, upon written request of any Participant or Beneficiary, furnish a copy of the latest updated summary plan description, and the latest annual report, any terminal report, any bargaining agreement, trust agreement, contracts, or other instruments under which this Plan is established or operated to the party making such request.

11.4—Special Disclosures.

Upon written request to the Committee once during any twelve (12) month period, a Participant or Beneficiary shall be furnished with a written statement, based on the latest available information, of the total benefits accrued, or the earliest date on which such benefits will become nonforfeitable.

Prior to the distribution of any benefits to which any Participant or Beneficiary may be entitled, he must be provided with a written explanation of the terms and conditions of the various distribution options that are available and must, in turn, file a written election with the Committee.

Upon termination of employment, an Employee who has been a Participant in the Plan is entitled to a written explanation of and accounting for any vested deferred benefits which have accrued to his account and of any applicable options regarding the disposition of those benefits. Such information will also be provided to the Social Security Administration by the Internal Revenue Service on the basis of information required to be reported by the Committee.

11.5—Employee Right to Comment.

Pursuant to rights granted by the Act and the Regulations issued pursuant to that authority, the Participants shall be advised with respect to, and given an opportunity to comment on, the application of the Plan for a ruling regarding:

(a) Initial qualification determination under the requirements of the Internal Revenue Code;

(b) Any material amendment to the Plan;

(c) Any partial or complete termination of the Plan.

11.6—Filing a Claim for Benefits.

A Participant or Beneficiary or the Employer acting in his behalf shall notify the Committee of a claim of benefits under the Plan. Such request may be in any form acceptable to the Committee and shall set forth the basis of such claim and shall authorize the Committee to conduct such examinations as may be necessary to determine the validity of the claim and to take such steps as may be necessary to facilitate the payment of any benefits to which the Participant or Beneficiary may be entitled under the terms of the Plan.

11.7—Denial of Claim.

Whenever a claim for benefits by any Participant or Beneficiary has been denied, a written notice, prepared in a manner calculated to be understood by the Participant, must be provided, setting forth the specific reasons for the denial and explaining the procedure for an appeal and review of the decision by the Committee.

11.8—Remedies Available to Participants.

A Participant or Beneficiary shall be entitled, either in his own name or in conjunction with any other interested parties, to bring such actions in law or equity or to undertake such administrative actions or to seek such relief as may be necessary or appropriate to compel the disclosure of any required information, to enforce or protect his rights, to recover present benefits under the Plan.

11.9—Protection From Reprisal.

No Participant or Beneficiary may be discharged, fined, suspended, expelled, disciplined, or otherwise discriminated against for exercising any right to which he is entitled or for cooperation with any inquiry or investigation under the provisions of this Plan or any governing law or Regulations.

No person shall, directly or indirectly, through the use or threatened use of fraud, force or violence, restrain, coerce or intimidate any Participant or Beneficiary for the purpose of interfering with or preventing the exercise of or enforcement of any right, remedy or claim to which he is entitled under the terms of this Plan or any relevant law or Regulations.

11.10—Mergers, Consolidations or Transfers.

In the case of any merger or consolidation with, or transfer of assets or liabilities to, any other plan after the date of enactment of the Employee Retirement Security Act of 1974, each Participant in the Plan will (if the Plan then terminated) receive a benefit immediately after such merger, consolidation, or transfer which will be equal to or greater than the benefit he would have been entitled to receive immediately before such merger, consolidation, or transfer if the Plan then terminated.

ARTICLE XII

MISCELLANEOUS

12.1—Contribution Not Recoverable.

Subsequent to an initial determination and ruling of the Commissioner of Internal Revenue that this Trust is a "qualified" trust as defined in Internal Revenue Code, Section 401, it shall be impossible for any part of the principal or income to be used for or diverted to purposes other than the exclusive benefit of such Participants or their beneficiaries.

In the event of the initial determination and ruling (regarding qualification of this Trust by the Commissioner of Internal Revenue) that this is not a qualified trust as defined in Internal Revenue Code, Section 401, the Company, at its election, may recover any of its contributions made prior to said ruling.

12.2—Limitation on Participants' Rights.

Participation in this Trust shall not give any employees the right to be retained in the Company's employ or any right or interest in this Trust other than as herein provided. The Company reserves the right to dismiss any employee without liability for any claim either against this Trust, except to the extent provided herein, or against the Company. All benefits payable hereunder shall be provided solely from the Trust, and the Company assumes no responsibility for the acts of the Trustees.

12.3—Nonassignability.

None of the benefits, payments, proceeds or claims of any Participant or Beneficiary shall be subject to any claim of any creditor, and, in particular, the same shall not be subject to attachment or garnishment or other legal process by any creditor, nor shall any such Participant or Beneficiary have any right to alienate, anticipate, commute, pledge, encumber, or assign any of the benefits or payments or proceeds which he may expect to receive, contingently or otherwise, under this agreement.

12.4—Federal Law Governs.

This Trust Agreement and the Trust hereby created shall be construed, administered, and governed in all respects under applicable Federal law, and to the extent that Federal law is inapplicable by the laws of the State of California; provided, however, that if any provision is susceptible of more than one interpretation, such interpretation shall

327

be given thereto as is consistent with this profit sharing plan and trust being an employees' profit sharing plan and trust within the meaning of the Internal Revenue Code, or corresponding provisions of subsequent revenue laws. If any provision of this instrument shall be held by a court of competent jurisdiction to be invalid or unenforceable, the remaining provisions hereof shall continue to be fully effective.

12.5—Time Limit.

In the event the validity of this Trust shall depend upon compliance with the rule against perpetuities, then it shall terminate upon the death of the last to die of such of the employees, participating in the Plan from time to time, who were living on the day of execution of this Agreement.

12.6—Headings No Part of Agreement.

Headings and subheadings in this Agreement are inserted for convenience of reference only. They constitute no part of the Agreement.

12.7—Instrument in Counterparts.

This Agreement has been executed in several counterparts, each of which shall be deemed an original, and said counterparts shall constitute but one and the same instrument, which may be sufficiently evidenced by one counterpart.

12.8—Successors and Assigns.

This Agreement shall inure to the benefit of and be binding upon the parties hereto and their successors and assigns.

12.9—Gender.

The masculine gender shall include the feminine, and wherever appropriate the singular shall include the plural or the plural may be read as the singular.

12.10—Liability.

No provision contained in this Plan shall be construed as relieving any officers, directors or Trustee, or member of any Committee, Board or other body acting on behalf of the BIG BUCKS, INC., a California corporation, **EMPLOYEES' PROFIT-SHARING PLAN AND**

TRUST of any liability. Trustees are subject to liability for negligence, wilful misconduct or for bad faith.

IN WITNESS WHEREOF, the Company has executed this Agreement on the <u>1st</u> day of <u>April,</u> 1979.

BIG BUCKS, INC., A California Corporation

By _____
President

And _____
Secretary

"Company"

APPROVED AS TO FORM:

By _____
Attorneys for Company

ACCEPTANCE OF TRUSTEE

HERBERT BUCKSUP does hereby accept the appointment as initial Trustee of the BIG BUCKS, INC., EMPLOYEES' PROFIT-SHARING PLAN AND TRUST AGREEMENT and agrees to perform all of the duties and obligations imposed by said Trust Agreement.

Dated: _____, 1979.

_____

BIG BUCKS, INC.
EMPLOYEES' PENSION TRUST
(Money-Purchase Plan)

BIG BUCKS, INC.

EMPLOYEES' PENSION TRUST
(Money-Purchase Plan)

TABLE OF CONTENTS

BIG BUCKS, INC.
EMPLOYEES' PENSION TRUST
(Money-Purchase Plan)

WHEREAS, BIG BUCKS, INC., A California Corporation, desires to create a pension trust for the exclusive benefit of its employees who qualify under the terms and conditions thereof;

NOW, THEREFORE, BIG BUCKS, INC., A California Corporation, hereby adopts a pension trust (money-purchase plan), as follows:

ARTICLE I

DESIGNATION OF TRUST AND DEFINITIONS

1.1—Title.

This pension plan and trust shall be known as the BIG BUCKS, INC., EMPLOYEES' PENSION TRUST (Money Purchase Plan). The Plan and Trust are designated and intended to qualify under the appropriate provisions of the Internal Revenue Code.

1.2—Definitions.

"Account" or "pension account" means the account maintained by the Committee for each Participant as required by Article IV.

"Anniversary Date" shall mean the last day of each fiscal year.

"Beneficiary" or "beneficiaries" means the person or persons last designated by a Participant as set forth in Section 2.3, or if there is no designated beneficiary, then to the Participant's surviving spouse, and if no surviving spouse, then equally to the surviving issue, and if none, then to the Participant's estate, or if there is no legal representative appointed to represent his estate within sixty (60) days after the Participant's death and his vested interest does not exceed Two Thousand Dollars ($2,000.00), to his heirs-at-law, under the laws of California then in force and effect.

"Committee" shall mean the Committee described in Article VI hereof.

"Company" shall mean BIG BUCKS, INC., A California Corporation.

"Compensation" shall mean the full regular basic salary and hourly wages, including overtime, bonuses, and commissions, but excluding health and welfare or any other payments before deductions authorized by the Employee or required by law to be withheld from the Employee by the Company.

"Employee" shall mean any person who is employed by the Company.

"Year of Service" for purposes of vesting and eligibility upon reemployment shall mean any twelve (12) month period during which an Employee has completed One Thousand (1,000) Hours of Service with the first twelve (12) month period to commence on the date of his employment. Year of Service for purposes of benefit accrual shall be the Plan Fiscal Year in which a Participant completes at least 1,000 Hours of Service, except that an Employee who first becomes a Participant pursuant to Section 2.1 shall be deemed to have completed a Year of

Service as of the Anniversary Date upon which he becomes a Participant.

A "One Year Break in Service" shall be deemed to occur in each twelve (12) month period following the employment commencement date or any anniversary thereof during which the Employee has no more than 500 Hours of Service.

"Hour of Service" shall mean each hour for which (1) an employee is paid, or entitled to payment, for performance of duties for the Company, (2) an employee is paid, or entitled to payment, for nonperformance of duties, and (3) back pay, irrespective of mitigation of damages, is either awarded or agreed to by the Company. Hours shall not be credited under both (3) and (1) or (2). Hours for non-performance of duties shall be credited in accordance with Department of Labor Regulations Section 2530.200b2(b). Hours shall be credited to the applicable computation period in accordance with Department of Labor Regulations Section 2530.200b2(c).

"Effective Date" shall mean February 1, 1979.

"Fiscal Year" shall mean each year beginning on the first day of February and ending on the last day of January.

"Participant" shall mean an Employee of the Company who has been admitted to participation in the Plan and for whom a portion of the Company contributions is allocated.

"Plan" or "Trust" shall mean the Employees' Pension Trust (Money Purchase Plan) set forth in this Agreement and all subsequent amendments thereto.

"Trustees" shall mean that person or those persons appointed to be Trustees by the Board of Directors of the Company. The initial Trustee shall be HERBERT BUCKSUP.

"The Act" shall mean the Employee Retirement Income Security Act of 1974, or any future amendments thereto.

"Fiduciary" shall mean any person who exercises any discretionary authority or control respecting the management or disposition of trust assets or has any discretionary authority or responsibility in the administration of this Plan.

"Named Fiduciary" shall mean the fiduciary or fiduciaries who are named in the Plan and who jointly or severally shall have authority to control and manage the operation and administration of the Plan.

"Investment Manager" shall mean fiduciary as defined in Section 3(38) of the Act, which fiduciary has fully complied with the provisions of Section 3(38) of the Act and who has provided the Committee and the Trustee with written acknowledgement that he has done so and that he is a fiduciary with respect to this Plan.

ARTICLE II

PARTICIPATION

2.1—Commencement of Participation.

All employees of the Company shall commence participation on the Anniversary Date coinciding with or following the expiration of six (6) months from their date of employment.

2.2—Certification by Company.

Within thirty (30) days after each Anniversary Date of the Plan, the Company shall transmit to the Committee certified lists of the employees entitled to participate in the Plan as of any such Anniversary Date. Such certified lists shall be in such form and contain such information as the Committee may desire, and except in the case of a mistake, such certified lists shall not be questioned by the Committee.

2.3—Enrollment of Participant and Designation of Beneficiary.

Upon receipt of notification from the Committee that he is a Participant in the Plan, an Employee may designate, in writing, the beneficiary whom he desires to receive the benefits provided by the Plan in the event of his death, such designation to be filed on the form provided for that purpose by the Committee. A Participant may from time to time change his designated beneficiary hereunder without the consent of such beneficiary by filing such designation in writing with the Committee; and the Committee, the Company and the Trustees shall be authorized to rely upon the designation last filed with the Committee in acting in accordance with the terms of this Agreement.

2.4—Duration of Participation.

Participation of a Participant shall continue during his subsequent employment until the Anniversary Date coinciding with or preceding the actual termination of his employment for any reason, including retirement, at which time it shall terminate. A Participant may not voluntarily withdraw from participation or receive any distribution of his benefits from the Plan.

2.5—Retirement.

The normal retirement date shall be the Anniversary Date coinciding with or next preceding the date of a Participant's sixty-fifth (65th) birthday. While this Plan provides for the Participant's normal retirement date, such Participant may continue his employment after that time with approval of the Company.

2.6—Participation After Normal Retirement Date.

If, by mutual agreement between the Participant and the Company's Board of Directors, the Participant continues in the service of the Company beyond his normal retirement date, he shall continue to participate in the Plan during such continued employment.

2.7—Reparticipation by Former Participant.

A former Participant shall become a Participant immediately upon his return to employ, if, (1) such former Participant had a nonforfeitable right to all or a portion of his account balance derived from Company contributions at the time of his termination; or, (2) the former Participant's Years of Service before his termination exceed the number of consecutive one-year breaks in service after such termination. A former Participant who did not have a nonforfeitable right to any portion of his account balance derived from Company contributions at the time of his termination shall be considered a new Employee for eligibility purposes if the number of consecutive one-year breaks in service equals or exceeds the aggregate number of Years of Service before such break.

ARTICLE III

COMPANY CONTRIBUTIONS

3.1—Obligation.

Concurrently with the execution of this instrument, the Company has paid to the Trustees the sum of One Hundred Dollars ($100.00) on account of its initial contribution to the trust and, subject to its rights under Article IX, will make additional contributions for each Fiscal Year in an amount determined as set forth in Section 3.3, said contributions to be held and administered by the Trustees, in trust, pursuant to the terms of this Agreement.

3.2—Payment.

All payments of contributions shall be made directly to the Trustees and may be made on any date or dates selected by the Company; provided, that the total annual contributions for each fiscal year shall be paid within the time allowed by the pertinent provisions of the applicable Federal Tax Laws to obtain a tax deduction for that year. The Trustees shall have no duty to demand payment of a contribution, and shall not be responsible for the accuracy thereof.

3.3—Company Contribution Formula.

The contribution to be made by the Company each year shall be equal to ten percent (10%) of the compensation paid to all Participants for such year. The contribution shall be made whether or not there are current or accumulated net profits. In the event of forfeitures pursuant to Section 4.3 of this Agreement, such forfeitures shall remain in trust and shall reduce the Company contributions required under this provision.

ARTICLE IV

ALLOCATION TO PARTICIPANTS' ACCOUNTS

4.1—Participant's Pension Account.

At the commencement of this Trust, the Committee shall open a separate account for each Participant, and as of each Anniversary Date of this Plan, the Committee shall open a separate account for each new Participant who shall have then become eligible to participate in the Plan and Trust.

4.2—Annual Contributions.

The Company's contributions plus forfeitures shall be allocated as of each Anniversary Date to the pension account of all Participants on the following basis:

(a) An amount equal to seven percent (7%) of each Participant's compensation in excess of taxable wage base for each year for purposes of Social Security contributions for such year shall be allocated to his pension account;

(b) the balance of the Company's contribution and the balance of forfeitures shall be allocated to the pension account of each Participant in the proportion that the amount of compensation received by him during such Fiscal Year bears to the total amount of compensation received by all Participants during such Fiscal Year.

The annual additions to a Participant's account (including the additions to any other defined contribution plan to which the Company contributes for such Participant's benefit) during any Fiscal Year shall not exceed the lesser of $25,000 (subject to any annual cost-of-living increases permissible pursuant to the terms of the Act or corresponding provisions of subsequent revenue laws and/or regulations) or twenty-five percent (25%) of such Participant's compensation from the Company during such Fiscal Year.

The term "annual additions" means the sum of:

(a) The Company's contribution;

(b) forfeitures reallocated to such Participant's account pursuant to Section 4.3 of the Plan; and

341

    (c) the lesser of:
- (i) one-half (½) of the Participant's contribution, or
- (ii) such Participant's contribution in excess of six percent (6%) of his compensation from the Company during the Fiscal Year.

Annual additions shall not include rollovers from a qualified plan or an individual retirement account. Any excess annual additions shall be placed in a suspense account and shall be treated as a forfeiture on the following Anniversary Date. The amount of the suspense account shall remain constant until such Anniversary Date.

4.3—Forfeitures.

Annually, as of each Anniversary Date, the forfeitures of the participating employees of the Company caused by a One Year Break in Service of each such Employee which occurs during the Plan Year ending on such Anniversary Date shall be allocated to the accounts of Participants, excluding Participants who became Participants on the Anniversary Date of such allocation, in the same manner as the Company's contribution.

4.4—Annual Revaluation.

Commencing with the Second Anniversary Date, the Committee shall revalue the account of each Participant so as to reflect any increase or decrease in the fair market value of the assets of the fund (including the income and earnings of, and expenditures from, the Fund) as of that Anniversary Date as compared with the value of the assets of the Fund as of the last preceding Anniversary Date, and such increase or decrease shall be allocated to the Participants in the proportion that the amount of the Participant's account bears to the total amount of all Participant's accounts of the Company as of the last preceding Anniversary Date. Neither the Company nor the Trustees nor any members of the Committee shall, in any manner or to any extent whatsoever, warrant, guarantee, or represent that the value of the Participant's account shall at any time equal or exceed the aggregate amount previously contributed thereto by the Company and the Participant.

4.5—Interim Revaluation.

The pension account of a Participant whose participation is terminated on other than an Anniversary Date shall be valued currently for the purpose of distribution only in the event of a substantial change in the fair market value of trust assets. In such case, the Committee shall determine, as of the end of the calendar month in which the participation of an employee terminated, the fair market value of the net trust assets in order to determine the percentage of increase or decrease in the fair market value of such assets when compared with the fair market value of such assets as of the preceding Anniversary Date. The cumulative amount allocated as of the preceding Anniversary Date to the pension account of such Participant shall, for the purpose of distribution only, be adjusted to reflect the increase or decrease, as the case may be, by multiplying such amount by the percentage so determined.

This interim revaluation shall not affect any amount to be forfeited under Section 5.3, and any increase or decrease so distributed or retained with respect to the pension account to the former Participant shall merely increase or decrease unallocated assets for the purpose of the annual revaluation required by Section 4.4.

Interim revaluations shall be made in a uniform and nondiscriminatory manner.

ARTICLE V

BENEFITS

5.1—Vesting of Company Contributions.

The interest of each Participant in the Company contributions account allocated to his benefit shall vest in accordance with the following provisions:

(a) If the employment of any Participant is terminated for any cause other than death, disability or retirement, such Participant shall have a nonforfeitable vested right in his Company contributions account determined as of the Anniversary Date coinciding with or next preceding the occurrence of a One Year Break in Service in accordance with the following schedule:

Years of Service with Company	Vested Interest
Less than 1 Year of Service	0%
1 Year but less than 2 Years of Service	20%
2 Years but less than 3 Years of Service	40%
3 Years but less than 4 Years of Service	60%
4 Years but less than 5 Years of Service	80%
5 Years or more of Service	100%

In computing the period of service for the purpose of determining the percentage of nonforfeitable vested interest, a Participant's entire service with the Company shall be taken into account.

(b) One Hundred Percent (100%) on reaching his Normal Retirement Date, death, a judicial declaration of his incompetence, or a determination by the Committee based upon competent medical evidence, that his employment is terminated because of his becoming totally and permanently, physically or mentally, incapacitated.

The vesting of a Participant's interest in whole or in part shall not preclude the allocations and evaluations provided for under Article IV.

5.2—Distribution of Benefits.

The benefit distributable to a Participant upon the termination of his participation or to the beneficiary or beneficiaries of a Participant who dies shall be the amount allocated to his account under Section 4.2, adjusted if necessary in accordance with Section 4.5, multiplied by the percentage of vested interest in accordance with Section 5.1; provided, however, that distribution shall not be made until a terminated Participant has incurred a One Year Break in Service.

When a Participant ceases to participate, the Committee shall, with reasonable promptness, determine in its discretion the method of distribution of the Participant's vested interest to commence not later than his Normal Retirement Date which it deems to be in the best interest of the Participant, and shall authorize the Trustees to distribute his interest in any of the following ways:

(a) A Participant who retires at his Normal Retirement Date shall be entitled to retirement income benefits in the form of a straight-life annuity.

In the event such Participant and his spouse have been married throughout a one (1) year period ending on the annuity starting date, payment of such annuity benefits shall be made in the form having the effect of a qualified joint and survivor annuity.

A qualified joint and survivor annuity required to be paid under this paragraph to a Participant and his spouse shall be a monthly amount which is reduced from but which will be actuarially equivalent to the monthly amount of the single life annuity to which such Participant would be otherwise entitled, but such reduction shall not exceed the estimated actuarial costs associated with providing qualified joint and survivor annuities.

The term "qualified joint and survivor annuity" means an annuity for the life of the Participant with a survivor annuity for the life of his spouse which is not less than one-half ($\frac{1}{2}$) nor more than one hundred percent (100%) of the annuity payable during the joint lives of the Participant and his spouse.

In the event a Participant dies on or after the date his Normal Retirement Age is attained while still in active service of the Company, or separates from service on or after his Normal Retirement Age is attained and thereafter dies before beginning to receive benefits under the Plan, the Participant's benefits will be paid in the form of a qualified joint and survivor annuity unless the Participant otherwise elects within the election period specified in the following paragraph.

Each Participant shall have a reasonable period (not less than 90 days) before the annuity starting date during which he may elect in writing (after receiving a written explanation of the terms and conditions of the joint and survivor annuity and the effect of an election under this paragraph) not to take the joint and survivor annuity. The election period shall not end more than 90 days before commencement of benefits but must end before commencement of benefits. Any election made during the election period is revocable during the election period.

(b) In the event the Participant elects not to take a joint and survivor annuity upon retirement at his Normal Retirement Date or in the event any Participant is terminated for any cause other than death, disability or retirement, the Committee may direct the Trustee to distribute the benefits to which a Participant is entitled in any of the modes of settlement set forth below or any combination thereof; provided that each such mode shall have the same present value:

(1) A cash lump sum; provided, however, that the benefits of a Participant cannot be cashed out without his written consent if the value of his accrued benefits is in excess of $1,750.00; or

(2) Substantially equal installments payable not less frequently than annually to commence not later than sixty (60) days subsequent to his retirement; provided, however, that the benefits to which the Participant is entitled must be paid over a period not exceeding the life expectancy of the Participant determined at the date of his retirement; provided further, that in the event distribution is to be made in the form of installments, the Committee shall direct the Trustee to segregate in a separate account an amount equal to the lump sum value and to invest it in United States Government obligations or to deposit it in an interest-bearing savings account of any bank, or to deposit it in an interest-bearing savings account of a federal savings and loan association. Any interest received thereon shall be distributed with the final installment of benefits. In the event a Participant dies prior to complete distribution of his installments, his Beneficiary shall be entitled to the balance; or

(3) A life annuity, which may be a straight-life annuity

or a joint and survivor annuity, with or without cash or installment refund, with or without a period certain, purchased from a legal reserve life insurance company. In the event a joint and survivor annuity is elected for a Participant, the present value of the annuity payable to the Participant must be more than 50 percent (50%) of the present value of the benefit payable to both the Participant and the joint annuitant; or

(4) Upon written request of the Participant or his Beneficiary, approved by the Committee, distribution of the lump sum value may be made in shares issued by a regulated investment company registered under the Investment Company Act of 1940, or shares of stock listed on a National Stock Exchange.

5.3—Non-Vested Interests.

If any Participant incurs a One Year Break in Service prior to death or retirement, such portion of the cumulative amount previously allocated to his account as of the coinciding or next preceding Anniversary Date if not vested shall be forfeited and allocated in the manner provided in Section 4.3.

5.4—Commencement of Benefits.

Notwithstanding anything contained herein to the contrary, the payment of benefits hereunder to any Participant shall commence not later than the sixtieth (60th) day after the latest of the close of the plan year in which:

(a) the date on which such Participant attains the earlier of age Sixty-Five (65), or the normal retirement age specified under the Plan,

(b) such Participant terminates his service with the Company.

No distribution shall be made until a former Participant has incurred a One Year Break in Service unless such former Participant is fully vested.

5.5—Loans to Participants.

The Committee is hereby specifically authorized to direct the Trustee to make loans to Participants or beneficiaries of this Plan. Such loans shall be available to all Participants and beneficiaries. Notwithstanding the foregoing, no loan shall be made pursuant to the provisions of this Section unless it bears a reasonable rate of interest and unless the repayment of such loan is adequately secured. Any such loan shall be repaid in full within five (5) years.

ARTICLE VI

THE COMMITTEE

6.1—Members.

The Board of Directors of the Company shall, by resolution, appoint a Committee of three (3) to be known as the Committee, who shall serve at the pleasure of the Company. Vacancies in the Committee arising by resignation, death, removal by the Company or otherwise shall be filled by the Company as soon as is reasonably possible after the vacancy occurs, and until a new appointment is made, the remaining members or member of the Committee shall have full authority to act. The Company shall file written notice of the names of the members of the Committee with the Trustee, and as changes take place in membership, the names of the new members. The initial members of the Committee shall be Herbert Bucksup, Betty Bucksup and Flo Cash.

Except as otherwise provided for herein, the Committee is the Named Fiduciary and Administrator of the Plan provided for by the Act, and shall have the authority to control and manage the operation and administration of this Plan.

6.2—Committee Action.

The Committee shall choose a Secretary who shall keep the minutes of the Committee's proceedings and all data, records and documents pertaining to the Committee's administration of the Plan. The Committee shall act by a majority of its members at the time in office and such action may be taken either by a vote at a meeting or in writing without a meeting. The Committee may by such majority action authorize its Secretary or any one or more of its members to execute any document or documents on behalf of the Committee, in which event the Committee shall notify the Trustees in writing of such action and the name or names of those so designated. The Trustees thereafter shall accept and rely conclusively upon any direction or document executed by such Secretary, member or members as representing action by the Committee until the Committee shall file with the Trustees a written revocation of such designation.

A member of the Committee who is also a Participant hereunder shall not vote or act upon any matter relating solely to himself.

6.3—Rights and Duties.

The Committee, on behalf of the Participants and their beneficiaries, shall enforce the Plan in accordance with its terms, shall be charged with the general administration of the Plan, and shall have all the powers necessary to accomplish those purposes, including but not by way of limitation, the following:

(a) To determine all questions relating to the eligibility of employees to participate;

(b) To compute and certify to the Trustees the amounts and kind of benefits payable to Participants and their beneficiaries;

(c) To authorize all disbursements by the Trustees from the Trust;

(d) To maintain all the necessary records for the administration of the Plan other than those maintained by the Trustees;

(e) To interpret the provisions of the Plan and to make and publish such rules for the regulation of the Plan as are not inconsistent with the terms hereof;

(f) To direct the Trustees in writing from time to time to purchase, retain, sell, or lease any property, real or personal, which the Committee may designate;

(g) To approve or disapprove investment changes recommended by the Trustees;

(h) The terms and provisions of this Plan shall not be administered in such a manner as to cause discrimination in favor of those employees who are officers, shareholders, persons whose principal duties consist of supervising the work of other employees, or highly compensated employees.

6.4—Information.

To enable the Committee to perform its functions, the Company shall supply full and timely information to the Committee on all matters pertaining to the compensation of all Participants, their continuous regular employment, their retirement, death, or the cause for termination of employment, and such other pertinent facts as the Committee may require; and the Committee shall furnish the Trustees such information as may be pertinent to the Trustees' administration of the Plan.

6.5—Compensation, Indemnity,
and Liability.

All expenses of the Committee shall be paid by the Company, and the Company shall furnish the Committee with such clerical and other assistance as is necessary in the performance of its duties.

The Company hereby indemnifies and saves harmless each member of the Committee against any and all expenses and liabilities arising out of his membership on the Committee, excepting only expenses and liabilities arising out of his own wilful misconduct or gross negligence.

ARTICLE VII

THE TRUSTEES

7.1—Acceptance by Trustees.

The Trustees shall execute a written instrument acknowledging their acceptance to act as Trustees hereunder and agreeing to perform the obligations imposed by this Agreement.

7.2—Single Fund.

All contributions to the Trust and all income or other property derived therefrom shall be held and administered by the Trustees as a single Trust Fund except as otherwise provided in this Agreement.

7.3—Investments.

The Trustees are hereby granted full power and authority:

(a) To invest and reinvest the trust fund or any part thereof in any manner directed by the Committee. Without limiting the generality of the foregoing, the Trustees may invest in bonds, notes, mortgages, commercial paper, preferred stocks, common stocks, or other securities, rights, obligations or property, real or personal, including shares and certificates of participation issued by investment companies or investments trusts.

(b) To retain in cash or other property unproductive of income, without liability for interest, so much of the Trust assets as may be determined to be necessary and proper; to deposit cash in any bank and select any bank as custodian; and to cause securities or other property to be held in their own names as Trustees for the BIG BUCKS, INC., EMPLOYEES' PENSION TRUST (Money Purchase Plan). The action of a majority of the Trustees is required to dispose of trust property (including the transfer or endorsement of checks and other negotiable paper and the drawing of checks, or other withdrawals of funds from the bank account of the Trust) or to gain access to the safety deposit box of the Trust. The Trustees shall cause all securities and other documents constituting a part of the Trust Estate to be deposited immediately in the Trust's safety deposit box.

(c) To manage, control, sell, convey, exchange, partition, divide, subdivide, improve and repair; to grant options and sell upon deferred payments; to lease without limit as to term for any purpose; to compromise, arbitrate or otherwise adjust claims in favor of or against the trust; to institute, compromise and defend actions and proceedings and to take any other action necessary or desirable in connection with the administration of the trust.

(d) To vote any stock, bonds or other securities of any corporation or other issuer at any time held in trust; otherwise to consent to or request any action on the part of any such corporation or other issuer; to give general or special proxies or powers of attorney, with or without power of substitution; to participate in any reorganization, recapitalization, consolidation, merger or similar transaction with respect to such securities in any voting trust, or with any protective or like committee, or with the Trustees, or with depositaries designated thereby, to exercise any subscription rights and conversion privileges; and generally to exercise any of the powers of an owner with respect to the stock or other securities or properties comprising the trust.

(e) Generally, to do all such acts, execute all such instruments, take all such proceedings, and exercise all such rights and privileges with relation to property constituting the trust fund as if the Trustees were the absolute owner thereof.

(f) Before the Trustees may invest in the securities of the Company, a majority of the Trustees and a majority of the Board of Directors of the Company shall pass a resolution that the Company is in sound financial condition. All loans made by the Trust shall be adequately secured.

(g) All investments shall be made in accordance with the provisions of Section 2261 of the California Civil Code, and the Trustees have the responsibility to ensure that said Section is complied with.

7.4—Controversy or Disagreement.

If any controversy arises with respect to this trust, the Trustees may retain the funds or property involved without liability pending settlement of the controversy. The Trustees may take action as directed by the Committee or as they deem advisable, whether by legal proceedings, compromise, or otherwise. The Trustee shall be under no obligation to take any legal action of whatever nature unless indemnified or held harmless to their satisfaction, as often as they shall require, against loss, cost, liability and expense.

7.5—Joinder of Parties.

In any action or other judicial proceedings affecting the trust, it shall be necessary to join as parties only the Trustee, the Committee and the Company, and no Participant or other persons having an interest in the trust shall be entitled to any notice or service of process. Any judgment entered in such a proceeding or action shall be binding upon all persons claiming under this trust.

7.6—Taxes.

If the whole or any part of the trust shall become liable for the payment of any estate, inheritance, income or other tax which the Trustees shall be required to pay, the Trustees shall have full power and authority to pay such tax out of any monies or other property in their hands for the account of the person whose interests hereunder are so liable. Prior to making any payment, the Trustee may require such releases or other documents from any lawful taxing authority as they shall deem necessary.

7.7—Employment of Counsel.

The Trustees may consult with legal counsel (who may be counsel for the Company) and shall be fully protected with respect to any action taken or omitted by them in good faith pursuant to the advice of such counsel.

7.8—Records.

The Trustees shall keep a full, accurate and detailed record of all transactions of the Trust which the Committee shall have the right to examine at any time during the Trustees' regular business hours. Within ninety (90) days following the close of the fiscal year of the Trust, the Trustees shall furnish the Committee with a statement of account. This account shall set forth all receipts, disbursements, and other transactions effected by the Trustees during said year and shall show the investments at the end of the year, including the cost of each item as carried on the books of the Trustees and the fair market value. The accounts of the Trustee shall be kept on an accrual basis of accounting. The Trustees shall provide each Participant with an annual statement of his account.

The Committee shall promptly notify the Trustees in writing of approval or disapproval of the account. The Committee's failure to disapprove the account within sixty (60) days after receipt shall be considered an approval. The Trustees may elect to have their account judicially settled.

The Trustees shall, in addition to the foregoing annual statement, render a comparable statement covering the period from the last annual statement to the date specified by the Committee, within ten (10) days after receipt of a request from the Committee for the purpose of making the interim evaluation in Section 4.5.

7.9—Notices and Directions.

Whenever a notice or direction is given to the Trustees, the instrument shall be signed in the name of the Committee as authorized in Section 6.2 or in the name of the Company by its Secretary, whichever is applicable, unless otherwise specifically authorized. The Trustees may act upon any such notice, resolution, order, certificate, opinion, telegram, letter or other document believed to be genuine and to have been signed by the proper party or parties and may act thereon without notice to any Participant.

7.10—Compensation and Indemnity.

The Company agrees to pay the Trustees for their services reasonable compensation as may from time to time be agreed upon, and to indemnify and save harmless the Trustees against all liabilities and costs, including specifically demands made by any individual claiming an interest hereunder, which they may incur in the lawful performance of their duties, including all actions taken at the direction of the Company or the Committee, whether or not such actions are authorized herein, except as to any liabilities arising from the Trustees' wilful misconduct or negligence or bad faith. If at any time any such amounts are not paid by the Company, the Trustees may pay the same from the trust assets then in their possession.

The Trustees shall not be compelled to do any act under this Agreement or commence or defend any suit in respect thereof unless indemnified to their satisfaction, as often as they shall require, against loss, cost, liability and expense.

7.11—Duty of Care.

The Trustees shall use ordinary care and reasonable diligence in the exercise of powers and performance of duties hereunder. They shall not be liable for following the direction of the Company or the Committee or, in the absence of directions, for the omission of any act as to which direction is required or authorized, or for any mistake of judgment or other action taken or omitted by them in good faith, or for any loss, unless resulting from their own wilful misconduct or negligence. If at any time the Committee should fail to give directions to the Trustees, the Trustees may act, and shall be protected in acting without such directions, in such manner as in their discretion seems appropriate and advisable under the circumstances for carrying out the purposes of this Plan and Trust Agreement.

7.12—Third Persons.

A third person dealing with the Trustees shall not be required to make any inquiry whether the Committee has instructed the Trustees, or the Trustees are otherwise authorized, to take or omit any action, or to follow the application by the Trustees of any money or property which may be paid or delivered to the Trustees.

7.13—Investment Management.

Except as hereinafter provided, the Committee shall be the Named Fiduciary with respect to the investment, management and control of the Trust assets with full discretion in the exercise of such investment, management and control. The Committee, by appropriate action, may appoint an Investment Manager to direct the investment and management of such assets of the Trust.

    (a) The Company may, by resolution of its Board of Directors, assume from the Committee and transfer to the Trustee or an Investment Manager the authority and duty to direct the investment and management of all or a portion of the Trust assets. A certified copy of any such Board resolution shall be delivered to the Trustee. Any transfer of investment and management authority to the Trustee or to an Investment Manager may be revoked upon receipt by the Trustee of a notice to that effect by the Company through its Board of Directors. The appointment, selection and retention of a qualified Investment Manager shall be solely the responsibility of the Committee or the Company, as the case may be. The Trustee is authorized and entitled to rely upon the fact that said Investment Manager is at all times a qualified Investment Manager, as defined in Section 3(38) of the Act, until such time as the Trustee has received a written notice from the

Company or Committee to the contrary, as well as to rely upon the fact that said Investment Manager is authorized to direct the investment and management of the assets of the aforesaid trust until such time as the Company or Committee, as the case may be, shall notify the Trustee in writing that another Investment Manager has been appointed in the place and stead of the Investment Manager named or, in the alternative, that the Investment Manager has been removed and the responsibility for the investment and management of the trust assets has been assumed by the Committee or has been transferred back to the Trustee, as the case may be.

(b) In the event the Committee is given full power and responsibility to direct the Trustee with respect to the investment and management of all or a portion of the assets of the Trust Fund, the Trustee shall not be liable nor responsible for losses or unfavorable results arising from the Trustee's compliance with proper directions of the Committee which are made in accordance with the terms of the Plan and Trust and which are not contrary to the provisions of any applicable Federal or State statute regulating such investment and management of the assets of an employee benefit trust. In the event that an Investment Manager has full authority and responsibility with respect to the investment and management of the trust assets, the Trustee shall not be liable nor responsible in any way for any losses or other unfavorable results arising from the Trustee's compliance with investment or management directions received by the Trustee from the Investment Manager. All directions concerning investments made by the Committee or the Investment Manager shall be signed by such person or persons, acting on behalf of the Committee or the Investment Manager, as the case may be, as may be fully authorized in writing; provided, however, that the transmission to the Trustee of such directions by photostatic teletransmission with duplicate or facsimile signature or signatures shall be considered a delivery in writing of the aforesaid directions until the Trustee is notified in writing by the Committee that the use of such devices with duplicate or facsimile signatures is no longer authorized. The Trustee shall be entitled to rely upon directions which which it receives by such means if so authorized by the Committee and shall in no way be responsible for the consequences of any authorized use of such device which use was not, in fact, known by the Trustee at the time to be unauthorized. The

Trustee shall be under no duty to question any directions of the Investment Manager not to review any securities or other property of the Trust constituting assets thereof with respect to which an Investment Manager has investment responsibility, nor to make any suggestions to such Investment Manager in connection therewith. The Trustee shall, as promptly as possible, comply with any written directions given by the Committee or an Investment Manager hereunder and, where such directions are given by photostatic teletransmission with facsimile signature or signatures, the Trustee shall be entitled to presume that any directions so given are fully authorized. The Trustee shall not be liable, in any manner nor for any reason, for the making or retention of any investment pursuant to such directions of the Investment Manager, nor shall the Trustee be liable for its failure to invest any or all of the Trust fund in the absence of such written directions. In any event, neither the Committee nor any Investment Manager referred to above shall direct the purchase, sale or retention of any assets of the Trust Fund if such directions are not in compliance with the applicable provisions of the Act and any Regulations or Rulings issued thereunder. No fiduciary shall permit the indicia of ownership of any of the Trust assets to be maintained at a location outside the jurisdiction of the District Courts of the United States, except as authorized by the Secretary of Labor.

(c) During such period or periods of time, if any, as the Committee or an Investment Manager is authorized to direct the investment and management of the trust assets, the Trustee shall have no obligation to determine the existence of any conversion, redemption, exchange, subscription or other right relating to any of said securities purchased of which notice was given prior to the purchase of such securities, and shall have no obligation to exercise any such right unless the Trustee is informed of the existence of the right and is instructed to exercise such right, in writing, by the Committee or the Investment Manager, as the case may be, within a reasonable time prior to the expiration of such right.

(d) During such period or periods of time, if any, as the Committee and an Investment Manager is authorized to direct the Trustee to purchase securities issued by any foreign government or agency thereof, or by any corporation domiciled outside the United States, it shall be the responsibility of the Committee or Investment Manager, as the case may be, to advise the Trustee, in writing, with respect to any laws or Regulations of any foreign countries or any United States territories or possession which shall apply, in any manner whatsoever, to such securities including, but not limited to, receipt of dividends or interests by the Trustee from such securities; and the Company does hereby agree to forever hold the Trustee harmless and indemnify the Trustee against any losses which may occur with respect to the Trust Fund which are occasioned by the failure to give such written notification to the Trustee.

7.14—Insurance.

Notwithstanding any other provisions of this Plan and Trust Agreement, in the event the Committee directs that any monies constituting assets of the Trust Fund shall be invested in policies of life insurance or annuity policies, either on an individual or a group basis, the Committee shall select the insurance company or companies with respect to which such investments shall be made and shall further direct such insurance company or companies to notify the Committee of all premiums due or to become due, the respective amounts of any said premiums [which shall not exceed fifty percent (50%) of the contributions allocated to a Participant's account in the case of ordinary life insurance or twenty-five (25%) in the case of term life insurance] and the respective dates when the same are due, whereupon the Committee shall verify the names of the individual Participants if the policies or annuities involved relate to the lives of individual Participants in the Plan, and the Committee shall thereupon deliver to the Trustee such premium notices together with the Committee's verification, as aforesaid, and a written direction to pay such premiums, no less than five (5) Bank working days prior to the date or dates any said premiums shall be due. In the event that the Committee does not strictly comply with the provisions of this Paragraph 7.14, time being of the essence thereof, the Trustee shall have no duty nor liability with respect to the payment of any of said premiums and shall be entitled to presume that the Committee has properly decided to permit such policies to lapse.

7.15—Method of Valuation.

Notwithstanding any other provisions contained in this Trust Agreement, the fair market value of assets in the trust shall be determined by the Trustee based upon such sources of information as it may deem reliable including, but not limited to, information report in (1) newspapers of general circulation, (2) standard financial periodicals or publications, (3) statistical and valuation services, (4) the records of securities exchanges, Investment Managers or brokerage firms or any combination thereof deemed by the Trustee to be reliable.

7.16—Fiduciary Responsibility.

Each of the fiduciaries under the Plan and Trust shall be solely responsible for its own acts or omissions. Except to the extent imposed by said Act, no fiduciary shall have the duty to question whether any other fiduciary is fulfilling all of the responsibilities imposed upon such other fiduciary by the Act, as the same may be amended from time to time, or by any Regulations or Rulings issued thereunder. No fiduciary shall have any liability for a breach of fiduciary responsibility of another fiduciary with respect to this Plan and Trust Agreement unless he participates knowingly in such breach, knowingly undertakes to conceal such breach, has actual knowledge of such breach and fails to take reasonable remedial action to remedy said breach or, through his negligence in performing his own specific fiduciary responsibilities which give rise to his status as a fiduciary, he has enabled such other fiduciary to commit a breach of the latter's fiduciary responsibilities.

7.17—Fiduciary Standard of Conduct.

Each fiduciary of the Plan shall discharge his duties solely in the interests of the Participants and their Beneficiaries. Each fiduciary of the Plan shall act with the care, skill, prudence, and diligence under the circumstances then prevailing that a prudent man acting in a like capacity and familiar with such matters would use in conducting an enterprise of like character and with like aims. Fiduciaries shall diversify Plan assets to minimize risk of large losses, unless under the circumstances it is clearly prudent not to do so.

7.18—Prohibited Transactions.

(a) Except as provided in subsection (c) of this Section 7.18, a fiduciary shall not cause the Plan to engage in a transaction if he knows or should know that such transaction constitutes a direct or indirect:

(1) Sale of exchange, or leasing of any property between the Plan and a party-in-interest; or

(2) Lending of money or extension of credit between the Plan and a party-in-interest; or

(3) Furnishing of goods, services or facilities between the Plan and a party-in-interest; or

(4) Transfer to, or use by or for the benefit of a party-in-interest, of any assets of the Plan; or

(5) Acquisition, on behalf of the Plan, of an Employer security or Employer real property.

(b) Except as provided in subsection (c) of this Section 7.18, a fiduciary shall not:

(1) Deal with the assets of the Plan to his own interest or for his own account; or

(2) In his individual or any other capacity act in any transaction involving the Plan on behalf of a party or represent a party whose interests are adverse to the interests of the Plan or the interests of its Participants or Beneficiaries; or

(3) Receive any consideration for his own personal account from any party dealing with such Plan in connection with a transaction involving the assets of the Plan.

(c) The prohibited transactions rules set forth in this Section 7.18 shall not prevent a plan fiduciary from:

(1) Receiving benefits from the Plan as a Participant or Beneficiary so long as the benefits are consistent with the terms of the Plan as applied to all other Participants and Beneficiaries;

(2) Receiving reasonable compensation for services to the Plan unless the fiduciary receives full-time pay from the Employer or Employee organization;

(3) Receiving reimbursement for expenses incurred; or

(4) Serving as an officer, employee, or agent of a party-in-interest; or

(5) Making payments to parties-in-interest for reasonable compensation for office space and legal, accounting and other services necessary to operate the plan; and

(6) Taking other actions pursuant to specific instructions and authorizations in the Plan governing document so far as consistent with all other fiduciary rules of the Act.

(d) For purposes of this Section, the term "party-in-interest" shall include, but not by way of limitation, the following:

(1) Any fiduciary or counsel of the Plan;

(2) A person providing services to the Plan;

(3) The Company; and

(4) A relative of any individual described in subparagraphs (1) and (2) above.

7.19—Liability Insurance.

The following parties may purchase and maintain liability insurance under the following terms and conditions:

(1) The Plan administrator, as an authorized expense of the Plan, to cover liability or losses occurring by reason of the act or omission of a fiduciary provided such insurance permits recourse by the Insurer against the fiduciary in the case of a breach of a fiduciary obligation by such fiduciary;

(2) a fiduciary, to cover liability from and for his own account;

(3) the Employer, to cover potential liability of one or more persons who serve in a fiduciary capacity with regard to the Plan.

7.20—Prohibition Against Certain Persons Holding Certain Positions.

No person who has been convicted of, or has been imprisoned as a result of his conviction of, robbery, bribery, extortion, embezzlement, fraud, grand larceny, burglary, arson, a felony violation of Federal or State law involving substances defined in Section 102(6) of the Comprehensive Drug Abuse Prevention and Control Act of 1970, murder, rape, kidnapping, perjury, assault with intent to kill, any crime described in Section 9(a)(1) of the Investment Company Act of 1940, a violation of any provision of the Employee Retirement Income Security Act of 1974, a violation of Section 302 of the Labor-Management Relations Act, 1947, a violation of Chapter 63 of Title 18, United States Code, a violation of Section 874, 1026, 1503, 1505, 1506, 1510, 1951, or 1954 of Title 18, United States Code, a violation of the Labor-Management Reporting and Disclosure Act of 1959, or conspiracy to commit any such crimes or attempt to commit any such crimes, or a crime in which any of the foregoing crimes is an element, shall serve or be permitted to serve:

(1) as an administrator, fiduciary, officer, trustee, custodian, counsel, agent, or employee of any employee benefit plan; or

(2) as a consultant to any employee benefit plan.

7.21—Bonding Requirements.

(a) Every fiduciary of the Plan and every person who handles funds or other property of the Plan shall be bonded, provided, however, that no bond shall be required of a fiduciary (or of any director, officer, or employee of such fiduciary) if such fiduciary:

(1) is a corporation organized and doing business under the laws of the United States or of any State;

(2) is authorized under such laws to exercise trust powers or to conduct an insurance business;

(3) is subject to supervision or examination by Federal or State authority; and

(4) has at all times a combined capital and surplus in excess of such minimum amount as may be established by regulations issued by the Secretary of Labor, which amount shall be at least $1,000,000.

(b) The amount of such bond shall be fixed at the beginning of each Fiscal Year of the Plan. Such amount shall not be less than ten percent (10%) of the amount of funds handled. In no event shall such bond be less than $1,000 nor more than $500,000, except that the Secretary of Labor, after due notice and opportunity for hearing to all interested parties, may prescribe an amount in excess of $500,000, subject to the ten percent (10%) limitation of the preceding sentence. Such bond shall provide protection to the Plan against loss by reason of acts of fraud or dishonesty on the part of the Plan official, directly or through connivance with others.

ARTICLE VIII

RESIGNATION AND REMOVAL OF TRUSTEE

8.1—Method and Procedure.

Any Trustee may resign at any time by delivering to the Company a written notice of resignation, to take effect at a date specified therein, which shall not be less than thirty (30) days after the delivery thereof, unless such notice shall be waived.

Any Trustee may be removed by the Company by delivery of a written notice of removal, to take effect at a date specified therein, which shall not be less than thirty (30) days after delivery thereof, unless such notice shall be waived.

The Company, upon receipt of or giving notice of the resignation or removal of a Trustee, shall promptly appoint a successor Trustee. While a vacancy exists, the remaining Trustee may perform any act which the Trustees are authorized to perform.

Upon the appointment of a successor trustee, all right, title and interest of such former Trustee in the assets of the trust and all rights and privileges under this Agreement theretofore vested in such Trustee shall vest in the successor Trustee, and thereupon all future liability of such Trustee shall terminate; provided, however, that the Trustee shall execute, acknowledge, and deliver all documents and written instruments which are necessary to transfer and convey the right, title and interest in the trust assets, and all rights and privileges to the successor trustee.

In the event of the resignation or removal of the initial trustee, the successor Trustee or Trustees may be one or more individuals and/or bank or trust company qualified and authorized to do business in the State of California.

ARTICLE IX

AMENDMENT AND TERMINATION

9.1—Amendments.

The Company shall have the right to amend this Trust from time to time, and to amend or cancel any amendments. Such amendments shall be stated in an instrument in writing executed by the Company, and this Agreement shall be amended in the manner and at the time therein set forth, and all Participants should be bound thereby; provided, however:

    (a) No amendments shall cause any of the assets of the Trust to be used for or diverted to purposes other than for the exclusive benefit of Participants or their beneficiaries;

    (b) No amendment shall have any retroactive effect so as to deprive any Participant of any benefit already vested, except that such changes, if any, as may be required to permit the Plan to meet the requirements of the Internal Revenue Code, or of the corresponding provisions of any subsequent revenue law, may be made to assure the deductibility for tax purposes of any contributions;

    (c) No amendment shall create or effect any discrimination in favor of Participants who are officers, shareholders, or whose principal duties consist of supervising the work of other employees, or highly compensated employees; and

    (d) No amendment shall increase the duties or liabilities of the Trustees without their written consent.

9.2—Discontinuance of Plan.

This Trust is irrevocable and it is the expectation of the Company that this Plan and the payment of contributions hereunder shall be continued indefinitely, but continuance of the Plan is not assumed as a contractual obligation of the Company, and the right is reserved at any time to reduce or discontinue contributions hereunder. In the event of complete discontinuance of contributions, each Participant shall have a vested and non-forfeitable interest in his pension trust account to the extent of one hundred percent (100%).

The Company may terminate this Plan at any time upon fifteen (15) days written notice to the Trustees. Upon termination or partial termination of the Plan, the entire interest of each of the affected Participants shall vest and become nonforfeitable to the extent of one hundred percent (100%) immediately. The Trustees shall, with reasonable promptness, liquidate all assets remaining in the Trust. Upon the liquidation of all assets, the Committee shall make, after deducting estimated expenses for liquidation and distribution, the allocations required under Article IV, where applicable, with the same effect as though the date of completion of liquidation were an Anniversary Date of the Plan. Following these allocations, the Trustee shall promptly, after receipt of appropriate instructions from the Committee, distribute in accordance with Section 5.2 to each former Participant a benefit equal to the amount credited to his account as of the date of completion of liquidation.

ARTICLE X

EMPLOYEE RIGHTS

10.1—General Rights of Participants and Beneficiaries.

The Plan is established and Trust Assets are held for the exclusive purpose of providing benefits for such Employees and their Beneficiares as have qualified to participate under the terms of the Company's Plan. Such benefits may be payable upon retirement, death, disability or termination of employment with the Company, subject to the specific provisions of the Plan.

Every Participant and Beneficiary receiving benefits under the Plan is entitled to receive, on a regular basis, a current, comprehensible and detailed written account of his personal benefit status and of the relevant terms of the Plan which provides these benefits.

10.2—Regular Reports and Disclosure Requirements.

Every Participant covered under the Plan and every Beneficiary receiving benefits under the Plan shall receive a summary plan description, summary of the latest annual report of the Plan, or such other information as may be required to be furnished by law, under any of the following circumstances:

(a) When the Plan is established, or any material modification or amendment is proposed or adopted;

(b) Within ninety (90) days after he becomes a Participant or begins to receive benefits under the Plan;

(c) Within two hundred and ten (210) days after the close of the Plan's Fiscal Year.

10.3—Information Generally Available.

The Committee shall make copies of the Plan description and the latest annual report and any bargaining agreement, trust agreement, contract or other instruments under which the Plan was established or is operated available for examination by any Plan Participant or Beneficiary in the principal office of the Committee and such other locations as may be necessary to make such information reasonably accessible to all interested parties, and subject to a reasonable charge to defray the cost of furnishing such copies, the Plan Committee shall, upon written request of any Participant or Beneficiary, furnish a copy of the latest updated summary plan description, and the latest annual report, any terminal report, any bargaining agreement, trust agreement, contracts, or other instruments under which this Plan is established or operated to the party making such request.

10.4—Special Disclosures.

Upon written request to the Committee once during any twelve (12) month period, a Participant or Beneficiary shall be furnished with a written statement, based on the latest available information, of the total benefits accrued, or the earliest date on which such benefits will become nonforfeitable.

Prior to the distribution of any benefits to which any Participant or Beneficiary may be entitled, he must be provided with a written explanation of the terms and conditions of the various distribution options that are available and must, in turn, file a written election with the Committee.

Upon termination of employment, an Employee who has been a Participant in the Plan is entitled to a written explanation of and accounting for any vested deferred benefits which have accrued to his account and of any applicable options regarding the disposition of those benefits. Such information will also be provided to the Social Security Administration by the Internal Revenue Service on the basis of information required to be reported by the Committee.

10.5—Employee Right to Comment.

Pursuant to rights granted by the Act and the Regulations issued pursuant to that authority, the Participants shall be advised with respect to, and given an opportunity to comment on, the application of the Plan for a ruling regarding:

(a) Initial qualification determination under the requirements of the Internal Revenue Code;

(b) Any material amendment to the Plan;

(c) Any partial or complete termination of the Plan.

10.6—Filing a Claim for Benefits.

A Participant or Beneficiary or the Employer acting in his behalf shall notify the Committee of a claim of benefits under the Plan. Such request may be in any form acceptable to the Committee and shall set forth the basis of such claim and shall authorize the Committee to conduct such examinations as may be necessary to determine the validity of the claim and to take such steps as may be necessary to facilitate the payment of any benefits to which the Participant or Beneficiary may be entitled under the terms of the plan.

10.7—Denial of Claim.

Whenever a claim for benefits by any Participant or Beneficiary has been denied, a written notice, prepared in a manner calculated to be understood by the Participant, must be provided, setting forth the specific reasons for the denial and explaining the procedure for an appeal and review of the decision by the Committee.

10.8—Remedies Available to Participants.

A Participant or Beneficiary shall be entitled, either in his own name or in conjunction with any other interested parties, to bring such actions in law or equity or to undertake such administrative actions or to seek such relief as may be necessary or appropriate to compel the disclosure of any required information, to enforce or protect his rights, to recover present benefits under the Plan.

10.9—Protection from Reprisal.

No Participant or Beneficiary may be discharged, fined, suspended, expelled, disciplined, or otherwise discriminated against for exercising any right to which he is entitled or for cooperation with any inquiry or investigation under the provisions of this Plan or any governing law or Regulations.

No person shall, directly or indirectly, through the use or threatened use of fraud, force or violence, restrain, coerce or intimidate any Participant or Beneficiary for the purpose of interfering with or preventing the exercise of or enforcement of any right, remedy or claim to which he is entitled under the terms of this Plan or any relevant law or Regulations.

10.10—Mergers, Consolidations or Transfers.

In the case of any merger or consolidation with, or transfer of assets or liabilities to, any other plan after the date of enactment of the Employee Retirement Income Security Act of 1974, each Participant in the Plan will (if the Plan then terminated) receive a benefit immediately after such merger, consolidation or transfer, which will be equal to or greater than the benefit he would have been entitled to receive immediately before such merger, consolidation, or transfer if the Plan then terminated.

ARTICLE XI

MISCELLANEOUS

11.1—Contribution Not Recoverable.

Subsequent to an initial determination and ruling of the Commissioner of Internal Revenue that this Trust is a "qualified" trust as defined in Internal Revenue Code, Section 401, it shall be impossible for any part of the principal or income to be used for or diverted to purposes other than the exclusive benefit of such Participants or their beneficiaries.

In the event the initial determination and ruling (regarding qualification of this Trust by the Commissioner of Internal Revenue) that this is not a qualified trust as defined in Internal Revenue Code Section 401, the Company, at its election, may recover any of its contributions made prior to said ruling.

11.2—Limitation on Participants' Rights.

Participation in this Trust shall not give any employees the right to be retained in the Company's employ or any right or interest in this Trust other than as herein provided. The Company reserves the right to dismiss any employee without liability for any claim either against this Trust, except to the extent provided herein, or against the Company. All benefits payable hereunder shall be provided solely from the Trust, and the Company assumes no responsibility for the acts of the Trustees.

11.3—Nonassignability.

None of the benefits, payments, proceeds or claims of any Participant or Beneficiary shall be subject to any claim of any creditor and, in particular, the same shall not be subject to attachment or garnishment or other legal process by any creditor, nor shall any such Participant or Beneficiary have any right to alienate, anticipate, commute, pledge, encumber, or assign any of the benefits or payments or proceeds which he may expect to receive, contingently or otherwise, under this agreement.

11.4—Federal Law Governs.

This Trust Agreement and the Trust hereby created shall be construed, administered, and governed in all respects under applicable Federal law, and to the extent that Federal law is inapplicable by the laws of the State of California; provided, however, that if any provision is susceptible of more than one interpretation, such interpretation shall be given thereto as is consistent with this pension plan and trust being an employees' pension plan and trust within the meaning of the Internal Revenue Code, or corresponding provisions of subsequent revenue laws. If any provision of this instrument shall be held by a court of competent jurisdiction to be invalid or unenforceable, the remaining provisions hereof shall continue to be fully effective.

11.5—Time Limit.

In the event the validity of this Trust shall depend upon compliance with the rule against perpetuities, then it shall terminate upon the death of the last to die of such of the employees, participating in the Plan from time to time, who were living on the day of execution of this Agreement.

11.6—Headings No Part
of Agreement.

Headings and subheadings in this Agreement are inserted for convenience of reference only. They constitute no part of the Agreement.

11.7—Instrument in Counterparts.

This Agreement has been executed in several counterparts, each of which shall be deemed an original, and said counterparts shall constitute but one and the same instrument, which may be sufficiently evidenced by one counterpart.

11.8—Successors and Assigns.

This Agreement shall inure to the benefit of and be binding upon the parties hereto and their successors and assigns.

11.9—Gender.

The masculine gender shall include the feminine, and wherever appropriate the singular shall include the plural or the plural may be read as the singular.

11.10—Liability.

No provision contained in this Plan shall be construed as relieving any officers, directors or Trustee, or member of any Committee, Board or other body acting on behalf of the BIG BUCKS, INC. EM-

PLOYEES' PENSION TRUST (Money-Purchase Plan) of any liability. Trustees are subject to liability for negligence, wilful misconduct or for bad faith.

IN WITNESS WHEREOF, the Company and the Trustee have caused this Agreement to be executed on the 1st day of April, 1979.

BIG BUCKS, INC., A California Corporation.

By _____

President

By _____

Secretary

APPROVED AS TO FORM:

By _____

Attorneys for Company

ACCEPTANCE OF TRUSTEE

HERBERT BUCKSUP does hereby accept his appointment as initial Trustee of the BIG BUCKS, INC., EMPLOYEES' PENSION TRUST (MONEY PURCHASE PLAN) and agrees to perform all of the duties and obligations imposed by said Trust Agreement.

DATED: _____, 1979.

_____

[¶908.4] What to Do After Plans Have Been Adopted

Once the plan or plans have been properly adopted, each plan should obtain an identification number from the IRS. They should be submitted to the District Director of the Internal Revenue Service to obtain from the Service a determination letter that states that the plans are qualified plans. The application should be made as soon as is practical; but must be made before the corporation files its Federal income tax return. Prior to submitting the plans to the Service, employees must be notified that the corporation has adopted the plans. They also must be informed of their rights in connection with the submission of the plan to the IRS.

The following documents must be prepared and submitted to plan participants, the IRS or the Department of Labor. Some of the documents may have to be submitted to more than one of the above.

☐ Notice to All Employees (see pages 376 to 379).
　　This must be posted in a conspicuous place and be posted prior to the time the plan is sent to the IRS.

☐ Forms 5301 and 5302 (see pages 380 to 391).
　　Application to IRS for a letter stating that the plans are qualified.

☐ Form 2848 (page 392).
　　This is a power of attorney which enables an attorney or CPA to act on the client's behalf in dealing with the IRS.

☐ Cover letter to IRS (page 395).
　　This accompanies the plans and requests a letter from the IRS stating that the plans are qualified.

☐ Summary Plan Description (see pages 397 to 420).
　　This document summarizes the provisions of the retirement plan. It must be given to each participant within 120 days after the plan has been adopted. A copy must also be filed with the Department of Labor.

☐ Form EBS-1 (see pages 422 to 433).
　　This form contains information regarding how the plan

will be administered. It must be filed with the Department of Labor within 120 days after the plan is adopted.

☐ Form 5500-C (see pages 436 to 441).

This is a form that must be filed with the IRS and the Department of Labor. It is an annual return that contains financial information relating to the operation of the plan.

These forms have been reproduced on the following pages. They have been filled in as if a corporation adopted the sample pension plan and profit-sharing plan which have been previously reproduced.

NOTICE TO

ALL EMPLOYEES

Name of Plan: BIG BUCKS, INC. EMPLOYEES
PENSION TRUST (MONEY-PURCHASE PLAN)
Plan I.D. #95-0000000

Name of Applicant: Applicant I.D. #95-0000000

BIG BUCKS, INC., A California
Corporation

Name of Plan Administrator: Administrative Committee for the Big
Bucks, Inc. Employees' Pension Trust

The application will be submitted to the District Director of the Internal Revenue at Los Angeles, California, for an advance determination as to whether or not the plan qualifies under section 401(a) of the Internal Revenue Code, with respect to initial qualification.

The employees eligible to participate under the plan are all fulltime employees with six (6) months of service on any Anniversary Date of the Plan.

The Internal Revenue Service has not previously issued a determination letter with respect to the qualification of this plan.

Each person to whom this notice is addressed is entitled to submit, or request the Department of Labor to submit, to the District Director described above a comment on the question of whether the plan meets the requirements for qualification under part I of Subchapter D of chapter 1 of the Internal Revenue Code of 1954. Two or more such persons may join in a single comment or request. If such a person or persons request the Department of Labor to submit a comment and that department declines to do so in respect of one or more matters raised in the request, the person or persons so requesting may submit a comment to the District Director in respect of the matters on which the Department of Labor declines to comment. A comment submitted to the District Director must be received by him on or before (45 days after Receipt by IRS). However, if it is being submitted on a matter on which the Department of Labor was first requested, but declined to comment, the comment must be received by the District Director on or before the later of (45 days later), or the 15th day after the day on which the Department of Labor notifies such person or persons that it declines to comment, but in no event later than (60 days later). A request of the Department of Labor to submit a comment must be received by that department on or before (25 days later), 1979, or, if the person or persons making the request wish to preserve their right to submit a comment to the District Director in the event the Department of Labor declines to comment, on or before (15 days later), 1979.

Additional informational material regarding the plan and the procedures to be followed in submitting, or requesting the Department of Labor to submit, a comment, may be obtained at 445 South Figueroa St., Los Angeles, Ca. 90071.

Additional informational material to be made available to interested parties:

1. Up-dated copy of Plan and related Trust Agreement.

2. Application for Determination to the Internal Revenue Service excluding Employees' Census (Form 5302).

3. Any additional document dealing with the application which is submitted by or for the applicant to the Internal Revenue Service, or furnished by the Internal Revenue Service to the Applicant.

4. Comment Procedure Statement.

A comment submitted by an interested party or parties to the District Director must be in writing, signed by such party or parties or by an authorized representative of such party or parties (as provided in §601.201 (e) (6) of the Internal Revenue Service Statement of Procedural Rules), be addressed to the District Director (described in subsection 034), and contain the following:

(a) The name or names of the interested party or parties making the comment;

(b) the name and taxpayer identification number of the applicant making the application;

(c) the name of the plan and the plan identification number.

(d) whether the party or parties submitting the comments are:

(i) employees eligible to participate under the plan,

(ii) former employees or beneficiaries of deceased former

employees who have a vested right to benefit under the Plan, or

(iii) employees not eligible to participate under the Plan.

(e) the specific matter or matters raised by the interested party or parties on the question whether the plan meets the requirements for qualification under Part I of Subchapter D of the Code, and how such matter or matters relate to the interests of such party or parties making such comment.

(f) the address of the interested party submitting the comment to which all correspondence, including a notice of the Internal Revenue Service's final determination with respect to qualification should be sent. (See Section 7476 (b) (5) of the Code.) If more than one interested party submits the comment, it must designate a representative for receipt of such correspondence and notice on behalf of all interested parties submitting the comment and state the address of such representative. Such representative shall be one of the interested parties submitting the comment or the authorized representative.

5. Request Procedure Statement.

(1) A request of the Department of Labor to submit a comment to the District Director must be in writing, signed as provided in the Comment Procedure Statement, addressed to the Director of the Office of Employee Benefits Security, Department of Labor, 200 Constitution Avenue, N.W., Washington, D.C. 20210, and contain the information prescribed in the Comment Procedure Statement. The address designated for notice by the Internal Revenue Service will be used by the Department of Labor in communicating with the party or parties submitting the request.

(2) If a request described in the preceding Paragraph 5 (1) is made and the Department of Labors sends a notice that it declines to comment on one or more matters raised in the request, the party or parties submitting the request may submit to the District Director at Los Angeles a comment in respect of any matter on which the Department of Labor declines to comment. Such comment must comply with the requirements described in the Comment Procedure Statement and include a statement that the comment is being submitted on matters raised in a request to the Department of Labor on which that department declined to comment.

(3) For purposes of requests of the Department of Labor,

Notice by the Department of Labor that it declines to comment shall be deemed given to the interested party designated to receive such notice when received by him.

(4) The contents of written comments submitted by interested parties to the Internal Revenue Service will not be treated as confidential material and may be inspected by persons outside the Internal Revenue Service, including the applicant for the determination. Accordingly, designations of material as confidential or not to be disclosed, contained in such comments, will not be accepted. Thus, an interested party submitting a written comment should not include therein material that he considers to be confidential or inappropriate for disclosure to the public. It will be presumed by the Internal Revenue Service that every written comment submitted to it is intended by the party or parties submitting it to be subject in its entirety to public inspection and copying.

[¶909] IRS FORMS 5301 AND 5302, AND POWER OF ATTORNEY (2848)

The IRS has printed forms which are to be used in connection with requesting a letter of determination for a retirement plan. In the case of a profit-sharing plan or money-purchase plan, these are Forms 5301 and 5302. Completed copies of these forms are prepared for each plan.

These forms can be copied directly unless changes are made in such items as vesting, in which case the form should be revised to reflect any such changes.

These completed forms can provide tremendous time saving—and saving time means more profit for your firm. Also, a client can be more easily advised.

To be able to deal with the Internal Revenue Service in the event any questions arise in connection with the plans, a power of attorney must be obtained from the client. This authorizes the attorney (or Certified Public Accountant) to act as the corporation's agent.

This form is numbered 2848 and is pre-printed by the government for your convenience. A reproduction has been prepared with all the necessary information.

Form **5301**

(Rev. June 1976)

Department of the Treasury
Internal Revenue Service

Application for
Determination for Defined Contribution Plan
For Profit-sharing, Stock Bonus and Money Purchase Plans
(Under sections 401(a), 405(a), 414(l) and 501(a) of the Internal Revenue Code)
This Form is Open to Public Inspection

For IRS Use Only

Case number ▶ ....

Issue date ▶ ....

EPMF status code ▶ ....

File folder
number ▶

▶ **Church and Governmental Plans.**—All items need not be completed. See instruction "B. What to File."

▶ Please complete every applicable item on this form. If an item does not apply, enter N/A.

1 (a) Name, address and ZIP code of employer	2 Employer's identification nur

1 (a) Name, address and ZIP code of employer

BIG BUCKS, INC.

445 South Figueroa Street

Los Angeles, CA 90071 | Telephone number ▶ (*213*) *620-0460*

(b) Name, address and ZIP code of plan administrator, if other than employer

Profit Sharing Plan Committee

445 South Figueroa Street

Los Angeles, California 90071

(c) Administrator's identification number ▶ *95-0000000*   Telephone number ▶ (*213*) *620-0460*

2 Employer's identification nur
95-0000000

3 Business code number
5931

4 Date incorporated or business comme
2/1/78

5 Employer's taxable year end
January

6 Determination requested for:

(a) (i) ☒ Initial qualification—date plan adopted ▶ *4/1/78*   (ii) ☐ Amendment—date adopted ▶ ....

(iii) If (ii) is checked, enter file folder number ▶ ....

(b) Were employees who are interested parties given the required notification of the filing of this application? . ☒ Yes ☐

(c) If this application involves a merger or consolidation with another plan, enter the employer identification number(s) and plan number(s) of such other plan(s) ▶

7 Type of entity: **(a)** ☒ Corporation   **(b)** ☐ Subchapter S corporation   **(c)** ☐ Sole proprietor   **(d)** ☐ Partners

(e) ☐ Tax exempt organization   **(f)** ☐ Church   **(g)** ☐ Governmental organization

(h) ☐ Other (specify) ▶

8 (a) Name of Plan *BIG BUCKS, INC. EMPLOYEES* **(b)** Plan number ▶ *002*   **(c)** Plan year ends ▶ *Jan*

PROFIT SHARING PLAN AND TRUST **(d)** Is this a Keogh (H.R. 10) plan? . . . . ☐ Yes ☒

AGREEMENT **(e)** If "Yes," is an owner-employee in the plan? . ☐ Yes ☐

9 (a) If this is an adoption of a master or prototype plan (other than Keogh) or a district approved pattern plan, enter name of such plan *N/A* **(b)** Letter serial number notification letter num *N/A*

10 Type of plan: **(a)** ☒ Profit-sharing   **(b)** ☐ Stock bonus   **(c)** ☐ Money purchase   **(d)** ☐ Target ben

11 Effective date of plan *2/1/78*	12 Effective date of amendment *N/A*	13 Date plan was communicated to employees ▶ *4/1/7*

How communicated? ▶ *Notice*

14 (a) Indicate the general eligibility requirements for participation under the plan and indicate the section and page number of plan or trust where each provision is contained:	Section and page number *	GOVERNME USE ONL

(i) ☐ All employees   (v) Length of service (number of years) ▶ *6 mos.*

(ii) ☐ Hourly rate employee only   (vi) Minimum age (specify) ▶ *2.1, p.6*

(iii) ☐ Salaried employee only   (vii) Maximum age (specify) ▶ ....

(iv) ☐ Other job class (specify) ▶ ....   (viii) Minimum pay (specify) ▶ ....

(b) Are the eligibility requirements the same for future employees? . . . . ☒ Yes ☐ No   *2.1, p.6*

If "No," explain ▶ ....

(c) Does the plan recognize service only with this employer? . . . . . . ☒ Yes ☐ No   *2.1, p.6*

If "No," explain ▶

15 Coverage of plan at (give date) ▶ *1/31/79*

Enter here the number of self-employed individuals ▶ *None*

	Number
(a) Total employed (if a Keogh plan, include all self-employed individuals)	3
(b) Exclusions under plan (do not count an employee more than once):	
(i) Minimum age or years of service required (specify) ▶	0
(ii) Employees included in collective bargaining	0
(iii) Nonresident aliens who receive no earned income from United States sources	0
(c) Total exclusions, sum of (b)(i) through (iii)	0
(d) Employees not excluded under the statute, (a) less (c)	3

* Of plan or trust or other document constituting the plan.

Under penalties of perjury, I declare that I have examined this application, including accompanying statements, and to the best of my knowledge and belief it is true, c and complete.

Signature ▶ _____ Title ▶ _____ Date ▶ _____

380

(Section references are to the Internal Revenue Code)			Number	GOVERNMENT USE ONLY
Coverage *(continued):*				
e) Ineligible under plan on account of (do not count an employee included in (b)):			/////	
(i) Minimum pay			0	
(ii) Hourly-paid			0	
(iii) Maximum age			0	
(iv) Other (specify) ▶			0	
f) Employees ineligible, sum of (e)(i) through (iv)			0	
g) Employees eligible to participate, line (d) less line (f)			3	
h) Number of employees participating in plan			3	
i) Percent of nonexcluded employees who are participating, (h) divided by (d) . . .		100 %	/////	
Complete (j) only if (i) is less than 70% and complete (k) only if (j) is 70% or more.			/////	
j) Percent of nonexcluded employees who are eligible to participate, (g) divided by (d)		%		
k) Percent of eligible employees who are participating, (h) divided by (g)		%	/////	
If (i) and (j) are less than 70% or (k) is less than 80%, see instructions.			/////	
l) Total number of participants, include certain retired and terminated employees, see instructions			3	

	Yes	No	Section and page number *	
Employee contributions:				
a) Are mandatory contributions limited to 6%, or less, of compensation? . . .			N/A	
b) Are voluntary contributions limited to 10%, or less, of compensation for all qualified plans? .	XX		4.1, p.11	
c) Are employee contributions nonforfeitable?	XX		6.1, p.18	
Employer contributions:				
a) Under a profit-sharing or stock bonus plan, are they determined under—				
(i) ☐ A definite formula *(ii)* ☒ An indefinite formula *(iii)* ☐ Both			3.3, p.9	
b) Under profit-sharing or stock bonus plans are contributions limited to—				
(i) ☐ Current earnings *(ii)* ☐ Accumulated earnings *(iii)* ☒ Combination			3.3, p.10	
c) Money purchase—Enter rate of contribution ▶				
d) State target benefit formula, if applicable ▶				

	Yes	No		
Integration:	/////	/////		
Is this plan integrated with Social Security or Railroad Retirement?	/////	XX		
If "Yes," see instructions.	/////	/////		

Vesting—Check the appropriate box to indicate the vesting provisions of the plan:

(a) ☐ Full and immediate

(b) ☐ Full vesting after 10 years of service

(c) ☐ 5- to 15-year vesting, i.e., 25% after 5 years of service, 5% additional for each of the next 5 years, then 10% additional for each of the next 5 years

(d) ☐ Rule of 45 (see section 411(a)(2)(C))

(e) ☐ For each year of employment, commencing with the 4th such year, vesting not less than 40% after 4 years of service, 5% additional for each of the next 2 years, and 10% additional for each of the next 5 years

(f) ☐ 100% vesting within 5 years after contributions are made (class year plans only)

(g) ☐ Other (specify and see instructions) ▶ _20% for each year of service_ 6.2, p.10

Administration:

(a) Type of funding entity: *(i)* ☒ Trust   *(ii)* ☐ Custodial account   *(iii)* ☐ Non-trusteed   3.2, p.9

   If you checked (i) or (ii), enter date executed ▶ _April 1, 1978_

(b) Enter name of trustee or custodian, if any ▶ _Herbert Bucksup_

	Yes	No		
(c) Does trust agreement prohibit reversion of funds to the employer?	XX		12.1, p65	
(d) Specify the limits placed on the purchase of insurance contracts, if any:	/////			
(i) Ordinary life ▶ _50% of account_	/////		8.14, p45	
(ii) Term insurance ▶ _25% of account_	/////		8.14, p45	
(iii) Other (specify) ▶	/////			
(e) If the trustees may earmark specific investments, including insurance contracts, are such investments subject to the employee's consent, or purchased ratably where employee consent is not required?	/////		N/A	
(f) Are loans to participants limited to their vested interests?		XX	6.6, p.26	
(g) If Puerto Rican trust, does it qualify for tax exemption under the laws of Puerto Rico? . . .			N/A	

plan or trust or other document constituting the plan.

	Yes	No	Section and page number *	GOVERN... USE O...

21 Requirements for benefits—distributions—allocations:

(a) Normal retirement age is ▶...65...... State years of service required ▶.............. | | | 2.5, p.7

(b) Early retirement age is ▶....None.... State years of service required ▶.............. | | | N/A

(c) If employer's consent is required for early retirement, are benefits limited to vested benefits? . | | | N/A

(d) (i) Does the plan provide that the payment of benefits, unless the employee elects otherwise, will commence not later than the 60th day after the latest of (1) the close of the plan year in which the participant attains the earlier of age 65, or the normal retirement age specified under the plan, (2) the close of the plan year in which occurs the 10th anniversary of the year in which participant commenced participation or (3) the close of the plan year in which the participant terminates his service with the employer? . . . . | XX | | 6.5, p.25

(ii) Does plan provide for payment of benefits if claim is not filed? . . . . . | XX | | 6.5, p.25

(e) Distribution of account balances may be made in:

(i) ☒ Lump sum (ii) ☒ Annuity contracts *Life expectancy* | | | 6.3, p.23

(iii) ☒ Substantially equal annual installments—not exceeding ▶..../..... years | | | 6.3, p.23

(iv) ☐ Other (specify) ▶

(f) If distributions are made in installments, are they credited with:

(i) ☐ Fund earnings

(ii) ☐ Interest at a rate of ▶..............% per year

(iii) ☒ Other (specify) ▶...*Bank interest (Current Rate)*..... | | | 6.3, p.24

(g) If insurance contracts are distributed, are the modes of settlement contained in the contracts limited to those provided under the plan? . . . . | | | N/A

(h) If plan provides for payment of annuity benefits, does the plan provide a joint and survivor benefit unless participant elects otherwise? . . . . | XX | | 6.3, p.21

(i) Are all optional modes of distribution of equal value? . . . . | XX | | 6.3, p.24

(j) If this is a stock bonus plan, are distributions made in employer stock? . . . | | |

(k) Other event permitting distribution (specify) ▶.............................. | | | 6.2, p.19

(l) If participants may withdraw their contributions or earnings, may such withdrawal be made without forfeiting vested benefits based on employer contributions? . . . . | XX | | 5.3, p.14

(m) Are contributions allocated on the basis of total compensation? . . . . . . | XX | | 5.3, p.14

If "No," see instructions.

(n) Are forfeitures allocated, in case of a profit-sharing or stock bonus plan, on basis of total compensation? . . . . | XX | | 5.3, p.14

If "No," explain how allocated.

(o) Are trust earnings and losses allocated on the basis of account balances? . . | XX | | 5.5, p.16

If "No," explain how allocated.

(p) In case of target benefit or other money purchase plan, are forfeitures allocated to reduce employer contributions? . . . . | | |

If "No," explain how allocated.

(q) Does plan provide for maximum limitation under section 415? . . . . . . | XX | | 5.3, p.15

(r) In the case of a merger or consolidation with another plan or transfer of assets or liabilities to another plan, will each participant be entitled to the same or greater benefit as if the plan had terminated? . . . . | XX | | 11.10 p64

(s) Does the plan prohibit the assignment or alienation of benefits? . . . . . | XX | | 12.3, p66

(t) Does the plan preclude divestment for cause? . . . . | | XX |

(u) Are trust assets valued at current value? . . . . | XX | | 5.6, p.16

(v) Are trust assets valued at least annually? . . . . | XX | | 5.6, p.16

If "No," explain when valued.

22 Termination:

(a) Is there a provision in the plan for terminating the plan and/or trust? . . . . | XX | | 10.2, p57

(b) Are the amounts credited to participants' accounts nonforfetiable upon termination or partial termination of the plan? . . . . | XX | | 10.2, p57

(c) Upon complete discontinuance of contributions under a profit-sharing or stock bonus plan are the employees' rights under the plan nonforfeitable? . . . . | XX | | 10.2, p57

* Of plan or trust or other document constituting the plan.

	Yes	No	GOVERNMENT USE ONLY
Miscellaneous:			
(a) Has power of attorney been submitted with the application (or previously submitted)? . . .	XX		
(b) Have you completed and attached Form 5302?	XX		
(c) Is the adopting employer a member of a controlled group of corporations or under commonly controlled trades or businesses? . . . . If "Yes," see instructions.		XX	
(d) Is any issue relating to this plan or trust currently pending before the Internal Revenue Service, the Department of Labor, the Pension Benefit Guaranty Corporation or any Court? . . . . If "Yes," attach explanation.		XX	

(e) Other qualified plans—Enter for each other qualified plan you maintain (do not include plans that were established under union-negotiated agreements that involved other employers): $Big Bucks, Inc.$

    (i) Name of plan ► _Employees' Pension Trust (Money Purchase Plan)_

    (ii) Type of plan ► _Pension_

    (iii) Rate of employer contribution, if fixed ► _10%_

    (iv) Benefit formula or monthly benefit ►

    (v) Number of participants ► _3_

	Yes	No	
In the case of a request on an initial qualification, have the following documents been included:			
(a) Copies of all instruments constituting the plan or joinder agreement?	XX		
(b) Copy of trust indenture?	XX		
(c) Evidence that retirement benefits for employees in 15(b)(ii) were the subject of good faith bargaining between employee representatives and employer(s)—where that has occurred and is the basis for excluding certain employees, see section 410(b)(2)(A)? . N/A			
In the case of a request involving an amendment, after initial qualification, have the following documents been included:			
(a) A copy of the amendment(s)?			
(b) A description of the amendment covering the items changed and an explanation of the provisions before and after the amendment?			
(c) A completely restated plan? †			
(d) A working copy of the plan in which there has been incorporated all of the previous amendments representing the provisions of the plan as currently in effect? †			
(e) Copies of all amendments adopted since the date of the last determination letter for which no determination letter has been issued by the Internal Revenue Service? †			

	Yes	No	Section and page number *
This section pertains to Keogh (H.R. 10) plans only:			
(a) Do owner-employees have the option to participate?			
(b) Does plan prohibit distribution of benefits to owner-employees before age 59½, except for disability?			
(c) Does plan prohibit excess contributions for self-employed individuals? . . .			
(d) Is a definition of earned income provided?			
(e) Are distributions of benefits to owner-employees required to commence not later than age 70½?			
(f) Are the self-employed individual participants covered only under this plan? . .			
(g) Does plan prohibit the allocation of forfeitures to self-employed individuals? .			

plan is being amended for the first time to conform to the participation and vesting standards of the Employee Retirement Income ecurity Act of 1974, or if the plan has been amended at least three times since the last restated plan was submitted, one of the ocuments specified under (c) or (d) must be attached.

If any item in 24 or 25 is answered "No," please explain.

plan or trust or other document constituting the plan.

If more space is needed for any item, attach additional sheets of the same size.

Employee Census

Form 5302 (Rev. June 1976)
Department of the Treasury
Internal Revenue Service

▶ Attach to application for determination—defined benefit and defined contribution plans.

Schedule of 25 highest paid participating employees for 12-month period ended ▶ January 31, 1978.

(Round off to nearest dollar)

Employer identification number 95-0000000

This Form is NOT Open to Public Inspection

Name of employer: BIG BUCKS, INC.

Line no.	Employee's last name and initials (List in order of compensation) (a)	Check — Officer or shareholder (b)	Percent of voting stock owned (c)	Age (d)	Years of service (e)	Annual Nondeferred Compensation — Used in computing benefits or employee's share of contributions (f)	Excluded (g)	Total (h)	Employee contributions under the plan (i)	Amount allocated under each other qualified plan of deferred compensation (j)	Defined Benefit — Annual benefit expected (k)	Defined Contribution — Employer contribution allocated (l)	Number of units, if any (m)	Forfeitures allocated in the year (n)
1	Bucksup, H.	XX	50%	50	1	80,000	-	80,000		11,272		8,728		None
2	Bucksup, B.	XX	50%	45	1	40,000	-	40,000		5,636		3,745		None
3	Cash, F.	XX	0%	40	1	30,000	-	30,000		4,227		2,527		None
4														
5														
6														
7														
8														
9														
10														
11														
12														
13														
14														
15														
16														
17														
18														
19														
20														
21														
22														
23														
24														
25														
Totals for above						150,000	-	150,000	None	21,135		15,000		None
Totals for all others (Specify number ▶)						None	-	None	None	None		None		None
Totals for all participants						150,000	-	150,000	None	21,135		15,000		None

575-199-2

384

Every employer or plan administrator ~ho files an application for determina-ɔn with respect to a defined benefit or defined contribution plan is required attach thereto this schedule, which ~ust be completed in all details.

Prepare the employee census for a ~rrent 12-month period. Generally, the 2-month period should be the em-~oyer's taxable year, a calendar year ~ the plan year.

Section 6104(a)(1)(B) provides gen-~ally that applications, filed with re-~ect to the qualification of a pension, ~ofit-sharing or stock bonus plan, shall ~e open to public inspection. However, ~ction 6104(a)(1)(C) provides that in-~rmation concerning the compensation ~ any participant shall not be opened ~ public inspection. Consequently, the ~formation contained in this schedule ~all not be made available to the pub-~, including plan participants and ~her employees of the employer who ~tablished the plan.

This schedule is to be used by the ~ternal Revenue Service in its analysis ~ an application for determination as ~ whether a plan of deferred compen-~tion qualifies under section 401(a) or ~05(a).

If there are fewer than 25 partici-~nts, list all the participants. Oth-~wise, only the 25 highest-paid partici-~nts need be listed.

~pecific Instructions

In column (a), list the participants in ~e order of compensation, starting ~ith the highest-paid participant fol-~wed by the next highest-paid partici-~nt, and so on.

In column (b), enter a check mark or an "X" to indicate that a participant is either an officer or a shareholder. If a participant is neither an officer nor a shareholder, make no entry in this col-umn for such participant.

In column (c), enter only the percent-age of voting stock owned by a partici-pant. For example, participant "P" owns 200 shares of voting stock of the employer's 5,000 shares outstanding. His percentage is 4% (200÷5,000). If a participant owns only nonvoting stock of the employer, make no entry in this column.

In column (d), enter the attained age of each participant as of the end of the year for which this schedule applies. For example, if a participant reached his 47th birthday on January 7, 1975, and the schedule covers the calendar year 1975, enter 47 for that participant.

In column (e), enter the number of full years of service of each participant with respect to employment with the employer, and any prior employer if such employment is recognized for plan purposes.

In column (f), enter the amount of each participant's compensation that is recognized for plan purposes in com-puting the benefit (in case of a defined benefit plan) or in computing the amount of employer contribution that is allocated to the account of each par-ticipant (in the case of a defined contri-bution plan). Do not include any portion of the employer contributions to this or any other qualified plan as compensa-tion for any participant.

In column (g), enter the amount of compensation that is not recognized for purposes of column (f). For ex-ample, if a participant received $12,500 compensation for the year, $1,000 of which was a bonus and the plan does not recognize bonuses for plan pur-

poses, enter $11,500 in column (f) and $1,000 in column (g).

In column (h), enter the total amount of compensation for the year for each participant. The amount entered in this column will be the sum of the amounts entered in columns (f) and (g) with re-spect to each participant. Again, do not enter any amount of employer contribu-tions made to this or any other qualified plan.

In column (i), enter the total amount of mandatory and voluntary contribu-tions made by each participant. If the plan does not provide for employee con-tributions of any kind, leave blank or enter "N/A."

In column (j), enter the portion of the employer's contribution (1) that is attributable to the cost for providing each participant's benefits under all plans other than this plan or (2) that is allocated to each participant's account under all plans other than this plan.

In column (k), enter the amount of benefit each participant may expect to receive at normal retirement age based on current information, assuming no future compensation increases. For ex-ample, under a 30% benefit plan, a participant whose benefit is based on annual compensation of $10,000 may expect an annual benefit of $3,000 ($10,000×30%) at retirement. In such case enter $3,000.

In column (l), enter the amount of the employer's contribution that is allo-cated to the account of each partici-pant.

In column (m), enter the number of units, if any, used to determine the amount of the employer contribution that is allocated to each participant.

In column (n), enter the amount of the forfeitures that is allocated to each participant, unless forfeitures are allo-cated to reduce employer contributions.

575-199-1

385

Form **5301**

(Rev. June 1976)

Department of the Treasury
Internal Revenue Service

Application for
Determination for Defined Contribution Plan
For Profit-sharing, Stock Bonus and Money Purchase Plans
(Under sections 401(a), 405(s), 414(l) and 501(a) of the Internal Revenue Code)

This Form is Open to Public Inspection

▶ **Church and Governmental Plans.**—All items need not be completed. See instruction "B. What to File."

▶ **Please complete every applicable item on this form. If an item does not apply, enter N/A.**

1 (a) Name, address and ZIP code of employer

BIG BUCKS, INC.
445 South Figueroa Street
Los Angeles, CA 90071 | Telephone number ▶ (213)

(b) Name, address and ZIP code of plan administrator, if other than employer

Pension Plan Committee
445 South Figueroa Street
Los Angeles, CA 90071

(c) Administrator's identification number ▶ *95-0000000*   Telephone number ▶ (*213*) *620-0460*

2 Employer's identification num
95-0000000

3 Business code number
5931

4 Date incorporated or business comme
2/1/78

5 Employer's taxable year ends
January 31

6 Determination requested for:

(a) (i) ☒ Initial qualification—date plan adopted ▶ *4/1/78*   **(ii)** ☐ Amendment—date adopted ▶

  (iii) If (ii) is checked, enter file folder number ▶

(b) Were employees who are interested parties given the required notification of the filing of this application? . ☒ Yes   ☐

(c) If this application involves a merger or consolidation with another plan, enter the employer identification number(s) and plan number(s) of such other plan(s) ▶

7 Type of entity: **(a)** ☒ Corporation   **(b)** ☐ Subchapter S corporation   **(c)** ☐ Sole proprietor   **(d)** ☐ Partners
 (e) ☐ Tax exempt organization   **(f)** ☐ Church   **(g)** ☐ Governmental organization
 (h) ☐ Other (specify) ▶

8 (a) Name of Plan *BIG BUCKS, INC. EMPLOYEE* **(b)** Plan number ▶....*001*...... **(c)** Plan year ends ▶ *Jan*
PENSION TRUST (MONEY PURCHASE PLAN) **(d)** Is this a Keogh (H.R. 10) plan? . . . . ☐ Yes ☒
 (e) If "Yes," is an owner-employee in the plan? . ☐ Yes   ☐

9 (a) If this is an adoption of a master or prototype plan (other than Keogh) or a district approved pattern plan, enter name of such plan   *N/A*

 (b) Letter serial number
  N/A notification letter num

 (c) ☒ Money purchase   **(d)** ☐ Target ben

10 Type of plan: **(a)** ☐ Profit-sharing   **(b)** ☐ Stock bonus

11 Effective date of plan
2/1/78

12 Effective date of amendment
N/A

13 Date plan was communicated to employees ▶ *4/1/78*
 How communicated? ▶ *Notice*

14 (a) Indicate the general eligibility requirements for participation under the plan and indicate the section and page number of plan or trust where each provision is contained:

			Section and page number	GOVERNM USE ONL
(i) ☒ All employees	**(v)** Length of service (number of years) ▶ *6 mos.*		*2.1, p.6*	
(ii) ☐ Hourly rate employee only	**(vi)** Minimum age (specify) ▶			
(iii) ☐ Salaried employee only	**(vii)** Maximum age (specify) ▶			
(iv) ☐ Other job class (specify) ▶	**(viii)** Minimum pay (specify) ▶			

 (b) Are the eligibility requirements the same for future employees? . . . . ☒ Yes ☐ No   *2.1, p.6*
  If "No," explain ▶

 (c) Does the plan recognize service only with this employer? . . . . . . ☒ Yes ☐ No   *2.1, p.6*
  If "No," explain ▶

15 Coverage of plan at (give date) ▶ *1/31/79*
 Enter here the number of self-employed individuals ▶ *None*

	Number
(a) Total employed (if a Keogh plan, include all self-employed individuals)	3
(b) Exclusions under plan (do not count an employee more than once):	
(i) Minimum age or years of service required (specify) ▶	0
(ii) Employees included in collective bargaining	0
(iii) Nonresident aliens who receive no earned income from United States sources . . .	0
(c) Total exclusions, sum of (b)(i) through (iii)	0
(d) Employees not excluded under the statute, (a) less (c)	3

* Of plan or trust or other document constituting the plan.

Under penalties of perjury, I declare that I have examined this application, including accompanying statements, and to the best of my knowledge and belief it is true, co
and complete.

Signature ▶ _____   Title ▶ _____   Date ▶ _____

(Section references are to the Internal Revenue Code)	Number	GOVERNMENT USE ONLY

Coverage (continued):

(e) Ineligible under plan on account of (do not count an employee included in (b)):

		Number
(i) Minimum pay		0
(ii) Hourly-paid		0
(iii) Maximum age		0
(iv) Other (specify) ▶		0
(f) Employees ineligible, sum of (e)(i) through (iv)		0
(g) Employees eligible to participate, line (d) less line (f)		3
(h) Number of employees participating in plan		3
(i) Percent of nonexcluded employees who are participating, (h) divided by (d) . . .	100 %	

Complete (j) only if (i) is less than 70% and complete (k) only if (j) is 70% or more.

| (j) Percent of nonexcluded employees who are eligible to participate, (g) divided by (d) . . . . | % | |
| (k) Percent of eligible employees who are participating, (h) divided by (g) . . . . | % | |

If (i) and (j) are less than 70% or (k) is less than 80%, see instructions.

| (l) Total number of participants, include certain retired and terminated employees, see instructions . . . . . | | 3 |

	Yes	No	Section and page number *
Employee contributions:			
(a) Are mandatory contributions limited to 6%, or less, of compensation? . . .			
(b) Are voluntary contributions limited to 10%, or less, of compensation for all qualified plans? . .			N/A
(c) Are employee contributions nonforfeitable?			

Employer contributions:

(a) Under a profit-sharing or stock bonus plan, are they determined under—
(i) ☐ A definite formula   (ii) ☐ An indefinite formula   (iii) ☐ Both

(b) Under profit-sharing or stock bonus plans are contributions limited to—
(i) ☐ Current earnings   (ii) ☐ Accumulated earnings   (iii) ☐ Combination

(c) Money purchase—Enter rate of contribution ▶ 10%   3.3, p.10

(d) State target benefit formula, if applicable ▶

Integration:

Is this plan integrated with Social Security or Railroad Retirement? XX   4.2, p.11
If "Yes," see instructions.

Vesting—Check the appropriate box to indicate the vesting provisions of the plan:
(a) ☐ Full and immediate
(b) ☐ Full vesting after 10 years of service
(c) ☐ 5- to 15-year vesting, i.e., 25% after 5 years of service, 5% additional for each of the next 5 years, then 10% additional for each of the next 5 years
(d) ☐ Rule of 45 (see section 411(a)(2)(C))
(e) ☐ For each year of employment, commencing with the 4th such year, vesting not less than 40% after 4 years of service, 5% additional for each of the next 2 years, and 10% additional for each of the next 5 years
(f) ☐ 100% vesting within 5 years after contributions are made (class year plans only)
(g) ☒ Other (specify and see instructions) ▶ 20% for each year of service   5.5, p.15

Administration:
(a) Type of funding entity: (i) ☒ Trust   (ii) ☐ Custodial account   (iii) ☐ Non-trusteed
If you checked (i) or (ii), enter date executed ▶ April 1, 1978   3.2, p.9
(b) Enter name of trustee or custodian, if any ▶ Herbert Bucksup

	Yes	No	
(c) Does trust agreement prohibit reversion of funds to the employer?	XX		11.1, p.8

(d) Specify the limits placed on the purchase of insurance contracts, if any:
(i) Ordinary life ▶ 50% of account   7.14, p.8
(ii) Term insurance ▶ 25% of account
(iii) Other (specify) ▶

(e) If the trustees may earmark specific investments, including insurance contracts, are such investments subject to the employee's consent, or purchased ratably where employee consent is not required?			N/A
(f) Are loans to participants limited to their vested interests?		XX	5.5, p.23
(g) If Puerto Rican trust, does it qualify for tax exemption under the laws of Puerto Rico? . . .			N/A

* plan or trust or other document constituting the plan.

	Yes	No	Section and page number *	GOVERNME USE ONL'

21 Requirements for benefits—distributions—allocations:

(a) Normal retirement age is ▶ _65_ State years of service required ▶ _0_ — | | | 2.5, p.7 |

(b) Early retirement age is ▶ .... State years of service required ▶ .... | | | N/A |

(c) If employer's consent is required for early retirement, are benefits limited to vested benefits? . | | | N/A |

(d) (i) Does the plan provide that the payment of benefits, unless the employee elects otherwise, will commence not later than the 60th day after the latest of (1) the close of the plan year in which the participant attains the earlier of age 65, or the normal retirement age specified under the plan, (2) the close of the plan year in which occurs the 10th anniversary of the year in which participant commenced participation or (3) the close of the plan year in which the participant terminates his service with the employer? . . . . | XX | | 5.4, p22 |

(ii) Does plan provide for payment of benefits if claim is not filed? . . . . . | XX | | 5.4, p22 |

(e) Distribution of account balances may be made in: | | | 5.2, p22 |

(i) [X] Lump sum (ii) [ ] Annuity contracts _life expectancy_ | | | 5.2, p20 |

(iii) [ ] Substantially equal annual installments—not exceeding ▶ ..../..... years

(iv) [ ] Other (specify) ▶..

(f) If distributions are made in installments, are they credited with:

(i) [ ] Fund earnings

(ii) [ ] Interest at a rate of ▶..............% per year

(iii) [ ] Other (specify) ▶ _Bank Interest_ .... | | | 5.2, p20 |

(g) If insurance contracts are distributed, are the modes of settlement contained in the contracts limited to those provided under the plan? . . . . | | | N/A |

(h) If plan provides for payment of annuity benefits, does the plan provide a joint and survivor benefit unless participant elects otherwise? . . . . | XX | | 5.2, p17 |

(i) Are all optional modes of distribution of equal value? . . . . | XX | | 5.2, p20 |

(j) If this is a stock bonus plan, are distributions made in employer stock? . . .

(k) Other event permitting distribution (specify) ▶ _Disability or Death_ | | | 5.1, p16 |

(l) If participants may withdraw their contributions or earnings, may such withdrawal be made without forfeiting vested benefits based on employer contributions? . . . . | XX | | N/A 4.2, p11 |

(m) Are contributions allocated on the basis of total compensation? . . . . . .
If "No," see instructions.

(n) Are forfeitures allocated, in case of a profit-sharing or stock bonus plan, on basis of total compensation? . . . .
If "No," explain how allocated. | | | N/A |

(o) Are trust earnings and losses allocated on the basis of account balances? . . | XX | | 4.4, p13 |
If "No," explain how allocated.

(p) In case of target benefit or other money purchase plan, are forfeitures allocated to reduce employer contributions? . . . .
If "No," explain how allocated. | | | N/A |

(q) Does plan provide for maximum limitation under section 415? . . . . . | XX | | 4.2, p12 |

(r) In the case of a merger or consolidation with another plan or transfer of assets or liabilities to another plan, will each participant be entitled to the same or greater benefit as if the plan had terminated? . . . . | XX | | 10.10, p59 |

(s) Does the plan prohibit the assignment or alienation of benefits? . . . . . | XX | | 11.3, p62 |

(t) Does the plan preclude divestment for cause? . . . . | | XX | |

(u) Are trust assets valued at current value? . . . . | XX | | 4.5, p13 |

(v) Are trust assets valued at least annually? . . . . | XX | | 4.5, p.13 |
If "No," explain when valued.

22 Termination:

(a) Is there a provision in the plan for terminating the plan and/or trust? . . . . | XX | | 9.2, p53 |

(b) Are the amounts credited to participants' accounts nonforfeitable upon termination or partial termination of the plan? . . . . | XX | | 9.2, p53 |

(c) Upon complete discontinuance of contributions under a profit-sharing or stock bonus plan are the employees' rights under the plan nonforfeitable? . . . . | | | N/A |

* Of plan or trust or other document constituting the plan.

	Yes	No	GOVERNMENT USE ONLY
Miscellaneous:			
(a) Has power of attorney been submitted with the application (or previously submitted)? . . .	XX		
(b) Have you completed and attached Form 5302?	XX		
(c) Is the adopting employer a member of a controlled group of corporations or under commonly controlled trades or businesses? . . . . If "Yes," see instructions.		XX	
(d) Is any issue relating to this plan or trust currently pending before the Internal Revenue Service, the Department of Labor, the Pension Benefit Guaranty Corporation or any Court? . . . . If "Yes," attach explanation.		XX	

(e) Other qualified plans—Enter for each other qualified plan you maintain (do not include plans that were established under union-negotiated agreements that involved other employers): *Big Bucks, Inc.*
   (i)   Name of plan ►*Employees Profit Sharing Plan*
   (ii) Type of plan ► *Profit Sharing*
   (iii) Rate of employer contribution, if fixed ►
   (iv) Benefit formula or monthly benefit ►
   (v)   Number of participants ► *3*

	Yes	No	
In the case of a request on an initial qualification, have the following documents been included:			
(a) Copies of all instruments constituting the plan or joinder agreement?	XX		
(b) Copy of trust indenture?	XX		
(c) Evidence that retirement benefits for employees in 15(b)(ii) were the subject of good faith bargaining between employee representatives and employer(s)—where that has occurred and is the basis for excluding certain employees, see section 410(b)(2)(A)? *N/A*			
In the case of a request involving an amendment, after initial qualification, have the following documents been included:			
(a) A copy of the amendment(s)?			
(b) A description of the amendment covering the items changed and an explanation of the provisions before and after the amendment?			
(c) A completely restated plan? †			
(d) A working copy of the plan in which there has been incorporated all of the previous amendments representing the provisions of the plan as currently in effect? †			
(e) Copies of all amendments adopted since the date of the last determination letter for which no determination letter has been issued by the Internal Revenue Service? †			

	Yes	No	Section and page number *
This section pertains to Keogh (H.R. 10) plans only:			
(a) Do owner-employees have the option to participate?			
(b) Does plan prohibit distribution of benefits to owner-employees before age 59½, except for disability?			
(c) Does plan prohibit excess contributions for self-employed individuals? . . .			
(d) Is a definition of earned income provided?			
(e) Are distributions of benefits to owner-employees required to commence not later than age 70½?			
(f) Are the self-employed individual participants covered only under this plan? . .			
(g) Does plan prohibit the allocation of forfeitures to self-employed individuals? .			

plan is being amended for the first time to conform to the participation and vesting standards of the Employee Retirement Income Security Act of 1974, or if the plan has been amended at least three times since the last restated plan was submitted, one of the documents specified under (c) or (d) must be attached.

If any item in 24 or 25 is answered "No," please explain.

plan or trust or other document constituting the plan.

If more space is needed for any item, attach additional sheets of the same size.

U.S. GOVERNMENT PRINTING OFFICE   e70—575-279

Employee Census

Form 5302
(Rev. June 1976)
Department of the Treasury
Internal Revenue Service

▶ **Attach to application for determination—defined benefit and defined contribution plans.**

Schedule of 25 highest paid participating employees for 12-month period ended ▶ January 31, 1978   (Round off to nearest dollar)

This Form is NOT Open to Public Inspection

Name of employer: BIG BUCKS, INC.

Employer identification number: 95-0000000

Line no.	(a) Employee's last name and initials (List in order of compensation)	Check (b) Officer or shareholder	(c) Percent of voting stock owned	(d) Age	(e) Years of service	(f) Used in computing benefits or employee's share of contributions	(g) Excluded	(h) Total	(i) Employee contributions under the plan	Amount allocated under each other qualified plan of deferred compensation	Defined Benefit Annual benefit expected	Defined Contribution Employer contribution allocated	Number of units, if any (m)	Forfeitures allocated in the year (n)
1	Bucksup, H.	XX	50%	50	1	80,000	-	80,000		8,728		11,272		None
2	Bucksup, B.	XX	50%	45	1	40,000	-	40,000		3,745		5,636		None
3	Cash, F.	XX	0%	40	1	30,000	-	30,000		2,527		4,227		None
4														
5														
6														
7														
8														
9														
10														
11														
12														
13														
14														
15														
16														
17														
18														
19														
20														
21														
22														
23														
24														
25														
Totals for above						150,000	-	150,000	None	15,000		21,135		None
Totals for all others (Specify number) ▶						None	-	None	None	None		None		None
Totals for all participants						150,000	-	150,000	None	15,000		21,135		None

General Instructions

(References are to the Internal Revenue Code)

Every employer or plan administrator who files an application for determination with respect to a defined benefit or a defined contribution plan is required to attach thereto this schedule, which must be completed in all details.

Prepare the employee census for a current 12-month period. Generally, the 12-month period should be the employer's taxable year, a calendar year or the plan year.

Section 6104(a)(1)(B) provides generally that applications, filed with respect to the qualification of a pension, profit-sharing or stock bonus plan, shall be open to public inspection. However, section 6104(a)(1)(C) provides that information concerning the compensation of any participant shall not be opened to public inspection. Consequently, the information contained in this schedule shall not be made available to the public, including plan participants and other employees of the employer who established the plan.

This schedule is to be used by the Internal Revenue Service in its analysis of an application for determination as to whether a plan of deferred compensation qualifies under section 401(a) or 405(a).

If there are fewer than 25 participants, list all the participants. Otherwise, only the 25 highest-paid participants need be listed.

Specific Instructions

In column (a), list the participants in the order of compensation, starting with the highest-paid participant followed by the next highest-paid participant, and so on.

In column (b), enter a check mark or an "X" to indicate that a participant is either an officer or a shareholder. If a participant is neither an officer nor a shareholder, make no entry in this column for such participant.

In column (c), enter only the percentage of voting stock owned by a participant. For example, participant "P" owns 200 shares of voting stock of the employer's 5,000 shares outstanding. His percentage is 4% (200÷5,000). If a participant owns only nonvoting stock of the employer, make no entry in this column.

In column (d), enter the attained age of each participant as of the end of the year for which this schedule applies. For example, if a participant reached his 47th birthday on January 7, 1975, and the schedule covers the calendar year 1975, enter 47 for that participant.

In column (e), enter the number of full years of service of each participant with respect to employment with the employer, and any prior employer if such employment is recognized for plan purposes.

In column (f), enter the amount of each participant's compensation that is recognized for plan purposes in computing the benefit (in case of a defined benefit plan) or in computing the amount of employer contribution that is allocated to the account of each participant (in the case of a defined contribution plan). Do not include any portion of the employer contributions to this or any other qualified plan as compensation for any participant.

In column (g), enter the amount of compensation that is not recognized for purposes of column (f). For example, if a participant received $12,500 compensation for the year, $1,000 of which was a bonus and the plan does not recognize bonuses for plan purposes, enter $11,500 in column (f) and $1,000 in column (g).

In column (h), enter the total amount of compensation for the year for each participant. The amount entered in this column will be the sum of the amounts entered in columns (f) and (g) with respect to each participant. Again, do not enter any amount of employer contributions made to this or any other qualified plan.

In column (i), enter the total amount of mandatory and voluntary contributions made by each participant. If the plan does not provide for employee contributions of any kind, leave blank or enter "N/A."

In column (j), enter the portion of the employer's contribution (1) that is attributable to the cost for providing each participant's benefits under all plans other than this plan or (2) that is allocated to each participant's account under all plans other than this plan.

In column (k), enter the amount of benefit each participant may expect to receive at normal retirement age based on current information, assuming no future compensation increases. For example, under a 30% benefit plan, a participant whose annual compensation of $10,000 may expect an annual benefit of $3,000 ($10,000×30%) at retirement. In such case enter $3,000.

In column (l), enter the amount of the employer's contribution that is allocated to the account of each participant.

In column (m), enter the number of units, if any, used to determine the amount of the employer contribution that is allocated to each participant.

In column (n), enter the amount of the forfeitures that is allocated to each participant, unless forfeitures are allocated to reduce employer contributions.

Form **2848**
(Rev. July 1976)
Department of the Treasury
Internal Revenue Service

Power of Attorney

(See the separate Instructions for Forms 2848 and 2848–D.)

Name, identifying number, and address including ZIP code of taxpayer(s)

BIG BUCKS, INC.
445 South Figueroa Street
Los Angeles, California 90071   (213) 620-0460

hereby appoints (Name, address including ZIP code, and telephone number of appointee(s)) (See Treasury Department Circular No. 230 as amended (31 C.F.R. Part 10), Regulations Governing the Practice of Attorneys, Certified Public Accountants, and Enrolled Agents before the Internal Revenue Service, for persons recognized to practice before the Internal Revenue Service.)

CASH & CAREY
Attorneys at Law
123 Best Street
Sunnyland, California
(213) 620-0460

as attorney(s)-in-fact to represent the taxpayer(s) before any office of the Internal Revenue Service for the following Internal Revenue tax matters (specify the type(s) of tax and year(s) or period(s) (date of death if estate tax)):

Seeking a ruling as to the qualification of the corporation's Employees' Pension Trust (Money Purchase Plan) and Employees Profit Sharing Plan and Trust.

The attorney(s)-in-fact (or either of them) are authorized, subject to revocation, to receive confidential information and to perform on behalf of the taxpayer(s) the following acts for the above tax matters:

(Strike through any of the following which are not granted.)

~~To receive, but not to endorse and collect, checks in payment of any refund of Internal Revenue taxes, penalties, or interest (see "refund checks" on page 2 of the separate instructions).~~

~~To execute waivers (including offers of waivers) or restrictions on assessment or collection of deficiencies in tax and waivers of notices of disallowance of a claim for credit or refund.~~

~~To execute consents extending the statutory period for assessment or collection of taxes.~~

~~To execute any release of any lien under section 7425 of the Internal Revenue Code.~~

~~To delegate authority or to substitute another representative.~~

Other acts (specify) .... *See above* ....

Send copies of notices and other written communications addressed to the taxpayer(s) in proceedings involving the above matters to (Name, address including ZIP code, and telephone number):

and
ROBERT P. CASH, 123 Best Street, Sunnyland, California 90071
(213) 620-0460

This power of attorney revokes all earlier powers of attorney and tax information authorizations on file with the same Internal Revenue Service office for the same matters and years or periods covered by this form, except the following:

(Specify to whom granted, date, and address including ZIP code, or refer to attached copies of earlier powers and authorizations.)

Signature of or for taxpayer(s)

If signed by a corporate officer, partner, or fiduciary on behalf of the taxpayer, I certify that I have the authority to execute this power of attorney on behalf of the taxpayer.

President

(Signature)	(Title, if applicable)	(Date)

(Signature)	(Title, if applicable)	(Date)

(The applicable portion of the back page must also be completed.)

Form **2848** (Rev. 7–76)

If the power of attorney is granted to an attorney, certified public accountant, or enrolled agent, this declaration must be completed.

   I declare that I am not currently under suspension or disbarment from practice before the Internal Revenue Service, that I am aware of Treasury Department Circular No. 230 as amended (31 C.F.R. Part 10), Regulations Governing the Practice of Attorneys, Certified Public Accountants, and Enrolled Agents before the Internal Revenue Service, and that:

   I am a member in good standing of the bar of the highest court of the jurisdiction indicated below; or
   I am duly qualified to practice as a certified public accountant in the jurisdiction indicated below; or
   I am enrolled as an agent pursuant to the requirements of Treasury Department Circular No. 230.

Designation (Attorney, C.P.A., or Agent)	Jurisdiction (State, etc.) or Enrollment Card Number	Signature	Date
Attorney	California	Robert P. Cash	6-30-78

If the power of attorney is granted to a person other than an attorney, certified public accountant, or enrolled agent, it must be witnessed or notarized below. (See Treasury Department Circular No. 230 as amended (31 C.F.R. Part 10), Regulations Governing the Practice of Attorneys, Certified Public Accountants, and Enrolled Agents before the Internal Revenue Service, for persons recognized to practice before the Internal Revenue Service.)

   The person(s) signing as or for the taxpayer(s):   (Check and complete one.)

☐ is/are known to and signed in the presence of the two disinterested witnesses whose signatures appear here:

---   ----------------------------
(Signature of Witness)   (Date)

---   ----------------------------
(Signature of Witness)   (Date)

☐ appeared this day before a notary public and acknowledged this power of attorney as a voluntary act and deed.

                                                                                    NOTARIAL SEAL
---   ----------------------------   (If required)
(Signature of Notary)   (Date)

[¶910] HOW TO SUBMIT DOCUMENTS TO THE IRS

The three IRS documents must be completed and signed, then the forms and the plans should be sent to the Service. The address will depend on where the corporation is located. A sample cover letter (see page 395) should accompany the submission of these materials to the IRS.

Internal Revenue Service
Chief, EP/EO Division
Post Office Box 2350
Los Angeles, California 90053

Attn: Pension Profit Sharing Plan Section

Re: BIG BUCKS, INC.

Gentlemen:

        Enclosed herewith please find the following documents:

    1. Profit Sharing Plan, together with
        Forms 5301, 5302, 2848, and Notice
        to Employees.

    2. Pension Trust (Money Purchase Plan)
        together with Forms 5301, 5302, 2848
        and Notice to Employees.

It is respectfully requested that a letter ruling issue
from your office regarding the subject plans being qualified
plans as defined in Section 401, that the contributions made
to the trusts by the employer are allowable deductions in
accordance with Section 404, and that the subject plans are
exempt from income tax pursuant to Section 501 of the Internal
Revenue Code.

                        Very truly yours,

                        Robert P. Cash

[¶911] SUMMARY PLAN DESCRIPTION

If the plans are approved as submitted, the client will receive a letter from the IRS stating that the plans constitute qualified plans for tax purposes. Retain the letter with the original plan so that it may be presented to an auditor in the event of a corporate audit by the IRS. In the event the IRS wants to have minor amendments to the plan, the person with the power of attorney will be contacted and informed of any requested changes. If the plans are submitted to the IRS within a time frame, assuming approval, any such amendments will be applied retroactively.

Once the plans have been adopted and approved by the IRS, there are certain periodic reports which must be filed with the Service and with the Department of Labor. Certain documents must be distributed to or made available to plan participants.

For example, participants must be given a document called a "Summary Plan Description." The form must comply with government regulations. The participants must receive the document within 120 days after the plan is adopted and a copy must be filed with the Department of Labor. A Summary Plan Description for each of the two sample plans is described below. Description for a Profit-Sharing Plan and Trust Agreement is shown on pages 397 to 408; the Plan Description for a Pension Trust is on pages 409 to 420.

SUMMARY PLAN DESCRIPTION

FOR THE

BIG BUCKS, INC.

EMPLOYEES' PROFIT-SHARING PLAN

AND TRUST AGREEMENT

Your Employer has established an employee benefit plan to supplement your income upon retirement. The Plan is provided without cost to you.

The purpose of this Summary Plan Description is to provide you with a description of the more important features of this Plan. The full legal Plan and Trust Agreement documents are available for your review in the Employer's officer at any time during regular business hours. You may also purchase copies of the legal documents if you so desire from the Plan Administrator. In the event of any difference between the formal legal documents and this summary, the formal legal documents, of course, will control.

If after reading this summary you have additional questions concerning the Plan, your Employer or the Plan Administrator will be happy to discuss them in greater detail.

TABLE OF CONTENTS

1. GENERAL INFORMATION

a) <u>Name of Plan:</u>   BIG BUCKS, INC. EMPLOYEES'
PROFIT-SHARING PLAN
AND TRUST AGREEMENT

b) <u>Name and Address of Employer:</u>   BIG BUCKS, INC.
445 South Figueroa Street
34th Floor
Los Angeles, Ca. 90071

c) The Employer Identification
Number Assigned by the Internal
<u>Revenue Service to the Employer:</u>   95-0000000

d) <u>The Plan Number:</u>   001

e) <u>Type of Retirement Plan:</u>   Profit-Sharing Plan

f) <u>Type of Administration of the Plan:</u>   Committee

g) <u>Plan Administrator:</u>

Committee of the Profit-Sharing Trust
c/o Big Bucks, Inc.
445 South Figuerora Street
34th Floor
Los Angeles, California 90071

A Committee appointed by the Board of Directors of the Company is the Plan Administrator and is charged with the general administration of the Plan. The Committee manages the Plan for the sole benefit of the Participants.

h) <u>Agent for Service of Legal Process:</u>

Any legal process relating to a claim that has been denied should be addressed to the attention of the Plan Administrator.

i) <u>Plan Trustee:</u>   HERBERT BUCKSUP

The assets contributed to the Plan are managed by the Trustee in the Trust Fund. The Trustee will invest the Trust Fund for the benefit of the Participants and will distribute to the Participants the benefits to which they are entitled upon retirement or as specified in the Plan.

j) Plan Year:

The twelve-month period commencing the first day of February and ending on the last day of January.

k) Normal Retirement Age:

Sixty-five years.

2. ELIGIBILITY

a) When and How Do I Begin to Participate?

You can become a Participant of the Plan on the Anniversary Date coinciding with or following six (6) months from the day you begin to work. However, if you are not working for the Company on this date, you will not become a Participant.

Each Anniversary Date is the key date in the operation of the Plan. The last day of the Plan Year is the Anniversary Date of the Plan. On each Anniversary Date:

1. The Company determines who is eligible to participate.
2. Your rights to your account will increase because of the process called "vesting." See Section 4.
3. Earnings or losses of the Trust Fund will be allocated to your account. See Section 3.

Within thirty days after you become a Participant, the Company will send your name to the Committee which manages the Plan. You will then be asked to fill out a Beneficiary Designation Form wherein you will name the person(s) to receive your account in the event of your death. You can name anyone you like, and you can name more than one person. The beneficiary of your account may be changed at any time you desire. It is important to review your Beneficiary Designation Form when you have changes in your family because the Plan Administrator must follow the instructions of your last Beneficiary Designation Form on file.

b) How Will I Cease to Be a Participant?

Generally you will continue to participate until one of the following happens:

1. Termination of Employment Followed by a One Year Break in Service
2. Normal Retirement
3. Permanent Disability
4. Death

The general requirements for normal retirement and disability are in Section 4 of this summary.

The phrase "One Year Break in Service" means a twelve month period measured from your date of hire or any anniversary thereof in which you work for five hundred (500) or fewer hours.

c) How Can I Regain My Status As a Participant?

If you were previously employed and were a Participant, then you will become a Participant again on your date of reemployment.

3. CONTRIBUTIONS TO PROFIT-SHARING PLAN

a) How Is the Company's Contribution Determined?

Each year the Company may, in its discretion and pursuant to resolution adopted by its Board of Directors, contribute a percentage of its profits to the Plan.

For purposes of this Plan, your compensation includes your full regular basic salary and hourly wages, including overtime, bonuses, and commissions, but excluding health and welfare or any other payments before deductions authorized by you or required by law to be withheld from you by the Company.

b) Who Will Share in the Company's Contribution?

All active Participants will share in the Company's contribution. In order to be an active Participant you must have at least 1,000 hours of compensated service during the Plan Year and continue to meet the Plan's eligibility requirements.

Participants who have less than 1,000 hours but more than 500 hours of compensated service are considered to be inactive and will not share in the Company's contribution or forfeitures. However, they will share in the Trust Fund net earnings, gains or losses.

c) How Is My Share of the Company Contribution Determined?

When you become a Participant, a Company Contribution Account will be opened in your name. Thereafter, a portion of the Company's contribution to the Plan will be credited to your Company Contribution Account. Your portion of the Company's contribution is based upon that percent which your compensation bears to the total compensation of all Participants.

You will share in any growth or decrease in the Trust Fund itself. On each Anniversary Date, the value of the Trust Fund will be revalued, and any increase or decrease in the value of the Trust Fund will be allocated to your account in the proportion that your account bears to the total of all accounts as of the preceding Anniversary Date.

d) May I Make Voluntary Contributions?

You may, if you desire, make voluntary contributions to the Plan, and a Voluntary Contribution Account will be opened in your name. The amount contributed may be an even percentage of your compensation. Also, the amount contributed by you cannot exceed 10% of the compensation paid to you since the commencement of your participation.

Your Voluntary Contribution Account will share in the investment experience of the Trust Fund. Upon your request, the Company will provide you with a Voluntary Contribution Election Form on which you may indicate how much you want to contribute. You may authorize the Company to deduct an amount from your paycheck each payday, and it will be contributed to your Voluntary Contribution Account. You can change or even stop the amount you want to personally contribute by notifying the Company in writing during the 30-day period before June 30 or December 31. But remember, you do not have to personally contribute to the Plan.

4. WHEN WILL YOUR ACCOUNT BE DISTRIBUTED?

Your account will be distributed after your employment with the Company ends.

Company Contributions

Retirement: If you retire, at your Normal Retirement Age, all of your account will be used for your benefit or will be payable to you.

Disability: If you become totally disabled (regardless of your age or length of service), all of your account will be used for your benefit or will be payable to you.

Death: If you die while employed (regardless of your age or length of service) or after your employment ends but before you have received all of your benefits, your beneficiary will be entitled to all of your account.

Termination of Employment Before Retirement: Your years of service with the Company determines how much of your Company Contribution Account belongs to you if you quit or are discharged. No benefits are payable upon termination of employment unless such termination results in a One Year Break in Service. If you incur a One Year Break in Service for reasons other than normal retirement or death, your interest and rights are as follows.

On such One Year Break in Service, you shall be vested in your Company Contribution Account balance in accordance with the following schedule:

Your Years of Service	Vested Interest
Less than 1 year	None
1 year	20%
2 years	40%
3 years	60%
4 years	80%
5 years or more	100%

Your vested Company Contribution Account balance at the date of your One Year Break in Service will continue to share in gains and losses and will be paid to you at what would have been your Normal Retirement Date.

However, upon your written request, the Plan Administrator may direct the Trustee to make distribution of your vested Company Contribution Account balance at an earlier date (but not prior to the date the break in service occurred).

You will be considered to have worked a Year of Service for each 12 month period beginning with the date of your employment in which you have performed 1,000 or more hours of service.

If you leave the Company before you are entitled to the full 100% value of your Company Contribution Account, the remainder of your

Company Contribution Account, after your "vested" share is distributed, will be allocated to the accounts of the remaining Participants.

Voluntary Contributions

Amounts which you voluntarily contribute to the Plan will share in the investment experience of the Trust Fund together with the Company's contributions. Your voluntary contributions will be distributed at the same time and in the same fashion as the Company contributions. Your voluntary contributions are not subject to vesting. You always have a right to the value of your voluntary contributions.

5. BENEFITS

a) What Are the Benefits I Will Receive from the Plan?

There are four basic benefits provided by the Plan: normal retirement, death, disability and termination.

Normal Retirement

You are entitled to a normal retirement benefit when you reach your Normal Retirement Age. Your Normal Retirement Age is 65 or the age attained when you actually retire, if later.

If you are married on your Normal Retirement Age and have been married to the same person for the preceding 12 months, then you will receive your benefit in the form of a joint and survivor annuity unless you elect otherwise.

Death

If you die while employed by the Company, your designated beneficiary will be entitled to receive a death benefit.

If you are a participant on the first day of the 120th month preceding your normal retirement date, then you may elect to have your benefit paid to your beneficiary in the form of a survivor annuity.

Disability

If you become totally and permanently disabled while employed by the Company, you are entitled to a disability benefit.

Termination

    If, after your employment has been terminated, you incur a One Year Break in Service, you will be entitled to receive a termination benefit.

    The amount of your benefit will be the value of your account balance which has become vested. See Section 4.

    The value of your account balance will depend on the following:

1. How long you have been a Participant in the Plan;
2. What your compensation has been;
3. How much the Company has contributed; and
4. How much growth has taken place as a result of investing all contributions.

    Because the Plan is a defined contribution plan, your benefits are not insured under Title IV of ERISA, and neither the Company nor the Plan's Trustee insure or guarantee the value of your benefits.

b) When and How May I Expect
   to Receive My Benefits?

    When you become entitled to receive a benefit, the Plan Administrator will value your account as of the last day of the Plan Year.

    Generally, normal retirement, death and disability benefits will commence as soon as is administratively possible following the end of the Plan Year in which the event occurred which entitled you to the benefit distribution.

    Your benefit may be paid to you or your designated beneficiary in the case of death in one or more of the following ways:

1. You may receive a nontransferable annuity contract purchased for you from a responsible life insurance company selected by the Committee. The annuity contract will provide for payments to commence when you attain Normal Retirement Age and, if you are unmarried, to continue throughout your lifetime. If you are married, the annuity shall be a Qualified Joint and Survivor Annuity unless you elect some other form of benefit. A Qualified Joint and Survivor Annuity means annuity payments for your life with a survivor annuity for the life of your spouse. Since the benefit takes two lives into consideration, payments made to you will generally be less than you would receive based

on your life alone. However, the present value of the total payments you and your spouse should receive will be equal to the present value of the payments you would receive if the annuity were based on your life alone;

or

2. A lump sum; or

3. A straight life annuity; or

4. Installment payments over a period of time.

While the exact method of distribution is up to the Plan Administrator, you or your beneficiary may request the Plan Administrator to make the distribution in the method of your choice. However, before making a request you are strongly urged to seek legal advice concerning the method which will be best for you.

6. PROCEDURE FOR CLAIMING BENEFITS

Filing a Claim for Benefits: You or your beneficiary or the Company acting on your behalf must notify the Committee of a claim for benefits under the Plan. The Committee will inform you of your benefits within a reasonable time.

Denial of a Claim: If a claim is wholly or partially denied, notice of the decision will be furnished to you or your beneficiary within a reasonable period of time after receipt of the claim by the Committee. The notice of decision will be set forth in writing and will provide:

1. Specific reasons for the denial;

2. Specific references to the pertinent Plan provisions on which the denial is based;

3. A description of any additional material to perfect the claim and an explanation of why such material is needed; and

4. The steps to be taken for review of the denied claim.

If you (or your beneficiary) disagree with the Committee's decision, you may request, in writing, a reconsideration of that decision from the Committee. All claims for benefits or requests for review of claim denials may be made by contacting the Committee. The Committee will provide a full and fair review of the decision, and notify you in writing of the results of that review.

7. <u>TAXES ON YOUR ACCOUNT ARE DEFERRED</u>

What kind of taxes do you have to pay in connection with your account? Under current tax laws, here is what happens:

Company Contributions are not taxable to you as they are credited to your Company Contribution Account. You do not report them as income. The money is subject to tax, however, when you receive it.

Voluntary Contributions have already had taxes paid on them; so you won't be taxed again on that money when it is repaid to you. However, any increase in the value of your Voluntary Contribution Account will be taxed when paid to you.

8. <u>RIGHTS OF PARTICIPATING EMPLOYEES</u>

As a Participant in the Plan, you are entitled to certain rights and protections under the Employee Retirement Income Security Act of 1974 (ERISA). ERISA provides that a Participant shall be entitled to:

1. Examine, without charge, at the plan administrator's office and at other specified locations, such as worksites and union halls, all plan documents, including insurance contracts, collective bargaining agreements and copies of all documents filed by the plan with the U.S. Department of Labor, such as detailed annual reports and plan descriptions.

2. Obtain copies of all plan documents and other plan information upon written request to the plan administrator. The administrator may make a reasonable charge for the copies.

3. Receive a summary of the plan's annual financial report. The plan administrator is required by law to furnish each participant with a copy of this summary annual report.

4. Obtain a statement telling you whether you have a right to receive a pension at Normal Retirement Age and if so, what your benefits would be at normal reitrement age if you stop working under the plan now. If you do not have a right to a pension, the statement will tell you how many more years you have to work to get a right to a pension. This statement must be requested in writing and is not required to be given more than once a year. The plan must provide the statement free of charge.

5. In addition to creating rights for plan participants, ERISA imposes duties upon the people who are responsible for the operation of the employee benefit plan. The people who operate your plan, called "fiduciaries" of the plan, have a duty to do so prudently and in the interest of you and other plan participants and beneficiaries. No one, including your employer, your union, or any other person, may fire you or otherwise discriminate against you in any way to prevent you from obtaining a (pension, welfare) benefit or exercising your rights under ERISA. If your claim for a (pension, welfare) benefit is denied in whole or in part, you must receive a written explanation of the reason for the denial. You have the right to have the plan review and reconsider your claim. Under ERISA, there are steps you can take to enforce the above rights. For instance, if you request materials from the plan and do not receive them within 30 days, you may file suit in a Federal court. In such a case, the court may require the plan administrator to provide the materials and pay you up to $100 a day until you receive the materials, unless the materials were not sent because of reasons beyond the control of the administrator. If you have a claim for benefits which is denied or ignored, in whole or in part, you may file suit in a state or federal court. If it should happen that plan fiduciaries misuse the plan's money, or if you are discriminated against for asserting your rights, you may seek assistance from the U.S. Department of Labor, or you may file suit in a Federal court. The court will decide who should pay court costs and legal fees. If you are successful, the court may order the person you have sued to pay these costs and fees. If you lose, the court may order you to pay these costs and fees, for example, if it finds your claim is frivolous. If you have any questions about your plan, you should contact the plan administrator. If you have any questions about this statement or about your rights under ERISA, you should contact the nearest **Area Office of the U.S. Labor-Management Services Administration, Department of Labor.**

SUMMARY PLAN DESCRIPTION

FOR THE

BIG BUCKS, INC.

EMPLOYEES' PENSION TRUST

(Money-Purchase Plan)

Your Employer has established an employee benefit plan to supplement your income upon retirement. The Plan is provided without cost to you.

The purpose of this Summary Plan description is to provide you with a description of the more important features of this Plan. The full legal Plan and Trust Agreement documents are available for your review in the Employer's office at any time during regular business hours. You may also purchase copies of the legal documents if you so desire from the Plan Administrator. In the event of any difference between the formal legal documents and this summary, the formal legal documents, of course, will control.

If, after reading this summary, you have additional questions concerning the Plan, your Employer or the Plan Administrator will be happy to discuss them in greater detail.

TABLE OF CONTENTS

1. GENERAL INFORMATION

a) <u>Name of Plan:</u>

BIG BUCKS, INC.
EMPLOYEES' PENSION TRUST
(MONEY-PURCHASE PLAN)

b) <u>Name and Address of Employer:</u>

BIG BUCKS, INC.
445 South Figueroa Street
34th Floor
Los Angeles, Ca. 90071

c) The Employer Identification
Number Assigned by the Internal
<u>Revenue Service to the Employer:</u>   95-0000000

d) <u>The Plan Number:</u>   002

e) <u>Type of Retirement Plan:</u>   Money-Purchase Plan

f) <u>Type of Administration of the Plan:</u>   Committee

g) <u>Plan Administrator:</u>

Committee of the Big Bucks, Inc.
Employees' Pension Trust
c/o Big Bucks, Inc.
445 South Figueroa St.
34th Floor
Los Angeles, California 90071

A Committee appointed by the Board of Directors of the Company is the Plan Administrator and is charged with the general administration of the Plan. The Committee manages the Plan for the sole benefit of the Participants.

h) <u>Agent for Service of Legal Process:</u>

Any legal process relating to a claim that has been denied should be addressed to the attention of the Plan Administrator.

i) <u>Plan Trustee:</u>   HERBERT BUCKSUP

The assets contributed to the Plan are managed by the Trustee in the Trust Fund. The Trustee will invest the Trust Fund for the benefit of the Participants and will distribute to the Participants the benefits to which they are entitled upon retirement or as specified in the Plan.

j) <u>Plan Year:</u>

The twelve-month period commencing the first day of February and ending on the last day of January.

k) <u>Normal Retirement Age:</u>

Sixty-five years.

2. <u>ELIGIBILITY</u>

a) <u>When and How Do I Begin to Participate?</u>

You can become a Participant of the Plan on the Anniversary Date coinciding with or following six (6) months from the day you begin to work. However, if you are not working for the Company on this date, you will not become a Participant.

Each Anniversary Date is the key date in the operation of the Plan. The last day of the Plan Year is the Anniversary Date of the Plan. On each Anniversary Date:

1. The Company determines who is eligible to participate.
2. Your rights to your account will increase because of the process called "vesting." See Section 4.
3. Earnings or losses of the Trust Fund will be allocated to your account. See Section 3.

Within thirty days after you become a Participant, the Company will send your name to the Committee which manages the Plan. You will then be asked to fill out a Beneficiary Designation Form wherein you will name the person(s) to receive your account in the event of your death. You can name anyone you like, and you can name more than one person. The beneficiary of your account may be changed at any time you desire. It is important to review your Beneficiary Designation Form when you have changes in your family because the Plan Administrator must follow the instructions of your last Beneficiary Designation Form on file.

b) <u>How Will I Cease to Be a Participant?</u>

Generally you will continue to participate until one of the following happens:

1. Termination of Employment Followed by a One Year Break in Service
2. Normal Retirement
3. Permanent Disability
4. Death

The general requirements for normal retirement and disability are in Section 4 of this summary.

The phrase "One Year Break in Service" means a twelve month period measured from your date of hire or any anniversary thereof in which you work for five hundred (500) or fewer hours.

c) <u>How Can I Regain My Status As a Participant?</u>

If you were previously employed and were a Participant, then you will become a Participant again on your date of reemployment.

3. <u>CONTRIBUTIONS TO PROFIT-SHARING PLAN</u>

a) <u>How Is the Company's Contribution Determined?</u>

Each year the Company must contribute an amount equal to 10% of the total compensation paid to all Participants for such Plan Year.

For purposes of this Plan, your compensation includes your full regular basic salary and hourly wages, including overtime, bonuses, and commissions, but excluding health and welfare or any other payments before deductions authorized by you or required by law to be withheld from you by the Company.

b) <u>Who Will Share in the Company's Contribution?</u>

All active Participants will share in the Company's contribution. In order to be an active Participant you must have at least 1,000 hours of compensated service during the Plan Year and continue to meet the Plan's eligibility requirements. Employment on the last day of the Plan Year (or on any other date for that matter) is not necessary in order to share in the Company's contribution.

Participants who have less than 1,000 hours but more than 500 hours of compensated service are considered to be inactive and will not share in the Company's contribution or forfeitures. However, they will share in the Trust Fund net earnings, gains or losses.

c) How Is My Share of the Company Contribution Determined?

When you become a Participant, a Company Contribution Account will be opened in your name. Thereafter, a portion of the Company's contribution to the Plan will be credited to your Company Contribution Account. Your portion of the Company's contribution is based on two calculations:

1) An amount equal to 7 percent of your compensation which is in excess of the social security wage base will be allocated to your Company Contribution Account; and

2) The remainder of the Company's contribution will be allocated to your Company Contribution Account based upon that percent which your compensation bears to the total compensation of all Participants.

You will share in any growth or decrease in the Trust Fund itself. On each Anniversary Date, the value of the Trust Fund will be revalued, and any increase or decrease in the value of the Trust Fund will be allocated to your account in the proportion that your account bears to the total of all accounts as of the preceding Anniversary Date.

4. WHEN WILL YOUR ACCOUNT BE DISTRIBUTED?

Your account will be distributed after your employment with the Company ends.

Company Contributions

Retirement: If you retire, at your Normal Retirement Age, all of your account will be used for your benefit or will be payable to you.

Disability: If you become totally disabled (regardless of your age or length of service), all of your account will be used for your benefit or will be payable to you.

Death: If you die while employed (regardless of your age or length of service) or after your employment ends but before you have received all of your benefits, your beneficiary will be entitled to all of your account.

Termination of Employment Before Retirement: Your years of service with the Company determine how much of your Company Contribution Account belongs to you if you quit or are discharged. No benefits are payable upon termination of employment unless such termination results in a One Year Break in Service. If you incur a One Year Break in Service for reasons other than normal retirement or death, your interest and rights are as follows.

On such One Year Break in Service, you shall be vested in your Company Contribution Account balance in accordance with the following schedule:

Your Years of Service	Vested Interest
Less than 1 year	None
1 year	20%
2 years	40%
3 years	60%
4 years	80%
5 years or more	100%

Your vested Company Contribution Account balance at the date of your One Year Break in Service will continue to share in gains and losses and will be paid to you at what would have been your Normal Retirement Date.

However, upon your written request, the Plan Administrator may direct the Trustee to make distribution of your vested Company Contribution Account balance at an earlier date (but not prior to the date the break in service occurred).

You will be considered to have worked a Year of Service for each 12 month period beginning with the date of your employment in which you have performed 1,000 or more hours of service.

If you leave the Company before you are entitled to the full 100% value of your Company Contribution Account, the remainder of your Company Contribution Account, after your "vested" share is distributed, will reduce the next required company contribution.

5. BENEFITS

a) What Are the Benefits
   I Will Receive from the Plan?

There are four basic benefits provided by the Plan: normal retirement, death, disability and termination.

Normal Retirement

You are entitled to a normal retirement benefit when you reach your Normal Retirement Age. Your Normal Retirement Age is 65 or the age attained when you actually retire, if later.

If you are married on your Normal Retirement Age and have been married to the same person for the preceding 12 months, then you will receive your benefit in the form of a joint and survivor annuity unless you elect otherwise.

Death

If you die while employed by the Company, your designated beneficiary will be entitled to receive a death benefit.

If you are a participant on the first day of the 120th month preceding your normal retirement date, then you may elect to have your benefit paid to your beneficiary in the form of a survivor annuity.

Disability

If you become totally and permanently disabled while employed by the Company, you are entitled to a disability benefit.

Termination

If, after your employment has been terminated, you incur a One Year Break in Service, you will be entitled to receive a termination benefit.

The amount of your benefit will be the value of your account balance which has become vested. See Section 4.

The value of your account balance will depend on the following:

1. How long you have been a Participant in the Plan;
2. What your compensation has been;
3. How much the Company has contributed; and
4. How much growth has taken place as a result of investing all contributions.

Because the Plan is a defined contribution plan, your benefits are not insured under Title IV of ERISA, and neither the Company nor the Plan's Trustee insure or guarantee the value of your benefits.

b) When and How May I Expect
   To Receive My Benefits?

When you become entitled to receive a benefit, the Plan Administrator will value your account as of the last day of the Plan Year.

Generally, normal retirement, death and disability benefits will commence as soon as is administratively possible following the end of the Plan Year in which the event occurred which entitled you to the benefit distribution.

Your benefit may be paid to you or your designated beneficiary in the case of death in one or more of the following ways:

1. You may receive a nontransferable annuity contract purchased for you from a responsible life insurance company selected by the Committee. The annuity contract will provide for payments to commence when you attain Normal Retirement Age and, if you are unmarried, to continue throughout your lifetime. If you are married, the annuity shall be a Qualified Joint and Survivor Annuity unless you elect some other form of benefit. A Qualified Joint and Survivor Annuity means annuity payments for your life with a survivor annuity for the life of your spouse. Since the benefit takes two lives into consideration, payments made to you will generally be less than you would receive based on your life alone. However, the present value of the total payments you and your spouse should receive will be equal to the present value of the payments you would receive if the annuity were based on your life alone;

or

2. A lump sum; or

3. A straight life annuity; or

4. Installment payments over a period of time.

While the exact method of distribution is up to the Plan Administrator, you or your beneficiary may request the Plan Administrator to make the distribution in the method of your choice. However, before making a request you are strongly urged to seek legal advice concerning the method which will be best for you.

6. PROCEDURE FOR CLAIMING BENEFITS

Filing a Claim for Benefits: You or your beneficiary or the Company acting on your behalf must notify the Committee of a claim for benefits under the Plan. The Committee will inform you of your benefits within a reasonable time.

Denial of a Claim: If a claim is wholly or partially denied, notice of the decision will be furnished to you or your beneficiary within a reasonable period of time after receipt of the claim by the Committee. The notice of decision will be set forth in writing and will provide:

1. Specific reasons for the denial;
2. Specific references to the pertinent Plan provisions on which the denial is based;
3. A description of any additional material to perfect the claim and an explanation of why such material is needed; and
4. The steps to be taken for review of the denied claim.

If you (or your beneficiary) disagree with the Committee's decision, you may request, in writing, a reconsideration of that decision from the Committee. All claims for benefits or requests for review of claim denials may be made by contacting the Committee. The Committee will provide a full and fair review of the decision, and notify you in writing of the results of that review.

7. TAXES ON YOUR ACCOUNT ARE DEFERRED

What kind of taxes do you have to pay in connection with your account? Under current tax laws, here is what happens:

Company Contributions are not taxable to you as they are credited to your company Comtribution Account. You do not report them as income. The money is subject to tax, however, when you receive it.

8. RIGHTS OF PARTICIPATING EMPLOYEES

As a Participant in the Plan, you are entitled to certain rights and protections under the Employee Retirement Income Security Act of 1974 (ERISA). ERISA provides that a Participant shall be entitled to:

1. Examine, without charge, at the plan administrator's office and at other specified locations, such as worksites and union halls, all plan documents including insurance contracts, collective bargaining agreements and copies of all documents filed by the plan with the U.S. Department of Labor, such as detailed annual reports and plan descriptions.

2. Obtain copies of all plan documents and other plan information upon written request to the plan administrator. The administrator may make a reasonable charge for the copies.

3. Receive a summary of the plan's annual financial report. The plan administrator is required by law to furnish each participant a copy of this summary annual report.

4. Obtain a statement telling you whether you have a right to receive a pension at Normal Retirement age and if so, what your benefits would be at normal retirement age if you stop working under the plan now. If you do not have a right to a pension, the statement will tell you how many more years you have to work to get a right to a pension. This statement must be requested in writing and is not required to be given more than once a year. The plan must provide the statement free of charge.

5. In addition to creating rights for plan participants, ERISA imposes duties upon the people who are responsible for the operation of the employee benefit plan. The people who operate your plan, called "fiduciaries" of the plan, have a duty to do so prudently and in the interest of you and other plan participants and beneficiaries. No one, including your employer, your union, or any other person, may fire you or otherwise discriminate against you in any way to prevent you from obtaining a (pension, welfare) benefit or exercising your rights under ERISA. If your claim for a (pension, welfare) benefit is denied in whole or in part, you must receive a written explanation of the reason for the denial. You have the right to have the plan review and reconsider your claim. Under ERISA, there are steps you can take to enforce the above rights. For instance, if you request materials from the plan and do not receive them within 30 days, you may file suit in a Federal court. In such a case, the court may require the plan administrator to provide the materials and pay you up to $100 a day until you receive the materials, unless the materials were not sent because of reasons beyond the control of the administrator. If you have a claim for benefits which is denied or ignored, in whole or in part, you may file suit in a state or Federal court. If it should happen that plan fiduciaries misuse the plan's money, or if you are discriminated against for asserting your rights, you may seek assistance from the U.S. Department of Labor, or you may file suit in a Federal court. The court will decide who should pay court costs and legal fees. If you are successful the court may order the person you have sued to pay these costs and fees. If you lose, the court may order you to pay these costs and fees, for example, if it finds your claim is frivolous. If you have any questions about your plan, you should

contact the plan administrator. If you have any questions about this statement or about your rights under ERISA, you should contact the nearest Area Office of the U.S. Labor-Management Services Administration, Department of Labor.

[¶912] FORM EBS-1

A form EBS-1 must be filed for each plan with the Department of Labor within 120 days after the plan is adopted. A completed EBS-1 for each of the sample plans is reproduced on pages 422 to 433.

U.S. Department of Labor

Labor-Management Services Administration—Office of Employee Benefits Security

Plan Description

Form approved

OMB No. 44—R1596

This form is prescribed under the reporting and disclosure provisions of Title I of the Employee Retirement Income Security Act of 1974 (ERISA). Code references are to the Internal Revenue Code of 1954.

NOTE: Due to the use of certain specialized terms, it is important to refer to the instructions on an item-by-item basis when completing the form. Answer each item, or enter "None" or "N/A" (Not Applicable), as appropriate.

A. Is this: ☒ an initial filing, OR

☐ an amended filing

Department of Labor Use ONLY	A	B	C	D	E	F	G	H	I

B. 1. If an amended filing, is this:

☐ a termination not involving a transfer of assets or liabilities to another plan

☐ a transfer of assets or liabilities to another plan involving a termination

☐ a transfer of assets or liabilities to another plan not involving a termination

☐ another amendment

2. If assets or liabilities were transferred to another plan, enter sponsor name, EIN and PN for other plan. _____

3. What is the effective date of the amendment?

N/A

Month	Day	Year

4. Does the amendment result in a reduction of accrued pension benefits to participants? ☐ Yes ☐ No

C. What was the date of the latest general distribution of a summary plan description to participants and beneficiaries receiving benefits under the plan? *To be distributed*

PART I ALL PLANS

1. (a) Name of sponsor (employer if for a single employer plan)

Big Bucks, Inc.

Address (number and street)

445 South Figueroa Street

City or town, State and ZIP code

Los Angeles, California 90071

1. (b) Employer identification number

9 5 0 0 0 0 0 0 0

1. (c) Telephone number

(213) 620-0460

1. (d) Employer taxable year ends

1/31/79

2. (a) Name of plan administrator (if other than sponsor)

Profit Sharing Committee

Address (number and street)

445 South Figueroa Street

City or town, State and ZIP code

Los Angeles, California 90071

1. (e) Business code number

5931

2. (b) Administrator's employer identification no.

9 5 0 0 0 0 0 0 0

2. (c) Telephone number

(213) 624-6654

3. Check appropriate box to indicate the type of plan entity (check only one box):

(a) ☒ Single-employer

(b) ☐ Plan of controlled group of corporation or common control employers

(c) ☐ Multiemployer plan

(d) ☐ Multiple-employer-collectively-bargained plan

(e) ☐ Multiple-employer plan (other)

4. (a) Name of plan: *BIG BUCKS, INC. EMPLOYEES' PROFIT SHARING PLAN AND TRUST AGREEMENT*

4. (b) Plan number 0 0 2

5. Department of Labor WP file number (if any) WP-	6. Initial effective date of plan			7. Ending date of plan's fiscal year	Month	Day
	Month	Day	Year			
None	2	1	78	*January 31, 1978*		

8. Number of active and retired participants and beneficiaries as of the end of the plan year (welfare plans complete only (a) (iii), (b), (c) and (d)):

(a) Active participants (employed or carried as active) (i) Number fully vested . . . . _0_

(ii) Number not fully vested . . . . . . _3_

(iii) Total . . . . _3_

(b) Retired participants receiving benefits . . . . _0_

(c) Participants separated from employment and entitled to future benefits . . . . _0_

(d) Subtotal, sum of (a), (b) and (c) . . . . _3_

(e) Beneficiaries receiving pension benefits . . . . _0_

(f) Total, (d) plus (e) . . . . _3_

Under penalties of perjury and other penalties set forth in the instructions, I declare that I have examined this report, including accompanying schedules and statements, and to the best of my knowledge and belief, it is true, correct and complete.

4/1/78

Date	Signature of plan administrator

9. Check at least one item in (a) or (b) and applicable items in (c):

   (a) ☐ Welfare benefit plan

   (b) Pension benefit plan:

      (i) Defined benefit plan—(Indicate type of defined benefit plan below):

         (A) ☒ Fixed benefit   (B) ☐ Unit benefit   (C) ☐ Flat benefit   (D) ☐ Other (specify) ▶ _____

      (ii) Defined contribution plan—(Indicate type of defined contribution plan below):

         (A) ☐ Profit-sharing   (B) ☐ Stock bonus   (C) ☐ Target benefit   (D) ☐ Other money purchase

         (E) ☐ Other (specify) ▶ _____

      (iii) ☐ Defined benefit plan with benefits based partly on balance of separate account of participant (section 414 of the Code)

      (iv) ☐ Annuity arrangement of a certain exempt organization or a governmental unit (section 403(b) of the Code)

      (v) ☐ Custodial account for regulated investment company stock (section 403(b)(7) of the Code)

      (vi) ☐ Trust treated as an individual retirement account (section 408(c) of the Code)

      (vii) ☐ Employee stock ownership plan not part of a qualified plan (section 301(d) of the Tax Reduction Act of 1975)

      (viii) ☐ Other (specify) ▶ _____

   (c) Other plan features:

      (i) ☐ Thrift-savings   (ii) ☐ Keogh (H.R. 10) plan

      (iii) ☐ Employee stock ownership as part of a qualified plan (check only if you checked a box in (b)(ii) above)

10. Is the plan administrator designated as agent for the service of legal process?   ☒ Yes   ☐ No
   If "No," enter the person designated:

Name _____

Business address (Number and street) _____

City, town or post office, State and ZIP code _____

11. Indicate the persons who perform functions for the plan. Mark X in all applicable boxes.

Function	Plan Sponsor (1)	Plan Administrator (2)	Trustee (3)	Insurance Carrier (4)	Other (Specify) (5)
(a) Receives and/or deposits contributions	☐	☐	☒	☐	☐ ____
(b) Maintains records of plan participants	☐	☒	☐	☐	☐ ____
(c) Authorizes payment of plan administrative expenses	☐	☒	☐	☐	☐ ____
(d) Pays plan administrative expenses	☒	☐	☐	☐	☐ ____
(e) Determines investment policy	☐	☒	☐	☐	☐ ____
(f) Invests plan assets	☐	☐	☒	☐	☐ ____
(g) Selects insurance carrier or service organization	☐	☒	☐	☐	☐ ____
(h) Selects corporate trustee	☒	☐	☐	☐	☐ ____
(i) Receives claims for benefits under the plan	☐	☒	☐	☐	☐ ____
(j) Determines eligibility of claimants for receipt of benefits	☐	☒	☐	☐	☐ ____
(k) Determines benefit amount	☐	☒	☐	☐	☐ ____
(l) Makes determination on appeal of claim denials	☐	☒	☐	☐	☐ ____
(m) Authorizes payment of benefits	☐	☒	☐	☐	☐ ____
(n) Makes payments of benefits	☐	☐	☒	☐	☐ ____

NOTE: Information furnished above will not be determinative as to whether a party is a fiduciary to a plan.

12. Is this a plan established or maintained pursuant to one or more collective bargaining agreements? ☐ Yes   ☒ No
DO NOT SUBMIT COPIES OF COLLECTIVE BARGAINING AGREEMENTS

13. Mark X in the appropriate box(es) which indicate the type of document(s) establishing or affecting the plan: **DO NOT SUBMIT COPIES OF PLAN DOCUMENTS**

   (a) ☒ Plan   (c) ☐ Regulations and rules

   (b) ☒ Trust   (d) ☐ Contracts (other than collective bargaining agreements)

14. This plan includes as participants (mark X in all applicable boxes):

   (a) ☒ All types of employees   (d) ☐ Employees covered by collective bargaining

   (b) ☐ Hourly employees   (e) ☐ Employees not covered by collective bargaining

   (c) ☐ Salaried employees   (f) ☐ Other (specify) _____

15. Indicate sources and methods of determining contributions to the plan (mark X in all applicable boxes):

Employer's Contribution	Employee's Contribution
(a) ☐ Fixed rate (i) ☐ Per hour	(h) ☒ Voluntary
(ii) ☐ Per day	☐ Mandatory
(iii) ☐ Per week	(i) ☐ Fixed rate (i) ☐ Per hour
(iv) ☐ Per month	(ii) ☐ Per day
(v) ☐ Per annum	(iii) ☐ Per week
(b) ☐ Based on profits . . . Formula	(iv) ☐ Per month
(c) ☒ Based on profits . . . Discretionary	(v) ☐ Per annum
(d) ☐ Percentage of payroll	(j) ☐ Percentage of compensation
(e) ☐ Actuarial rate of determination	(k) ☐ Part of dues to union
(f) ☐ None	(l) ☐ Assessment by union
(g) ☐ Other (specify)_____	(m) ☐ None
_____	(n) ☐ Other (specify)_____

16. Indicate the method used for the accumulation of assets and for disbursement of benefits (mark X in all applicable items):

Type of funding entity:	Accumulation of Assets (1)	Disbursement of Benefits (2)
(a) Trust (benefits provided in whole from trust funds)	☒	☒
(b) Trust or arrangement providing benefits partially through insurance and/or annuity contracts	☐	☐
(c) Trust or arrangement providing benefits exclusively through insurance and/or annuity contracts	☐	☐
(d) Custodial account described in section 401 (f) of the Code and not included in (c) above	☐	☐
(e) Other (specify)_____	☐	☐

17. Indicate procedure for presenting claims for benefits and review of claims which are denied (mark X in all applicable boxes):

(a) Does the plan provide a procedure for presenting initial claims for benefits?   ☒ Yes   ☐ No

(b) Does the claimant have to initiate action for review of claims which have been denied?   ☒ Yes   ☐ No

(c) Indicate by marking X in the applicable boxes, the plan official or other person who makes decisions on claims and the plan official or other person who makes determinations on appeals of claims denied in whole or in part.

	Claims (1)	Appeals of Claims Denied (2)
(i) Administrator	☒	☒
(ii) Board of Trustees	☐	☐
(iii) Employer	☐	☐
(iv) Insurance Company	☐	☐
(v) Other (specify)_____	☐	☐
(vi) None	☐	☐

(d) Does the plan provide for independent arbitration of claim denials?   ☐ Yes   ☒ No

(e) If the benefits under the plan are collectively bargained, is there provision for binding arbitration of claims?   ☐ Yes   ☐ No

PART II PLANS WITH PENSION PROVISIONS

18. Indicate the general eligibility requirements for participation under the plan:

(a) Age _None_ Service _6 months_ Number of years or Age _N/A_ Service _N/A_ Number of years

(b) Maximum age (after which employees are not admitted) (specify) _____

(c) Other (specify) _____

19. Indicate the general vesting provisions of the plan for employer contributions:

(a) Vesting Schedule:

(i) ☐ Full (100%) and immediate

(ii) ☐ Full (100%) vesting after 3 years of service

(iii) ☐ Full (100%) vesting at 10 years of service

(iv) ☐ Rule of 45; (5 years of service and where the sum of the participant's age and years of service equal or exceed 45)

(v) ☐ 25% vesting after 5 years, 5% additional for each of the next 5 years, and 10% additional for each of the next 5 years

(vi) ☐ Full (100%) vesting within 5 years after contributions are made (Class Year Plan Only)

(vii) ☐ For each year of employment, commencing with the 4th such year, vesting not less than 40% after 4 years of service, 5% additional for each of the next 2 years, and 10% additional for each of the next 5 years

(viii) ☒ Other (describe) _20 percent per year_

(b) Check if you exclude the following years of service under the vesting provisions of the plan:

(i) ☐ Years of service before age 22

(ii) ☐ Years of service for period during which the employee declined to contribute to plan requiring employee contributions

(iii) ☐ Years of service during which the employer did not maintain the plan or a predecessor plan

20. Does the plan have any features of portability or reciprocity with:

(a) Employer(s) participating under the plan? ☐ Yes ☒ No

(b) Employer(s) not participating under the plan? ☐ Yes ☒ No

21. Indicate how length of service is determined for participation, vesting and full benefit accrual:

(a) Mark X in the appropriate boxes to indicate the computation period:

Participation	Vesting	Full Benefit Accrual
(i) ☒ Employment commencement date	(iii) ☐ Calendar year	(vi) ☐ Calendar year
(ii) ☐ Other (specify)_____	(iv) ☐ Plan year	(vii) ☒ Plan year
_____	(v) ☐ Other (specify)_____	(viii) ☐ Other (specify)_____
		(ix) ☐ Not applicable

(b) Indicate hours required for one year of service for purposes of participation, vesting and full benefit accrual:

Participation	Vesting	Full Benefit Accrual
_1000_ (Hours)	_1000_ (Hours)	_1000_ (Hours)

(c) Mark X in the appropriate boxes to indicate whether employees are credited for hours:

	Participation (1)	Vesting (2)	Full Benefit Accrual (3)
(i) Actually worked	☒	☐	☐
(ii) Sickness	☐	☐	☐
(iii) Vacation	☐	☐	☐
(iv) Disability	☐	☐	☐
(v) Layoff	☐	☐	☐
(vi) Other_____	☒	☒	☒

22. Does the plan contain break in service rules? ☐ Yes ☒ No

(a) Mark X in the appropriate boxes to indicate the computation period for a break in service:

Participation	Vesting
(i) ☐ Employment commencement date	(iv) ☐ Calendar year
(ii) ☐ Plan year	(v) ☐ Plan year
(iii) ☐ Other (specify)_____	(vi) ☐ Other (specify)_____

(b) Indicate the minimum number of hours needed to avoid a break in service:

Participation	Vesting	Full Benefit Accrual
_____ (Hours)	_____ (Hours)	_____ (Hours)

425

23. Mark X in all applicable boxes for which the plan provides benefits and mark X or otherwise complete the information indicating the requirements for attaining the benefits provided.

Type of Benefit	Requirements for Benefits				
	No age or Service (1)	Age Only (2)	Service Only (3)	Combination Age and Service (4)	Other (5)
(a) ☐ Normal Retirement	☐	_65_ Yrs	_____ Yrs	_____ Yrs _____ Yrs	☐
(b) ☐ Early Retirement	☐	_____ Yrs	_____ Yrs	_____ Yrs _____ Yrs	☐
(c) ☐ Deferred Vested	☐	☐	☐	☐	☐
(d) ☐ Disability	☐	_____ Yrs	_____ Yrs	_____ Yrs _____ Yrs	☐
(e) ☐ Death	☐	_____ Yrs	_____ Yrs	_____ Yrs _____ Yrs	☐

24. (a) Mark X in the block which best describes the basis on which normal retirement benefits under the plan are computed and fill in the dollar or percentage figures as appropriate:

  (i) ☐ Money Purchase

  (ii) ☐ _____ % of the employee's earnings for each year of service

  (iii) ☐ _____ % of the employee's required contributions

  (iv) ☐ _____ % of the employee's earnings on which contributions to Social Security are required up to $ _____
       and _____ % of the balance of earnings for each year of service

  (v) ☐ _____ % of the employee's earnings for each year of service less _____ % of primary social security benefits

  (vi) ☐ $_____ Per month for each year of service

  (vii) ☐ _____ % of earnings not related to service

  (viii) ☐ $_____ Per month not related to earnings or service

  (ix) ⊠Other (describe) _Profit Sharing-Discretionary to 15% of Compensation_

(b) Mark X in the block which best describes the years of earnings used to compute normal retirement benefits   N/A

  (i) ☐ Career Average   (iii) ☐ Terminal Average - 5 years

  (ii) ☐ Terminal Average - 3 years   (iv) ☐ Terminal Average - 10 years

            (v) ☐ Other (specify) _____

25. (a) Are there any circumstances causing:

  (i) Ineligibility to participate once having become eligible?   ☐ Yes ⊠ No
  (ii) Denial, loss, forfeiture or suspension of benefits once having become vested or in pay status?   ☐ Yes ⊠ No

(b) If the circumstances are other than re-employment under the plan or break in service, explain__N/A_____

26. For plans that provide retirement income benefits in the form of a lifetime annuity:

  (a) Does the plan provide for a qualified joint and survivor annuity upon attainment of normal
      retirement age or actual retirement?   ⊠ Yes ☐ No
  (b) If the plan provides for early retirement, does the plan provide a joint and survivor annuity
      election at the earliest date on which a participant is eligible for early retirement benefits?   ☐ Yes ☐ No

27. What is the disposition of an employee's own contribution if his participation in the plan ends before benefits are received (mark X in all applicable boxes):

	Death (1)	Withdrawal (2)	Disqualification (3)
(a) Contribution returned without interest	☐	☐	☐
(b) Contribution returned with interest.	☐	☐	☐
(c) Contribution not returned (explain) _____	☐	☐	☐
(d) Other (specify) _____	☐	☐	☐

PART III PLANS WITH WELFARE PROVISIONS

28. Mark X in all applicable boxes for which the plan provides benefits and mark X or otherwise complete the information indicating the requirements for attaining the benefits provided: N/A

Type of Benefit	Requirements for Benefits		
	Immediate (1)	Waiting Period (Specify) (2)	Other (3)
HEALTH			
(a) ☐ Hospital	☐		
(b) ☐ Convalescent care	☐		
(c) ☐ Home health care	☐		
(d) ☐ Surgical	☐		
(e) ☐ Medical	☐		
(f) ☐ Maternity	☐		
(g) ☐ Major medical	☐		
(h) ☐ Dental	☐		
(i) ☐ Prescription drugs (out of hospital)	☐		
(j) ☐ Diagnostic X-ray and laboratory services (out of hospital)	☐		
(k) ☐ Vision care	☐		
(l) ☐ Other health benefit (specify)_____	☐		
OTHER WELFARE			
(a) ☐ Life insurance	☐		
(b) ☐ Accidental death and dismemberment	☐		
(c) ☐ Temporary disability income (accident and sickness)	☐		
(d) ☐ Long term disability	☐		
(e) ☐ Supplementary unemployment benefits	☐		
(f) ☐ Severance pay	☐		
(g) ☐ Apprenticeship and other training	☐		
(h) ☐ Scholarship	☐		
(i) ☐ Prepaid legal services	☐		
(j) ☐ Other (except health) specify_____	☐		

29. Indicate circumstances (other than termination of employment or retirement) causing ineligibility, denial, loss, forfeiture or suspension of welfare benefits: N/A

(a) ☐ Illness   (c) ☐ Strikes

(b) ☐ Layoffs   (d) ☐ Other (specify)_____

PART IV ALL PLANS

30. Give the name and address of each fiduciary (including trustee) to the plan.

Name	Address
Herbert Bucksup	445 South Figueroa Street, L.A., Calif.
Betty Bucksup	445 South Figueroa Street, L.A., Calif.
Flo Cash	445 South Figueroa Street, L.A., Calif.

427

U.S. Department of Labor
Labor-Management Services Administration—Office of Employee Benefits Security

Plan Description

Form approved
OMB No. 44—R1596

This form is prescribed under the reporting and disclosure provisions of Title I of the Employee Retirement Income Security Act of 1974 (ERISA). Code references are to the Internal Revenue Code of 1954.

NOTE: Due to the use of certain specialized terms, it is important to refer to the instructions on an item-by-item basis when completing the form. Answer each item, or enter "None" or "N/A" (Not Applicable), as appropriate.

A. Is this: ☒ an initial filing, OR
☐ an amended filing

Department of Labor Use ONLY	A	B	C	D	E	F	G	H	I

B. 1. If an amended filing, is this:

☐ a termination not involving a transfer of assets or liabilities to another plan

☐ a transfer of assets or liabilities to another plan involving a termination

☐ a transfer of assets or liabilities to another plan not involving a termination

☐ another amendment

2. If assets or liabilities were transferred to another plan, enter sponsor name, EIN and PN for other plan. _____

3. What is the effective date of the amendment?
   N/A

Month	Day	Year

4. Does the amendment result in a reduction of accrued pension benefits to participants? ☐ Yes ☐ No

C. What was the date of the latest general distribution of a summary plan description to participants and beneficiaries receiving benefits under the plan? *To be distributed*

PART I ALL PLANS

1. (a) Name of sponsor (employer if for a single employer plan)	1. (b) Employer identification number
Big Bucks, Inc.	9 5 0 0 0 0 0 0 0
Address (number and street)	1. (c) Telephone number
445 South Figueroa Street	(*213*) *620-0460*
City or town, State and ZIP code	1. (d) Employer taxable year ends
Los Angeles, California 90071	*1/31/79*
2. (a) Name of plan administrator (if other than sponsor)	1. (e) Business code number
Pension Trust Committee	*5931*
Address (number and street)	2. (b) Administrator's employer identification no.
445 South Figueroa Street	9 5 0 0 0 0 0 0 0
City or town, State and ZIP code	2. (c) Telephone number
Los Angeles, California 90071	(*213*) *624-6654*

3. Check appropriate box to indicate the type of plan entity (check only one box):

(a) ☐ Single-employer

(b) ☐ Plan of controlled group of corporation or common control employers

(c) ☐ Multiemployer plan

(d) ☐ Multiple-employer-collectively-bargained plan

(e) ☐ Multiple-employer plan (other)

4. (a) Name of plan: *BIG BUCKS, INC. EMPLOYEES' PENSION TRUST (MONEY PURCHASE PLAN)*	4. (b) Plan number	0 0 1

5. Department of Labor WP file number (if any) WP: *None*	6. Initial effective date of plan Month Day Year *2 1 78*	7. Ending date of plan's fiscal year *January 31, 1978*	Month	Day

8. Number of active and retired participants and beneficiaries as of the end of the plan year (welfare plans complete only (a) (iii), (b), (c) and (d)):

(a) Active participants (employed or carried as active) (i) Number fully vested . . . . _-0-_

(ii) Number not fully vested . . . . . . _3_

(iii) Total . . . . _3_

(b) Retired participants receiving benefits . . . . _-0-_

(c) Participants separated from employment and entitled to future benefits . . . . _-0-_

(d) Subtotal, sum of (a), (b) and (c) . . . . _3_

(e) Beneficiaries receiving pension benefits . . . . _-0-_

(f) Total, (d) plus (e) . . . . _3_

Under penalties of perjury and other penalties set forth in the instructions, I declare that I have examined this report, including accompanying schedules and statements, and to the best of my knowledge and belief, it is true, correct and complete.

4/1/78

Date	Signature of plan administrator

9. Check at least one item in (a) or (b) and applicable items in (c):

  (a) ☐　Welfare benefit plan

  (b)　Pension benefit plan:

    (i)　Defined benefit plan—(Indicate type of defined benefit plan below):

      (A) ☐　Fixed benefit　　(B) ☐　Unit benefit　　(C) ☐　Flat benefit　　(D) ☐　Other (specify) ▶ _____

    (ii)　Defined contribution plan—(Indicate type of defined contribution plan below):

      (A)☒　Profit-sharing　　(B) ☐　Stock bonus　　(C) ☐　Target benefit　　(D) ☐　Other money purchase

      (E) ☐　Other (specify) ▶ _____

    (iii) ☐　Defined benefit plan with benefits based partly on balance of separate account of participant (section 414 of the Code)

    (iv) ☐　Annuity arrangement of a certain exempt organization or a governmental unit (section 403(b) of the Code)

    (v) ☐　Custodial account for regulated investment company stock (section 403(b)(7) of the Code)

    (vi) ☐　Trust treated as an individual retirement account (section 408(c) of the Code)

    (vii) ☐　Employee stock ownership plan not part of a qualified plan (section 301(d) of the Tax Reduction Act of 1975)

    (viii) ☐　Other (specify) ▶ _____

  (c)　Other plan features:

    (i) ☐　Thrift-savings　　(ii) ☐ Keogh (H.R. 10) plan

    (iii) ☐　Employee stock ownership as part of a qualified plan (check only if you checked a box in (b)(ii) above)

10.　Is the plan administrator designated as agent for the service of legal process?　　☒ Yes　　☐ No
If "No." enter the person designated:

Name _____

Business address (Number and street) _____

City, town or post office, State and ZIP code _____

11.　Indicate the persons who perform functions for the plan. Mark X in all applicable boxes.

Function	Plan Sponsor (1)	Plan Administrator (2)	Trustee (3)	Insurance Carrier (4)	Other (Specify) (5)
		Persons Performing Function			
(a) Receives and/or deposits contributions	☐	☐	☒	☐	☐ ___
(b) Maintains records of plan participants.	☐	☒	☐	☐	☐ ___
(c) Authorizes payment of plan administrative expenses . .	☐	☒	☐	☐	☐ ___
(d) Pays plan administrative expenses	☒	☐	☐	☐	☐ ___
(e) Determines investment policy	☐	☒	☐	☐	☐ ___
(f) Invests plan assets.	☐	☐	☒	☐	☐ ___
(g) Selects insurance carrier or service organization	☐	☒	☐	☐	☐ ___
(h) Selects corporate trustee	☒	☐	☐	☐	☐ ___
(i) Receives claims for benefits under the plan	☐	☒	☐	☐	☐ ___
(j) Determines eligibility of claimants for receipt of benefits	☐	☒	☐	☐	☐ ___
(k) Determines benefit amount	☐	☒	☐	☐	☐ ___
(l) Makes determination on appeal of claim denials	☐	☒	☐	☐	☐ ___
(m) Authorizes payment of benefits	☐	☒	☐	☐	☐ ___
(n) Makes payments of benefits	☐	☐	☒	☐	☐ ___

NOTE: Information furnished above will not be determinative as to whether a party is a fiduciary to a plan.

12.　Is this a plan established or maintained pursuant to one or more collective bargaining agreements?　　☐ Yes　　☒ No
DO NOT SUBMIT COPIES OF COLLECTIVE BARGAINING AGREEMENTS

13.　Mark X in the appropriate box(es) which indicate the type of document(s) establishing or affecting the plan: **DO NOT SUBMIT COPIES OF PLAN DOCUMENTS**

  (a) ☒ Plan　　　　　　　　　　(c) ☐ Regulations and rules

  (b) ☒ Trust　　　　　　　　　　(d) ☐ Contracts (other than collective bargaining agreements)

14.　This plan includes as participants (mark X in all applicable boxes):

  (a) ☒ All types of employees　　　　　　(d) ☐ Employees covered by collective bargaining

  (b) ☐ Hourly employees　　　　　　　　(e) ☐ Employees not covered by collective bargaining

  (c) ☐ Salaried employees　　　　　　　　(f) ☐ Other (specify) _____

15. Indicate sources and methods of determining contributions to the plan (mark X in all applicable boxes):

Employer's Contribution	Employee's Contribution
(a) ☐ Fixed rate (i) ☐ Per hour	(h) ☐ Voluntary
(ii) ☐ Per day	☐ Mandatory
(iii) ☐ Per week	(i) ☐ Fixed rate (i) ☐ Per hour
(iv) ☐ Per month	(ii) ☐ Per day
(v) ☐ Per annum	(iii) ☐ Per week
(b) ☐ Based on profits . . . Formula	(iv) ☐ Per month
(c) ☐ Based on profits . . . Discretionary	(v) ☐ Per annum
(d) ☒ Percentage of payroll	(j) ☐ Percentage of compensation
(e) ☐ Actuarial rate of determination	(k) ☐ Part of dues to union
(f) ☐ None	(l) ☐ Assessment by union
(g) ☐ Other (specify)_____	(m) ☒ None
	(n) ☐ Other (specify)_____

16. Indicate the method used for the accumulation of assets and for disbursement of benefits (mark X in all applicable items):

	Accumulation of Assets (1)	Disbursement of Benefits (2)
Type of funding entity:		
(a) Trust (benefits provided in whole from trust funds)	☒	☒
(b) Trust or arrangement providing benefits partially through insurance and/or annuity contracts	☐	☐
(c) Trust or arrangement providing benefits exclusively through insurance and/or annuity contracts	☐	☐
(d) Custodial account described in section 401 (f) of the Code and not included in (c) above	☐	☐
(e) Other (specify)_____	☐	☐

17. Indicate procedure for presenting claims for benefits and review of claims which are denied (mark X in all applicable boxes):

(a) Does the plan provide a procedure for presenting initial claims for benefits?   ☒ Yes   ☐ No

(b) Does the claimant have to initiate action for review of claims which have been denied?   ☒ Yes   ☐ No

(c) Indicate by marking X in the applicable boxes, the plan official or other person who makes decisions on claims and the plan official or other person who makes determinations on appeals of claims denied in whole or in part.

	Claims (1)	Appeals of Claims Denied (2)
(i) Administrator	☒	☒
(ii) Board of Trustees	☐	☐
(iii) Employer	☐	☐
(iv) Insurance Company	☐	☐
(v) Other (specify)_____	☐	☐
(vi) None	☐	☐

(d) Does the plan provide for independent arbitration of claim denials?   ☐ Yes   ☒ No

(e) If the benefits under the plan are collectively bargained, is there provision for binding arbitration of claims?   *N/A*   ☐ Yes   ☐ No

PART II PLANS WITH PENSION PROVISIONS

18. Indicate the general eligibility requirements for participation under the plan:

(a) Age_ *none* _Service_ *6 months* _or Age_ *N/A* _Service_ *N/A* _
                                Number of years   Number of years

(b) Maximum age (after which employees are not admitted) (specify) _____

(c) Other (specify) _____

19. Indicate the general vesting provisions of the plan for employer contributions:

    (a) Vesting Schedule:

      (i) ☐ Full (100%) and immediate

      (ii) ☐ Full (100%) vesting after 3 years of service

      (iii) ☐ Full (100%) vesting at 10 years of service

      (iv) ☐ Rule of 45: (5 years of service and where the sum of the participant's age and years of service equal or exceed 45)

      (v) ☐ 25% vesting after 5 years, 5% additional for each of the next 5 years, and 10% additional for each of the next 5 years

      (vi) ☐ Full (100%) vesting within 5 years after contributions are made (Class Year Plan Only)

      (vii) ☐ For each year of employment, commencing with the 4th such year, vesting not less than 40% after 4 years of service, 5% additional for each of the next 2 years, and 10% additional for each of the next 5 years

      (viii) ☐ Other (describe) _20 percent per year_

    (b) Check if you exclude the following years of service under the vesting provisions of the plan:

      (i) ☐ Years of service before age 22

      (ii) ☐ Years of service for period during which the employee declined to contribute to plan requiring employee contributions

      (iii) ☐ Years of service during which the employer did not maintain the plan or a predecessor plan

20. Does the plan have any features of portability or reciprocity with:

    (a) Employer(s) participating under the plan?   ☐ Yes   ☒ No

    (b) Employer(s) not participating under the plan?   ☐ Yes   ☒ No

21. Indicate how length of service is determined for participation, vesting and full benefit accrual:

    (a) Mark X in the appropriate boxes to indicate the computation period:

Participation	Vesting	Full Benefit Accrual
(i) ☒ Employment commencement date	(iii) ☐ Calendar year	(vi) ☐ Calendar year
(ii) ☐ Other (specify)_____	(iv) ☒ Plan year	(vii) ☐ Plan year
_____	(v) ☐ Other (specify)_____	(viii) ☐ Other (specify)_____
		(ix) ☐ Not applicable

    (b) Indicate hours required for one year of service for purposes of participation, vesting and full benefit accrual:

Participation	Vesting	Full Benefit Accrual
_1000_ (Hours)	_1000_ (Hours)	_1000_ (Hours)

    (c) Mark X in the appropriate boxes to indicate whether employees are credited for hours:

	Participation (1)	Vesting (2)	Full Benefit Accrual (3)
(i) Actually worked	☒	☒	☒
(ii) Sickness	☒	☒	☒
(iii) Vacation	☒	☒	☒
(iv) Disability	☒	☒	☒
(v) Layoff	☒	☒	☒
(vi) Other_____	☐	☐	☐

22. Does the plan contain break in service rules?   ☐ Yes   ☒ No

    (a) Mark X in the appropriate boxes to indicate the computation period for a break in service:

Participation	Vesting
(i) ☐ Employment commencement date	(iv) ☐ Calendar year
(ii) ☐ Plan year	(v) ☐ Plan year
(iii) ☐ Other (specify)_____	(vi) ☐ Other (specify)_____

    (b) Indicate the minimum number of hours needed to avoid a break in service:

Participation	Vesting	Full Benefit Accrual
_____ (Hours)	_____ (Hours)	_____ (Hours)

23. Mark X in all applicable boxes for which the plan provides benefits and mark X or otherwise complete the information indicating the requirements for attaining the benefits provided.

Type of Benefit	Requirements for Benefits				
	No age or Service (1)	Age Only (2)	Service Only (3)	Combination Age and Service (4)	Other (5)
(a) ☐ Normal Retirement	☐	_65_ Yrs	_____ Yrs	_____ Yrs _____ Yrs	☐
(b) ☐ Early Retirement	☒	_____ Yrs	_____ Yrs	_____ Yrs _____ Yrs	☐
(c) ☐ Deferred Vested	☒	☐	☐	☐	☐
(d) ☐ Disability	☒	_____ Yrs	_____ Yrs	_____ Yrs _____ Yrs	☐
(e) ☐ Death	☒	_____ Yrs	_____ Yrs	_____ Yrs _____ Yrs	☐

24. (a) Mark X in the block which best describes the basis on which normal retirement benefits under the plan are computed and fill in the dollar or percentage figures as appropriate:

    (i) ☒ Money Purchase

    (ii) ☐ _____ % of the employee's earnings for each year of service

    (iii) ☐ _____ % of the employee's required contributions

    (iv) ☐ _____ % of the employee's earnings on which contributions to Social Security are required up to $ _____
          and _____ % of the balance of earnings for each year of service

    (v) ☐ _____ % of the employee's earnings for each year of service less _____ % of primary social security benefits

    (vi) ☐ $_____ Per month for each year of service

    (vii) ☐ _____ % of earnings not related to service

    (viii) ☐ $_____ Per month not related to earnings or service

    (ix) ☐ Other (describe) _____

(b) Mark X in the block which best describes the years of earnings used to compute normal retirement benefits

    (i) ☐ Career Average   (iii) ☐ Terminal Average - 5 years

    (ii) ☐ Terminal Average - 3 years   (iv) ☐ Terminal Average - 10 years

        (v) ☐ Other (specify) _____

25. (a) Are there any circumstances causing:

    (i) Ineligibility to participate once having become eligible?   ☐ Yes   ☒ No

    (ii) Denial, loss, forfeiture or suspension of benefits once having become vested or in pay status?   ☐ Yes   ☒ No

(b) If the circumstances are other than re-employment under the plan or break in service, explain _N/A_____

26. For plans that provide retirement income benefits in the form of a lifetime annuity:

(a) Does the plan provide for a qualified joint and survivor annuity upon attainment of normal retirement age or actual retirement?   ☒ Yes   ☐ No

(b) If the plan provides for early retirement, does the plan provide a joint and survivor annuity election at the earliest date on which a participant is eligible for early retirement benefits?   _N/A_   ☐ Yes   ☐ No

27. What is the disposition of an employee's own contribution if his participation in the plan ends before benefits are received (mark X in all applicable boxes):   *N/A*

	Death (1)	Withdrawal (2)	Disqualification (3)
(a) Contribution returned without interest	☐	☐	☐
(b) Contribution returned with interest	☐	☐	☐
(c) Contribution not returned (explain)_____	☐	☐	☐
(d) Other (specify)_____	☐	☐	☐

PART III PLANS WITH WELFARE PROVISIONS

28. Mark X in all applicable boxes for which the plan provides benefits and mark X or otherwise complete the information indicating the requirements for attaining the benefits provided: *N/A*

Type of Benefit	Immediate (1)	Waiting Period (Specify) (2)	Other (3)
HEALTH			
(a) ☐ Hospital	☐		
(b) ☐ Convalescent care	☐		
(c) ☐ Home health care	☐		
(d) ☐ Surgical	☐		
(e) ☐ Medical	☐		
(f) ☐ Maternity	☐		
(g) ☐ Major medical	☐		
(h) ☐ Dental	☐		
(i) ☐ Prescription drugs (out of hospital)	☐		
(j) ☐ Diagnostic X-ray and laboratory services (out of hospital)	☐		
(k) ☐ Vision care	☐		
(l) ☐ Other health benefit (specify)_____	☐		
OTHER WELFARE			
(a) ☐ Life insurance	☐		
(b) ☐ Accidental death and dismemberment	☐		
(c) ☐ Temporary disability income (accident and sickness)	☐		
(d) ☐ Long term disability	☐		
(e) ☐ Supplementary unemployment benefits	☐		
(f) ☐ Severance pay	☐		
(g) ☐ Apprenticeship and other training	☐		
(h) ☐ Scholarship	☐		
(i) ☐ Prepaid legal services	☐		
(j) ☐ Other (except health) specify_____	☐		

29. Indicate circumstances (other than termination of employment or retirement) causing ineligibility, denial, loss, forfeiture or suspension of welfare benefits: *N/A*

(a) ☐ Illness   (c) ☐ Strikes

(b) ☐ Layoffs   (d) ☐ Other (specify)_____

PART IV ALL PLANS

30. Give the name and address of each fiduciary (including trustee) to the plan.

Name	Address
Herbert Bucksup	*445 South Figueroa Street, L.A., Calif.*
Betty Bucksup	*445 South Figueroa Street, L.A., Calif.*
Flo Cash	*445 South Figueroa Street, L.A., Calif.*

[¶913] ANNUAL REPORTING FORMS

The final forms to be filed are Internal Revenue Service and Department of Labor forms 5500-C for each plan with fewer than 100 participants. These forms must be filed annually. See completed forms on pages 436 to 441.

Annual Return/Report of Employee Benefit Plan

(With fewer than 100 participants)

This form is required to be filed under sections 104 and 4065 of the Employee Retirement Income Security Act of 1974 and sections 6057(b) and 6058(a) of the Internal Revenue Code, referred to as the Code.

1978

This Form is
Open to Public
Inspection

For the calendar plan year 1978 or fiscal plan year beginning _____, 1978 and ending _____, 19___

File original of this form, including schedules and attachments, completed in ink or type.

▶ Do not file this form for Keogh (H.R. 10) plans with fewer than 100 participants and with at least one owner-employee participant. File Form 5500-K instead.
▶ Governmental plans and church plans (not electing coverage under section 410(d) of the Code). Do not file this form. File Form 5500-G instead.
▶ Pension benefit plans, unless otherwise excepted, complete all items. Annuity arrangements of certain exempt organizations, and individual retirement account trusts of employers complete only items 1 through 6, 9 and 10.
▶ Certain welfare benefit plans are not required to file this form—see instructions.
▶ Welfare benefit plans required to file this form do not complete items 7(a), 7(c), 17, 18, 20 and 22.
▶ Plan number—Your 3 digit plan number must be entered in item 5(c); see instruction 5(c) for explanation of "plan number."
▶ If any item does not apply, enter "N/A."

1 (a) Name of plan sponsor (employer if for a single employer plan) BIG BUCKS, INC.	**1 (b)** Employer identification number 95 ⦙ 0000000
Address (number and street) 445 South Figueroa Street	**1 (c)** Telephone number of sponsor (213) 620-0460
City or town, State and ZIP code Los Angeles, California 90071	**1 (d)** Employer taxable year ends Month 1 Day 31 Year 19
2 (a) Name of plan administrator (if other than plan sponsor) Profit Sharing Plan Committee	**1 (e)** Business code number 5931
Address (number and street) 445 South Figueroa Street	**2 (b)** Administrator's employer identification no. 95 ⦙ 0000000
City or town, State and ZIP code Los Angeles, California 90071	**2 (c)** Telephone number of administrator (213) 620-0460

3 Name, address and identification number of ☐ plan sponsor and/or ☐ plan administrator as they appeared on the last return/report filed for this plan if not the same as in 1 or 2 above ▶ ...... Same

4 Check appropriate box to indicate the type of plan entity (check only one box):
- **(a)** ☒ Single-employer plan
- **(b)** ☐ Plan of controlled group of corporations or common control employers
- **(c)** ☐ Multiemployer plan
- **(d)** ☐ Multiple-employer-collectively-bargained plan
- **(e)** ☐ Multiple-employer plan (other)

5 (a) (i) Name of plan ▶ BIG BUCKS, INC., EMPLOYEES' PROFIT SHARING PLAN AND TRUST
   (ii) ☐ Check if name of plan changed since the last return/report.
   (iii) ☒ Check if plan year was changed since last return/report.

5 (b) Effective date of plan
February 1, 1978

5 (c) Enter three digit plan number ▶ 0 0 1

6 Type of plan:
- **(a)** ☐ Defined benefit
- **(b)** ☒ Defined contribution
- **(c)** ☐ Welfare benefit
- **(d)** ☐ Other (specify) ▶ ....

7 (a) Active participants: **(i)** Fully vested ...0... **(ii)** Partially vested ...3... **(iii)** Nonvested ...0... **(iv)** Total ▶ | 3

		Yes	No
(b) Total participants: **(i)** Beginning of plan year ▶ ...3... **(ii)** End of plan year ▶	3		
(c) During the plan year, has any participant(s) separated from service with a deferred benefit (if "Yes," see instructions)?			XX
8 Was this plan amended in this plan year?			XX
9 Plan termination information: N/A			
(a) Was this plan terminated during this plan year or any prior plan year?			
(b) If "Yes," were all trust assets distributed to participants or beneficiaries or transferred to another plan?			
(c) If item 12 is to be checked "Yes" and 9(a) is "Yes," has a notice of intent to terminate been filed with PBGC?			
10 (a) In this plan year, was this plan merged or consolidated into another plan or were assets or liabilities transferred to another plan?			XX

If "Yes," identify other plan(s):
(b) Name of plan(s) ▶ _____

(c) Employer identification number(s)	**(d)** Plan number(s)

(e) Has Form 5310 been filed with IRS? . . . . ☐ Yes ☒ No

Under penalties of perjury and other penalties set forth in the instructions, I declare that I have examined this report, including accompanying schedules and statements, and to the best of my knowledge and belief it is true, correct, and complete.

Date ▶ _____   Signature of employer/plan sponsor ▶ _____

Date ▶ _____   Signature of plan administrator ▶ _____

436

11 Indicate funding arrangement:

    (a) [X] Trust **(b)** [ ] Fully insured **(c)** [ ] Combination **(d)** [ ] Other (specify) ▶ _____

    (e) If (b) or (c) are checked enter number of Schedule A's (Form 5500) which are attached . . . . ▶

12 Is the plan covered under the Pension Benefit Guaranty Corporation termination insurance
program? . . . . [ ] Yes [X] No [ ] Not determined

13 Plan assets and liabilities at the beginning and the end of the plan year (list all assets and liabilities at current value). A plan with
no trust and which is funded entirely by allocated insurance contracts which fully guarantee the amount of benefit payments should
check box and not complete this item . . . . [ ]

Note: *Include all plan assets and liabilities of a trust or separately maintained fund. If more than one trust/fund, report on a
combined basis. Include all insurance values except for the value of that portion of an allocated insurance contract which
fully guarantees the amount of benefit payments. Trusts with no assets at the beginning and the end of the plan year enter
zero on line 13(g). Round off amounts to nearest dollar.*

Assets	Beginning of year		End of year	
	a. Party-in-interest	b. Total	c. Party-in-Interest	d. Total
(a) Cash		0		21,135.00
(b) Receivables		0		0.00
(c) Investments—(i) Government securities .		0		0.00
(ii) Pooled funds/mutual funds . . .		0		0.00
(iii) Corporate (debt and equity instruments) .		0		0.00
(iv) Real estate and mortgages . . .		0		0.00
(v) Other		0		0.00
(d) Buildings and other depreciable property . . .		0		0.00
(e) Unallocated insurance contracts . . .		0		0.00
(f) Other assets		0		0.00
(g) Total assets, sum of (a) through (f) . .		0		21,135.00
Liabilities and Net Assets				
(h) Payables		0		0.00
(i) Acquisition indebtedness				0.00
(j) Other liabilities				0.00
(k) Total liabilities, sum of (h) through (j)				0.00
(l) Net assets, (g) minus (k)				21,135.00

14 Plan income, expenses and changes in net assets during the plan year:

Note: *Include all income and expenses of a trust(s) or separately maintained fund(s) including any payments made for allocated insurance contracts. Round off amounts to nearest dollar.*	a. Amount	b. Total
(a) Contributions received or receivable in cash from—		
(i) Employer(s) (including contributions on behalf of self-employed individuals) .	0	
(ii) Employees	0	
(iii) Others	0	None
(b) Noncash contributions (specify nature and by whom made) ▶	0	
	0	0.00
(c) Earnings from investments (interest, dividends, rents, royalties)		0.00
(d) Net realized gain (loss) on sale or exchange of assets		0.00
(e) Other income (specify) ▶		0.00
(f) Total income, sum of (a) through (e)		0.00
(g) Distribution of benefits and payments to provide benefits—		
(i) Directly to participants or their beneficiaries	0	
(ii) To insurance carrier or similar organization for provision of benefits (including prepaid medical plans)	0	
(iii) To other organizations or individuals providing welfare benefits	0	0.00
(h) Interest expense		0.00
(i) Administrative expenses (salaries, fees, commissions, insurance premiums) . .		0.00
(j) Other expenses (specify) ▶		0.00
(k) Total expenses, sum of (g) through (j)		0.00
(l) Net income, (f) minus (k)		0.00
(m) Changes in net assets—(i) Unrealized appreciation (depreciation) of assets . .	0	
(ii) Other changes (specify) ▶	0	0.00
(n) Net increase (decrease) in net assets for the year (l) plus (m)		21,135.00
(o) Net assets at beginning of year (line 13(l), column b)		0.00
(p) Net assets at end of year, (n) plus (o) (equals line 13(l), column d)		21,135.00

15 Has there been any change since the last report in the appointment of any trustee, accountant, insurance carrier, enrolled actuary, administrator, investment manager or custodian? . . . . □ Yes ☒ No

If "Yes," explain and include the name, position, address and telephone number of the individual who left or was removed by the plan ▶ _____

_____

_____

			Yes	No
16 (a) Surety company name ▶	XYZ SURETY COMPANY			
(b) Amount of bond coverage ▶	$ 5,000.00	(c) Was any loss discovered during plan year? . . .		XX

17 Information about employees of the employer at end of the plan year. (Plans not purporting to satisfy the percentage tests of section 410(b)(1)(A) of the Code complete only (a) below and see instructions):

(a) Total number of employees	3
(b) Number of employees excluded under the plan because of:	
(i) Minimum age or years of service	0
(ii) Employees on whose behalf retirement benefits were the subject of collective bargaining	0
(iii) Nonresident aliens who receive no earned income from United States sources	0
(iv) Total excluded, sum of (i), (ii) and (iii)	0
(c) Total number of employees not excluded, (a) less (b)(iv)	3
(d) Employees ineligible (specify reason) ▶ _____	0
(e) Employees eligible to participate, (c) less (d)	3
(f) Employees eligible but not participating	0
(g) Employees participating, (e) less (f)	3

18 Is this plan an adoption of a: N/A

	Yes	No
(a) □ Master/prototype, (b) □ Field prototype, (c) □ Pattern, (d) □ Model plan, or (e) □ Bond purchase plan? .		
If "Yes," enter the four or eight digit IRS serial number (see instructions) ▶		

19 Did any person who rendered services to the plan receive, directly or indirectly, compensation from the plan in the plan year? . . . . ▶ . . . . | | XX

If "Yes," see instructions for information required.

20 (a) Is this a defined benefit plan subject to the minimum funding standards for this plan year? . . . . . . | | XX

If "Yes," attach Schedule B (Form 5500).

(b) Is this a defined contribution plan, i.e. money purchase or target benefit, subject to the minimum funding standards? (If a waiver was granted see instructions) . . . . | | XX

If "Yes," complete (i), (ii) and (iii):

(i) Amount of employer contribution required for the plan year . . . . |

(ii) Amount of contribution paid by the employer for the plan year under section 412 of the Code . . .

Enter date of last payment by employer . . . . ▶ Month ...1........ Day ..31...... Year ..79....... |

(iii) Funding deficiency, excess, if any, of (i) over (ii) (file Form 5330 to pay tax on deficiency) . . . . | 0

	Yes	No
21 (a) Did any non-exempt transaction, involving plan assets, involve a person known to be a party-in-interest? . . .		XX
If (a) is "Yes," attach a list of such transactions in the same format as is shown in the instructions.		
(b) Were any loans by the plan or fixed income obligations due the plan in default as of the close of the plan year or classified during the year as uncollectable?		XX
(c) Were any leases to which the plan was a party in default or classified as uncollectable during the plan year? . .		XX

Complete this item only if you answered "Yes," to item 12.

22 Did one or more of the following reportable events or other events requiring notice to the Pension Benefit Guaranty Corporation occur during this plan year? . . . .

If "Yes," complete (a) through (i) below.

(a) Notification by the Internal Revenue Service that the plan has ceased to be a plan as described in Section 4021(a)(2) of ERISA or a determination by the Secretary of Labor of non-compliance with Title I of ERISA . . .		
(b) A decrease in active participants to the extent specified in the instructions		
(c) A determination by the Internal Revenue Service that there has been a termination or partial termination of the plan within the meaning of Section 411(d)(3) of the Code		
(d) An inability to pay benefits when due		
(e) A distribution to a Substantial Owner to the extent specified in the instructions		
(f) An alternative method of compliance has been prescribed for this plan by the Secretary of Labor under Section 110 of ERISA		
(g) A cessation of operations at a facility to the extent specified in the instructions		
(h) A withdrawal of a substantial employer		
(i) An amendment which may cause the benefit payable to any participant to be decreased		

Form 5500-C
Department of the Treasury
Internal Revenue Service

Department of Labor
Pension and Welfare Benefit Programs

Pension Benefit Guaranty Corporation

Annual Return/Report of Employee Benefit Plan
(With fewer than 100 participants)

This form is required to be filed under sections 104 and 4065 of the Employee Retirement Income Security Act of 1974 and sections 6057(b) and 6058(a) of the Internal Revenue Code, referred to as the Code.

1978

For the calendar plan year 1978 or fiscal plan year beginning _____ , 1978 and ending _____ , 19____

File original of this form, including schedules and attachments, completed in ink or type.

▶ Do not file this form for Keogh (H.R. 10) plans with fewer than 100 participants and with at least one owner-employee participant. File Form 5500-K instead.

▶ Governmental plans and church plans (not electing coverage under section 410(d) of the Code). Do not file this form. File Form 5500-G instead.

▶ Pension benefit plans, unless otherwise excepted, complete all items. Annuity arrangements of certain exempt organizations, and individual retirement account trusts of employers complete only items 1 through 6, 9 and 10.

▶ Certain welfare benefit plans are not required to file this form—see instructions.

▶ Welfare benefit plans required to file this form do not complete items 7(a), 7(c), 17, 18, 20 and 22.

▶ Plan number—Your 3 digit plan number must be entered in item 5(c); see instruction 5(c) for explanation of "plan number."

▶ If any item does not apply, enter "N/A."

1 (a) Name of plan sponsor (employer if for a single employer plan) 　　　　BIG BUCKS, INC.	**1 (b)** Employer identification number 95 ┊ 0000000
Address (number and street) 　　　445 South Figueroa Street	**1 (c)** Telephone number of sponsor (213) 620-0460
City or town, State and ZIP code 　　　Los Angeles, California 90071	**1 (d)** Employer taxable year ends Month 1　Day 31　Year 19
2 (a) Name of plan administrator (if other than plan sponsor) 　　　Pension Trust Committee	**1 (e)** Business code number 5931
Address (number and street) 　　　445 South Figueroa Street	**2 (b)** Administrator's employer identification no. 95 ┊ 0000000
City or town, State and ZIP code 　　　Los Angeles, California 90071	**2 (c)** Telephone number of administrator (213) 620-0460

3 Name, address and identification number of ☐ plan sponsor and/or ☐ plan administrator as they appeared on the last return/report filed for this plan if not the same as in 1 or 2 above ▶ ___Same___

4 Check appropriate box to indicate the type of plan entity (check only one box):

(a) ☒ Single-employer plan　(c) ☐ Multiemployer plan　(e) ☐ Multiple-employer plan (other)

(b) ☐ Plan of controlled group of corporations or common control employers　(d) ☐ Multiple-employer-collectively-bargained plan

5 (a) (i) Name of plan ▶ BIG BUCKS, INC. EMPLOYEES' PENSION TRUST (Money Purchase Plan) 　　(ii) ☐ Check if name of plan changed since the last return/report. 　　(iii) ☐ Check if plan year was changed since last return/report.	**5 (b)** Effective date of plan February 1, 1978 **5 (c)** Enter three digit plan number ▶ 0 ┊ 0 ┊ 2

6 Type of plan:

(a) ☐ Defined benefit　(b) ☒ Defined contribution　(c) ☐ Welfare benefit　(d) ☐ Other (specify) ▶ _____

7 (a) Active participants: (i) Fully vested ___0___ (ii) Partially vested ___3___ (iii) Nonvested ___0___ (iv) Total ▶ | 3

(b) Total participants: (i) Beginning of plan year ▶ ___3___ (ii) End of plan year ▶ | 3

	Yes	No
(c) During the plan year, has any participant(s) separated from service with a deferred benefit (if "Yes," see instructions)?		XX
8 Was this plan amended in this plan year?		XX

9 Plan termination information:　N/A

(a) Was this plan terminated during this plan year or any prior plan year? . . . .

(b) If "Yes," were all trust assets distributed to participants or beneficiaries or transferred to another plan? . . .

(c) If item 12 is to be checked "Yes" and 9(a) is "Yes," has a notice of intent to terminate been filed with PBGC? . .

10 (a) In this plan year, was this plan merged or consolidated into another plan or were assets or liabilities transferred to another plan? . . . . | XX

If "Yes," identify other plan(s):

(b) Name of plan(s) ▶ _____

	(c) Employer identification number(s)	(d) Plan number(s)

(e) Has Form 5310 been filed with IRS? . . . . ☐ Yes ☒ No

Under penalties of perjury and other penalties set forth in the instructions, I declare that I have examined this report, including accompanying schedules and statements, and to the best of my knowledge and belief it is true, correct, and complete.

Date ▶ _____　Signature of employer/plan sponsor ▶ _____

Date ▶ _____　Signature of plan administrator ▶ _____

439

11 Indicate funding arrangement:
    (a) ☒Trust **(b)** ☐ Fully insured **(c)** ☐ Combination **(d)** ☐ Other (specify) ▶_____
    (e) If (b) or (c) are checked enter number of Schedule A's (Form 5500) which are attached . . . . . ▶

12 Is the plan covered under the Pension Benefit Guaranty Corporation termination insurance
    program? . . . . ☐ Yes ☒ No ☐ Not determined

13 Plan assets and liabilities at the beginning and the end of the plan year (list all assets and liabilities at current value). A plan with
    no trust and which is funded entirely by allocated insurance contracts which fully guarantee the amount of benefit payments should
    check box and not complete this item . . . . ☐

    Note: *Include all plan assets and liabilities of a trust or separately maintained fund. If more than one trust/fund, report on a
    combined basis. Include all insurance values except for the value of that portion of an allocated insurance contract which
    fully guarantees the amount of benefit payments. Trusts with no assets at the beginning and the end of the plan year enter
    zero on line 13(g). Round off amounts to nearest dollar.*

Assets	Beginning of year a. Party-in-Interest	Beginning of year b. Total	End of year c. Party-in-Interest	End of year d. Total
(a) Cash		0		15,000
(b) Receivables		0		0
(c) Investments—*(i)* Government securities .		0		0
(ii) Pooled funds/mutual funds . . .		0		0
(iii) Corporate (debt and equity instruments) .		0		0
(iv) Real estate and mortgages . . .		0		0
(v) Other		0		0
(d) Buildings and other depreciable property . . .		0		0
(e) Unallocated insurance contracts . . .		0		0
(f) Other assets		15,000		15,000
(g) Total assets, sum of (a) through (f) . .		0		0
Liabilities and Net Assets				
(h) Payables		0		0
(i) Acquisition indebtedness				0
(j) Other liabilities				0
(k) Total liabilities, sum of (h) through (j)				0
(l) Net assets, (g) minus (k)				0

14 Plan income, expenses and changes in net assets during the plan year:

	a. Amount	**b. Total**
Note: *Include all income and expenses of a trust(s) or separately maintained fund(s) including any payments made for allocated insurance contracts. Round off amounts to nearest dollar.*		
(a) Contributions received or receivable in cash from—		
(i) Employer(s) (including contributions on behalf of self-employed individuals) .	0	
(ii) Employees	0	
(iii) Others	0	None
(b) Noncash contributions (specify nature and by whom made) ▶_____	0	
	0	0
(c) Earnings from investments (interest, dividends, rents, royalties)		0
(d) Net realized gain (loss) on sale or exchange of assets		0
(e) Other income (specify) ▶_____		0
(f) Total income, sum of (a) through (e)		0
(g) Distribution of benefits and payments to provide benefits—		
(i) Directly to participants or their beneficiaries	0	
(ii) To insurance carrier or similar organization for provision of benefits (including prepaid medical plans)	0	
(iii) To other organizations or individuals providing welfare benefits	0	0
(h) Interest expense		0
(i) Administrative expenses (salaries, fees, commissions, insurance premiums) . .		0
(j) Other expenses (specify) ▶_____		0
(k) Total expenses, sum of (g) through (j)		0
(l) Net income, (f) minus (k)		0
(m) Changes in net assets—*(i)* Unrealized appreciation (depreciation) of assets . .		
(ii) Other changes (specify) ▶_____		0
(n) Net increase (decrease) in net assets for the year (l) plus (m)		15,000.
(o) Net assets at beginning of year (line 13(l), column b)		0
(p) Net assets at end of year, (n) plus (o) (equals line 13(l), column d)		15,000.

15 Has there been any change since the last report in the appointment of any trustee, accountant, insurance carrier, enrolled actuary, administrator, investment manager or custodian? . . . . ☐ Yes ☒No

If "Yes," explain and include the name, position, address and telephone number of the individual who left or was removed by the plan ▶ --

----

		Yes	No
16 (a) Surety company name ▶ __XYZ SURETY COMPANY__			
(b) Amount of bond coverage ▶ $ 5,000.00 (c) Was any loss discovered during plan year? . . .			XX

17 Information about employees of the employer at end of the plan year. (Plans not purporting to satisfy the percentage tests of section 410(b)(1)(A) of the Code complete only (a) below and see instructions):

(a) Total number of employees	3
(b) Number of employees excluded under the plan because of:	
(i) Minimum age or years of service.	0
(ii) Employees on whose behalf retirement benefits were the subject of collective bargaining	0
(iii) Nonresident aliens who receive no earned income from United States sources	0
(iv) Total excluded, sum of (i), (ii) and (iii)	0
(c) Total number of employees not excluded, (a) less (b)(iv)	3
(d) Employees ineligible (specify reason) ▶----------------------------------	0
(e) Employees eligible to participate, (c) less (d)	3
(f) Employees eligible but not participating	0
(g) Employees participating, (e) less (f)	3

18 Is this plan an adoption of a: N/A

	Yes	No
(a) ☐ Master/prototype, (b) ☐ Field prototype, (c) ☐ Pattern, (d) ☐ Model plan, or (e) ☐ Bond purchase plan? .		
If "Yes," enter the four or eight digit IRS serial number (see instructions) ▶		

19 Did any person who rendered services to the plan receive, directly or indirectly, compensation from the plan in the plan year? XX

If "Yes," see instructions for information required.

20 (a) Is this a defined benefit plan subject to the minimum funding standards for this plan year? XX

If "Yes," attach Schedule B (Form 5500).

(b) Is this a defined contribution plan, i.e. money purchase or target benefit, subject to the minimum funding standards? (If a waiver was granted see instructions) XX

If "Yes," complete (i), (ii) and (iii):

(i) Amount of employer contribution required for the plan year . . . .

(ii) Amount of contribution paid by the employer for the plan year under section 412 of the Code . . . .

Enter date of last payment by employer . . . . ▶ Month .....1...... Day ...31..... Year .79..

(iii) Funding deficiency, excess, if any, of (i) over (ii) (file Form 5330 to pay tax on deficiency)   0

	Yes	No
21 (a) Did any non-exempt transaction, involving plan assets, involve a person known to be a party-in-interest? . . .		XX
If (a) is "Yes," attach a list of such transactions in the same format as is shown in the instructions.		
(b) Were any loans by the plan or fixed income obligations due the plan in default as of the close of the plan year or classified during the year as uncollectable?		XX
(c) Were any leases to which the plan was a party in default or classified as uncollectable during the plan year? . .		XX

Complete this item only if you answered "Yes," to item 12.

22 Did one or more of the following reportable events or other events requiring notice to the Pension Benefit Guaranty Corporation occur during this plan year? . . . .

If "Yes," complete (a) through (i) below.

(a) Notification by the Internal Revenue Service that the plan has ceased to be a plan as described in Section 4021(a)(2) of ERISA or a determination by the Secretary of Labor on non-compliance with Title I of ERISA . . .

(b) A decrease in active participants to the extent specified in the instructions . . . .

(c) A determination by the Internal Revenue Service that there has been a termination or partial termination of the plan within the meaning of Section 411(d)(3) of the Code . . . .

(d) An inability to pay benefits when due . . . .

(e) A distribution to a Substantial Owner to the extent specified in the instructions . . . .

(f) An alternative method of compliance has been prescribed for this plan by the Secretary of Labor under Section 110 of ERISA . . . .

(g) A cessation of operations at a facility to the extent specified in the instructions . . . .

(h) A withdrawal of a substantial employer . . . .

(i) An amendment which may cause the benefit payable to any participant to be decreased . . . .

Index

[References are to paragraph (¶) numbers]

Documents (*contd*)
  stock restriction agreement, 907
  submission to IRS, 910
  Summary Plan Description, 911
  Wage Continuation Plan, 905
Domestic corporation, 301
Double tax, 300
Drafting legal documents
  (*see* Documents)

E

Early disposition, 507.2
Earnings, excess, 603
Earnings ratio, 107
Economic benefits, 102
Employee benefit plans, 800–807.4
  (*see also* Fringe benefits)
Employee Stock Ownership Plans,
  806
Employment contract, 906
Equity, establish, 701
Estate and gift tax:
  book value, 603
  cross-purchase agreements, 603
  don't undervalue stock, 603
  establish successor trustee, 604
  excess earnings, 603
  gift program, 601.1
  installment purchase, 603
  life insurance, 603
  living trust, 604
  minimize, 601
  minimizing estate taxes, 604
  minority discount, 603
  prior sales of stock, 603
  professional appraisals, 603
  purpose of estate planning, 600
  redemptions, 602
    complete, procedure, 602.1
    taxes and expenses,
      administration, 602.2
  transfer of stock upon death,
    604
  value of key employees, 603
  valuing stock, 603
Estate planning, 109
Excess cash, 510.2

Excess earnings, 603
Existing business, 508
Expansion, 202.2
Expenses:
  business and personal, 100
  organizational, 513.5

F

Factories Investment Corp., 202.3
Family, Subchapter S, 300
Filing fees, 111
Film rents, 202.5
Financial needs, personal, 100
Financial ratios, 107
Financing, 107
Fixed-property ratio, 107
Flexibility:
  corporation, 202.1
  multiple corporations, 513.3
Focht v. Commissioner, 508.4
Foreign income, 303
Forms:
  documents
    (*see* Documents)
  EBS-1, 912
  2553, 302.1
  2848, 909
  5301 and 5302, 909
Fotocrafters, Inc., 202.3
Fringe benefits:
  combination of plans, 803
  defined benefit pension plan, 802
  disability insurance, 807.2
  employee death benefit, 807.4
  ESOT or ESOP, 806
  increased benefits, 803, 804
  life insurance, 807.3
  medical reimbursement plan,
    807.1
  money-purchase pension plan,
    801
  multiple corporations, 804
  profit sharing or pension, 804
  partnership, 201.3
  profit-sharing plans, 800
  salary continuation plan, 807.2
Funds, surplus, 100